# Daily Guideposts 2011

New York, New York

*Daily Guideposts 2011*
Published by Guideposts
16 East 34th Street
New York, New York 10016
www.guideposts.com

Copyright © 2010 by Guideposts. All rights reserved.

This book, or parts thereof, may not be reproduced, stored in a retrieval system, or transmitted in any form or by any means, electronic, mechanical, photocopying, recording or otherwise, without the written permission of the publisher.

Acknowledgments

Every attempt has been made to credit the sources of copyrighted material used in this book. If any such acknowledgment has been inadvertently omitted or miscredited, receipt of such information would be appreciated.

All Scripture quotations, unless otherwise noted, are taken from *The King James Version of the Bible*.

Scripture quotations marked (cev) are taken from *Holy Bible: Contemporary English Version*. Copyright © 1995 American Bible Society.

Scripture quotations marked (esv) are taken from the Holy Bible, English Standard Version, copyright © 2001 by Crossway Bibles, a division of Good News Publishers. Used by permission. All rights reserved.

Scripture quotations marked (msg) are taken from *The Message*. Copyright © 1993, 1994, 1995, 1996, 2000, 2001, 2002 by Eugene H. Peterson.

Scripture quotations marked (nas) are taken from the *New American Standard Bible*, copyright © 1960, 1962, 1963, 1968, 1971, 1972, 1973, 1975, 1977, 1995 by the Lockman Foundation. Used by permission.

Scripture quotations marked (ncv) are taken from *The Holy Bible, New Century Version*. Copyright © 2005 by Thomas Nelson, Inc. Used by permission. All rights reserved.

Scripture quotations marked (niv) are taken from *The Holy Bible, New International Version*. Copyright © 1973, 1978, 1984 International Bible Society. Used by permission of Zondervan Bible Publishers.

Scripture quotations marked (nkjv) are taken from *The Holy Bible, New King James Version*. Copyright © 1997, 1990, 1985, 1983 by Thomas Nelson, Inc.

Scripture quotations marked (nlt) are taken from the *Holy Bible*, New Living Translation. Copyright © 1996. Used by permission of Tyndale House Publishers, Inc., Wheaton, Illinois 60189. All rights reserved.

Scripture quotations marked (nrsv) are taken from the *New Revised Standard Version Bible*. Copyright © 1989 by the Division of Christian Education of the National Council of the Churches of Christ in the U.S.A. Used by permission. All rights reserved.

Scripture quotations marked (rsv) are taken from the *Revised Standard Version of the Bible*. Copyright © 1946, 1952, 1971 by Division of Christian Education of the National Council of Churches of Christ in the U.S.A. Used by permission.

Scripture quotations marked (tlb) are taken from *The Living Bible*. Copyright © 1971 by Tyndale House Publishers, Wheaton, Illinois 60187. All rights reserved.

"Reader's Room" by Hannah Beiler, Gloe Bertram, Joan Boyer, Linda Brantley, Allene DeWeese, Ruth Hefner, Jo Kruger, Bobby Lee, Carolyn Malion, Janetta Messmer, Linda Parent and Joann Woosley are reprinted with permission from the authors.

Andrew Attaway's photo by Doug Snyder. Brian Doyle's photo by Jerry Hart. Oscar Greene's photo copyright © 2001 by Olan Mills, Inc. Edward Grinnan's photo by Jane Wexler. Rick Hamlin's photo by Nina Subin. Roberta Messner's photo by Jan D. Witter/Camelot Photography. Elizabeth Sherrill's and John Sherrill's photos by Gerardo Somoza.

Cover design by Faceout Studio
Cover photo by Istock
Interior design by Lorie Pagnozzi

Monthly page opener photos by Corbis
Indexed by Patricia Woodruff
Typeset by Aptara

Printed and bound in the United States of America
10 9 8 7 6 5 4 3 2 1

## INTRODUCTION

The book you're holding in your hands is a very special one—the thirty-fifth annual edition of *Daily Guideposts*. Thirty-five years ago, then-Guideposts Books editor Fred Bauer got the idea for a new kind of devotional, one that would give readers fresh material for prayer and reflection every day of the year. Fred wrote that first book (and its 1978 successor) himself and was rewarded by the enthusiastic response of nearly 190,000 readers. Over the succeeding years, *Daily Guideposts* has grown from one man's work into a collaborative effort (fifty-five writers this year!), and has sold more than twenty million copies. Most important of all, over those years, we've become a family—readers and writers sharing together, every day, in Scripture, reflection and prayer.

To celebrate these thirty-five years, our theme for 2011 is "Growing in Love." Our writers, including such longtime favorites as Elizabeth and John Sherrill, Marion Bond West, Oscar Greene, Carol Kuykendall and Daniel Schantz, will let you know how God has helped them grow in their relationships with family and friends, on the job and at home, and in their walk with Him. And our *Daily Guideposts* family is growing too: This year we welcome Anne Adriance of Oldwick, New Jersey. Anne is a senior vice president at Guideposts and the mother of two college-age sons.

While this year is a time of celebration for us here at Guideposts, it's also a sad one. Fred Bauer, who not only started *Daily Guideposts* but was a treasured contributor to all of our volumes through 2010, passed away on September 17, 2009. All of us who knew Fred will miss his generous spirit, his quick wit, and his deep love for God, family and country that shone out from everything he wrote. Please keep his beloved Shirley, their children and grandchildren, and the whole Bauer family in your prayers.

And now, come along with us on this special journey through all the days of our thirty-fifth anniversary year!

---

*DAILY GUIDEPOSTS* DEVOTIONALS IN YOUR IN-BOX
Receive each day's devotional in your in-box or read it online!
Visit DailyGuideposts.com/DGP2011 and enter this code:
DGP2011

## SPECIAL FEATURES

### A PATH TO SIMPLICITY  8

Join Roberta Messner at the beginning of each month as she shows how downsizing her cabin led her to a new perspective on life.

### TO SAY GOOD-BYE  19

For thirty-seven years, the church her husband David pastored had been at the center of Pam Kidd's life. At the middle of every month, join Pam as she learns to say good-bye to the people and places she has grown to love.

### ADVICE FROM AUNT ANNIE  31

At the end of each month, learn how a chance discovery in Penney Schwab's basement opened a window into the inmost heart of her father's oldest sister—and the lessons of a life well lived.

### WHEN THE HEART NEEDS HEALING  43

When his fiancée ended their engagement, Brock Kidd found a spark of hope amid the ashes of his dreams. In February, learn how a shattered love made room for a renewed relationship with the people around him—and with God.

### JOURNEY IN THE DARK  62

Throughout the year, Brigitte Weeks shares her struggle with depression, and the people, places and prayers that helped get her through it.

### FREE TO LOVE, FREE TO FOLLOW  119

In Holy Week, Marilyn Morgan King will take you on Mary Magdalene's journey from fear and self-reproach to the courage to stand at the foot of the Cross.

### LETTERS FROM THE HEART  225

In July, Marion Bond West shows you how a casual postcard turned sorrow to joy and an Oklahoma professor and a Georgia widow into a loving couple.

### TIME ON THE RIVER  293

As John and Elizabeth (Tib) Sherrill prepared to move from their home of fifty years, they decided to bring things full circle by returning to their very first home in Geneva, Switzerland. In September, John recounts some of the lessons he learned on the trip.

### THE ONE WHO IS TO COME  358

The Bible gives many descriptions of the Savior, but perhaps the most revealing are when Jesus says, "I am...." During Advent, Mary Brown ponders these seven images of Jesus.

# January

*And thou shalt love the
Lord thy God with all thine
heart, and with all thy soul,
and with all thy might.*

—Deuteronomy 6:5

## January

### Sat 1

*Immediately his mouth was opened and his tongue was loosed, and he began to speak, praising God.* —Luke 1:64 (NIV)

On the fourth evening of a five-day silent retreat, I realized that the next day I'd finally be able to speak again. I decided to make sure I said something worthwhile. I thought about the woman who had single-handedly prepared and served all of our meals and then washed the dishes. I hadn't been able to say "thank you" all week. Yes, *thank you* would make very appropriate first words.

However, the next morning during the church service before breakfast, I was surprised when the minister announced the "passing of the peace," something we hadn't done on the retreat because it required speaking to each other. The woman in the pew in front of me turned and said, "God's peace be with you," and I replied with deep emotion, "And God's peace be with you." As I spoke, a warm feeling went through me. Though they weren't what I'd planned, those were wonderful first words.

Many times during a normal day I have a chance to offer "first words." What are my first words when I get out of bed in the morning, when my husband Gordon arrives home from work, when I walk into a meeting, or when I run into someone in the grocery store? All of these can be just as golden as my first words after a silent retreat. They're all opportunities to say first words of God's blessing and peace.

> *Dear Holy Spirit, before I say anything else in this new year, help me to remember to speak Your words first.*
> —Karen Barber

Editor's Note: *As we begin our walk through a new year, please take time to share what God has been doing in your life. Jot down your reflections on the "Seeds of Love" journal pages at the end of every month.* If you'd like more space to record your thoughts, try our new *Daily Guideposts Journal*.

## January

### Sun 2

*Him we proclaim, warning everyone and teaching everyone with all wisdom, that we may present everyone mature in Christ.* —COLOSSIANS 1:28 (ESV)

Our eight-year-old daughter Maggie sometimes has trouble controlling her feelings. One day not too long ago, she'd been having a minitantrum, and her eleven-year-old sister Mary, much annoyed, said, "Maggie, you're acting like a six-year-old!"

"Well, I'm *immaturing*," Maggie replied.

There are days when I wonder if I'm "immaturing" too, days when I'm surly and snappy to those around me, days when I "allow" myself to have that pistachio muffin or those two or four or six cookies, days when the words don't easily pour out onto the computer screen and those urgent papers somehow just sit on my desk, days when my Bible seems too heavy to take off the shelf, days when I wonder whether I'm sixty-two or sixteen or maybe even six.

The beginning of a new year is the perfect time to remind myself that life, like the calendar, keeps going forward. The year 2010 isn't coming back again, much less 1964. And no matter how many years are given to me, my goal is the same: to become more like my Lord—to look to Christ, to live in Christ, to be conformed to Christ.

So it's time to pick myself up and start again, to put a lock on my tongue, stay away from the bakery, clean out the in-box and keep the Word in my heart. Maybe by this time next year, I can look back and say that in some small way, I've grown—or my wife and my children and my co-workers can say, "At least this year he hasn't 'immatured.'"

*Lord, this year, for Maggie and for me, I make Paul's prayer my own: "That we ... may grow up into him in all things, which is the head, even Christ" (Ephesians 4:14–15).*
—ANDREW ATTAWAY

*January*

## 🌿 A PATH TO SIMPLICITY

*Mon 3*  "*Do not store up for yourselves treasures on earth....*"
—Matthew 6:19 (NAS)

**LOSING MY WAY**

All I knew is I wanted my sweet little cabin back. I began to lose it when one of the decorating magazines I worked for asked me to produce a regular feature called "The Salvage Sleuth." I was to be a detective, visiting estate sales and flea markets and purchasing discards on the cheap. Then I was to transform them into one-of-a-kind home furnishings.

I was in my element. *Rescue, reuse, repair, rethink* became my keywords. When I spotted a wooden washboard, I envisioned a kitchen message center. Corbels from a Victorian home? Ideal adornments for a shelf. And that antique rope bed I snared at a yard sale could easily be reconfigured into a bench. With the red-checked upholstery fabric I found, it would work for country, cottage or eclectic settings. Magazine sales would surely soar.

The stuff piled up and up and up. First I filled a potting shed and then a guest cottage. My basement followed. After all, I needed to purchase such finds when I found them. And then the unthinkable happened: In the midst of the recession, the magazine folded. Suddenly I was nobody's Salvage Sleuth—and I owned a whole lot of junk.

There was nothing to do but pray. And there couldn't have been a better solution. God literally sent a woman to help me: Kay needed antique props for an event she was hosting. She would load them, transport them, refurbish them and sell them, all for the privilege of using them.

Jesus warned about hoarding treasures. But even when we lose our way with the trappings of this world, He stands ready to do a brand-new thing.

*Precious Jesus, no matter what fix I find myself in, You are there.*
—Roberta Messner

## January

### Tue 4

*Wisdom has built her house, she has set up her seven pillars. She has slaughtered her beasts... she has also set her table.*
—Proverbs 9:1–2 (RSV)

Over the past couple of years, I've become a Food Network junkie. I can watch those TV chefs for hours, hoping that one or another of their lessons will somehow improve my own cuisine.

My favorite show is called *Chopped*, where four chefs are thrown into competition. In each round, they get a basket of surprise ingredients (say, flank steak, grape juice, goat cheese and lemongrass) and a tight time frame (twenty minutes for the appetizer, thirty minutes for entrée and dessert) in which they have to create a dish that includes all of them. After each round, one chef gets "chopped" from the contest. The whole thing is a crazy, wild test of their creativity, their patience and their ability to apply, in a superhigh-pressure situation, the lessons they've learned in meals past.

Reality is no game show, but there are parallels between what those chefs have to do and how we are called to respond to the unpredictability of life. Every day is a basket of surprise ingredients: the traffic, a colleague's sour mood, an unexpected project, a toothache, a kind word from a stranger. So what will I make with my daily basket? Will I respond to adversity with frustration or with aplomb? Will I react to good news with humility or gloating?

When I was a child, my grandmother would tell me that Proverbs has thirty-one chapters so that I could read one each day of the month. Its admonitions are to the faithful life as knife skills are to cookery. And the lessons within come straight from the only One we can call life's Master Chef.

*Lord, when life seems to have heaped too much on my plate,*
*help me to step back and take time in Your Word.*
—Jeff Chu

## January

### Wed 5
*Pray without ceasing.* —I THESSALONIANS 5:17

For years, I'd heard that drinking eight glasses of water a day would be good for my health, so I felt pretty noble when I finally made it my New Year's resolution.

But as I walked into the kitchen one night, I was stunned to see my cat washing his face by scooping water out of my glass, dashing it on his face and circling his wet face with his paw. His bowl of water went untouched.

*Just how long has he been doing this? Could I have caught some cat disease?* I raced to the phone to call my vet, praying, *Please, God, let her answer right away. I could be seriously ill right now!*

She answered on the first ring—*Thank You, God.* "What's wrong with your cat?" she asked.

"Oh, it's not about Junior," I said. "It's about me. I just discovered that he has been scooping out water from my drinking glass to wash his face. What should I do?"

There was a moment's pause and then she said, "Keep your water in the refrigerator." I could swear I heard her chuckle as she hung up the phone.

"What a waste of time and worry," I said to the vet when she was examining Junior during his next regular checkup.

"But not a waste of prayer," she commented. "Prayer is never wasted."

I've thought about what she'd said many times since then. Though it was something silly, that odd situation had led me to pray. If only I could stay as connected to God all the time. Now there's a subject for a resolution.

*God, may I be inspired to pray more often, over big matters and small, so that I may become closer to You.*
—LINDA NEUKRUG

*January*

**Thu 6**  *Then, opening their treasure chests, they offered him gifts of gold, frankincense, and myrrh.* —MATTHEW 2:11 (NRSV)

I collect Christmas books. Between Thanksgiving and Epiphany, I try to read them all. One is reserved for today.

When I turn to the drawing accompanying the story, I'm distressed all over again. It's a stark pen-and-ink depiction of a bent old man riding on a camel. In the distance, three figures are hanging on crosses.

The story is an ancient, heartrending legend about one of the wise men who visited the baby Jesus, the one who brought myrrh, a precious ointment for healing and anointing the dead. It takes place thirty years after his encounter with the newborn Child. In the prime of his life when he first found Jesus, he is now aged and crippled. He painfully dismounts at the foot of the Cross to leave the same gift again: myrrh to anoint the dead and broken body of his King.

Though this story moves me to tears each year, it's the one I carry forward into the year with a determined joy. As the whirl and waiting of Christmas fades, I don't want to forget why Jesus was born. Following Him and His parents to Bethlehem is easy; following Him to Jerusalem, Gethsemane, Golgotha and the tomb is not so easy.

So where's the joy? The joy is in knowing what happens after. And each year, I imagine that the aged wise man, waiting at an inn for the strength to return home, stayed in Jerusalem long enough to learn the rest of the story.

*Jesus, let me be always ready to give You the gift of myself: my heart, my mind, my body, my actions, my prayers, my faith, my love.*
—MARCI ALBORGHETTI

## January

### Fri 7

*If we hope for what we do not yet have, we wait for it patiently.*
—Romans 8:25 (niv)

My five-year-old grandson Drake is allergic to peanuts. We found this out a few years ago when his first peanut butter sandwich was followed by his first trip to the emergency room. The doctor told us that there was a small chance Drake might outgrow this allergy. We've all prayed that might be the case, but we've also educated Drake about his "problem" and taught him that he cannot eat everything others may be eating.

Last month Drake was retested. His three-year-old brother Brock was tested for nut allergies too. The week before the procedure, Drake was smiling and wiggling with excitement. "Nina, I'm going to have a test and I might not be allergic. If I'm not allergic, I'm coming to your house to eat peanut butter!" But when the nurse called with the results, Drake was still allergic to nuts. Brock, however, was not.

A few days ago, the boys and I were heading home from preschool. From the backseat, Drake said, "Nina, can you guess who's not allergic to nuts? No, it's not me. It's Brock!" I glanced in the rearview mirror to see Drake pointing to Brock, a big smile on his face. We drove in silence for a few minutes before Drake continued. "I will be tested again when I am six. Maybe I will not be allergic that time. And then, Nina, I will come to your house and eat peanut butter."

Hope—pure, unadulterated hope. Drake was happy knowing that his desire could still come to pass. He would wait expectantly. And in the meantime, he'd celebrate his brother's good fortune.

I'm going to try (again) this year to do as the Apostle Paul admonishes: to hope, to believe and to wait—patiently. It shouldn't be too hard. After all, I have Drake to show me how it's done.

*Father, I wait for Your perfect timing in my life.*
—Mary Lou Carney

## January

### Sat 8
*"In his hand is the life of every creature and the breath of all mankind."* —Job 12:10 (NIV)

This morning I took my time getting ready for the day. I showered, put on some comfortable clothes, and headed to the kitchen for a cup of coffee and a look at my to-do list. The weekend was still full of possibilities, ripe with potential to do the things on my list. My family was still asleep upstairs, and our dog Nellie wagged a morning greeting and trotted ahead of me, eager for her breakfast.

As I looked at my planner, I remembered it was my father's birthday, and I made a note to call him. Despite a stroke fifteen years ago and triple bypass surgery more recently, he seems a man half his age, with tireless energy, a love of work, an impish demeanor and a caring heart.

As the day went on, I checked off many of the to-do's on my list and found some I'd need to leave for another day. The afternoon had begun to wane by the time I saw the notation on my planner. I'd almost forgotten to call Daddy on his birthday! Immediately I dialed the number.

"I outlived my father!" Daddy said with joy in his voice.

"What?" I responded, confused by his comeback to my birthday greeting.

"I've lived two months longer than my father did. He died two months before his seventy-seventh birthday," he explained. All at once, I realized how the thought of his father's death must have hung over him as he approached his own seventy-seventh birthday. Then in the very next moment, Daddy was delightedly sharing a story of his fort-building project with one of his grandsons. Once again, he'd chosen life, stepping into the next opportunity to work and share and love and contribute to his family and to all those around him in whatever ways God presented him.

*Dear God, help me always to be grateful for the gift of being alive, and use it to bring light and life wherever I go.*
—Anne Adriance

## January

### Sun 9

*Yet those who wait for the Lord ... will mount up with wings like eagles....* —Isaiah 40:31 (NAS)

I find the literal translations in the margin of my Bible fascinating. They can transform the text. In Psalm 139, David asks God to search his heart. Verse 24 is commonly read, "And see if there be any wicked way in me." The literal meaning of "wicked way" is "way of pain." I ask myself, "How and where am I causing pain to myself or others?"

In Psalm 139:3 (NAS), "You scrutinize my path" is literally, "You winnow my journeying." When I watch the harvesting in our Midwest farm country, I see the chaff separated from the grain in the winnowing process. How wonderful it is to know that God is with me on my journey, helping me to let go of the unnecessary and to hang on to the essential.

Proverbs 22:6 (NAS) reads, "Train up a child in the way he should go." The margin translates "the way he should go" as "according to his way." That was the parenting style I followed—giving each child's distinctive spirit both guidance and freedom.

In Philippians 4:11 (NAS), "content" in Paul's "I have learned to be content" is literally "self-sufficient." As I reach to make greater use of my talents and abilities, this passage assures me that healthy independence is a natural part of trusting God.

Most recently I discovered Colossians 3:10 (NAS)—"the new self who is being renewed" in the Creator's image. The margin suggests "renovated." I am God's ongoing beautification project!

What other exciting finds await me as I discover the nitty-gritty of God's good news?

*Jesus, Your name Emmanuel—"God with us"—*
*literally fills me with wonder.*
—Carol Knapp

## January

### Mon 10

*You are the God who performs miracles; you display your power among the peoples.* —Psalm 77:14 (NIV)

For two years, medication had been successful in helping our daughter Maria manage her Crohn's disease, minimizing the flare-ups of colon pain and allowing her to lead an almost-normal life. Then, when she began eighth grade, the medication stopped working and she experienced intense pain that was debilitating and unpredictable. She missed a lot of school, and by Christmas break she was in the hospital.

I'd been praying for her all through her illness, but now I decided I hadn't been bold enough. I would pray for a miracle. Her doctor was talking to us about a stronger medication, but we were scared by its possible side effects. So every day I told God, "I'm praying for a miracle for Maria." I fully believed I would get it.

Maria left the hospital feeling better, but nothing prevented the continuing flare-ups. I kept praying. Then one day I spoke with the mother of a teenage girl who had been taking the stronger medication for several months. The family had determined that the risks of the disease outweighed the risks of the medication. And the girl was flourishing. "It's been a miracle treatment for us," the mother said.

*I've been praying for a miracle healing for Maria,* I thought, *but can't God also heal through the gift of medicine? Maybe this is our miracle.*

It was. The new medication helped Maria regain control of her life. And I learned a valuable lesson: Faith isn't about God giving me answers I've already decided on; it's about believing that God has answers of His own.

*Forgive me, Lord, for being so slow to trust You.*
*Thank You for Your unending love.*
—Gina Bridgeman

*January*

*Tue 11*  *He shall grow up before him as a tender plant, and as a root out of a dry ground....* —ISAIAH 53:2

There's an old patch of wood that we keep unpainted in our back room near the storage cabinets.

The dates and names start at the bottom, a little more than three feet above the ground, in childish handwriting. The writing becomes more secure when the names rise higher, and it's positively mature well above five feet. There's William on 9-12-99 and then William a foot higher on 5-10-03. Timothy seems to make the same rapid progress a little behind his older brother. Mom and Dad never seem to change. I never rise above five feet eleven inches, but the boys leapfrog over each other until you see them leap above their mother—a strong black line to mark the milestone—and then they rise above their father, leaving him in the dust.

Then the writing stops—no more updates; no need for more. But the old marks are still there, and I can glance at them when I'm getting down the gardening shears or looking for a screwdriver. My friend Tib reminds me that the one prayer God never answers is "Please, let nothing change." When I cling too tightly to the past, I can look at this record of how the boys grew until they towered over me. So many answers to prayer in indelible ink. Someday we'll have to move from this home, but I hope the new owners can make their own marks of progress along the wood.

*Lord, let me look forward, always remembering the love that has been with me all along.*
—RICK HAMLIN

## *January*

### Wed 12

*Forgetting what is behind and straining toward what is ahead, I press on toward the goal to win the prize for which God has called me heavenward in Christ Jesus.*
—Philippians 3:13–14 (NIV)

During my dancing days, Miss McB, our ballet mistress, was a firm taskmaster. Rehearsals were exhausting; she insisted we get the choreography exactly right.

My challenge was the thirty-two *fouettes* required of the ballerina in *Swan Lake*. These were a rapid, whipping motion of the leg, done *en pointe* (on the toes). Toward the end of rehearsal, I was so tired that I frequently fell. Miss McB would have none of it.

"Continue!" she'd bellow in her deep, authoritative voice. Bone weary, I would pick myself up and start again. Needless to say, the practice paid off; the performance went well, without a tumble.

Lately I've been weary to the point of exhaustion. It seems the older I get, the less energy I have. "You need to walk," my friend Bess urged. "The exercise will build up your stamina. I'll meet you at the corner. We'll take it slowly. First once around the block, then twice and so on." She should know. She goes around the block several times for a two-mile daily walk.

Once went well, twice was a drag, and when it came to the mile mark of three times around, I felt I just couldn't make it. Then Miss McB's voice echoed in my ear: "Continue!"

"All right, Fay! One mile a day is a good beginning," said Bess.

*When my soul is weary and my faith tends to falter, I hear Your voice, Lord, saying, "Press on, press on!"*
—Fay Angus

## January

### Thu 13

*After this, the word of the Lord came to Abram in a vision: "Do not be afraid, Abram. I am your shield, your very great reward."* —Genesis 15:1 (NIV)

I was peeling potatoes at the kitchen sink and listening to my four-year-old grandson Frank. He was in the next room, deep into one of the imaginative stories he loves to tell with his box of "people."

This time Frank's people were in a snake-infested jungle. Wild animals were all around them. They were lost. "It was getting dark," he said in a stage whisper, "and they were very scared." There was a long pause, and I was all ears, wondering how Frank would get his people out of this mess.

Finally, in a loud voice, he announced, "But God was with them."

I stopped, potato peeler in midair, wondering how God would bring the people out. But there was only silence. I tiptoed to the doorway and saw Frank putting the people back in the box. I don't know what was in Frank's mind or why the story ended there. *Perhaps he couldn't figure out an ending and so took the easy way out of leaving it with God*, I thought, smiling.

I went back to peeling potatoes and pondering a problem that seemed to have no solution. But Frank's unfinished ending kept going 'round and 'round in my head. "But God was with them." Finally I heard the truth of it.

*Lord God, You Who are the Alpha and the Omega, the Beginning and the End, help me to stay with You in the here and now.*
—Shari Smyth

*January*

## ✸ TO SAY GOOD-BYE

*Fri 14*  *I will clothe thee with change....* —ZECHARIAH 3:4

**THE SHAPE OF CHANGE**

"David, I'm running behind," I said to my husband. "Would you please slice the mushrooms for the salad?"

A few minutes later, our family was gathered around the kitchen table. "Mom, what are these round things in the salad?" our son Brock asked.

"Some new kind of vegetable?" our daughter Keri chimed in.

"They have a texture like mushrooms," Keri's husband Ben said.

I looked down at the salad and laughed. "Great. I ask your dad to slice the mushrooms and he invents a totally new way to do it!" In all my years of cooking I'd never seen mushrooms cut in perfect rounds. They looked like big full moons floating in a sky of greens.

Later, while I was cleaning the dishes, a rush of apprehension swept across my heart. David was retiring as pastor of Hillsboro Presbyterian Church after thirty-seven years. We were so young when we came, and it had been our life for so long; now our future was uncertain.

I caught sight of a last white circle of mushroom clinging to a plate. "I'm like you," I whispered. "My life is taking a completely new shape. I have no idea who I'll become."

David reappeared from the porch where he'd been saying good-bye to the kids. "Guess I flunked Mushroom Cutting 101," he said.

"*Hmm*, I don't know," I answered, holding that last mushroom moon up to the light. "Maybe change is good. It's actually kind of pretty, don't you think?"

*Father, a transition is coming. Reshape me as You would have me be.*
—PAM KIDD

*January*

## Sat 15

*"So get to work, and may the Lord be with you!"*
—I Chronicles 22:16 (TLB)

After Captain Chesley Sullenberger landed his commercial jet safely in the Hudson River a couple of years ago, he was interviewed by several reporters. One of them asked, "When you realized you were going down, did you pray?"

He hesitated. "I thought of nothing else but flying the plane."

At first I was surprised by his answer, but the more I thought about it, the more I appreciated his honesty. As a pilot myself, I understand how much concentration it takes to fly a plane, even when there's no emergency. When things go wrong, it's time for action, not conversation.

Action is a kind of physical prayer, I think, and the airplane itself is a good example of how it works. On the ground, an airplane is the slowest and most awkward of creatures, hard to steer. But when it picks up speed and the wind hits the control surfaces, it suddenly becomes the most agile of all transports. You can steer it with the merest touch. Not until it gets into action can it be guided well.

Many kinds of prayer exist, all of them useful. There's a place for the all-nighter, with tears. There's a place for table graces and a time for the "flare prayer," when you cry out, "Dear God, help me!" But there's also a time for the wordless prayer, when you get up off your knees and get to work. When I do that, I can feel His wind beneath my wings.

*Forgive me, Lord, but I can't talk right now. I have a plane to fly.*
—Daniel Schantz

*January*

## Sun 16

*Do not withhold your mercy from me, O Lord; may your love and your truth always protect me.* —Psalm 40:11 (NIV)

A while ago, I spoke at a church in northeast Mississippi. Three days later, I received an e-mail from a man who had attended the service. He said that he had enjoyed my message but that wasn't the reason he was writing to me. "My ten-year-old daughter said this was the first time she had ever really listened to and understood what a preacher was saying. She has never commented to me in any way about a sermon before, other than to say she never understands what's being said."

He went on to say that he asked her what she remembered most about the sermon. She said she remembered that she can always get another chance with God.

What a great reminder that God's mercy to me is so great that He allows me to share His Word. And even greater is the way He allowed the light of His great love to open the eyes of a ten-year-old girl, who on that day understood that she serves a God of mercy.

*Thank You, Father, for understanding who we are and choosing to accept our childlike faith.*
—Dolphus Weary

---

### READER'S ROOM

Each day I remind myself that this is the day God has made and I am going to rejoice and be glad. When I feel overwhelmed, I try to remind myself that God has plans for me to prosper and that He has not given me a spirit of timidity but of power. —*Bobby Lee, Albion, Michigan*

*January*

## Mon 17

*Let all the nations gather together, and let the peoples assemble....* —Isaiah 43:9 (RSV)

When I taught high school history, one of my favorite units was the civil rights movement. We studied the far-reaching impact of the Montgomery, Alabama, bus boycott; the historic march across the Edmund Pettus Bridge in Selma, Alabama; the significance of the sit-ins at the Woolworth's lunch counter in Greensboro, North Carolina; and Martin Luther King Jr.'s famous "I Have a Dream" speech at the Lincoln Memorial. We always finished the unit with a field trip to a 1950s-themed diner located across town.

The girls dressed up in poodle skirts, and the boys wore cuffed denim jeans and penny loafers. They sat in booths and ordered hamburgers and milkshakes. Some students checked out the rock-and-roll music on the vintage jukebox, while others stepped onto the dance floor to try out the jitterbug steps they'd learned in class.

One year I looked out across the diner. Four of my African American students had chosen to eat at the lunch counter.

"Lance," I called out to one of them, "why aren't you all sitting at a booth?"

He swiveled around on his stool and stood up. "Mrs. B," he announced, getting everyone's attention, "my friends and I are sitting here at the lunch counter simply because we can."

The diner quieted down for a moment. One student called out, "Way to go, Lance!" Then a man at the end of the lunch counter stood up and began to clap. One by one the students joined in until everyone—students, customers and waitresses—was standing up and applauding.

*Thank You, Gracious Father, for leaders like Dr. King,*
*whose courage, vision and sacrifice gave us so*
*many of the freedoms that we enjoy today.*
—Melody Bonnette

*January*

## Tue 18

*The hearing ear and the seeing eye, the Lord has made them both.* —Proverbs 20:12 (RSV)

"Quid hoc ad aeternitatem?" as St. Bernard of Clairvaux used to mumble when faced with the usual parade of tumult and travail. "What does it matter in the light of eternity?"

And yet, with total respect for eternity, don't we love our problems, considering the alternative? The blizzards of bills I can never pay in toto, the surly son, the dismissive daughter, the moist shabby house held together by duct tape and blackberry vines, the battered moaning car, the shivering pains in my back, the grim brooding debts, the dark thread of fear that I might not have been the best dad, the feeling sometimes in the dark reaches of the night that maybe there was a better husband for my wife if only she had stayed in the game a little longer, and the most pressing problems, the ones that haunt me every minute of the blessed week: the health and joy of our kids and the fragility of their future....

But there are sweet, glorious moments when I realize that the things that keep us awake at night could be the greatest gifts we can ever get. Soon enough, as real time is accounted, we'll be with old St. Bernard, and what we will want more than anything, even there, in the incomprehensible Light, on the Ocean of Love, is to be in a chair late at night, worried, rocking a sick child, knowing that that child needs and wants you more than any other person in the history or future of the world. All the way to heaven *is* heaven, as another mumbling saint said—despite the muddy potholes along the road.

> *Lord, I ask politely for the kind of eyesight that sees the glory of the muddy road.*
> —Brian Doyle

*January*

## Wed 19

*He hath filled the hungry with good things....*
—LUKE 1:53

Mary's been in the kitchen again. A juicy apple pie appeared while I was at a meeting today. I didn't peel an apple or put on an oven mitt.

I'm happy that my eleven-year-old enjoys cooking. I like it, too, but for the past decade my three-times-a-day food adventures have been more duty than pleasure. Then this fall I discovered a free syllabus for a kitchen science course through MIT's Open Courseware, ordered the book and printed out the assignments. Mary and I have been happily working our way through the class ever since.

We've made Death by Chocolate cookies and learned that for centuries Europeans only used chocolate as a bitter drink. We mashed avocados for guacamole after reading that they've been cultivated for seven thousand years. My favorite food fact so far, though, is that the substance released when we cut into an onion dissolves in our eyes and makes sulfuric acid. No wonder it stings!

I enjoy foodie details. They make cooking interesting and I learn more than how to create a dish. But what I secretly relish about this little class at home is having a shared interest with my daughter. Nothing is quite as tasty as a good relationship, especially during these challenging *tween* years.

As pans clatter in the kitchen (Mary's stirring up macaroni and cheese for lunch), I stop to consider what interests God and I have in common. A lot of what absorbs my mind and heart each day doesn't draw me closer to Him. Perhaps I need to set up a different curriculum to work on that.

*Lord, train my heart to love what interests You.*
—JULIA ATTAWAY

*January*

## Thu 20

*Let love of the brethren continue. Do not neglect to show hospitality to strangers....* —Hebrews 13:1–2 (NAS)

It was storming—a wet, cold and foggy day in Macon, Georgia. I had five minutes to reach my freshman class as I rushed across a parking lot, carrying my briefcase and hunched under my golf umbrella. The umbrella was huge, big enough to shelter three people. It billowed like a sail in the wind, nearly lifting me off the ground.

As I cut between parked cars, a door suddenly swung open in front of me and a young woman stepped out. She hadn't seen me and I nearly ran over her. Both of us stood, apologizing in the pouring rain.

She was in her thirties, perhaps a young mother working on a graduate degree in education. She had no umbrella or raincoat, just a wool parka with a hood. Between awkwardly stammered apologies, I held up my umbrella and said, "You're really getting soaked. Can I walk you to your class?"

Her eyes grew wide and she stepped closer, lugging her backpack; now two strangers huddled under a portable tent, sloshing through puddles together. In the minute that we walked together, she asked me if I was a professor and I asked if she was a schoolteacher. When she nodded, we had reached the education building. Hurrying through a glass door, she offered a quick and muffled thank-you and I went on my way.

The intersection of our lives only lasted seconds, but it left a series of questions in my mind: *Who was that? What is her story? Did she think I was forward to offer my umbrella? Should I have spoken? Was this the right thing to do?*

Offering a kind word, a smile, an umbrella may feel awkward and embarrassing, but God often uses such moments to touch hearts and build bridges.

*Father, when there is little time to think, may I smile instead of frown, encourage instead of criticize, offer help and not walk on by.*
—Scott Walker

## January

### Fri 21

*And when you turn to the right or when you turn to the left, your ears shall hear a word behind you saying, "This is the way; walk in it."* —Isaiah 30:21 (NRSV)

The phone rang in the middle of a Friday morning. It was my husband's neuro-oncologist. "I've got some bad news," he told me. "The MRI shows that Lynn's brain tumor is back."

Nearly four years earlier, Lynn had been diagnosed with brain cancer. Following surgery, radiation and chemotherapy, he lived a fairly normal life with no evidence of disease. We traveled, he continued to work at his law firm, and we spent good times with our children and grandchildren. We were almost ready to pronounce him cured—until this MRI.

Some parts of this new journey seem so familiar:

*Gather information and make choices.* This time Lynn's tumor is inoperable and radiation will not work. Our only medical hope is aggressive chemotherapy. We agree to go for it but realize the physical realities will end his law career.

*Set up systems.* Get the every-other-week chemo appointments on the calendar and plan the rest of our lives around this new priority.

*Tell others.* Choose the simplest language to describe the news for family, friends and our church.

*Face our fears.* This time the fears seem bigger. The cancer affects the brain functions more. The side effects of chemo are greater. The statistics are not as good. Yet, as I look back at our earlier journey down this same unpredictable path, I remember how we discovered surprising doses of God's hope all along the way.

There's a saying: "Remember in the dark what you learned in the light." But as we begin this journey again, I'm remembering in the dark what I learned in the dark: that God gives us enough light to direct our paths, one step at a time, and what we need when we need it most.

*Lord, as we begin this journey with cancer again, I trust You and will look for those doses of hope.*
—Carol Kuykendall

### Sat 22

*January*

*Now return to the Lord your God, For He is gracious and compassionate, Slow to anger, abounding in lovingkindness And relenting of evil.* —Joel 2:13 (NAS)

It was a cold Saturday in January, and I was busy doubting God—again. My mind took off on a worry tangent while my husband played in the yard with his parakeets. Rick raises the birds in an outdoor aviary behind our house. An elderly friend couldn't take care of them and knew that Rick would do a good job. Right now, there are about forty brightly colored birds chirping in our backyard. The parakeets love our usually warm Georgia weather, and during the winter Rick keeps a heat lamp inside their home and covers it with plastic.

I spotted a lime green parakeet perched high in a pine tree out back. Somehow he'd escaped. "He won't survive on his own," Rick told me.

"You can't catch him up there," I said. "What are you going to do?"

"He'll come back."

I doubted that the bird would return, but I kept my mouth shut.

Later that afternoon, as Mr. Parakeet sat on the aviary door handle, Rick eased up behind him with a net and helped him back to safety. Mr. Parakeet's family and friends chattered to welcome their prodigal home.

There have been times in my life when I've let worry, vain imagination and negative talk take me far from God. Like that bird, I've run wild and fast with fear, as far as I could go. But flying solo isn't fun for long. And each time I've returned, God has always been there to welcome me home to safety.

*Father, You alone are my safe haven, my hope, my peace, my salvation.*
—Julie Garmon

*January*

## Sun 23

*Love each other with brotherly affection and take delight in honoring each other.* —ROMANS 12:10 (TLB)

In a recent sermon, our pastor Kevin mentioned an encounter he'd had with my husband Wayne. No one in church realized he was talking about Wayne, but I did.

Kevin had stopped by our house on a quick errand for his wife, and Wayne had asked him in for a cup of coffee. Kevin was in a hurry and declined; he had a meeting scheduled, places to go and people to see. Wayne didn't think anything of it and neither did I.

Then on Sunday morning Kevin talked about the incident. He said he had been so busy doing the *work* of the church that he'd forgotten to *be* the church. He'd missed an opportunity to get to know one of his flock better and he regretted it.

That set me to thinking about how many opportunities I've missed because I was in a hurry to get somewhere. How many people has God planted in my path whom I was in too much of a hurry to notice?

As an old saying has it, "You may be the only Bible someone will ever read." If that's the case, I want to make sure I represent the living Christ in a way that honors Him.

*Father God, help me to live my life in such a way that people will see my faith in the love I show others.*
—DEBBIE MACOMBER

*January*

## Mon 24

*All the days ordained for me were written in your book before one of them came to be.* —Psalm 139:16 (NIV)

Visiting a museum, I paused in front of a picture by the surrealist René Magritte. In the painting, an artist sits before an easel, staring at an egg placed on a table. On the canvas, though, he's not painting an egg but a feathered, full-grown bird.

Puzzling, when there were more than enough puzzles in my life just then! My husband and I were trying to sell our home of fifty years in the worst housing market in decades. Moving near family in another state meant leaving not only friends, but longtime doctors and dentists, service people, our church. How could we ever find replacements for these things? Which belongings could we take to a small apartment? How would we manage if the house didn't sell?

I turned away from Magritte's perplexing painting and then looked again. The artist in the picture, clearly, was painting not what he saw but what he knew. The beak, the claws, the feathered wings on his canvas—all this, in time, would develop from an egg. The artist saw the end from the beginning.

*I'm seeing only the egg*, I thought, *things as they are at present. I can't see the life-in-the-making that will someday take shape. But there's an Artist at work in my life, and every life, One Who sees the completed picture and knows the people, the places, the specifics of a future still invisible to me.*

*Help me put anxiety aside, Father, and watch Your brush at work on the finished portrait.*
—Elizabeth Sherrill

*January*

## Tue 25

*Everyone who competes in the games goes into strict training. They do it to get a crown that will not last; but we do it to get a crown that will last forever.*
—I Corinthians 9:25 (NIV)

"What would happen if you stopped exercising?" a friend teasingly asked the other day.

I tried to laugh the question off, but in truth it made me feel self-conscious and a little guilty. I am a bit compulsive about getting to the gym every day. If I'm traveling, I make sure the hotel I'm booked into has a good exercise room. If I skip a day—or two, God forbid—I'm edgy and out of sorts. Even if I get to bed late, I'll still drag myself to the gym in the morning.

What made me uncomfortable, I think, was the suggestion in my friend's query that exercise controlled me, that I was a slave to my routine and there was something selfish and self-centered about it. Couldn't some of that gym time be better spent?

That morning while I toweled off after a cycling class, I was worried enough to say a prayer: *God, if I'm too focused on this gym thing, if I've become some kind of gym rat instead of just trying to take care of the body You gave me, let me know.* It would be hard, but I could change, I told myself as I walked to work.

The first e-mail I opened was a very pleasant surprise: My friend had sent me an article about the newest findings on exercise. Well-exercised rats, apparently, are better able to handle stress and adapt to difficult situations than their sedentary rodent brethren. "Just stumbled across this," my friend's message said. "Guess it answers my question!"

And my prayer. Yet my friend's inquiry was a legitimate one. Routines can trap us sometimes, and it's always good to question them. Still, now when someone calls me a gym rat, I won't get so worried.

*Lord, thank You for friends who keep me honest and for answers to prayer that reassure me.*
—Edward Grinnan

*January*

## ADVICE FROM AUNT ANNIE

**Wed 26**   *What a wonderful inheritance! I will bless the Lord....*
—Psalm 16:6–7 (TLB)

### AUNT ANNIE'S BOX

"My pleasant task," wrote Aunt Annie, "was to entertain the children. I thought they would enjoy playing Pass the Seashell.... The children took turns listening to my conch shell and relating what it said. Imagine my surprise when my six-year-old niece Penney announced, 'The seashell said Aunt Annie is an old maid!'"

I always thought of Aunt Annie, my father's oldest sister, as the stereotypical spinster. She came to our house for holiday dinners and we visited her, but when she died, I realized I'd never made the effort to really get acquainted.

Then God gave me a second chance when I found a cardboard box that had been tucked away in my basement since the day after Aunt Annie's funeral. The box contained copies of nearly two thousand verses, articles and stories she'd had published over a fifty-eight-year period.

The real Aunt Annie came alive as I pored over the contents of the box. Her life had been filled with friends and students; she was a lay visitor for her church, actively helping her neighbors; she traveled extensively. She often wrote about family, so I learned something about our history and even about myself. Best of all, I received advice for living that's still relevant today.

All of us have family, neighbors and friends with memories and stories that deserve to be told, heard, remembered and shared. These life experiences enable us to better understand and appreciate ourselves, each other and God.

*Thank You, Lord, for my inheritance in You. Help me*
*be faithful in passing on the faith.*
—Penney Schwab

*January*

## Thu 27

*Through wisdom is an house builded....*
—Proverbs 24:3

As the building contractor drove away, I turned to my wife Carol and said, "Well, that's strike three." Three times during the past month, a contractor had come to look over our garage, which we hoped to convert into a home office. Space was tight in our small house, and even though we had rearranged it, I was tired of typing in the cramped den while the kids watched television just a few feet away. The garage was roomy and bright; it would make a perfect workspace.

There was only one hitch: a long crack in the foundation. Ordinarily, this could be easily repaired, but the garage abuts a neighbor's retaining wall, making it impossible to bring in earth-moving equipment. All three contractors had shaken their heads on seeing the problem. One never got back to us; the second came up with a plan that would involve seriously disturbing our neighbor; the third proposed a solution that would cost double our budget.

I was terribly disappointed. I had dreamed about this office for years, drawing multiple plans for where to put the new door, skylight and built-in bookshelves, visiting countless furniture stores to select the right desk and couch—all for naught.

I was sitting in the living room, mulling over my ruined hopes, when Carol and the children popped into the room. "We have an idea," Carol said. "You know that space in the basement filled with junk? If we clear it out, paint the walls and install some lights, it will make a nice little office. It's small, but it would be cozy and cheerful. And the kids and I will do all the work!"

What could I say? I stood up and hugged them all, not because they had solved my problem, but because they'd shown me that while the foundation of our garage is cracked, the foundation of our family is solid to the core.

*Thank You, Father, for the priceless gift of family love.*
—Philip Zaleski

*January*

**Fri 28** *He guides me along right paths....*
—Psalm 23:3 (NLT)

One winter afternoon, preoccupied with some problems I couldn't get a grip on, I decided to take a break and visited the Metropolitan Museum of Art, a mile or two from my apartment. An hour later I went down the steps of the museum into a swirling snowstorm. *What fun to walk home through Central Park!* I thought. *Maybe the freshly falling snow will give me a new perspective.*

I'd walked home this way many times before and could do it in my sleep. Or so I thought. But as the snow swirled thicker and faster, I could barely see the walkway in front of me, much less the Manhattan skyline around the park that I use to keep my sense of direction. At some point in the obliterating whiteness, I realized I'd taken a path in the wrong direction and literally couldn't see where I was going. I felt a moment of panic. Where was I? I thought I knew my way, but now I felt surprisingly disoriented.

*Holy Spirit, where am I?* I took a deep, stinging breath, and something I'd read in Anne Lamott's book *Traveling Mercies* came to me: In faith we "stumble along toward where we think we're supposed to go, bumbling along, and here is what's so amazing—we end up getting exactly where we're supposed to be."

As the wind blew and the snow swirled even more vigorously, I calmed down and heard the creak of old-fashioned swing chains clanking in the wind. Now I knew just where I was, at a playground on the north side of the Great Lawn in a beautiful grove of pine trees. I'd gotten off track, but I eventually would end up exactly where I was supposed to be.

I felt that way about my unresolved problems as well.

*Dear God, help me to trust You wherever I wander.*
—Mary Ann O'Roark

*January*

## Sat 29

*Jerusalem remembers all her precious things that were from the days of old....* —LAMENTATIONS 1:7 (NAS)

Despite my best intentions, our house is always a little messy. Cracker crumbs speckle the living room rug, toothpaste fingerprints smear the bathroom mirror and toy cars hide under the couches. Evidence that we have a toddler and an infant is everywhere.

I was complaining to my mom about housework, telling her that my laundry is an ever-growing mountain no matter how hard I try to keep up, when Solomon rubbed his fingers on the windows I'd just cleaned. I shook my head and sighed. "It's no use," I said.

"Listen," my mom said, "before you know it, all of this will be a memory. So try to enjoy it."

"Enjoy fingerprints?" I asked, rolling my eyes as I picked up a puzzle piece that had strayed outside its box.

"Some day," Mom said, "you'll look at your clean house and miss these days."

I'll admit I still grumble when I pass my cloudy windows. But now, before I get out the glass cleaner, I try to find the blessing in it all, when my house is clean and my windows are crystal clear, to make a memory of that little handprint.

*Lord, the next time I reach for the vacuum cleaner, remind me that someday this mess will be a memory.*
—SABRA CIANCANELLI

*January*

## Sun 30 *"She has done what she could...."* —Mark 14:8 (NAS)

I guess *the special music is just an oversight,* I thought, as I skimmed the church bulletin that Sunday. *Becky certainly won't be playing for us today.*

Just last week I had opened an urgent e-mail that arrived on our church's prayer chain. "Please pray for Becky. She slipped and fell on a patch of ice. Her right wrist is crushed with bones broken in two places."

My heart sank. Becky was one of our church pianists, an accomplished musician with a promising career ahead of her. "Please guide the surgeons and bless her future," I prayed.

Now here she was, her arm in a cast supported by a sling, cheerfully thanking the congregation for their support and encouragement. "And no, that is not a mistake in the bulletin," she said, as if in answer to my thoughts. "I've been looking for music composed for one hand, and I'm going to play something for you." And then Becky swung onto the piano bench and, using only her left hand, she performed a beautiful classical piece that blessed us all.

It made me think, *If my abilities were suddenly reduced by half, would I still seek to serve God as joyfully and thankfully as Becky?*

*Lord, thank You for the inspirational examples of people who serve You despite their limitations.*
—Alma Barkman

*January*

## Mon 31

*Then little children were brought to Jesus for him to place his hands on them and pray for them.*
—Matthew 19:13 (NIV)

It's been a long time since I spent an extended period in high school. Occasionally I've visited to meet with students for an hour or two, but now I've committed myself to work for almost two months with a group of high schoolers.

When I pull up to the school, I'm nervous. It has a bad reputation and its academic scores are probably the worst in the city. But when I walk through the heavy metal doors, pass the metal detectors and see the smiling faces, I realize that they are children just like mine and each one is like the child I used to be.

They are a little shy at first and sit in their separate cliques, but like a mother hen I gather them all together. They are African American and Latina, but soon we are one big family. My plan is not to teach but to listen; I want to give them a place where they can say what's on their minds and where they will learn to respect one another. By the second week, they are asking, "Can we start writing now, Miss Foster?"

They tell me stories of broken homes, family arguments and immigration. They tell stories of abuse. One teenager wants to leave her family home, preferring to live in foster care. They find the courage, even the shy ones, to read their stories out loud. They encourage each other, tease each other and support each other. They read things so emotionally honest that I want to cry.

The children we pass by every day—at malls, in subways, on the street, in parks and in libraries making too much noise—carry burdens we do not imagine. Writing is not enough, I think, so when I'm away from them I pray:

*Lord, bless all the children of the world and help us to remember that they belong to Your family and to our families as well.*
—Sharon Foster

*January*

**SEEDS OF LOVE**

1 _____

2 _____

3 _____

4 _____

5 _____

6 _____

7 _____

8 _____

9 _____

10 _____

11 _____

12 _____

13 _____

14 _____

15 _____

*January*

16 ___

17 ___

18 ___

19 ___

20 ___

21 ___

22 ___

23 ___

24 ___

25 ___

26 ___

27 ___

28 ___

29 ___

30 ___

31 ___

# February

*Beloved, let us love one another:
for love is of God....*

—I John 4:7

*February*

## ❧ A PATH TO SIMPLICITY

*Tue 1*  *Pride goes before destruction....* —PROVERBS 16:18 (NAS)

**RELINQUISHING PRIDE**

The recession was continuing to take its toll. When more of the decorating magazines I'd worked for ceased publication, I took another good, hard look around my cabin. In the twenty years I'd styled homes for photography, I'd seriously blurred the boundaries between work and home. Besides the countless props I owned, my shelves were lined with hundreds of books on interior design and my basement served as a library of photographs of clients' homes and published articles.

Somewhere along the way, I'd lost my sense of priorities. Worst of all, the clutter—all necessary for the job I'd held—drained my physical, mental and creative energy. I learned that clutter makes everything more complicated. It also makes you disorganized, lowers your self-esteem, robs your peace, takes a toll on your most precious relationships and leaves little room for new ones.

The first step in reclaiming my cabin meant relinquishing my pride. For two decades I'd prided myself on having any reference an editor or client requested. When a call came to style a home, I could do it with props I single-handedly owned. I also prided myself on being a perfectionist.

But now all that stuff simply defeated me. Making decisions as to what to keep and what to throw away, sell or give away is hard work. In my struggle to rid myself of meaningless materials, the fear of not "doing it right" immobilized me.

Then a wiser Voice broke through my prideful confusion: *If you can begin it, you can do it, Roberta. Don't sabotage yourself before you even start.* By taking that first, tentative step, I was energized to take another, and then another.

*I give my pride to You, Lord Jesus. Help me to strive
for excellence, not perfection.*
—ROBERTA MESSNER

*February*

## Wed 2

*In all labour there is profit....* —Proverbs 14:23

When the Hervey Grammar School across the street became a condominium, the school's rest area remained intact. This crescent-shaped cement structure was built by parents and volunteers around a flagpole where children gathered to celebrate holidays.

In February, a huge storm dumped inches of snow on our town. Early the next morning, James, our eight-year-old next-door neighbor, was in the rest area shoveling for all he was worth.

*What is he doing?* I wondered. *No one would want to sit out there in the bitter cold.*

After breakfast, I went out to remove the snow from our car. James was still working. On my way back to the house, I yelled over to him, "James, you're awfully busy!"

He looked up and said, "Yes. I'm building the biggest snowman ever!" I looked at the snow pile that had grown as tall as he was.

I was surprised to see James still working in the late afternoon. Then I noticed that he wasn't alone: His dad was there shoveling too. Now the snow pile was as tall as Dad.

James had a dream, and he spent all day fulfilling it. When he was tired, help came. His efforts produced a huge snow pile that would remain for weeks.

I turned from the window feeling I had been taught a lesson. To fulfill my dreams I would have to make the first move; then God would send help.

*Patient Provider, You used little James to carry Your words to me.*
—Oscar Greene

*February*

**Thu 3**  *And all the women that were wise hearted did spin with their hands....* —EXODUS 35:25

Of all the on-the-job training I've had over the years, learning to use a spinning wheel at the Canterbury Shaker Village was the most satisfying. Right away, however, I found that spinning isn't as easy as experienced spinners make it look. First, pump the treadle with one or two feet, depending on the wheel. Once you have the rhythm to keep the wheel spinning, grasp the fleece in your left hand and gently feed fibers from your right to create smooth, even yarn—and keep pumping! My initial attempts looked more like popcorn (fibers too loose) strung on wire (fibers too tight), but the spinners never gave up on me.

Thanks to them, I've learned that different kinds of sheep provide different textures of wool: Some are soft as silk, while some don't belong close to the skin. I've learned that fibers from alpacas, llamas and rabbits all have their merits when blended together, such as merino wool for warmth and Angora for softness. No matter what the fiber, it has to be carded (brushed) before it can be spun into a strong yarn.

Though I don't have my own spinning wheel and can barely knit, I was invited to knit twice a month with these friendly women, who really know what they're doing. (One even raises her own sheep!) After making eleven scarves, all exactly the same stitch, I now have enough confidence to begin a hat with Joyce's guidance and circular needles. My spinning friends will help me to make sure it fits and doesn't itch. We'll laugh when we miscount, unravel the mistakes, and try again. More importantly, after ten years of feeling disconnected from the Wyoming home I left behind, my fiber-artist friends have wound me into their midst. I take comfort in their friendship—warm and strong as the yarns they spin.

*Dear God, You bless us with enduring friendships.*
—GAIL THORELL SCHILLING

*February*

## WHEN THE HEART NEEDS HEALING

**Fri 4** — *Give thanks unto the Lord, call upon his name, make known his deeds among the people.* —I CHRONICLES 16:8

**DAY 1: GO AND TELL**

"Brock, you have to tell this story," my client Judy said. "You have to tell it to everyone."

I'd been telling her what had been happening over the past six months: a broken engagement; a seemingly futile trip to Freeport in the Bahamas; an overwhelming feeling that redemption would be found in the fulfillment of a dream from a childhood filled with reading Ernest Hemingway and Jack London; a once-in-a-lifetime adventure in Mozambique from which I'd returned a new man who was making a new beginning.

Judy had seen miracles before. She had moved to my hometown of Nashville, Tennessee, after her husband lost a two-year battle with cancer.

"You know, Brock, I used to pray that God would take care of him," Judy said. "It wasn't until after he was gone that a friend helped me realize that God had actually answered my prayers. He had taken care of my husband, just not in the way I'd wanted Him to. Sounds like God has taken care of you, too, Brock. You owe it to Him to let people know what has happened to you."

Judy was right. I had already shared my story with a few other people, and they had similar responses. But I was beginning to see that this wasn't just a personal, sometimes painful, story about a relationship gone bad; it was about finding a fuller, more abundant life.

*Lord, how can I have gone in such a short time from the depths of heartbreak to a new life of service? Only by Your grace.*
—BROCK KIDD

*February*

## ☙ WHEN THE HEART NEEDS HEALING

*Sat 5*  *In the day when I cried thou answeredst me....* —Psalm 138:3

**DAY 2: BROKEN PROMISE, BROKEN HEART**

"Brock, we're just too different. I can't really love you. The engagement is over."

It was early in the morning, and my fiancée and I were sitting on the front porch of my house. For the past few days she had been withdrawn, not wanting to see me. Now I sat stunned as she got up, went to her car and drove away.

Numb, I changed into my suit and headed to the office. That afternoon, my company was launching an offering and we had until 8:00 PM to get the details entered in our brokerage system. I managed to muster up enough adrenaline to get the job done. But when the rush was gone, I was desolated.

I arrived in the office early the next morning and soon realized I needed to get away. I was almost incoherent on the phone; my computer screen was a flashing irritant.

The phone rang. "Brock, a Beth Baxter is here to see you."

"Oh yeah, I'll be right down." Somehow I had forgotten to put the appointment on my calendar. Beth, a psychiatrist, is an old family friend. I lumbered down the stairs to greet her. "Hi, Beth! So glad you're here."

As Beth and I went over her investments, I was amazed at how hard it was to concentrate on them. She asked, "So how are you, Brock? You must be getting excited about the wedding!"

I explained what had happened, and as we talked, I could feel the pain loosening its grip on me. As I walked her out, she gave me a hug. I had experienced my first full-blown meltdown, and here was the one person I knew best qualified to help.

*Lord, when I didn't know where to turn, You sent me a miracle—*
*a small one perhaps, but a miracle nonetheless.*
—Brock Kidd

DAILY GUIDEPOSTS

*February*

## WHEN THE HEART NEEDS HEALING

*Sun 6*  *To give unto them beauty for ashes....* —Isaiah 61:3

**DAY 3: AN OCEAN OF TEARS**

My engagement had ended suddenly, and I felt as though I was on the edge of a breakdown. I had to get out of town.

My sister Keri had found a trip leaving for the Bahamas later that day. Before I knew it, I was on Grand Bahama Island, parked on a beach chair, looking out at the emerald green ocean. I stared for hours, not moving, as the waves rolled back and forth. And then came the crying.

After my second day, I started taking walks down the beach, thinking about why this had happened. My faith was one of the most important things that had come between my fiancée and me; she was unable to respect my belief in God. I thought I could save her from a life of emptiness and show her the hope and happiness that faith can bring. That's why God was putting her with me, my family and our church. In my mind, the stage was being set for God to show up. But to her, He never did.

As I got a good distance down the beach, I began to talk to God. "How could You let this happen to us? This was all about You, after all! It was all there for her...." I was sobbing now, stumbling; the sun streaming red and pink lights throughout the stark blue sky. As the ocean continued its ebb and flow, the tide seemed to roar, *Why?*

I was screaming now. "I'm dead inside, God! There's nothing left! If You're there, how can You get me through this pain? What can You possibly give me?"

Suddenly, everything stopped: the sound of the ocean, the wind, my anger. Into my mind, clear and instantly focused, came one word: *You.*

*Lord, You have redeemed me and claimed me and
given me a strength that is not my own.*
—Brock Kidd

*February*

## WHEN THE HEART NEEDS HEALING

*Mon 7*  *As the hart panteth after the water brooks, so panteth my soul after thee, O God.* —PSALM 42:1

**DAY 4: A SPACE FOR RENEWAL**

As I was leaving the Bahamas, what I needed to do suddenly became very clear: I was to sell the engagement ring and go to Africa—alone. Normally, trips like this are planned at least a year ahead of time. The logistics for this one would take a miracle. But I believed if it was truly meant to be, it would somehow happen. I e-mailed my family from the airport and my father was the first to respond. "Great plan, Brock! I'll call Bill. He went several years ago and may have a contact."

By the time I got home to Nashville, Tennessee, my father had the number of a professional guide in Mozambique and my mother had bought me a new copy of Ernest Hemingway's *Green Hills of Africa*. A card from my sister was in the mailbox. On the front was a quote from Louis L'Amour: "There will come a time when you believe everything is finished. That will be the beginning."

Then the phone rang. "Brock," said a heavily accented voice, "this is Simon from Mozambique. Your dad gave me the dates you can join us. I only have one three-week period open the rest of the year and that happens to be it. Since that's all that I have open, if you book now, I'll give you twenty-five percent off the whole trip."

"Absolutely, Brock," the chairman of my company said. "Take a month off if you need to." My sister had a list of quotes on flights to get me to Mozambique, where I was to take a three-hour flight deep into the African bush. Before I knew it, the die was cast. In the meantime, I was planning on spending a lot of time with my son Harrison and hoping that God would somehow show me how to heal all these wounds.

*I know You are everywhere, Father, but sometimes I need unfamiliar surroundings to hear You more clearly.*
—BROCK KIDD

*February*

## ❀ WHEN THE HEART NEEDS HEALING

*Tue 8*   *Fear thou not, for I am with thee....* —Isaiah 41:10

**DAY 5: INTO THE WILD**

"Welcome to the bush, Brock," my guide Bryn said as I got off the plane in the interior of Mozambique. The setting was magnificent, as exotic and wild as anything I'd ever dreamed.

Our days began before sunrise with a quick breakfast and then the tracking: almost ten miles a day, surrounded by elephants, impalas, kudus, zebras, warthogs and baboons. The adventure was there. But why was *I* there?

On the seventh day, we got up at 4:30 in the morning to find a group of dagga boys, mature bull buffalo that spend most of their time away from the herd. We followed them for hours and at one point got caught in a ditch surrounded with thicket and dozens of angry female buffalo. Suddenly, a large buff stuck her head into the bush where we were hiding and stomped her feet. Fortunately, she left the bush and didn't charge us.

As the herd around us trampled off suddenly, we left our hideout. "*Shoomba!*" Bryn whispered, pointing to the reason the buffalo had left. There, fifteen yards from us, was a large lion. As he bounded over the hill, we heard his incredibly powerful roar. "We'll stay clear of this area for the rest of the day," Bryn said. That was fine with me.

Soon we were hot on the trail of a very large bull with big horns, the biggest we had seen. Bryn estimated he weighed more than 1,800 pounds.

While I was enjoying all of this excitement, I had a sick feeling of worry that I wouldn't be able to come through when I needed to. I began to shake. I started mentally repeating the Lord's Prayer, not just by rote, but fully conscious that I was saying it to God. After all that had happened, I was once again letting God into my heart.

*Lord, it's when I'm thrown back on myself that I find my need for You.*
—Brock Kidd

*February*

## WHEN THE HEART NEEDS HEALING

*Wed 9*  *Now be strong...for I am with you, saith the Lord of hosts.*
—HAGGAI 2:4

### DAY 6: A HEART MADE WHOLE

We spotted our great bull buffalo, along with two smaller bulls, in a thicket several hundred yards away in the Mozambique bush. It took my guide Bryn and me more than an hour, crouching and crawling, to get closer to the giant animals. *What if I begin to shake again?* I thought.

As we slowly climbed the hill to where the bulls were gathered, I started to pray again, and suddenly I began to hear "Amazing Grace" in my head, as if it were being sung by my grandfather and the other people I've known who are now in heaven. Tears of joy were running down my face; I wiped them away as we got closer to where the big bulls were.

As we set up in front of the thicket, we realized that the bulls had spotted us. I kept praying, worried about the shaking. I could barely see the giant bull through the thicket, some fifty yards away. Then he turned and faced us. The bull was looking directly at me now, into my eyes, and he started to stomp. *Dear God, please be with me,* I prayed.

Suddenly I felt a calm come over me. My body was tingling; the bull was staring into my eyes, and I was staring right back into his. Although I could feel my heart pounding, I wasn't shaking at all. I had never felt a sense of such peace. *This is why I've come,* I thought. *Not for the buffalo or the adventure, but for God—to have Him in my heart again.*

As I looked at the great old bull, I whispered under my breath, "My strength is in You, God."

All I heard was an answering whisper in my heart: *I am always here.*

> *Lord, help me to remember that underneath all my fears,*
> *You are there to be my strength.*
> —BROCK KIDD

*February*

## WHEN THE HEART NEEDS HEALING

*Thu 10*   *"Whoever believes in me, as the Scripture has said, streams of living water will flow from within him."*
—John 7:38 (NIV)

### DAY 7: A FATHER'S MESSAGE

It was a glorious sunrise in the bush. The sky was a burning orange, and now the noises around me were comforting. I felt that I had started a new life. I began to record the sunrise, talking out loud to Harrison, speaking a message I felt suddenly called to send. "Harrison, when you grow up and become a man, there will be times when you will be sad and maybe angry, and maybe your heart will feel like it's broken and you won't think you'll ever be happy again.

"Growing up, I was very blessed to have Mimi and Big Dad for my parents. One of the greatest gifts they gave me was a strong heart. You have that same strong heart. Just ask Mimi or Big Dad, Uncle Ben or Aunt Keri, and they will tell you.

"Harrison, now I know why I came to Africa. It was to share my story—our story—with you and the lesson it taught me. Every one of God's children has been given a cup. Even in our saddest and hardest times, God is always there with a pitcher overflowing with the water of life, but it's up to us to pick ourselves up, go out into the world and hold our cup up to God. He will fill it to overflowing with His power and love, and we will be happy once again.

"I am so glad to have you for my son. I love you, buddy."

I turned off the camera. It was time to go home.

*Lord, in Your mercy, even my tears can become the water of life.*
—Brock Kidd

*February*

## WHEN THE HEART NEEDS HEALING

*Fri 11*  *Oh that men would praise the Lord for his goodness....*
—PSALM 107:15

**DAY 8: THE NEW LIFE**

As my plane touched down in Nashville, Tennessee, I experienced a passing wave of sadness. I thought of my ex-fiancée and all those who build walls that keep out God. And then something happened: A wave of anticipation swept over me, and I knew that the minute my feet touched ground, a new beginning was ripe for the picking. New priorities were already shaping up, and in the next weeks I acted on them. When my son Harrison was with me, night walks replaced video games and I began to talk to him more about God and the goodness of our lives.

The responsibility of serving my clients became a privilege. I resigned from the boards of two organizations so I could give more time to a third that serves needy children in our community. My church was preparing for an uncertain new season with the retirement of my father, who had served as minister for thirty-eight years. As an elder, I was asked to chair a new committee focused on reenergizing the church and spreading the good news. An assignment I would have laughed at six months ago suddenly became my calling.

A part of me will always linger in the African bush, where I came eye to eye with all the horror the world holds in the form of the terrifying charge of a Cape buffalo. And I'll always hold fast to the knowledge that even though disappointments, dangers and fears will come, God is always with me. But just as important as my time there was that day sitting across the table from my client Judy: "Brock, you have to tell this story," she said to me.

I hope I will spend my life remembering—and living—both.

*Father, even the scars I carry in life are reasons to sing Your praises.*
—BROCK KIDD

*February*

## Sat 12

*Hezekiah trusted in the Lord, the God of Israel. There was no one like him among all the kings of Judah, either before him or after him.* —II KINGS 18:5 (NIV)

Last year was a tough time, jobwise. I work for a large publishing company that was suffering from budget cuts and a lack of advertisers, the people responsible for putting pages in the books. Every month, it seemed, a large wave of pink slips arrived and more e-mail notifications were sent of impending layoffs, shuttered magazines and farewell lunches for departing co-workers.

At first I had dreams in which I saw myself working through the night. I'd wake in the morning and take medicine for the jaw pain I'd developed from grinding my teeth. And while work had once been a blissful place for seeing friends and exchanging ideas, it was now a tense place where everyone wondered what this Friday's company update would bring.

I sat at home one weekend, worried about what would become of my department, my co-workers and my source of income, when it hit me: I was doing my very best. I was performing well at work, arriving on time and producing content that exceeded the goals set by my boss. What more could I do? At that moment, I gave my fears over to God and felt a wave of welcome peace wash over me.

When I returned to work on Monday after a delightfully dream-free weekend, I found that I could sit down and work through the day without worrying about the gossip whirling around me about who might be the next to go. I could only be responsible for myself, and with hard work and faith in God's plan, I knew I'd be fine.

*Remind me, Lord, to give my worries to You and to trust You when I do.*
—ASHLEY KAPPEL

*February*

## Sun 13

*And now these three remain: faith, hope and love. But the greatest of these is love.* —I Corinthians 13:13 (NIV)

The other day I received a valentine with the above verse printed inside and suddenly I recalled a long-ago Sunday school teacher who'd quoted this particular passage. "It's part of the 'love chapter,'" she told us, "the thirteenth chapter of Eye Corinthians."

We kids, of course, weren't Bible scholars, but we did know that the Roman numeral isn't pronounced "Eye."

Probably no one can giggle like fifteen-year-old girls. So when my friend Virginia whispered, "Good thing it wasn't from Eye Eye Corinthians," she precipitated more snickers. The teacher's dark look in our direction subdued us somewhat, so we resorted to note-writing about some other Bible books.

Virginia passed "Eye Eye Timothy" to me. I returned the paper with "Eye Eye Peter." St. John's three epistles prompted another exchange, "Eye Eye Eye John." While searching the Bible's table of contents, we discovered eight other Old or New Testament books with Roman numerals in their titles, so in the process we did learn something and our time wasn't completely wasted.

*Thank You, heavenly Father, for Your assurance that love is the greatest virtue of all. So it really doesn't matter whether our name is Timothy, Peter, John or any other—we're still Your kids.*
—Isabel Wolseley

*February*

## Mon 14

*"Love one another. As I have loved you, so you must love one another."* —JOHN 13:34 (NIV)

Last night I helped my grandsons get valentines ready for their preschool party. The cards, which featured a variety of bright characters, had to be pulled apart at perforated seams. Small heart stickers were included to hold the folded cards together.

We were pushing the bedtime limit, sitting at the kitchen table in a circle of overhead light. Drake, five, laboriously printed his name over and over. His brother, three, attached heart stickers, while his daddy wrote BROCK on all of his cards. My job was licking all sixty-eight envelopes.

Brock finished his stack first, and as he was leaving to go up to bed, he came over to Drake and stuck a red heart sticker on his brother's shirt. Drake stopped his printing and looked at the small bright spot of color on his sleeve. "Look, Nina," he said, "Brock gave me this. He must love me."

Sometimes we grown-ups make love way more complicated than it needs to be. A simple gesture, a kind touch, an unexpected card can all say, "I care about you." And, of course, so can a bright red heart sticker.

*Father, thank You for loving me unconditionally. Help me pass that love along today to someone who needs it.*
—MARY LOU CARNEY

*February*

## Tue 15

*"Cursed is the one... who depends on flesh for his strength.... But blessed is the man who trusts in the Lord...."*—JEREMIAH 17:5–7 (NIV)

It's easy to feel independent when you live in rural Colorado. We raise our own vegetables in the summer and forget that we buy produce the rest of the year. I built our house and ignore the fact that I purchased all the materials from a lumberyard. I depend on no one to drive to and from town, even though I didn't build the truck I drive. I feel, deep in my heart, that I'm a strong, independent man. But as Jeremiah also observed, "The heart is deceitful above all things" (Jeremiah 17:9, NIV).

Last January was cold and snowy. By the middle of the month, only my truck could make it up our unplowed hill. At the end of the month, another two feet of snow fell in one day. My four-wheel-drive truck was now as useless as our car. We prayed for help.

Our neighbors saw a road grader clearing the road above our hill and said to the driver, "Our neighbors are trapped. Can you clear the road to their driveway?" My wife and I were overjoyed. Both vehicles could now get out; we were independent again... for a week! Then a severe storm in early February left us buried beneath thirty inches of new snow. More prayers, same neighbors, different driver, different grader and so on, until spring—blessed spring—arrived.

I now feel, deep in my heart, that I am a weak, dependent man. During storms I count on neighbors and strangers. And at all times I put my faith in the Lord.

*Thank You, God, for forgiving me when I forget to trust in You.*
—TIM WILLIAMS

*February*

## Wed 16

*The heavens are telling the glory of God; they are a marvelous display of his craftsmanship.* —PSALM 19:1 (TLB)

It was a dream come true for me. My snowbird friends Kathy and Lenny had called to ask if I'd like to go for a sail on a yacht.

"Would I? Are you kidding? I'd be happy just to take a tour of a boat like that on land!"

Kathy's sister Joanne lives in a condominium near the water, and she has a friend who has a friend who owns the boat. "Joanne said we could bring some friends, so we're inviting you and Jack," Kathy said.

The perfect, warm, sunny February day was magical. The yacht was like a luxury condo on water, with two bedrooms, a full-sized kitchen and a living room. We dined on shrimp, stuffed mushrooms and canapés that we'd all brought to share. Later we docked and had an early supper at a fashionable waterside restaurant. It was a grand experience all right, but when I learned that it cost the captain a thousand dollars every time he took out his boat, I nearly swallowed my tongue.

Later, when I thought about that day, I had to admit that what I loved the most wasn't the boat or the rich life associated with it; the best part was the two dolphins that discovered our wake and followed us for miles, jumping for joy every few minutes as the wake of the 1,600-horsepower engine propelled them upward and outward.

Those two happy dolphins reminded me of me when I'm floating on my back or splashing with abandon in the warm waters of the Gulf of Mexico without a care in the world. No expensive marine gas, no insurance to pay, no upkeep; just me, the Gulf, warm air and sunshine. It's all I need and it's all free, thanks to our great Creator.

*Father, for the heavenly gifts of nature that You provide, I thank You.*
—PATRICIA LORENZ

*February*

## Thu 17

*"You're blessed when you care. At the moment of being 'care-full,' you find yourselves cared for."*
—MATTHEW 5:7 (MSG)

Recently I woke up missing my children and grandchildren. They know I don't need anything, and they don't often send letters or call.

I was indulging in a grand pity party, so I prayed, confessing my whiny self-absorption. Then I read the Beatitudes to see what Jesus said would make His followers feel blessed. My eye stopped at "You're blessed when you care."

I decided to care for everyone I met that day. *Maybe everyone like me needs to be heard,* I thought. *So to care for the people I meet today the way God does, I can let them tell me about their lives.*

It was a remarkable day. At each of my appointments, I asked the receptionists and nurses for their names. At the restaurant, I asked the waiter for his name and introduced myself and my wife to him.

I didn't preach or force conversation on people, and not everyone responded. But the simple act of really listening to the people I encountered had a striking effect: God had filled my day with warm and caring people.

*Lord, when I make my days full of simple caring, I really do feel cared for. Thank You for the blessing.*
—KEITH MILLER

*February*

## Fri 18

*And gather her that was driven out....*
—Zephaniah 3:19

We were not going to get another cat. Two were enough, especially since our cats were always "inside only" cats, and the house was just not that big. We already shared it with Tau, nineteen, and Chi, nearly nine. Besides, our dog Hobo weighed seventy-five pounds and would likely intimidate a new animal.

Then a tortoiseshell kitten wandered up the driveway. She was a tiny little thing, but not in bad shape. We tried to ignore her.

The kitten moved onto our deck, and suddenly all the birds we fed regularly were in some peril. So we were forced to feed her to keep her from chasing them. And every time we took food out to her, she meowed and purred and rubbed against us and was generally too adorable for words. We didn't so much weaken as fall completely apart, resolutions forgotten. We took her to the vet, got a clean bill of health and brought her home. We were warned that because she'd been an outdoor cat, she would always try to escape.

To our surprise, she not only didn't want to go out, but she took over the house. In two days, she knew every room, every stick of furniture; it was all hers. Oh, she liked to look out the windows, but it was clear that being inside and part of our family had been her goal from the beginning.

It's still a bit of a battle. Tau is too old to play, and he lets her know that with no hesitation when she tries to entice him. Chi would rather the kitten caught fire; there is much hissing and growling when she comes anywhere near her. And Hobo is upset at being bossed around by a five-pound cat. But we're all adjusting.

*We are grateful for the reminder, God, that Your plans always make ours look puny.*
—Rhoda Blecker

*February*

## Sat 19
*For we walk by faith, not by sight.* —II CORINTHIANS 5:7

I used to play hockey without a helmet. (I know, I know: dumb. Neither evolution nor intelligent design can explain how I got this far.) In any case, an errant stick caught me near the eye and down I went.

I was on all fours, watching the blood pool inside my eyelid. *Dear God, I think I lost my eye.* Then I had a second thought: *What will people think of me when I tell them what happened?* This was followed by a final thought: *Dude, you've got bigger problems than what other people think.*

Thankfully the blood was from my lid, and the damage to the cornea was mighty painful but not permanent. Still, I was unable to open my bandaged eyes for a while.

Not seeing for a spell teaches some harsh lessons. Healing takes time, you can rely on others for help, and Saint-Exupéry's *Little Prince* was correct: What's essential is invisible to the eye.

I hate to use the pun "insight," but there you have it. And that might be the toughest lesson of all, straight from Dorothy's mouth in *The Wizard of Oz*: Whatever you learn comes from someplace inside. If you're worried about what others may think of you, then, dude, you've got bigger problems.

*Lord, You are the only other Whose opinion really counts.*
—MARK COLLINS

---

### READER'S ROOM

Recording my thoughts each day in the journal pages helps to unlock what I hear and feel in my own spirit. Then each month I review the truths I have received in a "nutshell." I crack them open and get the goodies they contain. —*Joan Boyer, Battle Creek, Michigan*

*February*

## ❋ TO SAY GOOD-BYE

*Sun 20*  ...*As one that mourneth for his mother.* —Psalm 35:14

**OUT OF THE SHADOWS**

The empty sanctuary of Hillsboro Presbyterian Church takes on a sort of golden glow in what remains of the day. The twilight falls in shafts across the pews. The big cross in the front casts shadows that seem to come alive with memories of the past. If God is my Father, then this church is most certainly my mother. For so many years, this has been my safe place and soon I'll have to leave.

In the Presbyterian tradition, when ministers leave a church, they leave completely. My husband has chosen to leave because he loves this church and he wants it to live on, strong and viable. He knows there's a danger in overstaying.

I walk down the aisle and place my hand on the arm of the pew where I raised my children, sat with my parents, suffered over wars, prayed for peace, found comfort, struggled to forgive, felt God. I breathe in the air of this place that holds the memories of beautiful souls. Who will remember Diane, forever young, giving her best to Hillsboro's people? Who will see Gail holding little Katie in her arms, or Kathleen or Rubye, Tommy Sue or Anne? I imagine them all here in this place that they loved—all gone, with only me to call their names.

But even in my grief, I feel the beginning of a breeze coming in from an unknown place. My thoughts expand to include those who have lost jobs or loved ones and, like me, experienced unexpected change. When circumstances turn our lives upside down, who decides what's an ending and what's a beginning?

My friend Deanna once wrote: "Only when you come to the end and leap out into the darkness will you discover that you have wings to fly."

*Father, even as I mourn what I'm losing, help me to fly, trusting You to take me to places that I haven't yet imagined.* —Pam Kidd

*February*

## Mon 21

*Like living stones be yourselves built into a spiritual house.... —*I Peter 2:5 (RSV)

Playing tour guide, I welcomed my niece and her young family to Washington, DC. When four-year-old Colin returned to New York, he gave his teacher a report of his trip. After naming creatures on display at the Natural History Museum, he noted seeing "a green man with a dog." His final comment: "And Mr. Lincoln just sits there."

The green man? The focal statue of FDR and his dog Fala at the Franklin Delano Roosevelt Memorial. And, of course, a stone-faced Abraham Lincoln strikes an impressive pose in his memorial, keeping watch over the National Mall. Colin also saw memorials to two Founding Fathers: the obelisk that commemorates George Washington and the dome that keeps the rain off the bronze statue of Thomas Jefferson.

Washington, DC, is full of stone and metal monuments to past heroes and presidents: Andrew Jackson, Ulysses S. Grant, Theodore Roosevelt, to name a few who are less conspicuous than the postcard scenes I showed Colin. But my local area, as well as yours, is also honored to be the home of what Oswald Chambers called "living monuments of God's grace": men and women and younger folk who pray and serve, help and hope, overcoming hardship and reaching out with encouragement.

They'll never receive the type of recognition we reserve for our national leaders. Most won't even be acknowledged by a plaque in a park, to say nothing of a chiseled likeness sitting regally in a marble chair. But these are the people who build strong communities and, multiplied from region to region, a strong nation. Today I intend to list a few names and send a few cards expressing my heartfelt thanks.

*Lord, thank You for the living monuments of Your grace who grace my neighborhood.*
—Evelyn Bence

*February*

## Tue 22

*A lazy fellow is a pain to his employers—like smoke in their eyes or vinegar that sets the teeth on edge.*
—Proverbs 10:26 (TLB)

Reliability is better than brilliance, in my opinion. Two of my college students demonstrate the difference.

One was a "whiz kid," the first one done with quizzes, who always scored 100 percent. His term paper was a masterpiece, but three days late. He was late to class twelve times and absent nine times. If I called on him to recite, he didn't hear me because he was texting his girlfriend. If I wanted him to lead a small group, I could count on him *not* to be there.

The other student was of average intelligence. He just squeaked by on the quizzes, and his term paper was unremarkable. However, he was the first one in the classroom every day and he never missed a single session. If I called on him, he was ready with a thoughtful answer. When I asked for volunteers to serve on a panel, his hand was the first one in the air. In the end, I gave him generous bonus points for his contributions.

The second student inspired me by his constancy. He made me feel that he was interested in learning by being the first one in the room. When I missed a class, he stopped me in the hall. "Where were you today, Mr. Schantz? We all missed you." He inspired me to be more responsible. I found myself getting my papers graded and back to students in record time.

Being reliable takes work and sacrifice, but it increases our value to those who depend on us.

*Lord, I want to be someone You can count on every day.*
—Daniel Schantz

*February*

## JOURNEY IN THE DARK

*Wed 23*    *"Abba, Father," he said, "everything is possible for you. Take this cup from me...."*
—Mark 14:36 (NIV)

**THE COMFORT OF FRIENDS**

"Father... please take this cup of suffering away from me," Jesus pleaded in the darkening Garden of Gethsemane. No one can know what pain and grief lay behind those words, but they came suddenly and unexpectedly into my mind when my therapist told me quietly but firmly, "It's time for electroconvulsive therapy, Brigitte. You are losing this battle." Depression has shadowed my life for years, yet I'd always imagined I could endure it into defeat.

But now it was hard to eat, a major task to pick up a ringing telephone and, even worse, hard to feel the usual blessings of affectionate children and incorrigibly winning grandchildren. ECT is feared for its ability to wipe out short-term memory. But did I have a choice?

I trusted my therapist, so I took medical leave from work, even though I felt life as I had known it might be over.

I underestimated something simple and powerful: friendship. Led by a fellow depressive, my friends closed around me. Alice drew up lists of who would take me to the hospital, who would make sure I got home and how to reach my doctors. I knew memory might leave me, so I bought a large red notebook and resolved to write down everything that happened before and during my treatment.

My notes tell me that my friends took time off work, rearranged their busy schedules, e-mailed one another with progress reports, brought me cupcakes and offered prayers. The curse of depression became the blessing of love.

*Thank You, Lord, for the faith and care of true friends.*
—Brigitte Weeks

*February*

### Thu 24

> "Why do you look at the speck of sawdust in your brother's eye and pay no attention to the plank in your own eye?"
> —MATTHEW 7:3 (NIV)

The thought was set on repeat in my mind. *I can't believe he hasn't written back yet!*

I had sent an e-mail to a fellow motivational speaker proposing a speech we could do together. I thought it was a pretty good idea, but apparently he didn't. Or, at least, he hadn't bothered to write back, so I assumed he didn't like it.

*But he could surely take a minute to reply and say so,* I thought.

Several other people had been ignoring my e-mails recently too: a friend from college whom I'd written to wish a happy birthday; a client I'd contacted with a question. What was wrong with these people? What was their problem?

Then one day I happened to be searching my e-mail archives when I came across a return e-mail from my motivational-speaker friend. He'd written to say he loved my idea and wanted to talk about it by phone. I searched a bit more and found that my friend with the birthday had written me back, too, and so had that client. But their e-mails had been deleted without my seeing them.

A quick investigation revealed that when I installed a computer program last month to get rid of spam (those unwanted commercial e-mails), I set it up incorrectly so that it was filtering out important messages too.

As I wrote apologies to my friends, I marveled at how easily I had blamed others without even considering that I might be the source of the problem. I resolved next time to examine my own faults first.

> *Lord, please help me to extend the hand of grace—*
> *not that of judgment—in my relationships.*
> —JOSHUA SUNDQUIST

*February*

## ⌛ ADVICE FROM AUNT ANNIE

*Fri 25*  Do things in such a way that everyone can see you are honest clear through. —ROMANS 12:17 (TLB)

**WILLIE'S PIG**

My father was the most honest man I've ever known. I still remember the time he drove more than forty miles to return two dollars we'd been undercharged at a café.

According to Aunt Annie, Daddy came by his honesty honestly. "Our father," she wrote, "was the most scrupulously honest person I have ever known." She went on to relate the story of a broken promise from Grandfather's childhood.

His dad gave him a runt pig to raise, promising that Grandfather could keep the money when it sold. Grandfather took special care of the pig for months, but his dad kept the sale price. "Willie's pig turned out to be Pa's hog," Grandfather said, shaking his head sadly. "My father was a good man in many ways, but after that, I resolved that I'd always be square, even in the little things."

I confess that the kind of honesty Grandfather and Daddy exemplified is sometimes difficult for me. As my family will testify, I like to make a good story better. There are times when I don't tell the whole truth. And I'm usually way less than honest when someone asks, "How do you think I look in this minidress?"

Remembering Willie's pig is helping me cultivate the deep-down honesty that should be a hallmark of everyone's life. Daily, I'm striving to stick to the facts, tell the whole story, and be truthful but tactful—even when a friend's dress is six inches too short.

*Lord Jesus, help me always to be square, even in the little things.*
—PENNEY SCHWAB

*February*

## Sat 26

*"If any want to become my followers, let them deny themselves and take up their cross daily and follow me."*
—LUKE 9:23 (NRSV)

Jump shot from fifteen feet away is *goooood!* Great play on defense.... Another shot, another basket—he's having a good day today!"

Maybe you heard those words, or some like them, on the basketball game you or someone in your family was watching last night or last week or last month. But they would also describe the way I played basketball today.

I play pickup basketball periodically down at the local college gym. I love the game, and the exercise is really good for me. I'm no star player by any description, but some days I'll make my share of shots, track down rebounds, play good defense.

But only on some days. Other days, like the one the week before, I have a hard time making any shots and too often simply find myself in the wrong place at the wrong time to help out teammates. I'm way too erratic. I just don't play enough to improve my skills and play well more consistently.

I'm discovering how much there is in common between my jump shot and my faith life, and this is the most important link: To do it effectively, you've got to do it regularly. No exceptions.

That's why I've made a new commitment this year to make time for consistent daily prayer and Bible reading—no exceptions, no excuses. It's because I want my faith to be better, stronger, more effective. All those missed jump shots have taught me how: Just do it, do it, do it, every day.

*Swish.*

*Give me the courage, the strength, the focus, O God, to learn about You and live for You every single day.*
—JEFF JAPINGA

*February*

## Sun 27

*Now choose life, so that you and your children may live and that you may love the Lord your God, listen to his voice, and hold fast to him. For the Lord is your life....*
—Deuteronomy 30:19–20 (niv)

When I first heard the voice of God, I was stunned, as if struck by lightning. I'd been participating in a small group discussion on having a personal relationship with God. His words were not audible, merely whispered deep within my soul. They were simple, yet they profoundly changed my life: *Hal, I love you. Won't you love me?*

Until then, I wasn't even sure God was real. But that encounter removed all my doubts, and I determined to learn all I could about this God Who loved me. So I began devouring the one source I felt would tell me everything I needed to know: the Bible.

Since that day thirty-nine years ago, God has spoken to me often, sometimes in quiet whispers, but mostly through Scripture. For instance, a passage in Deuteronomy suddenly sprang to life, leading me to leave my job as a newspaper reporter in Hawaii and move to California, not knowing what lay ahead. After I obeyed, I became a Bible smuggler for Brother Andrew. Later I joined *Guideposts* magazine, as God continued to guide.

My experience isn't unique. From books I've read and friends who've shared their own spiritual journeys with me, I've learned that God desires a personal relationship with each of us. And so, with much anticipation, I continue to seek Him in prayer and in His Word and listen for what He wants to tell me.

*Father, thank You for the Voice that assures me of Your constant love.*
—Harold Hostetler

*February*

## Mon 28
*He healeth the broken in heart, and bindeth up their wounds.* —PSALM 147:3

I realized this week that I'm a broken person carrying the scars of childhood traumas. At work, a man's suggestive comments and aggressive behavior had become so disturbing that I'd grown afraid. When he followed me outdoors one night with even more to say, I went a little crazy. "Get away from me!" I screamed over and over, my throat hurting. "Get away from me! *GET AWAY FROM ME!*" He switched to derision, and what followed was a regular hullabaloo when my boss came out, alerted by all the hollering.

The ruckus left me badly shaken. *What's the matter with me?* I wondered. *I thought I was a bigger person than this. And doesn't God expect better of me?*

I thought of my granddaughter. Last month, two-year-old Evelyn broke her leg. When her dad called to tell me, the news made me sick to my stomach. The next day when she arrived at my house, asleep in her car seat, curls spilling down over her face, I nearly cried. Life is so fragile. We break so easily.

Today, Evelyn is limping about in her cast, God's healing process slowly at work. None of us expect more of her than she's capable of. We carry her when she can't manage. Isn't this what God does for us? For me? Doesn't He feel "sick to His stomach" when we break, when our psyches and souls suffer pain?

> *Dear God, help me to trust Your healing process, slow as it may seem, knowing that You don't expect more of me than I'm capable of and that You carry me when I can't manage on my own.*
> —BRENDA WILBEE

*February*

**SEEDS OF LOVE**

1

2

3

4

5

6

7

8

9

*February*

10 _____

11 _____

12 _____

13 _____

14 _____

15 _____

16 _____

17 _____

18 _____

19 _____

*February*

20 ___

21 ___

22 ___

23 ___

24 ___

25 ___

26 ___

27 ___

28 ___

# March

*This is my commandment,
That ye love one another,
as I have loved you.*

—John 15:12

*March*

## A PATH TO SIMPLICITY

*Tue 1*  *There is an appointed time for everything.... A time to weep and a time to laugh....* —ECCLESIASTES 3:1, 4 (NAS)

**SEEING THE HUMOR IN THINGS**

I thought I was making real progress in my path toward a simpler life when the unexpected happened: My laundry room and walk-in closet flooded, thanks to century-old pipes. In a panic, I lugged hangers full of my best clothes upstairs to a clear spot in the living room. Over in a corner were more piles of clothes, brought from my parents' home to sort for a charitable donation.

"Ask for help when you need it," I'd recently read in a how-to book on de-cluttering. Desperate, I telephoned James, who'd rescued a friend from an array of household disasters. "Don't you worry, ma'am," he told me. "We'll get 'er done."

By eleven o'clock, James was knocking on the front door of the cabin. I ushered him into the living room, although not much living had been done there of late. "Excuse the mess," I began. "But I guess that's why you're here."

James gazed wide-eyed from one end of the living room to the other. The space was jam-packed with clothes; you could hardly see the glistening log walls with their gray mortar chinking. I was filled with shame that I'd allowed my cabin, the one spot on earth that was mine alone, to fall into such a state. There wasn't even an empty chair to offer my willing worker. Then James piped up: "Got any thirty-six thirty-two blue jeans?"

*Oh no! James thinks my home is a store!* I began to laugh...and laugh...and laugh.

My father's pants were precisely what James had in mind. "Let's get to work and see what we can find," I said.

*Thank You, God, for helpers who come to my rescue—with humor.*
—ROBERTA MESSNER

*March*

## Wed 2

*And let us consider one another to provoke unto love....*
—HEBREWS 10:24

A new employee was crying in the ladies' room of the bookstore where I work. "What's wrong?" I asked.

"A customer yelled at me because I hadn't heard of Dostoevsky. And then I couldn't spell it right, so he yelled again. I'm ready to quit!"

"Oh, does that bring back memories of my first days on the job," I told her.

"Something this bad happened to you?" she asked.

"Let me tell you the story of *The Red Pumpernickel*," I said. "A man rushed in during my first month on the job. 'I need this book right away, *The Red Pumpernickel*. My kid needs it for school.' I looked it up. Nothing.

"When I told him that I'd come up with nothing, he rolled his eyes and said that he wanted to speak to a manager. I was sure that the manager would know the book right off the bat. *God, don't let the manager fire me on the spot,* I prayed. But the manager looked as mystified as I was.

"The man continued to holler. 'My kid said it's required, and everyone would have heard of it. He said it was written by some kind of royalty.'

"*School. Required reading. Royalty.* Something clicked.

"'Sir, could you mean *The Scarlet Pimpernel* by Baroness Orczy?'"

The newbie gasped. "Did he apologize?"

"No," I said, "but as he stormed off with the book, his face was as red as a—"

"Pumpernickel," we both said at the same moment, and the two of us were off in gales of laughter.

"I thought I was the only one who felt so . . . inadequate," she told me. "I feel so much better now."

"So go back out there," I said. "And if you need any help, don't hesitate to ask me. I've become an expert."

*When someone is hurting and feels alone, God, remind me of those healing words, "I've been there too. I understand."*
—LINDA NEUKRUG

DAILY GUIDEPOSTS

## March

### Thu 3

*The Sovereign Lord is my strength; he makes my feet like the feet of a deer, he enables me to go on the heights....*
—HABAKKUK 3:19 (NIV)

For twenty-seven years, I had the privilege of serving as president of Mendenhall Ministries, a rural Christian community organization. For the past eleven years, I served as executive director and then president of Mission Mississippi. When I stepped down as president, the Mission Mississippi board allowed me to remain in a part-time position.

It was quite a change to move from being *the* decision maker to being just one of the people in the room. It sounds great to be able to serve without all the responsibility, but in practice it isn't easy to adjust. I'm asking God to give me wisdom to deal with these changes.

Habakkuk 3:19 has become a particularly important Scripture for me in this season of my life. I'm learning how to trust this sovereign Lord as I go on this journey. And my God is giving me the strength to walk without the titles, the position or the authority, and to live out the meaning of being a servant, not just in theory, but in practical reality.

*Lord, help me to continue to learn how to depend on You, and help me to offer everything to You, including my pride.*
—DOLPHUS WEARY

---

### READER'S ROOM

I have always known that God loves me, but only in the past year have I realized how very much! It seems that the bond has grown sweeter, and I am more confident in Who He says He is and in His enduring promises. I'm learning to praise Him as David encourages us to do: "Seven times a day do I praise thee..." (Psalm 119:164).

—*Ruth Hefner, Duncan, Oklahoma*

## Fri 4

*"Get up, pick up your pallet and walk."*
—John 5:8 (NAS)

I have this theory: I think most of us struggle with at least one big thing in life. For me, it's fear. Fear trips me up over and over. It's weird. If I allow even one pip-squeak of fear to tiptoe through my thoughts, it stirs up others.

*What if my mind goes blank when I'm speaking in front of a crowd of people?*
*What if this mole isn't just a mole?*
*What if . . . ? What if . . . ? What if . . . ?*

Fear has been my enemy for as long as I can remember. When I'm really honest with myself, I have to admit that it feels more natural to worry and be afraid. Maybe I get charged on the energy. Who knows?

Sometimes—many times—I'll write in my prayer journal, "Jesus, I know I must be wearing You out with this same old, same old." And I sense Him smiling at me, laughing in a kind, relaxed sort of way. As I read these words from John 5:8, I can almost hear Him say:

"Get up, pick up your pallet and walk, Julie. You don't have to stay in fear, all huddled under the sheets today. You've been stuck here on your pallet before, remember? Get up, girl. Get out of that sickbed. You have a life to live. There's freedom, if you want it."

When I choose to take Jesus' hand and let Him lead me, the fear scrams. Every single time.

*Lord, I'm reaching for Your hand today. Let's dance again.*
—Julie Garmon

## March

### Sat 5

*Out of the ground the Lord God caused to grow every tree that is pleasing to the sight and good for food....*
—Genesis 2:9 (NAS)

In my book of Grandma Moses' paintings, there's a depiction of a thriving woodland titled "Sugaring Off." I entered a similar scene late last winter at my ninety-one-year-old friend Ken's farm. As the afternoon sun shone through the trees, my family followed his friends, the Cherrys, through the underbrush from maple to maple, as if we were playing tree tag.

Using a power drill, we bored into each sugar maple, quickly hammering a spile (a metal spigot) into the opening. We dangled old pails once used by Ken's father from the spiles, and clear, pure sap began to drip into the buckets. As it dripped, we caught it in our hands and tasted it. "I'm drinking from a tree," I said with a sigh of awe.

We left our pails to fill overnight and collected others that were brimming and loaded them onto an ATV to haul them to the Cherrys' home, where we'd get to see the rest of the process. As we were leaving, a great horned owl watched us from a nest high in a tree.

In the Cherrys' backyard, the sap was poured through a strainer and then into a large vat on a wood-burning stove. It would boil for hours to yield the syrup—one gallon of syrup from forty gallons of sap! Final treats awaited inside: maple syrup ice cream sundaes and a bottle of the "amber gold" to carry home.

*The Psalmist says, "O taste and see that the Lord is good" (Psalm 34:8).*
*I have, Lord, and You are!*
—Carol Knapp

*March*

## Sun 6

*In bygone days he permitted the nations to go their own ways, but he never left himself without a witness; there were always his reminders—the kind things he did such as sending you rain and good crops and giving you food and gladness.*
—Acts 14:16–17 (TLB)

When I was a child, we said grace before every meal at home. I still do. But we never said grace in a restaurant or public eating place, and for most of my life it was something that I just wouldn't do. If the person I was dining out with said grace, I was a little embarrassed.

But something happened in Savannah, Georgia, that changed my thinking. While we were waiting to get into the popular Mrs. Wilkes Dining Room, my friend Jack and I met two gentlemen, Joe from Alabama and Dan from Savannah. Lifelong friends, they'd been English teachers together for years.

We struck up a conversation, and once inside the restaurant I was delighted that Joe and Dan would be joining us at our table. You see, everyone eats with strangers at Mrs. Wilkes. There are eight tables, each seating ten people, and each table is filled before the next one opens up.

Just as the food started appearing, Joe told our group that Mrs. Wilkes, who had originally run a boardinghouse on the site, had a long-standing tradition that grace must be said before the guests ate. And so we all bowed our heads as Joe blessed the day, the gathering of strangers, our special time together and the marvelous array of food before us.

Somehow that meal, with its twenty-seven different bowls and platters of to-die-for, mouth-watering Southern home cooking, was the most pleasant dining experience of my life, thanks to the new friends we made—and to Joe's blessing, which taught me not to be embarrassed to express my faith and gratitude in public.

These days I say grace before *every* meal.

*Lord, help me to thank You for my blessings out loud, every day, in every way and everywhere.*
—Patricia Lorenz

## March

### Mon 7

*Why art thou cast down, O my soul? and why art thou disquieted within me? hope thou in God: for I shall yet praise him, who is the health of my countenance, and my God.*
—Psalm 42:11

It was a gray, chilly day; even my eleven-year-old daughter Mary, who seems to have been born smiling, was a little subdued as we walked from our apartment building toward the subway that would take us to her ballet class. But as we turned right and crossed the street, Mary suddenly perked up. "There's SPEDBUMP!" she said happily, pointing to a Smart Car parked near the corner. Its bright yellow body, hardly bigger than a golf cart, shone out amid the dull colors of the other parked cars.

We don't know who owns the little car that we've seen around the neighborhood for the past six months, so we refer to it by the eight capital letters stamped on its license plate—as much of SPEED BUMP as would fit, I guess. I don't know exactly why my daughter and I are cheered up by it, but somehow we always are. Maybe it's its eye-popping vivid color, like a sudden splash of Technicolor sunshine on the black-and-white street, or its diminutive size, or its silly but somehow appropriate name, or a combination of all three. SPEDBUMP never fails to make us feel better.

I've been struggling with sadness lately, but even on my darkest days, I can't help but see a little light when I pass by SPEDBUMP. I smile, slow down, quiet my racing thoughts, and find space for a little prayer of praise and thanksgiving. Amid the stresses and strains of city life, what else is a speed bump for?

*Lord, thank You for the little signs of hope all around me.*
—Andrew Attaway

## March

### Tue 8

*O Lord, truly I am your servant....* —PSALM 116:16 (NIV)

"Pick a day at work this week," our Sunday school teacher said, "and apply yourself to your job as if you're working for the Lord instead of for your boss." I picked Tuesday, thinking, *I'm my own boss. This will be easy.* I work at home doing a variety of things: managing our rental property, writing, filling orders for my prayer study program, running a nonprofit and leading a prayer service at church.

On Tuesday morning I breezed through the rental business, answered e-mails and filed the disorganized papers I'd been carelessly sticking in my prayer service notebook. Then, after lunch, I got a call from a bed-and-breakfast canceling our reservations for the next weekend. That launched me into a forty-five-minute online search for another place. Then an e-mail came in with a sale offer from a linen store. I clicked the Web site, shopped, tried to order and had to call the toll-free number because of trouble with the promotion code. When I finally completed the order, another forty-five minutes had gone by.

Realizing that I'd gone off mission for at least an hour and a half, I left my office chair, sat on the top of the steps, put my hand on my forehead and told the Lord I was sorry for wasting His time. Then I went back into my office, determined to get back to work for the best Boss in the universe.

*Dear Lord, help me work faithfully for You in everything that I do today.*
—KAREN BARBER

## March

### Wed 9

*Now your attitudes and thoughts must all be constantly changing for the better.* —EPHESIANS 4:23 (TLB)

I have a notorious sweet tooth. Not only do I enjoy sampling desserts, I enjoy baking them and experimenting with recipes. So it's no small sacrifice for me to give up sweets for Lent.

This past Lent I had lunch with a friend, and when it came time to order dessert, she asked me what looked good.

"Everything," I told her and then explained that because it was Lent I was abstaining. "Giving up something goes way back to my childhood. Don't you?"

"I used to," she explained, "but I've had a change of heart."

That intrigued me. "How do you mean?"

"Well," she said, "I decided that instead of giving up something, I would *do* something."

This was sounding better by the moment. "Give me an example," I said.

"I send a shut-in a card or make an overdue phone call to a friend or relative."

"That's great."

"At first it seems like a task, but I come away feeling better about life. I don't think it's a bad thing to give up something for Lent, but I've discovered that the things I do become habits and that makes a positive change in my life."

I'm looking to make positive changes in my life too. I'll continue to abstain from desserts during Lent because it's good for me and I appreciate them more at Easter, but from now on, I'm going to do something too.

*Lord, open my eyes to the needs of others and show me how I can make a difference during Lent and all year round.*
—DEBBIE MACOMBER

*March*

**Thu 10** *So then, as we have opportunity, let us do good to all....*
—GALATIANS 6:10 (RSV)

My friend Osie sat in her chair and chatted away as the nurse filled a pint-sized container with Osie's blood. It was her first time donating, and it wasn't as bad as she thought it would be. The nurse was a sweetheart, it was practically painless, and the juice and cookies hit the spot. "Thank you so much," Osie said as she prepared to leave.

"Oh no," said the nurse, "thank you!"

Osie felt great knowing she'd done something that day that might save a life. That's just her nature: always generous, delighted to serve and happy to know she's made a difference.

A week later, my friend was riding her bike to school and was struck by a van. People surrounded Osie and made frantic calls to 911 as she lay motionless on the ground. She tried to get up but realized she couldn't move, and then the commotion around her faded into darkness. Osie had broken her thigh, her pelvis and her ankle, but her most serious injury was the internal bleeding. When she went into surgery, her blood level was critically low. She would need a transfusion.

Her mother remembered how Osie had happily shared her experience of giving blood. When she told the doctors, the search was on to locate her donation. Hours later, the selfless gift Osie had given to save a life saved her very own.

*Dear God, reveal to me a selfless act that I can do today.*
—KAREN VALENTIN

## March

### Fri 11

*Thou shalt love thy neighbour as thyself....* —MARK 12:31

I knew from the sound of his voice over the phone that our grandson had bad news. The manager of the electronics store had fired him, he said, for telling a customer that for her needs, the cheap cell phone was as good as the expensive one she was looking at.

"This reminds me a lot," I told him, "of a job your grandfather lost sixty years ago. Like you, we were badly in need of money, so he went to work selling health insurance."

Often I'd go with John on his evening round of calls. Armed with addresses and a map of Louisville, Kentucky, we'd locate a street number in some ramshackle part of town and knock on a door with a torn screen. The "prospects" who'd answered the company's ad were mostly poor and visibly impressed by the elaborately embossed insurance form John would pull from a briefcase. While I tried to coax a smile from wide-eyed children, John would go through the presentation learned in a weeklong training course, concluding with the "sales-clinching maneuver" of uncapping his fountain pen.

But John also had discovered that for certain family situations, another company offered better coverage. Instead of handing the prospect the pen, he would lay out this other option. After six months, with exactly two sales to his record, John was fired.

"Both you and your grandfather," I told a very discouraged young man, "put the interests of others before your own. You can lose a job that way, but you'll keep the integrity that will fit you for the work God has waiting for you somewhere."

*Help me to think of my neighbor first, Father, in all I do today.*
—ELIZABETH SHERRILL

## March
### Sat 12

*Hatred stirs up strife, but love covers all offenses.*
—Proverbs 10:12 (NRSV)

My husband Charlie and I spend part of the year in Sausalito, California. The residents cultivate elaborate gardens where flowers bloom year-round, the bay sparkles, the sidewalks are immaculate, green parks abound, and residents and tourists alike act as if no one else exists.

"What am I, invisible?" I groused one day under my breath, maneuvering around yet another knot of people blocking the sidewalk. Moments before, I'd been all but shoved into the road by a young couple peering up at a mansion on the hillside. And the day before, I'd gingerly avoided two menacing dogs who'd taken over the path while their owners sipped lattes and compared purchases from a nearby gourmet shop.

I set my mouth in a thin line, gritted my teeth and moved on, staring straight ahead. If I could get through the next intersection, I'd reach the quiet, lovely part of the walk. Suddenly a child started shrieking that her father had bought her the wrong flavor ice cream. I bared my teeth, smiling grimly at this further display of selfishness.

A woman, drinking coffee on a bench, caught my eye and smiled back. It was a pleasant, gentle smile, and it knocked the boulder-sized chip right off my shoulder. She'd smiled simply because she'd seen me smile, and it made me wonder what would happen if I put aside my outrage and acted like who I was: someone out for a walk in one of the most beautiful places in the world.

Tentatively, I began smiling at everyone I met. Lo and behold, most smiled back, some even spoke, and all but one person responded.

And that one person? Well, I'm sorry to say that he reminded me of myself... an hour earlier.

*Father, help me to remember that I reap what I sow.*
—Marci Alborghetti

## March

### Sun 13

*But lay up for yourselves treasures in heaven... For where your treasure is, there will your heart be also.*
—Matthew 6:20–21

There's a church out West that I occasionally visit on my travels. When I first visited a few years ago, the congregation was meeting in a simple, linoleum-floored building filled with young families and folding chairs. Today, the congregation has a soaring, almost cathedral-like space. It has well-cushioned pews, plush carpeting and a sophisticated audiovisual system befitting an aspiring megachurch. It also has a huge debt.

On my last visit, the pastor's face was somber. "We're facing a million-dollar balloon payment on our church's loan," he told his congregation toward the end of the service. "But God is going to give us a field goal with ten seconds to play. I know He is."

The Lord promises to provide. But the pastor's half-joking exhortation to his flock—"If anyone has an extra million lying around, now would be an opportune time to give"—made me ponder what exactly God promises. To us, as well as to the church, He promises what we need, not what we want. And when Paul writes in his letter to the Ephesians about a strong church, he refers to love and patience, not sumptuous sanctuaries.

Did that church stretch beyond its means? I don't know. But in that pastor's words I heard a warning to be wise about our finances. Jesus' call for His followers to store up treasure in heaven, not on earth, applies to us collectively as well as individually.

*Lord, when I've fixed my mind on earthly treasures,*
*help me to lift up my eyes and look to You.*
—Jeff Chu

*March*

## Mon 14
*A man's mind plans his way, but the Lord directs his steps.*
—Proverbs 16:9 (RSV)

I was leading a series of journaling workshops on a beautiful college campus in western Pennsylvania. I'd led workshops for a day or a weekend but never for a full week, and I was a little nervous. Could I come up with enough ideas and energy to engage the participants for that long?

Classes were held in a dazzling new building with state-of-the-art technology. As impressive as all this was, my heart sank as I walked in: A podium with microphones stood at the center, with seats curving up and around in tiers; the class was spread out with some people up front, others midway and some on the upper edges with laptops.

Addressing the class from my podium like a chief of state, I led them in some exercises that I hoped would break the ice and get us to relax so we could share honestly and freely with each other. The class went okay, but it was stiff and formal; I was lecturing and the class was merely "reciting." *This isn't working*, I thought. *How can I get through this week?*

That night I slept fitfully, praying, *Holy Spirit, help me. This isn't working.* When I woke up that morning, a voice spoke in my mind gently but firmly: *You're the teacher. You can change how the class is set up.*

When I walked into class that day, some of the group was clustered together in the front rows, talking. "Stay here," I said, putting my notebooks on the table among them. "Come on down," I said to the others in the upper rows. "Let's all sit together."

From that point on, the whole class, including me, sat close together at the front of the room, writing, journaling, reading to each other, laughing, crying, sharing—close and real, pouring our hearts out on paper.

*Holy Spirit, please help me to remember that if something isn't working, with God's help, I can change things.*
—Mary Ann O'Roark

*March*

## Tue 15

*If we confess our sins, he is faithful and just and will forgive us our sins....* —I JOHN 1:9 (NIV)

As I sifted through my mail, I almost threw the cream-colored envelope on the junk-mail pile. Then I noticed Photo Radar Program boldly stamped in black. Even before I opened it, I knew I was busted.

Sure enough, the letter inside had not one, but three pictures that identified me as guilty of "excessive speed of thirty-three miles per hour in a twenty-mile-per-hour school zone." I remembered the moment several weeks ago when the flash of the camera caught me by surprise on an unfamiliar street. I didn't even realize there was a school a couple of blocks away; no children were around and no other cars. Besides, I was running late for a doctor's appointment.

But here was the incriminating evidence. The first picture showed my car approaching the camera. The second was a close-up of my face. The last photo clearly revealed my license plate on the back of the car.

The letter contained lots of small print about my options. Immediate payment of the fine would "close the matter," or I could report somewhere to "set the matter for a trial at a later date." Or I could wait until I was issued a second summons, which would nearly double the fine.

I left the envelope on my desk for several days because I didn't want to deal with it. But every time I saw it, my guilty feelings grew. Yesterday I finally picked it up, reread the fine print, wrote out a check and stuffed it in the envelope. Later, as I dropped it in the mailbox, I dropped my sense of guilt as well. After all, the letter promised that "payment closes the matter."

*Lord, You are the One Who promised that "payment closes the matter."*
*Help me live in the light of that truth.*
—CAROL KUYKENDALL

## TO SAY GOOD-BYE

**Wed 16**  *Thou shalt guide me....* —PSALM 73:24

**A PRESENCE IN THE DARK**

Dot's house is dark. The curtains are drawn and the old radio crackles with static. Her face is the brightest light in the room as I settle down with her on the ancient couch. We talk of her childhood, her marriage, her ninety-eight years. Under my breath, I'm chastising God: *Why do You leave her here alone?*

"Dot, are you sure you're okay, living by yourself?"

"For sure. I have my church friends," she says, "and my neighbors are always coming by."

She pauses. Her voice softens, as though she's ready to share a secret. "At night, I go to my room and sit on the side of my bed and wait. Then the boy comes and I talk to him."

"What boy, Dot?" I ask, looking for some sign of confusion on her face. But her eyes are clear and steady.

"Oh, Pam, you know, the boy—the one who went to Bethlehem to see the star." I sense that I'm on hallowed ground.

"It's so quiet and peaceful in my room. The boy loves the dark peacefulness of the night. I ask him why I'm still here. He doesn't say a thing." She pauses. "I wonder if they have forgotten me and he just smiles. 'Is there something I'm supposed to do?' I ask. But he still doesn't answer. He just waits with me until I fall asleep."

I have come to comfort Dot, but I leave comforted. Surely in the way that suits her best, God is with her, helping her endure, until her day of transition comes.

*Father, be present with us, our steady Guide,*
*pointing out the way You want us to go.*
—PAM KIDD

*March*

*Thu 17*   *And of his fulness have all we received, and grace for grace.*
—John 1:16

My big sister is a major card-sender—birthdays, anniversaries, Valentine's, St. Patrick's Day, you name it and Mary Lou graces my mailbox with a card. She never forgets. Me, I'm a slacker. I'll buy the occasional greeting card but never seem to actually get around to sending it. The convenience and instant gratification of e-cards has made it only slightly more likely that I'll send one.

But I love Mary Lou's cards. My birthday just wouldn't be complete without her greeting, or Valentine's Day without the burst of a heart-red envelope in my mailbox. I don't even need to decipher her left-handed scrawl to know it's from her. And she's the only one who actually mails me a St. Patrick's Day card (in a green envelope).

Mary Lou has been a world-class big sister to me all my life, ever since she got to name me after her favorite uncle (Hi, Uncle Ed!) because she was so upset about our mother having to go to the hospital and have me. I'm the baby of the family, and you know what that means. I got away with a lot of stuff the other kids never could. A little spoiled, you might say—just a little.

And maybe all these years later Mary Lou is still spoiling me a bit. Not that I deserve it. I'm too old. Yet Mary Lou's cards keep coming. They remind me of grace: We don't necessarily deserve it; it just comes. Maybe it's God's way of spoiling His children just a bit.

Next time the occasion arises, I'm sending Mary Lou a card. I wonder if she'll recognize my handwriting.

*I'm blessed, Lord, in so many ways I don't deserve. Thank You for the miracle of Your grace and for world-class big sisters.*
—Edward Grinnan

## Fri 18

*He will make her wilderness like Eden, and her desert like the garden of the Lord....* —Isaiah 51:3

"Stephen, that's the kind of thing we need to pray about," I counseled my five-year-old.

"I don't like to pray!" he replied petulantly.

"Why not?"

"I can't ever hear what God says!"

Stephen had a point. When you're little and think in concrete terms, it's not easy to hear God's voice. It's not easy to hear God even if you're an adult.

I'm finding it tough to pray these days. I do it, but I tend to be forgetful and easily distracted. Frankly, a lot of the time I feel like I'm talking to myself.

I once read that God allows us "dry" times like this so that we come to love Him for Himself and not for spiritual comfort. That makes sense, but it's not much fun. I've sometimes wondered how people without faith get through life, and now I know.

Except I *do* have faith, and though I'm not feeling nourished by it, I still have to live what I believe. I pray, I read Scripture, I serve others. Compared to the rich, fertile land I used to know, this desert I'm passing through seems bereft of life. But it's not. It was in the desert that God fed His people with manna; it was in the desert that water flowed from the rock. The desert may be an uncomfortable place for those of us accustomed to plenty, but it's certainly as sacred as anywhere else.

It's quieter in the desert too. That means I have to be quieter so that I can hear God's voice. I have to hush the voices of discontent and doubt and distraction, and listen carefully. That's hard work. But it's God's work—the work He's given me for now.

*Father, Who still art in heaven, hallowed be Thy name.*
—Julia Attaway

## March

### Sat 19

*Then I heard the voice of the Lord saying, "Whom shall I send? And who will go for us?..."* —Isaiah 6:8 (NIV)

When my elderly neighbor Anne signed up for the hospital's emergency call system, I agreed to be her first responder. One night last week, just as I was drifting off to sleep, Anne activated the little black box that hangs around her neck. After asking her a few questions to assess the problem, the operator phoned me. "She's stranded on the stairs. Can you go help her?"

When I unlocked Anne's door, I found her standing about a third of the way up the staircase, desperately clutching the railing. She immediately exclaimed, "I called them and they're coming."

I smiled to hear her skewed explanation of how the emergency call system works. Ever so gently I corrected her. "You called them. And I came."

As I calmed Anne's nerves and steadied her body, I slowly eased her up the stairs. I stayed long enough to help her into bed.

Apparently I wasn't the impressive rescuer Anne was expecting to come and "save the day." I thought of the many times I've prayed for help and been surprised at God's provision. I expect mighty mercies; the forthcoming aid looks commonly familiar. I call God; He deploys a neighbor.

Before I returned home, Anne squeezed my hand. "What would I have done without you? Thank you, my dear."

*And thank You, Lord, for reminding me that I have a role to play on Your response team.*
—Evelyn Bence

*March*

## Sun 20

*And we have a priceless inheritance—an inheritance that is kept in heaven for you....* —I Peter 1:4 (NLT)

I arrived early at church one Sunday morning, wanting some time to sit quietly. Lately, it seemed that church was the only place I could do that. As soon as I settled in, though, my mind began to race through my to-do list: *Work late next week until the newest projects are finished. Pick up the grandkids from school tomorrow. Ask the children if they want to come for dinner Saturday night. Bake snacks for vacation Bible school.* I sighed, shaking my head. *My life is just too busy,* I thought.

Just then Stephanie sat down in the pew in front of me. After her high school graduation, she'd enrolled in an out-of-state college and I'd not seen her for a while.

"Hi, Stephanie," I said, giving her a hug. "I heard you made the marching band. Congratulations! How's your first year going?"

"Great!" she'd exclaimed. "But I'm really, really busy. I knew it would be a lot of work, but it was even more than I anticipated. There is no time for anything else, just classes, studying and lots and lots of band practice."

"Wow," I replied, "sounds pretty challenging, especially for a freshman. Are you going to continue doing it?"

"Oh, of course!" she said with a big smile. "It's all worth it for Game Day!"

*Lord, may the anticipation of an eternal life with You make the challenges in my life always worth it.*
—Melody Bonnette

## March

### Mon 21

*To every thing there is a season, and a time to every purpose under the heaven.* —ECCLESIASTES 3:1

As I look back over my life, I can see that it's divided into distinct, though related, seasons. Sometimes they merge slowly, almost inconspicuously, together. At other times, a new season starts or ends with jarring suddenness.

A couple of years ago, the winds of a new season blew quietly but vibrantly into my life. I was ordained as a pastor at age twenty-four and now, at age fifty-eight, I sensed that my years as a parish minister were gently coming to completion. This pastoral chapter of thirty-four years had been marvelous and fulfilling. Yet, as I looked toward the future, I knew that I wanted to assist college students in catching a glimpse of their dreams. It was time for a new generation to confront the challenges of the future; I wanted to help them do so.

In July 2009, I joined the faculty of my alma mater, Mercer University in Macon, Georgia, to become the founding director of a new institute, The Institute of Life Purpose. The institute designs and offers courses, seminars and service opportunities to help young people gain self-knowledge and a better understanding of their unique purpose in life. If young adults can be captivated by an inspiring vision, they will be empowered to make our world a better place.

There is a season that we all reach when we begin to live not so much for ourselves but for the next generation: handing them the baton, motivating and empowering them to do significant things. Not to enter this season gladly is to stop growing and become lost in your own aging process. But to join hands with energetic youth and open doors for their advance is to know the joy of the return of spring and fresh venture.

*Lord, use my time with young people to bring back springtime to my heart.*
—SCOTT WALKER

*March*

## Tue 22
*You faithfully answer our prayers with awesome deeds, O God our savior....* —PSALM 65:5 (NLT)

The view of New York City from the thirty-second floor was breathtaking, even on a cloudy day. I could see the Willis Avenue Bridge that crosses from Manhattan into the Bronx and the FDR Drive, jammed with slowly moving rush-hour traffic. For miles around I saw buildings of all sizes, neighborhood stores and people going about their business on the crowded sidewalks.

My wife Elba and I were with our daughter for the signing of her first apartment lease. Christine had been praying for a home of her own in the city; Elba and I also had been praying that Christine would find a good, safe place, just right for her. It had been a long, frustrating process, and many times Christine had said, "At this rate, I'm never going to get my own place!"

"Yes, you will," Elba assured her. "Just give it time. Keep on praying!"

We listened attentively as the manager explained the terms of the lease and the rules and regulations. I glanced across the table; Christine was beaming with joy.

"We have security cameras all over the building and security guards at all entrances," the manager explained. That was just what my wife and I needed to hear.

On our way out, Elba turned to me. "God certainly answered our prayers," she said.

He certainly had: It was the right apartment, at the right location, with the right security, at the right price and at just the right time—God's time.

*You are awesome, God! Thank You for answering our prayers.*
—PABLO DIAZ

EDITOR'S NOTE: *We invite you to join us a month from today, on April 22, as we pray for all the needs of our Guideposts family at our annual Guideposts Good Friday Day of Prayer. Send your prayer requests to Day of Prayer, PO Box 5813, Harlan, IA 51593-1313, fax them to (845) 855-1178, call them into (845) 704-6080 (Monday through Friday, 7:00 AM to 10:00 PM EDT) or visit us on the Web at OurPrayerGoodFriday.org.*

*March*

## Wed 23

*Who can understand his errors? cleanse thou me from secret faults.* —PSALM 19:12

I crammed my cereal bowl, spoon and juice glass into the overcrowded dishwasher, thinking to myself, *Carol is sure going to have trouble fitting in her dishes when she has breakfast.*

I brushed my teeth, picked up my bag and then went back into the kitchen to kiss her before heading out to work. To my surprise, she was unloading the dishwasher.

"I just put my dirty dishes in there," I warned her.

"But these dishes are already clean," she said. "I turned on the dishwasher after dinner last night."

"But," I stammered, "the door was unlatched this morning..."

"I opened it before I went to bed," she said. "I took out a glass."

"My breakfast dishes aren't clean."

"Which ones are they?"

I peered into the upper rack. "Here," I said. "This bowl...and this juice glass."

"What about your spoon?" she asked.

"It's on the bottom rack." I looked at all the spoons in there. No way would I be able to pick out the one that was slightly dirty.

"I'll find it," she said.

"Okay." I leaned over to kiss her. "I'll be home for dinner."

She kissed my cheek back. "See you later."

A marriage is founded on constant scenes of forgiveness. Even for husbands who don't notice that they're putting a dirty cereal bowl, juice glass and spoon in a completely clean dishwasher.

*Forgive me for all my faults, Lord. You more than anyone know what they are.*
—RICK HAMLIN

## March

### Thu 24

*For in him we live, and move, and have our being....*
—Acts 17:28

For the past several weeks, I've been taking a digital photography class at the local university. It's a continuing education course, designed for adults who want to increase their knowledge without doing enough work to earn college credit. It didn't seem too intimidating.

But only twenty minutes into the first class, I was seriously thinking of bolting. We were each asked to state our name, tell why we signed up for the class and show our camera. One by one the rest of the people in the room began unzipping leather camera cases and taking out serious black cameras and big pricey lenses. I clutched my tiny crocheted string purse (the one with the pink and yellow embroidered flowers) and, when my turn came, I pulled out my camera: a tiny little thing... a tiny hot pink little thing.

But I stuck it out, and while some of what the professor said went over my head, I still learned a lot. And I couldn't help thinking how much photography is like life. He advised us to:

- *Get up close.* You miss a lot when you don't get really involved with what you're shooting.
- *Try a new perspective.* You'll be surprised how different things look from a fresh angle.
- *Don't be afraid to blur backgrounds.* Concentrate on what's important.

Yet the piece of advice I liked best was the first one he gave us. "Ninety percent of the quality of the picture is the person taking it." Not the camera or the lens—the person.

Those words remind me that what happens to us isn't nearly as important as how we respond to what happens to us. The power is in the person. In who she is and Whose she is.

I can't wait to see what I—and my tiny hot pink camera—can do!

*Empowered by You, Lord, I face the future unafraid.*
—Mary Lou Carney

## March

### Fri 25

*Like arrows in the hand of a warrior, So are the children of one's youth.* —PSALM 127:4 (NAS)

Going through my old notebooks, I find a scrap of paper with one line scribbled on it, apparently in a terrific hurry: *This girl I liked who I didn't think liked me—she does.* And the whole scene floods back into my mind so powerfully that I sit down, near tears.

Suddenly it is nine years ago, and I am at the dinner table with my son, then age six. He is telling me about what happened at school today, how he lost his shoe that morning in the gutter, and how he and his twin brother started a tunnel through the playground hedge, and how one boy in his class smells like frogs, and how he finally learned how to whistle, and how Mom gave him a candy bar for no reason. And then he says, gently, confidentially, shyly, "Dad, this girl I liked who I didn't think liked me—she does."

I remember that we sat at the table for a long time that evening, and that I had the rare wit not to ask her name, and that there was a look on my son's face that no one can ever explain—but you know the look, and so do I. The words we could use to try to explain that look, or the look on my face as I stared at the sweet round boy—there aren't any words that fit, and all the words we throw at those looks just fall to the floor slumped in jumbles and heaps. "This girl I liked who I didn't think liked me—she does." Isn't that one of the greatest sentences ever?

*Dear Lord, thank You for small boys, and for girls who like them, and for parents who sit there agape in tears at the extraordinary, one-time-only grace of children.*
—BRIAN DOYLE

*March*

*Sat 26* *No one who continues to sin has either seen him or known him.*
—I JOHN 3:6 (NIV)

My son Ross was organizing a cabinet full of old videotapes, many from my first job as a TV news reporter. You can imagine the fun my children had looking at their twenty-something mother in 1980s clothes and hairstyle.

"You look so different, Mom," Ross said.

Maria agreed. "You don't even sound like you," she said.

Well, it *was* a long time ago. But as I explained to them, I was fresh out of school, so I often copied successful reporters as I learned how to do the job. It made me think, *Who have I been copying lately?*

Our culture is loaded with so-called role models in sports, politics and entertainment. And it's easy to get caught up in wanting to copy the beautiful people in magazines, with their flawless faces and fabulous clothes. But the verse from I John popped out at me: To really know Jesus is to want to copy Him in real, practical ways. The way He took Himself away from the noise and crowds to spend time with God; the way He included the excluded; the way He challenged the accepted rules when He knew they were wrong, such as healing on the Sabbath or talking to the Samaritan woman.

Once I began looking for them, I discovered "role-model moments" throughout the Gospels. Now, instead of thinking, *Jesus was perfect and I could never be like Him,* I can see the "how to" that's contained in His story.

*Lord, help me to recognize the ways I can
become more Christlike every day.*
—GINA BRIDGEMAN

## March

### Sun 27

*Bless the Lord, O my soul, And forget none of His benefits.*
—Psalm 103:2 (NAS)

When it came time one Sunday for "sermons from the floor," Lena indicated that she wanted to speak into the roving microphone, and I could tell by her twinkling brown eyes that she had something special to say.

Over a year ago Lena had been diagnosed with an aggressive form of cancer, and for several months we missed her in church as she underwent a series of chemotherapy treatments. But now she was back with a clean bill of health, and as she began to speak, I rejoiced with her as she quoted from Psalm 103:2–4: "'Bless the Lord, O my soul, and forget not all his benefits: Who forgiveth all thine iniquities; who healeth all thy diseases... who crowneth thee with lovingkindness...' *and a wig!*"

Chuckles rippled throughout the congregation. Then Lena went on to describe the awful humiliation of losing her hair due to chemotherapy and how the provision of a suitable hairpiece had restored some of the confidence so severely drained by cancer.

When I cut my hair twenty years ago and donated it for people with the disease, I never thought about God using my gift to "crown" someone else with loving-kindness. Thanks to Lena, I have a new appreciation for the way God takes the little things we give or do and uses them to bless others.

*Thank You, Lord, for multiplying the efforts we make on Your behalf.*
—Alma Barkman

*March*

# ⌛ ADVICE FROM AUNT ANNIE

**Mon 28** *"Don't do your good deeds publicly, to be admired...."*
—Matthew 6:1 (TLB)

**FLAPPING WINGS**

My Aunt Annie's box contained some short pieces she'd clipped from other authors' writings. My favorite is this one (author unknown):

> There is a deacon in our church who is oh so pious! At every opportunity he speaks of his perfect attendance at services, his gifts to the building fund, his compassionate service to other members. Finally, the quietest woman in our congregation said, "I don't mind having angels in our midst, but I do hate to hear them flap their wings."

I pinned the clipping on my bulletin board, thinking maybe I'd share it with a couple of "angels" I knew. But before I got the chance, I heard flapping noises coming from deep inside my heart! While it was true that I rarely tooted my own horn, there were many occasions when I'd acted, spoken or given more from a desire to be recognized by others than to please God: Once I joined a church committee just because it was prestigious; I washed all the dishes after a dinner meeting to be sure everyone knew I always did my share of the work; I even gave to a charity to have my name on the donor list.

All of these actions were good ones. Committees need involved members, dishes must be washed, and charities can't do good works without money. Many times I should gladly do a task simply because it has to be done. After all, is dishwashing really anyone's particular calling? At the same time, it's crucial that I be honest with myself about my motives. Serving Christ to get recognition from others is really nothing more than silent bragging.

*Forgive me, Father, when I "flap my wings" instead of*
*serving because I want to please You.*
—Penney Schwab

## March

### Tue 29

*Lord, you have been our dwelling place throughout all generations. Before the mountains were born or you brought forth the earth and the world, from everlasting to everlasting you are God.* —Psalm 90:1–2 (NIV)

"Oh, Mom, I wish you could see the mountains. They're all around us!"

I was visiting my daughter Laura in Mukilteo, Washington, a little harbor town on Puget Sound. A thick fog shrouded the towering mountains she kept trying to describe. "Over there is Mt. Rainier and there's Mt. Olympia and down there are the Cascades," she said, pointing into what appeared as damp, gray nothingness.

The fog persisted. On the final morning of my visit, I was in my motel room, packing to go home, when Laura raced in, her face lit with excitement. "Mom, come outside!" We hurried through the revolving doors into a world transformed by brilliant sunshine. I caught my breath. There, in all their glory, stood the mountains. Towering and rugged, their snow-capped peaks dazzled the blue sky.

*Such an awesome presence and it's been here all along, hidden from sight,* I thought, *like the powerful, protecting, presence of God.* He's all around us, more real than the mountains. But the fog of despair, the shroud of grief can make it seem as if He's gone. Yet, if I patiently tune my ear and believe His Word, I'll hear His voice through the fog saying, "I am with you always" (Matthew 28:20, NIV).

*Lord God, You Who are the Alpha and the Omega, the Beginning and the End, help me to stay with You in the here and now.*
—Shari Smyth

*March*

*Wed 30*  So the Lord said to him, *"What* is *that in your hand?"*
—Exodus 4:2 (NKJV)

The most popular technology in my classroom is an old-fashioned, hand-cranked pencil sharpener. I have to empty the shavings almost every day.

Who could have predicted that a stick of cedar seven inches long would be so useful for so many years to so many people: writers and editors, teachers and test takers, artists and composers, carpenters and puzzle masters?

Perhaps the greatest virtue of the pencil is its abundance. I'm never more than ten feet from a pencil. Almost three billion of them are manufactured every year in America alone.

The pencil is a good metaphor for one of the most treasured of character traits: availability. If I want to be a more valuable and useful person, I need to be more available.

"Will you teach my Sunday school class while I'm on vacation?"

"Yes, I can do that."

"Can I talk to you for a few minutes; it's important."

"Sure, have a seat."

"Could you give me a hand with these groceries?"

"You bet."

I don't need a college degree, movie-star looks or money in the bank to be more useful. I just need to be handy.

When I say *yes*, I become a pencil in the hand of God and He can write His story through me.

*Yes, God, whatever You want me to do today, the answer is* yes.
—Daniel Schantz

## March

### Thu 31

*Then was our mouth filled with laughter....*
—Psalm 126:2

"We may be facing a recurrence of the cancer," the doctor said evenly. It was clear he had said this to a lot of people, but this time he was talking about my husband. I sat on the spare chair in the examining room, stunned. We thought the surgery had got it all.

"What do we do?" Keith asked.

The doctor gave us a couple of alternatives, but all I heard was the word *radiation*. My mother had had radiation treatment years before and had died shortly thereafter. I felt as if all the joy had just been sucked out of me.

Keith opted for the radiation. They sent us to the radiation oncologist and his staff. Very professional people planned out his program—eight weeks, five days a week—and I grew more depressed, more afraid. They detailed all the possible side effects. I was trying my best not to burst into tears.

Then they referred us to the cancer support coordinator. She was the social worker at the treatment center, and her job was to give us information about all the programs that could help us feel better during Keith's treatment. In her cheery office, she piled pamphlets, brochures and brightly colored flyers on Keith, who is most assuredly not a joiner. She chatted on about all the groups, not seeming to notice when Keith's lips started to twitch. Neither of us could have gotten a word in edgewise.

All at once, the absurdity of the situation struck me and I started choking to keep from laughing. Suddenly, everything wasn't so overwhelmingly terrible. It may not have happened in the way she had in mind, but the "Sunshine Lady" had accomplished her purpose.

*Thank You, God, for a sense of humor and for someone who turns it on when I don't expect it to be functioning.*
—Rhoda Blecker

*March*

**SEEDS OF LOVE**

1 _____

2 _____

3 _____

4 _____

5 _____

6 _____

7 _____

8 _____

9 _____

10 _____

11 _____

12 _____

13 _____

14 _____

15 _____

*March*

16 _____

17 _____

18 _____

19 _____

20 _____

21 _____

22 _____

23 _____

24 _____

25 _____

26 _____

27 _____

28 _____

29 _____

30 _____

31 _____

# April

*And walk in love, as Christ also hath loved us, and hath given himself for us an offering and a sacrifice to God....*

—EPHESIANS 5:2

*April*

## ❧ A PATH TO SIMPLICITY

*Fri 1*    *These things I remember and I pour out my soul within me....*
—P<small>SALM</small> 42:4 (<small>NAS</small>)

**LETTING GO OF THE PAST**

I thought that downsizing my cabin would largely be a matter of muscles and sweat. I wasn't prepared for the grief that would accompany many of the decisions of what to keep, what to sell or give away, and what to toss. I was literally exhuming my life. As I riffled through the endless outdated papers in my office file cabinet to make a place for current projects, a light blue ticket to *Beauty and the Beast* tumbled to the hooked rug.

I recalled the day as if it had just happened. I'd traveled from West Virginia to New Jersey for a meeting. When the meeting broke up on Saturday afternoon, I took the ferry to New York City to see a matinee.

I found my seat, five rows from the front. As the instruments tuned up prior to the performance, I listened to voices coming from the seats behind me. A father was explaining what to expect to a little girl. "Hear that music? It's coming from the orchestra pit. Look, there's the conductor." The father's voice was exquisitely patient.

I turned ever so slightly for a better look. The girl and her father were living out the dream of my life: to go somewhere fun with my daddy all to myself. Daddy worked for the railroad, and with four of us kids, he accepted all the extra shifts he could get. He once took us all to the circus. But a day out with just Daddy and me? Never.

Now I had a choice: to ruminate about all the *could haves*, *should haves* and *would haves*, or to be thankful for the things that were.

I placed the torn ticket in the box labeled "Keep" and vowed to hold all the things my hardworking father did right as a keepsake in my heart.

*Thank You for an earthly father, Lord, who loved me in his own way.*
—R<small>OBERTA</small> M<small>ESSNER</small>

## April

### Sat 2
*"Freely you have received, freely give."*
—MATTHEW 10:8 (NIV)

For the past forty-four years, my wife Ruby and I have lived in a seven-room house. Through all that time, we've been reluctant to discard anything. As a result, we have an abundance of books, clothes, small appliances and other household items. Yet I still can't drive past a yard sale.

To me, yard sales resemble the marketplaces of biblical times: safe places where people can visit, exchange ideas and make new friends. At every sale, I find a warm welcome, courtesy and delightful conversation. I have to admit I don't need another thing—in fact, I feel I should be holding a weekly yard sale myself—but the buyer's joy is searching and hoping to find a treasure. For me, it's always notepaper, books or some good writing pens. But I tell myself, "Isn't that attractive? If I can't use it, I can always give it away."

The next time I visit a yard sale, I'll try to have a different mission. I'll seek things for others: a book long out of print, dishes no longer manufactured, a rare cast-iron toy—anything I know my friends are hungering for. And I'll begin to discard some of our nearly half a century's accumulation.

*Dear Jesus, whenever I stop at a yard sale, remind me that sharing is a ministry where everyone receives.*
—OSCAR GREENE

*April*

## ✸ JOURNEY IN THE DARK

*Sun 3*  *The apostles often met together and prayed with a single purpose in mind....* —ACTS 1:14 (CEV)

**THE PRAYERS OF THE PEOPLE**

Depression is a fierce enemy, making it a struggle just to stand up, get dressed and walk around. In living with it, the name of the game is to look and act ordinary. So while I was waiting for my treatment, I decided to go to church.

St. Bartholomew's Church on New York City's Park Avenue is a beautiful building, always full of life, children, music and people from every corner of a great city. The opening hymn, "O Sacred Head Sore Wounded," about Jesus' Crucifixion, made me feel ashamed to feel so wretched, to be suffering while clothed, fed, and surrounded by loving family and friends. Phrases from my down-to-earth English childhood came back to me: "Snap out of it, dear. Pull yourself together."

*I am trying, Lord,* I would say to myself.

And then the service moved on to the Prayers of the People, asking for help for the hungry, poor and oppressed of the world, the sick and suffering, "and those we name now." And the names rolled out, none familiar to me, but each carrying a hidden history. And then, "Brigitte Weeks," said the lay minister.

*They are praying for me. All those strangers, row upon row, are praying for me.*

We hear so much about the power of prayer. Now I felt it wrapping around me, easing the stress in my shoulders, unclenching my hands. The depression wasn't gone—there was no miracle cure—but a day that before had been cold and gray was now soft and warm.

*Thank You, Lord, for that caring congregation that
lifted my spirit with their prayers.*
—BRIGITTE WEEKS

*April*

## Mon 4

*"And lo, I am with you always, even to the end of the age."*
—MATTHEW 28:20 (NAS)

When I was a teenager, my brother and sister and I liked to gather around my five-foot-three mother. We'd look around as if searching for her and ask in jest, "Hey, have you seen Mom? Where's Mom?"

Poor Mom. And soon, poor me. My days of towering over my children are numbered. Elizabeth has stabilized at about my mother's height, but John and Mary are already there and they still have a long way to grow. Maggie's always been an Amazon and towers over her peers. Only little Stephen (who's still in size four) is likely to be looking up to me for a while.

Suddenly, I'm a mom of big kids. My conversations are no longer punctuated by dashes after a two-year-old. I don't have a baby for whom I need to carry a set of clean clothes. My shoulder bag is lighter; the stains on the laundry are fewer. Instead of having toddlers with ten short meltdowns a day, I have teenagers who condense their angst into occasional three-hour marathons.

Life is different; I'm different too. I've grown more understanding in some ways and crankier in others. I listen more and talk less. I have less energy. I have more time to myself. And as I reach middle age, I wonder, *Do I know God better than I did a decade ago? If I could go back in time for an afternoon, would my faith back then be richer or poorer than it is now?*

I ponder this (I ponder more nowadays) and conclude that perhaps I'm asking the wrong question. I've grown up with God, walked and talked with Him all these years. Most likely, faith has its own flavor and texture over time, in the way that being a mother of toddlers is different from being a mother of teens.

> *Jesus, thank You for being beside me all these years.*
> *Help me love You more, always more.*
> —JULIA ATTAWAY

*April*

*Tue 5*  "Man looks at the outward appearance, but the Lord looks at the heart." —I Samuel 16:7 (NIV)

The request came via e-mail: "And you'd be speaking in my barn...." Barn?

One thing I've learned from giving motivational speeches for a living is that the venue can make or break a presentation. A speech in a brightly lit theater with great acoustics will be much more effective than one given from the corner of a school cafeteria—and I've done plenty of the latter.

When I got that request to speak in a barn, I imagined myself presenting from a stage made of stacked hay bales, my voice competing with the sounds of farm animals—a total disaster. It was for an old friend, though, so I said yes.

A few days later, when I pulled up in the driveway and saw the outside of the barn, I thought my worst fears had been confirmed. It was an old wooden structure that had obviously endured several generations of heavy use.

My friend ran over and greeted me.

"When was this place built?" I asked.

"Eighteen fifty-two," he said. "But we restored it last year."

Restored it indeed. When we walked in, I discovered that instead of listening to animal noises, I was hearing soft music from ten speakers hanging in the rafters. Rather than hay, the stage was polished wood, illuminated with an array of lights. In short, the so-called barn was, on the inside, one of the best performance venues I'd seen in months.

As I looked over my notes, I wondered how often I make judgments based on a cursory glance at an outward appearance. I walked onstage, asking God to help me avoid making the same mistake with my audience that I had made with that barn.

*God, give me the discernment to care about hearts and souls rather than stereotypes and appearances.*
—Joshua Sundquist

*April*

## Wed 6

*When he calls to me, I will answer him....*
—Psalm 91:15 (RSV)

"G.O.D." read the large red letters on the side of the semi barreling past us on the New Jersey Turnpike. "Guaranteed Overnight Delivery. Phone 1-800-Dial-God."

"I don't think that's funny," I groused to my husband John. Driving the turnpike always had a dampening effect on my sense of humor. "How ridiculous! As though God promises instant answers!"

John and I knew better. We were right then on our way home from Washington, DC, where the husband of a dear friend who'd struggled for years with multiple sclerosis had been out of work now for fourteen months. I couldn't count the number of prayers that we, their church and many others had poured out for this couple. We'd stormed heaven day after day, month after month. Still no job, still no change in the relentless progress of the disease. No overnight answers here!

Or were there? I remembered how we'd marveled as we drove away that morning at how cheerful they both seemed. When we'd joined them for their nightly prayer time the evening before, you'd have thought they were the most carefree people in the world: a simple laying of their situation before God and then almost an hour of praise songs and thanksgiving. And they'd waved us on our way today with smiles that seemed to come from the heart. Or from God?

Maybe, in fact, He does guarantee a swift answer to our prayers. Not just overnight, but the minute we turn to Him. Maybe the knowledge of His presence is the first, best answer to every prayer.

*Let me feel Your nearness, Father, as I pray.*
—Elizabeth Sherrill

## April

### Thu 7

*Land that drinks in the rain... receives the blessing of God. But land that produces thorns and thistles is worthless....*
—Hebrews 6:7–8 (NIV)

Our twenty acres of high mountain desert land in Colorado produces thorns and thistles. The young thistles thrive in the shade of the sagebrush, but soon the thistle roots absorb the sparse rain and the sagebrush dies.

I have never been able to protect all twenty acres from the yearly invasion of thistles. Putting on leather gloves and pulling up hundreds of thistle plants every spring is a tiring job. I'll do whatever is necessary to protect the land closest to me, my lawn. I do what I can with the two or three acres that surround our home, but sometimes the thistles put on seed heads before I can uproot them. Then there's the acreage south of the large arroyo that bisects our property. I try to help the sagebrush in this area, too, and although I can't fix the damage caused by the thistles growing so far from my home, I'm a better person for having tried.

It's the same with the people around me. When my sons lived at home, I did whatever I could to keep them safe. I joined our local fire department to help protect the people in our community. And when churches were being burned in Alabama, I joined a group and traveled far from home to help a congregation there rebuild. Could I make that little church so far away safe and secure? Of course not. But I'm a better person for having tried.

*Dear God, thank You for blessing my efforts as well as my results.*
—Tim Williams

## April

### Fri 8

*Sarah said, "God has brought me laughter, and everyone who hears about this will laugh with me."* —GENESIS 21:6 (NIV)

I was in a doctor's waiting room when I noticed that the man next to me, reading a magazine, was making some strange noises trying to stifle a laugh. Concerned for his well-being, I began to watch him out of the corner of my eye. First he stopped up a giggle and then a little bigger laugh. Then he made a noise like *zrggggg-ah* as the stifling became nearly impossible.

Smiling, I turned to him and said, "You need to laugh out loud or you might explode." Given permission, he burst out in a loud guffaw. And when he laughed, I laughed, even though I had no idea what was so funny.

"Oh, thanks," he said. "I just couldn't help it."

It turned out he was reading an article about how men and women are different, and when I asked him to read some of it to me, we both laughed—this time out loud.

Laughter is such potent medicine; there's no doubt it's a gift from God. That day showed me how easily it comes, too, if I let it. And like all good gifts, it's so much better when it's shared.

*Lord, open my eyes and ears to the laughter that's bubbling up around me today.*
—GINA BRIDGEMAN

## April

### Sat 9

> May the favor of the Lord our God rest upon us; establish the work of our hands for us—yes, establish the work of our hands.
> —Psalm 90:17 (NIV)

Spring has sprung in New York City, or more accurately *pounced*, with temperatures predicted to reach the eighties today and the nineties tomorrow. Debates about global warming aside, that's more like summer. Just last week the temperatures were dipping into the thirties at night, and folks were bemoaning what a cold spring we were having. My wife Julee left me a note on the fridge this morning, reminding me to clean the air conditioner filters.

Today I have a lot to do (in addition to those filters): Go to the gym, take winter clothing to the cleaners for storage (closet space is at a premium in New York City), pick up a few things for a business trip on Monday, pay bills (least favorite chore), take Millie to dog park (most favorite chore) and pick up dog food (Millie's favorite chore), shop for groceries, drop car off for servicing. And since I haven't gotten to any of them yet, I'm feeling a sense of urgency verging on panic.

Yet in this season of getting things done, taking a minute to give thanks for the blessing of a busy day is not a bad idea. Yes, we all feel overwhelmed and hopelessly behind at times. There are moments when I feel I will never catch up. But the fact that there is so much for me to do, that my days are so packed with life is a gift, a form of grace.

> *As hectic as things sometimes seem, God, let me never forget that You are always at the center of my day. Thank You for the gift of being busy.*
> —Edward Grinnan

## Sun 10

*April*

*"My Father is glorified by this, that you bear much fruit...."*
—John 15:8 (NRSV)

Working in the yard one day, I gave a tug to a sagging limb on our big maple tree. Instead of bending and springing back the way branches usually do, there was a muffled crack and the whole limb came crashing down. I didn't know I could jump that fast, but I got out of the way.

It started me thinking about what, at any time, might be above my head, which perhaps explains why I peered nervously at the ceiling of the church when our repair project was announced the next day. For a guy who had nearly been hit the day before by a huge tree limb, the thought of putting ten tons of steel up in the rafters as a way to stabilize the walls was not comforting—until I had a conversation with a fellow church member who was an engineer.

"It's all a matter of how things are attached to each other," he said. "Ten tons of steel over your head, properly installed, not only won't fall down, it will help prevent the whole building from falling on your head."

It makes me wonder if engineering is a pretty good image for our faith. If we stay firmly connected to God—with prayer, Bible reading and service—we can do remarkable things with our lives; we can "bear much fruit." But get disconnected and we're likely to fall, just like that tree branch that almost hit me on the head.

*I want to produce the deeds that come from staying connected to Christ. Guide me, oh, God, today and each day.*
—Jeff Japinga

*April*

## Mon 11

> *There is the sea, great and broad, In which are swarms without number, Animals both small and great.*
> —Psalm 104:25 (NAS)

In Florida, we take our manatees very seriously, protecting the slow-moving gentle giants every way we can. Averaging ten feet long and a thousand pounds, manatees have a face only a mother could love.

I swam with a manatee once in the Weeki Wachee River. It was the most mesmerizing, thrilling experience I'd ever had until I visited Apollo Beach. There, every November 1 through April 15, hundreds of manatees leave Tampa Bay when the water temperature falls below sixty-eight degrees and swim into the narrow, clean, warm-water discharge canal beside Tampa Electric's Big Bend Power Station.

The electric company not only provides sanctuary for these manatees each winter, but they've also built an admission-free park where visitors can view the manatees from a long nature boardwalk. They've also constructed an education building, a manatee museum and butterfly gardens on the grounds.

My daughter Jeanne, granddaughter Adeline, my friend Jack and I went to see the manatees just a few days before the viewing area closed for the season. One of the guides said there hadn't been any in sight all week because the water in the bay had warmed up. But that morning we saw at least two dozen of the amazing creatures poking their funny-looking noses up out of the water every few minutes.

As I stood on the boardwalk enjoying the sight, I remembered how I felt when I made my own trek from Wisconsin to Florida nearly five years earlier. I, too, was searching for warmer waters and a warmer life. And just like the manatees, I was surrounded by like-minded people, also anxious to warm up from the cold, snowy north, people who welcomed me and provided loving companionship on my journey.

> *Lord, encourage me to keep making new friends and to find joy and warmth in the companionship they provide.*
> —Patricia Lorenz

## TO SAY GOOD-BYE

*Tue 12*  *Forgive us... as we forgive....* —MATTHEW 6:12

**LESSONS IN FORGIVENESS**

Years from now, when I look back over my time as a preacher's wife, most of my memories will be peppered with laughter and happiness, gratitude and lasting love. But anyone who's ever been involved in a church knows that wedged between the caring and concern, the giving and serving, we all have our rough edges.

"The preacher's wife never even bothers to speak to me."

"If you knew what I know, you wouldn't think she was so great!"

"And where was she when I was scrubbing the parish house kitchen last week?"

"She might think everybody likes her, but I know different."

Criticism, even when deserved, stings like a bee. Sometimes I have to cut myself a bit of slack and realize that it's impossible to be everything to everybody, every minute of the day. Sometimes I have to recognize that I've done something that hurt someone's feelings.

Beyond taking responsibility for messing up in my relationships with others, there's a more unfortunate truth: Sometimes, even in a church, people can be cruel. But it might surprise you to hear that this dark side of the church has become one of my greatest sources of light. It's taught me to forgive, and there's something about forgiving that's pure magic. No wonder Jesus stressed forgiveness so often in His teachings.

To forgive another is one of the nicest gifts you can ever give yourself. It sets you free, clears the cobwebs from your heart, removes the dread from your spirit and gives you back your laugh. Thirty-seven years as a preacher's wife and it's one of the best things I've learned: No matter how tiny or huge the hurt, forgive!

*Father, Your plan is perfect! Only through forgiving*
*can we feel Your unending forgiveness.*
—PAM KIDD

## April

### Wed 13

*Remember now thy Creator in the days of thy youth....*
—ECCLESIASTES 12:1

"Well, what about *your* undergraduate career?"

It's a question my college students ask, and I have yet to give them an honest answer—well, an *unvarnished* answer. I can tell them quite honestly that it was a long time ago (accurate) and I don't remember (also accurate), but I'm not about to tell them why.

It's odd: I turned eighteen, and suddenly it was deemed that I could vote, go off to war, drive past midnight, stay out all hours. But I wasn't ready for any of that. I doubt many of us are. Instead, I pinballed from one mistake to another, bouncing indelicately through late adolescence with all its attendant charms and dangers. I would love, love, love to steer my students clear of the subterranean rocks and riptides that threaten their journey; I cannot. They'll have to find them for themselves.

And now my oldest daughter is in college and my middle daughter is ready to join her. Well, *not* ready, but as ready as she'll ever be. My experienced, postcollegiate heart often finds itself in my throat as I watch my kids venture out together: me waving from the shore, trying to warn them of the terrible currents that they must navigate themselves, and whispering prayers like every traveler and every parent who seeks guidance from something beyond the stars.

*Lord, help me not to be the only one who learns from my mistakes.*
—MARK COLLINS

---

### READER'S ROOM

On Easter Sunday, watching an amazing portrayal of Peter from the Last Supper to the Resurrection, I realized that the disciples' question, "Is it I, Lord?" could be answered "Yes" by everyone—Judas, of course, but also Peter, with his denials, and those who ran away. And me?

—*Joann Woosley, LaBelle, Florida*

*April*

## ☼ FREE TO LOVE, FREE TO FOLLOW

*Thu 14*   *... Mary called Magdalene, out of whom went seven devils.*
—LUKE 8:2

**THURSDAY BEFORE PALM SUNDAY: HIDING FROM JESUS**

This morning I woke from a dream in which a young woman with long dark hair and ocean blue eyes, wearing a blue robe and sandals, met me on the mountain behind our home.

"My name is Mary," she said. *"I'm from Magdala, a village on the shore of the Sea of Galilee.*

*"I loved the man Jesus from the first day I saw Him, but I couldn't imagine actually talking to Him, for my sins seemed beyond pardon. So I hid myself in the crowds that gathered around Him. I listened and I watched and I began to feel a great longing in my heart to be near Him.*

*"Then one day Jesus offered forgiveness to all those who were truly sorry for their sins. I certainly didn't have the nerve to ask such a thing.*

*"That was when a stunning thing happened: Jesus' eyes caught mine and held them in a gaze so loving that it seemed He saw right through me. Without my saying a word, He moved through the crowd toward me and laid both hands on my head. Then He called to the pain inside of me—the depression, the jealousy, the anger, the resentments, hatreds, fears and pride—and as each one left me, I actually felt it happen! Suddenly, my soul felt as light and free as a soaring gull, and I couldn't hold back my tears of joy.*

*"Never again will I hide from Him! The moment I become aware of darkness within me, I'll stop whatever I'm doing, close my eyes and remember that moment in which His soft brown eyes engaged my eyes ... and I'll ask His forgiveness, knowing that to ask is to receive."*

*Jesus, healer of body and soul, please shine Your light of forgiveness into my heart to banish the darkness there.*
—MARILYN MORGAN KING

*April*

## ✸ FREE TO LOVE, FREE TO FOLLOW

*Fri 15*   *The Son of man hath power on earth to forgive sins....* —MARK 2:10

**FRIDAY BEFORE PALM SUNDAY: FORGIVEN!**

In my dream, I am walking with Mary Magdalene along the shore of the Sea of Galilee. We take off our sandals and feel the wet sand between our toes as Mary continues her story.

*"I cried tears of relief when Jesus set me free from my inner darkness. I wanted to thank Him, but dusk was descending now, the crowd was dispersing and Jesus was nowhere in sight. One of the last people to leave told me that Jesus was having supper at the home of a Pharisee named Simon.*

*"Without thinking it through, I went to Simon's house. I found my Lord reclining on a couch and I knelt down before Him. My tears started falling on His bare feet, so I used them to wash away the dust of the road, kissing His feet again and again. Then I dried them with my hair. The Pharisee stood over me, glaring his disapproval. Noticing his condemning look, Jesus told Simon a parable about a creditor who forgave two debtors: one who owed him much and one who owed little. He ended by turning to me and saying, 'Her sins—and they are many—have been forgiven, so she has shown me much love. But a person who is forgiven little shows only little love.'*

*"Then Jesus said to me, 'Your faith has saved you; go in peace'"* (Luke 7:50, NLT).

Now I see, Mary. It's not that I'm forgiven because I love; it's the other way around! I can truly love because I'm forgiven!

*Please forgive me, Jesus, for the sins I'm aware of and for those I hide even from myself. I trust Your forgiveness will free me to love more truly.*
—MARILYN MORGAN KING

*April*

## ✹ FREE TO LOVE, FREE TO FOLLOW

**Sat 16** *And certain women . . . ministered unto him of their substance.*
—LUKE 8:2–3

**SATURDAY BEFORE PALM SUNDAY:
A PRECIOUS PRIVILEGE**

Tonight I dream again of walking along the seashore with Mary of Magdala. Tonight an unspoken question is in my heart: *How best can I follow Jesus?* As we gaze across the water, Mary says:

"After that evening at Simon's house, Jesus and His disciples were leaving to spread the good news of forgiveness and love. My friends and I desperately wanted to go along. I'll never forget the day I asked Jesus, trembling as I spoke, 'Please, my Lord, would you consider allowing my friends and me to go along with you?'

"Jesus knew our hearts. 'Yes,' He said. That was how it happened that my friends and I were given the privilege of being witnesses to His teachings on the kingdom of God, watching as He healed the sick, cast out demons and even raised Lazarus from the dead. Such miracles were beyond understanding, but we saw them with our own eyes.

"We weren't wealthy, but we did have some means and wanted to share it for His sake. But more important, we were forgiven sinners, so we knew what it meant to love in spirit. We ministered to Jesus by providing food when it was needed, finding places to sleep and caring for His needs as best we could. Of course, some people thought it was improper for us to travel with Him, but Jesus didn't let it concern Him. How authentic, how genuine He is!"

As I listen to Mary, the answer to my question forms in my heart: *Give what you have; be who you are.*

*Jesus, Lord, I ask Your forgiveness for the part of me that is inauthentic. Please make me more genuine, like You and Mary Magdalene.*
—MARILYN MORGAN KING

*April*

## ✸ FREE TO LOVE, FREE TO FOLLOW

*Sun 17*  *And they that went before, and they that followed, cried, saying, Hosanna; Blessed is he that cometh in the name of the Lord.* —MARK 11:9

**PALM SUNDAY: A SHAWL IN HIS PATH**

In my dream, I am standing by a city gate. Pieces of palm branches litter the ground; the remains of what must have been a large crowd is making its way out of the city to the surrounding villages. As I turn to walk back into the city, I see Mary Magdalene, her eyes wide with excitement.

"*It's such a thrilling time!*" she says. "*We've been going from town to town where Jesus has been teaching, telling life-changing stories in parables, performing heart-leaping miracles of healing. Wherever He went, crowds followed Him.*

"*Then, knowing something we do not understand, Jesus turned with great determination toward Jerusalem. He sent two disciples ahead to get a donkey that He arranged to ride on into the great city. (I think,* Now isn't that just like Him to choose to ride on a lowly donkey!*) His followers gathered palm branches, waving them before Him and throwing their garments on the road. With a feeling of wild abandonment, I tossed my shawl before Him and watched the donkey walk over it.*

"*I'm beginning to discover what it means to live fully by the grace of God. I have clutched life to me for as long as I can remember and locked myself in, afraid of losing something dear. Today I see that life is something to be joyfully used up in serving God and our brothers and sisters. Part of the glory of this day has been its lack of restraint, its high and unbridled devotion.*"

*Jesus, I want to cry with Mary, "Hosanna!*
*Hosanna! Hosanna in the highest!"*
—MARILYN MORGAN KING

*April*

## ❖ FREE TO LOVE, FREE TO FOLLOW

**Mon 18**  *My house shall be called . . . the house of prayer. . . .* —MARK 11:17

**MONDAY OF HOLY WEEK: ANGER**

As I encounter Mary of Magdala in my dream tonight, she seems troubled.

"I can hardly believe what I saw today at the temple just the day after my Jesus had ridden into the holy city, so humbly and yet so triumphantly!

"Standing outside, I saw Him angrily stride into the outer court of the temple, cast out the people buying and selling there, overturn the tables of the money changers and the seats of those selling doves. Then He spoke: 'Is it not written, My house shall be called the house of prayer? But you have made it a den of thieves.'

"Never before have I seen Him so angry!"

I share your surprise, Mary. Jesus' actions in the temple raise a question in me: *Is anger ever justified?* I remember once confessing my anger to a minister. His reply surprised me: "May God deliver you from the *sting* of your anger but not from the *protection* of it."

I have since come to know that there are times when anger serves. Now, when I feel anger within me, I ask God, "Does this anger serve in some unmistakable way? Or does it just sting the other person . . . and me?" I know this only helps when I take time to listen for His guidance. When I fail to listen and let my anger guide me instead, it stings both me and the one with whom I'm angry.

*When I feel anger rising in me, Father, may I remember to ask,*
*"Does this anger serve or sting?" Then may I listen for*
*Your wisdom and follow Your truth.*
—MARILYN MORGAN KING

*April*

## ☀ FREE TO LOVE, FREE TO FOLLOW

*Tue 19*  "She has done a beautiful thing to me." —Mark 14:6 (RSV)

**TUESDAY OF HOLY WEEK: SACRED EXTRAVAGANCE**

Tonight I find myself in a village outside the walls of Jerusalem. Light and the sounds of conversation come from an open doorway. By the doorway, Mary Magdalene stands, her face flushed with joy.

"I was so distressed that I couldn't eat," she says. "The longing to be near Jesus was so strong, I felt I had to do something. So once again I acted on an impulse. I bought an alabaster jar of perfumed ointment and ran all the way to the home of Simon the leper, where Jesus was having a meal. Without even knocking, I marched right into the house, stood behind Jesus at the table, broke the jar and poured the balm on His head. I can't imagine how I had the courage to do such a thing, but I did it!

"The reaction from the disciples and their host was immediate. I think it was Judas who said, 'Why wasn't this ointment sold and the money given to the poor?'

"I began trembling, but again Jesus saw into my heart. And what do you suppose he said? 'She has done a beautiful thing to me.... She has done what she could; she has anointed my body beforehand for burying. And truly, I say to you, wherever the gospel is preached in the whole world, what she has done will be told in memory of her' (Mark 14:6, 8–9).

"Yes, it was extravagant, but in the light of God's unthinkable gift of His Son, how could I do less?"

*Father, teach me to give without holding back, just because*
*I love. Give me the courage to follow my heart.*
—Marilyn Morgan King

*April*

## ☀ FREE TO LOVE, FREE TO FOLLOW

*Wed 20*  The Son of man shall be betrayed into the hands of men: And they shall kill him.... —MATTHEW 17:22–23

### WEDNESDAY OF HOLY WEEK: THE PASSOVER SUPPER

In my dream, I am again inside the walls of Jerusalem. Mary Magdalene greets me in front of a two-story house.

*"I wasn't with Jesus at the Passover supper,"* Mary tells me, *"but I talked with Peter when he came out. He said that when all of them were assembled, Jesus began to wash their feet!*

*"'Then Jesus said something that troubled me,' said Peter. 'Jesus said that before the cock crows, I will deny him three times! I simply can't believe that! Finally, Jesus made the shocking statement that one of us would betray him. We all protested, but we realized that Jesus knows things unknown to us.'*

*"Then Peter told me that after all of these dire predictions, Jesus also reassured them with these words: 'I will not leave you comfortless: I will come to you. Yet a little while, and the world seeth me no more; but ye see me: because I live, ye shall live also. At that day ye shall know that I am in my Father, and ye in me, and I in you'"* (John 14:18–20).

Mary's eyes are radiant as she tells this part of the story. *"Imagine your own heart being home to Christ in God—the place where Jesus feels most loved and welcomed, the place where He truly lives!"*

*Beloved Jesus, when I feel alone, I'll remind myself of Your promise not to leave me comfortless. I know it's true. Welcome home! Welcome home!*
—MARILYN MORGAN KING

*April*

## ☼ FREE TO LOVE, FREE TO FOLLOW

*Thu 21*   *Then all the disciples forsook him, and fled.*
—MATTHEW 26:56

**MAUNDY THURSDAY: GETHSEMANE**

I don't know where you were, Mary Magdalene, on that night when Jesus took Peter and the two sons of Zebedee with Him into the garden of Gethsemane and asked them to "tarry ye here and watch with me." Matthew says Jesus became exceedingly sorrowful, "went a little farther, and fell on his face and prayed, saying, 'O my Father, if it be possible, let this cup pass from me: nevertheless, not as I will, but as thou wilt'" (Matthew 26:39).

Isn't it surprising, Mary, that our Lord would ask to be released from the death He knew He must face?

*"Oh, but it shows His humanness!"* Mary replies. *"He knew His death by crucifixion would be agonizing and He was human enough to desire escape from the horror of it."*

Yes, you're right, Mary. And His statement at the end of His Gethsemane prayer is worthy beyond all vulnerabilities: "Not my will but thine."

I have a friend Anna who ends every prayer with these words: "This, Lord, or something better." Though her words are different, it's really the same prayer Jesus prayed, don't you think?

*Father of us all, Your will is always better than I can know to ask.*
*So I join in Jesus' prayer: Not my will but Thine—always.*
—MARILYN MORGAN KING

*April*

## ✺ FREE TO LOVE, FREE TO FOLLOW

**Fri 22**  *Daughters of Jerusalem, weep not for me, but weep for yourselves....* —LUKE 23:28

### GOOD FRIDAY: MARY'S SECRET

Mary Magdalene, in my dream we are walking together along the street of great sorrow with Jesus. I feel as though my heart is being squeezed in a vice. I don't want to see Him suffer! And you, Mary, who have known Him and loved Him, how can you possibly bear to watch Him being nailed to the cross? Surely you must feel every pounding of iron on iron, cold and piercing, in your own hands and feet!

Yet here you are with Jesus to the bitter end, as His cross is lifted up on the Mount of Olives. John is here, too, but where are the other eleven? They have deserted Him! But not you, Mary. Here you stand with His mother and John and the jeering crowd. You are stronger than the men! You are not turning away from Jesus' agony. What is your armor, beloved friend of Jesus?

*"He gave me the freeing gift of forgiveness. He defended me when I washed His feet with my tears. He allowed me to travel with Him. I watched His miracles, listened to His parables, and when I anointed His head with oil, He said I had done a beautiful thing. Through all of this, I've been holding a secret within my heart: Jesus loves me too! How could I not be here, loving Him with all my heart? Oh, listen! He's about to speak."*

*"Father, forgive them; for they know not what they do"* (Luke 23:34).

*Father forgive me, too, for Mary's secret is also mine.*
—MARILYN MORGAN KING

EDITOR'S NOTE: *We invite you to join us today as we observe our annual Good Friday Day of Prayer. Guideposts Prayer Ministry prays daily for each of the prayer requests we receive by name and need. Join us at www.OurPrayerGoodFriday.org and learn how you can request prayer, volunteer to pray for others or contribute to support our ministry.*

*April*

## ☀ FREE TO LOVE, FREE TO FOLLOW

**Sat 23** *And I will raise him up at the last day.* —JOHN 6:40

**HOLY SATURDAY: AT THE TOMB**

I knew I'd find you here in the garden, Mary Magdalene, at the end of the long Sabbath. I've learned, from being with you, that you love Jesus above all else. I also know you are grieving after yesterday's ordeal of watching your beloved bleed to death. As you watched His body being taken down, wrapped in linen and laid in the sepulchre, did you wonder if you'd ever see Him again? Watching the men roll the heavy stone over the opening must have felt like a prison door slamming on you.

"*Oh, but you see, through it all I have known something!*" Mary's voice is firm and full of certainty. "*When Jesus answered His accusers by saying, 'Destroy this temple, and in three days I will raise it up,' I knew He meant His own body—the temple of God. Though I agonized over His suffering yesterday, not for a minute did I ever doubt that I would see Him again. And of that I am still certain. Last evening my friends and I prepared spices and ointments for His body. And today we rested, as the Sabbath requires. Yet now that it's sundown, I am here this evening just to be near to Him. And yes, I grieve, but I am not discouraged. I believe in Him.*"

Mary and I stand in silence now here by the tomb. The moon is almost full; a soft spring breeze cools the air. The sky holds its breath, awaiting the stars, as Mary and I pray together:

*Heavenly Father, our hearts are open, awaiting Your Son's Resurrection.*
—MARILYN MORGAN KING

*April*

## ✹ FREE TO LOVE, FREE TO FOLLOW

*Sun 24*  He calls his own sheep by name... and his sheep follow him because they know his voice. —JOHN 10:3–4 (NIV)

**EASTER: NO GREATER LOVE**

I find you weeping, Mary, by the tomb of your beloved Jesus. So I must ask you: Where is the certainty of belief in Him that you expressed yesterday?

*"I weep because someone has taken away His body, and we don't know where it is!"*

I stand off to the side to let Mary have some time alone. A man, probably the gardener, approaches her and says, *"Woman, why weepest thou? Whom seekest thou?"*

She answers, *"Sir, if you have carried Him somewhere else, tell me where you have laid him and I will take him away."*

Then the man responds with one simple word: *"Mary."*

I know that voice!

*"Rabboni!"*

She reaches out to embrace Jesus but He tells her not to touch Him, *"for I am not yet ascended to my Father: but go to my brethren and say unto them, I ascend to my Father, and your Father: and to my God, and your God."*

Mary looks back at me and smiles as she races from the garden. *Mary, my heart cries out, thank you for showing me anew your God Who is also my God.*

As I turn in my sleep, a shaft of early morning sun touches my eyelids.

*Jesus, the Father has raised You up, and Mary of Magdala is surely with You now. May I too one day join Your blessed company.*
—MARILYN MORGAN KING

*April*

## Mon 25

*And they worshipped him, and returned to Jerusalem with great joy.* —LUKE 24:52

My family followed British traditions, so when I was a child, we celebrated Easter Monday as a holiday, continuing to rejoice in the risen Christ. It was a fun day, a no-school, no-mail-delivery, banks-closed day; an eat-as-many-of-your-eggs-and-chocolate-bunnies-as-you-like day. It usually culminated in a neighborhood picnic with a raw-egg toss, a tug-of-war, sack races and, for whoever wanted to join in, a soccer game.

Christ's suffering was over, His victory won. The gates of our eternal life were flung open. Paul Amundson of the Fellowship of Merry Christians put it best when he said that Easter ought to be "a giggle till your socks fall off kind of day." I join him in his vote for laughter and a raucous good time—all the way through Easter Monday.

*Blessed Redeemer, risen Lord,*
*Now and forevermore adored.*
*Rejoice my soul and sing,*
*Praise and glory to Christ our King.*
—FAY ANGUS

## *April*

### Tue 26

*I tell you, now is the time of God's favor, now is the day of salvation.* —II CORINTHIANS 6:2 (NIV)

A few weeks ago, our oldest son Sam told us that he'd been thinking about taking a year off from college, perhaps in a program abroad. I was glad he was looking for new challenges, but I felt a pang of sadness at the thought that he might be so far away.

Today, I sat on a plane next to Sam's brother Ned, traveling home from a cross-country trip to visit several universities as he decides where he'll spend his next four years. It's been a wonderful trip for my husband Matt and me as we watched Ned experiencing the world opening up before him and imagining his future in exciting new ways. Yet today, as we sat side by side in companionable silence, I felt sad knowing he wouldn't be beside me much in the coming year.

Before long, the in-flight movie commenced and together we watched the story of a man, his wife and family and mischievous Labrador retriever. It reminded me so much of our own family and Nellie, our delightful and very poorly trained black Lab! But when a scene opened with a veterinarian in it and the dog lying on a table, I found tears streaming down my face. Our Nellie is ten years old, and I immediately thought about the fact that we may not have too many more years with her.

Then I looked over at Ned; I was sharing a wonderful moment in his life. My husband was by my side, holding my hand. I would get to see Sam again next weekend. And when I walked through the door of our house tonight, Nellie would come bounding to greet me, with a big doggy grin and a wag that made her whole body wiggle.

*Dear God, please help me to live in the here and now, to experience this moment and all the love I feel in it to its fullest, and bring that love to all I do today.*
—ANNE ADRIANCE

*April*

## Wed 27

*Surely goodness and love will follow me all the days of my life....* —Psalm 23:6 (niv)

The automatic doors of the cancer center swooshed open before me, and I entered, feeling a familiar mixture of hope and dread. I turned right down the long hall. I knew the routine: Check in, take a seat and fill out the information sheet.

"Why are you here today?" *Regular checkup for stage-four ovarian cancer.*

"Pain level, on a scale of 1 to 10." *Circle number 2 because I don't have much pain.* In fact, I've been doing amazingly well since my diagnosis nearly four years ago when I was given a two-year life expectancy and told that stage-four ovarian cancer is not curable. It always comes back.

That's when I made a "bucket list" of things I still wanted to do and lived with an urgency that comes with a diagnosis like mine. I even thought of some of the things I *wouldn't* have to do, like paint and update the kids' bedrooms because they were long gone. After all, no one expected me to do that while fighting cancer, right?

But surprise! I didn't die. And so far, I haven't had a recurrence.

Soon I was ushered into a room where my doctor examined me and gave me another good report. "I'd like to break the record for being your longest surviving patient," I told her.

"That would be about twelve years out," she said with a smile. "Go for it!"

So I walked out of the cancer center with a new goal and a lot of new white space for more entries on my bucket list:

- Master "self-checkout" at the grocery store.
- Figure out how to organize about thirty photo albums and boxes of old negatives.
- Paint and update the kids' bedrooms.

I'm determined to keep adding entries, with lots more hope than dread.

*Lord, I trust You to number my days. In the meantime, I'm going to live well.*
—Carol Kuykendall

*April*

## Thu 28

*Her husband has full confidence in her and lacks nothing of value.* —Proverbs 31:11 (NIV)

"How's this speed?" Brian, my soon-to-be husband, asked as we settled into our run. It was a beautiful day, and I'd been so excited about the warm weather that I'd agreed to an after-work jog with Brian, an avid daily runner who also played basketball, lifted weights and swam. I tend to walk more than run, so I was grateful that the pace he'd found was somewhere between my comfort level (a stroll) and his (a sweat-inducing workout).

"Perfect," I said, careful to draw steady breaths.

Our wedding was only a month away, and we were using our precious time together to enjoy a long sunset run and simply savor each other's company. We covered a lot of ground and a lot of topics during that hour as we caught up on the daily details of our lives, something made difficult by our long-distance engagement.

At intervals, Brian would speed up or slow down, always asking me if the pace was okay and gently pulling me back if I started to push beyond my comfort level.

I looked at this man beside me, the one I'd loved for years and was due to marry in a matter of weeks, and thanked God for giving me a partner who challenges me, loves me and protects me, at times from myself, both in our relationship and in day-to-day life. Though he's faster than I am and much stronger, I know that he'll lead us as a team, be it toward heaven or simply on the straight stretch to our own back door.

*A good man may be hard to find, but a great one is like a needle in a haystack. Thank You, God, for creating a partner with whom I can run the true marathon: the race to Your kingdom.*
—Ashley Kappel

*April*

## ADVICE FROM AUNT ANNIE

*Fri 29*  *And he had a Book of Remembrance drawn....*
—MALACHI 3:16 (TLB)

**GOD'S AUTOGRAPHS**

Autograph books are nearly obsolete in this age of instant messaging, Twitter and cell phones. But family autograph books were common when my Aunt Annie was a girl. People wrote and collected brief notes and signatures to help them remember special moments and keep current on all the branches of the family tree.

Aunt Annie believed that God autographs the world in ways that remind us of Him. "God writes of His serenity in the moon-clad waters of Lake Erie," she wrote, "and of His majesty in Zion Canyon. His perfect design for the universe can be seen in a garden pansy, and fields of ripening wheat testify to His bountiful care for His children."

I've been making an extra effort to read God's autographs and I'm finding them everywhere. One day, shortly after my retirement, I missed my friends and wondered if they ever thought of me. During my walk that evening, a burst of golden monarch butterflies literally surrounded me, giving testimony to God's closeness. I saw God's hand in the kindness of those who prayed and called when my granddaughter Olivia suffered a concussion in a bicycle accident.

Best of all is the promise that I found in my Bible: "I will write my laws into their minds and...put my laws in their hearts...." (Hebrews 10:16, TLB). Wow! God loves me so much that He will actually autograph my heart so I can learn His will and follow Him more closely.

*Awesome God, thank You for surrounding us with*
*abundant reminders of Your love.*
—PENNEY SCHWAB

## Sat 30 — *April*

*Praise him with the sound of the trumpet: praise him with the psaltery and harp.* —PSALM 150:3

I used to wonder why my parents and their friends went into such exaggerated paroxysms of enjoyment whenever they heard big-band tunes like "String of Pearls" or "Sing, Sing, Sing." Not that I didn't like them myself—it's just that what I heard didn't fully explain the tear in the eye, the elbow in the ribs or the infectious foot-tapping that came over anyone who had been in their late teens when they first heard those tunes.

Then not long ago I was listening to the car radio and I was suddenly transported back to my own late teens. All at once I was driving the family station wagon over a mustard-drenched hill near San Francisco on a rainy Easter weekend. The Golden Gate Bridge was in the background, high school graduation was in the foreground, and I felt the rich thrill of possibilities ahead of me as Roberta Flack sang, "Killing Me Softly with His Song."

That's what music will do—take you back to former days. It's the pleasure I find when I sing hymns. When I hear "The Church's One Foundation," I'm reminded of the small gathering of family and friends that sang it at our wedding. "Holy, Holy, Holy" takes me back to my boyhood church and the devotion of our tireless organist transposing the last verse up a half step. With "Onward Christian Soldiers," I recall the memorial service for a dear friend who won a valiant spiritual battle in her losing war against cancer.

In church we use the phrase "a cloud of witnesses" to describe the believers who have preceded us and whom we will follow. They hover about me in familiar songs.

*I praise You, Lord, for the gift of music.*
—RICK HAMLIN

# April

**SEEDS OF LOVE**

1 _____

2 _____

3 _____

4 _____

5 _____

6 _____

7 _____

8 _____

9 _____

10 _____

*April*

11 _____

12 _____

13 _____

14 _____

15 _____

16 _____

17 _____

18 _____

19 _____

20 _____

21 _____

*April*

22 _____

23 _____

24 _____

25 _____

26 _____

27 _____

28 _____

29 _____

30 _____

# May

*As the Father hath loved me,
so have I loved you:
continue ye in my love.*

—John 15:9

## May

### Sun 1

*But if any widow has children or grandchildren, let them first learn to show piety at home and to repay their parents; for this is good and acceptable before God.* —I Timothy 5:4 (NKJV)

Even though it was one of those gorgeous days in Florida, I was feeling lonely and left out because it was my son Michael's thirty-seventh birthday and he was a thousand miles away in Cincinnati, Ohio.

I missed all four of my children and their families, scattered in California, Wisconsin and Ohio. I was feeling envious of my snowbird friends who only come to Florida for the winter and then head back north to be near their kids and grandkids.

I'd already left two messages on Michael's home phone and two on his cell phone. *Where is he?* I'd sung "Happy Birthday" off-key—twice—and I wanted to talk to my son!

Finally, late that night, I checked my messages and there was a long, over-the-top-happy message from Michael. "Mom, it's been a great day! We all went to church. Then Amy and the kids took me out to brunch and then home, where I opened gifts. Thanks for the shirts and the tie—they're terrific! Then I got to play golf with a good friend all afternoon on a perfect, gorgeous day. Right now I'm relaxing in my hammock, Amy's baking my birthday cake, the pizza's on its way, and later I'm going to go play basketball. Mom, sometimes I feel like an old man, but my wonderful wife and kids made this such an extra-special day for me that I can't complain. I even loved your singing. Call me! I love you!"

I couldn't have topped that day for my son, no matter what I did. I didn't get to hug him in person, but that phone call sure made me feel like I'd been hugged.

*Lord, help me to treasure every phone call, e-mail, letter and visit with my kids and to be grateful they're all on their own making their own happiness.*
—Patricia Lorenz

*May*

## A PATH TO SIMPLICITY

*Mon 2*    *"I do not say to you, up to seven times, but up to seventy times seven."* —MATTHEW 18:22 (NAS)

**FORGIVING MYSELF**

Today, in going though my "Keep" pile, I counted fourteen pairs of scissors: hot pink ones, neon green ones, tiny enamel babies I bought to clip thread, heavy-duty sewing models able to cut through any fabric. Some of the scissors are still in their original packages, a few I recognize as ones I purchased to give away (I guess I never did get around to it), and others I stocked in drawers throughout the cabin so I'd always have a pair handy.

And then there's the sunflower yellow jacket I bought at a clothing outlet for twelve dollars. The sleeves were too long, but it was a deep discount. The problem is, when I got it home, I realized the alteration was too complicated for me and my old sewing machine. I never did take the jacket to the tailor, and now it's hopelessly out of style. I never wore the yellow and black beads I bought to go with it, either.

I tossed the jacket and beads in the "Giveaway" pile and admonished myself. *Think of the food you could've bought for the hungry with all the money you wasted, Roberta.*

I wipe away tears of regret as I face the sin of my waste. *Dear Lord,* I pray, *help me to be more careful with money in the future. Please forgive me.*

And He does, of course. Now the task at hand is to forgive myself. In the meantime, know anyone who could use a good pair of scissors?

> *Self-condemnation is spiritual clutter, Lord. Help me*
> *to forgive myself seventy times seven.*
> —ROBERTA MESSNER

## May

### Tue 3

*And we urge you, brethren, to recognize those who labor among you... and to esteem them very highly in love for their work's sake....* —I Thessalonians 5:12–13 (NKJV)

Some of my college students are from countries where teachers are held in high regard, and it's the custom to show them appreciation and respect.

James, from Burma, would come up after class to shake my hand and say, "Thanks for being my teacher." He invited me to his home for supper.

Thanh, from Vietnam, constantly wrote thank-you notes to her teachers, no less wonderful for her broken English.

Thilini, from Sri Lanka, left platters of cookies in professors' offices.

Ricardo, from Haiti, led the senior class in putting on a lavish teacher-appreciation banquet in the auditorium. They cooked the meal and served it and then presented each teacher with a gift and a beautiful plaque. Nothing like it had ever been done in the history of the school.

At the end of my last class this year, students began to applaud, loud and long. It was the first time in forty-one years of teaching that I had ever received applause, and I suddenly felt the need to use my hanky.

Giving thanks is a small deed with an enormous payoff. It's like putting a coin in a jukebox. Soon the whole room is singing and dancing.

*Lord, help me to see clearly who really needs my appreciation and then to give it generously.*
—Daniel Schantz

Editor's Note: *Take a look back at your "Seeds of Love" journal pages, and let us know how God's love has been working in your life this year. Send your letter to* Daily Guideposts *Reader's Room, Guideposts Books, 16 East 34th Street, New York, New York 10016. We'll share some of what you tell us in a future edition of* Daily Guideposts.

# May

## Wed 4
*Whether we live therefore, or die, we are the Lord's.*
—Romans 14:8

I am walking in the woods, spring violets peeking through the dead leaves, when suddenly I recall a childhood memory. I am ten years old. Mother, an apron tied over her work dress, is talking to me. "I think we could grow some violets here," she says, pointing to a shady spot.

I stare at the bare patch of ground near the corner of our farmhouse.

"We could dig them in the woods." Already she is moving toward the tractor shed for the shovel.

Soon Mother and I are headed through the gate toward the back pasture and the woods that border it. I am not sure how much help my small hands will be, but I like being with Mother, being a part of whatever she suggests we do together. We easily find a patch of violets, and Mother begins to dig. Carefully I wrap the plants in the newspaper we've brought and nest them into a small basket.

"I think that will be enough, don't you?"

I nod.

The month of May is a difficult one for me. Next Sunday is Mother's Day; a week later, it's Mother's birthday; and the end of the month brings Memorial Day. Those first few Mays after Mother's death, I could scarcely comprehend how one small set of squares on the calendar could hold so much sadness.

My grief has mellowed over the years. The hurt is more like a tender spot than it is a gaping wound. Life has gone on. The violets Mother and I dug and replanted that spring took hold and bloomed every year until we sold that farm and moved to another. I like to think they might be blooming still.

*You are Lord of life and death. I place myself—and my loved ones—in Your eternal care.*
—Mary Lou Carney

## May

### Thu 5

*He named it Ebenezer, saying, "Thus far has the Lord helped us."* —I Samuel 7:12 (NIV)

It was my turn to help conduct a service at our church for the National Day of Prayer. I briefly prayed out loud about some of the problems facing our nation and let silence fall after each prayer so that those attending could add their own. During one of the silences, I heard a very faint but distinct tune that I immediately recognized as "Come Thou Fount of Every Blessing" by Robert Robinson (1735–1790).

I opened my eyes to see where the melody was coming from. The choir director and pianist were both sitting in a front pew with their eyes closed. The tune lasted for a single verse and then stopped. During the next silence, I listened again. All I heard was the sound of someone's bracelet clanking and people stirring in their seats.

After the service I asked others if they'd heard the tune, and many said yes. Since recorded music is often quietly played in the sanctuary before and after services, I double-checked with the woman working the sound system. She told me that no recordings were being played.

What made the whole experience more mysterious was that this wasn't the first time we'd heard the melody in the silent sanctuary. Once, on a Thursday night, our prayer group heard the same single verse of "Come Thou Fount of Every Blessing." Wondering if it had been some sort of message from God, we took out a hymnbook and read the words. Verse 2 begins, "Here I raise mine Ebenezer; Hither by thy help I'm come." The message is a reminder of how far we have come through God's help.

I can't explain where the mysterious music came from, but I do know how appropriate the message is for National Day of Prayer. There are many good people everywhere praying for our country. And those faithful prayers have brought us through thus far.

*"Come, Thou Fount of every blessing, Tune my heart to sing Thy grace."*
—Karen Barber

## May

### Fri 6

*Then he said to me, "Write, 'Blessed are those who are invited to the marriage supper of the Lamb'". . . .*
—Revelation 19:9 (NAS)

My Aunt Elizabeth (Betty) Blackstone died last spring at the age of 103. She was exceptionally witty, and I had scrambled to jot her quips on scraps of paper during our times together. At her funeral, swallowing tears as I read her witticisms out loud in the cemetery chapel, Aunt Betty seemed vibrantly present in her thoughts and words.

"The Lord is always good to us, but sometimes we don't notice."

"Now this is Monday, isn't it? Hooray, I got it right! I just never know."

"My Bill's gone on to heaven ahead of me—he always could beat me first."

"I could look at my children's faces and see a beautiful view."

"It's a great life if you don't weaken, if you don't give up what you were meant to do."

"If I'm going to stick around on earth this long, then I better take the consequences!"

"The Lord gives us songs. Here I am 101, and He keeps giving them to me. I just want to share the fellowship."

I concluded my reading with Aunt Betty's vision of heaven: "One of the first things I will hear is music. Just think, all the family and friends I'll get to see. Heavenly gates will open and we'll go in—oh my, we'll shout with joy! To meet the Lord is going to be enough—too much—more than anything I've ever done in my life."

*Jesus, oh for a faith that rejoices to meet You!*
—Carol Knapp

## May

### Sat 7

*The Lord is your keeper....* —PSALM 121:5 (NKJV)

Bringing in the groceries from the car, my husband stopped me at the door. "You have to see this," Tony said, leading me to our clothesline. "Be careful. Don't touch."

I followed him to the old tote bag that we keep pinned to the line to hold clothespins. Inside was a neatly wound bundle of sticks.

"I was hanging out clothes," Tony said, "and put my hand in. There's a nest inside the tote with little eggs. Can you believe it?"

Later that day when I took the clothes off the line, I stood on tiptoe and looked inside the tote. A startled wren flew out. It landed in a nearby oak and watched as I walked toward the house. While I folded the clothes, I worried that I'd frightened the bird and that she would abandon her eggs. Later, washing the dishes, I looked out the window at the clothesline, hoping to see a sign of the bird, but the tote was still.

That night, rain poured onto our tin roof and woke me up. I thought of the mother bird and her nest. *Please keep the bird and her eggs safe,* I prayed.

The next morning and every time after, when I felt the need to go check on the birds, I prayed instead. Days later, as we barbecued, I saw the mother bird fly into the tote. A symphony of chirps erupted. As hard as it was not to peek, I held off going near.

For almost two weeks the mother bird flew to and from the tote, and each time she arrived, the bag came to life with music. When enough time had passed and there was no sign of the mother bird, I cautiously stood on tiptoe and looked. An empty nest never looked so good!

*Dear Lord, help me to remember that sometimes as much as I want to help, my efforts are best spent putting my trust in You.*
—SABRA CIANCANELLI

## May

### Sun 8

*The four had the same form, their construction being something like a wheel within a wheel.* —EZEKIEL 1:16 (NRSV)

Years back, a TV ad touted Life Savers as "a part of living." In my childhood, the wheel-shaped candies seemed a part of loving. My mother carried a green-on-silver roll of Wint-O-Greens in her pocketbook. She kept the white mints for one purpose: to pull out during church and pass down the pew. Each of us children would peel back the wrap from one candy and hand along the ever-shortening coil. Mom would take one herself before slipping the remainder back in her purse. Even when I visited as a grown-up, if Mom forgot our ritual, during the sermon I would playfully tap her bag and silently tease, *Please*. And at her funeral, I distributed Wint-O-Greens—in memoriam—along the family rows.

Like mother, like daughter. This morning, as I settled in to listen to the sermon, I reached into my purse to retrieve a partial roll of Life Savers. When I didn't find it in its usual compartment, I rummaged feverishly. I didn't relax until my fingers grasped the misplaced mints. I slipped the familiarly shaped candy into my mouth. Of course I tasted the wintergreen flavoring. But today I also savored a suggestion of appreciation: for my mother and little kindnesses she afforded her children; for the family circle that remains unbroken, even though she has passed through this life to the next.

*Lord, thank You for my mother's many small gifts,*
*which I choose to remember as circles of grace.*
—EVELYN BENCE

## May

### Mon 9

*"Please test your servants for ten days: Give us nothing but vegetables to eat and water to drink."* —Daniel 1:12 (NIV)

Last night I dreamed of cookies—not the store-bought kind or even the bakery kind. These were the kind my son-in-law Paul bakes and sells: large oatmeal cookies with raisins, walnuts and white chocolate chunks.

So why am I dreaming of his cookies? I guess because I'd love one right now. But I won't have one; I'm dieting. When I stepped on the scale a few months ago and saw the numbers had edged up a bit, I knew it was time.

Sticking to my diet has taken a lot of discipline. I live close to New Orleans, a city known for its cuisine. As much as I wanted the French Market beignets with powdered sugar for breakfast, I ate a bagel instead. Turning down the Mardi Gras king cake was difficult. At lunch, I ate salads instead of the fried shrimp po'boys that everyone else ordered. *This is no fun,* I thought.

But then something changed: The discipline I practiced with my eating habits began to show up in other areas too. I started getting up early to read my Bible and pray before work; I walked through my neighborhood in the evenings; I even caught up with my correspondence.

I know now that the added weight reflected an undisciplined lifestyle. I needed to make better choices with food, exercise and my free time. It hasn't been easy, but I'm grateful for the experience. I've lost a few extra pounds and gained a whole lot of insight.

*Lord, may I be mindful that when I say* no *to an unhealthy lifestyle, I'm saying* yes *to You.*
—Melody Bonnette

## May

### Tue 10

*"Dear woman, why do you involve me?" Jesus replied, "My time has not yet come."* —JOHN 2:4 (NIV)

Mom and I were hard at work planning the finer details of my upcoming wedding. As we hurried around town orchestrating transportation for guests, finalizing the reception menu and making sure someone was at the church early to turn on the air-conditioning (the wedding was in May in Alabama, after all), I began to feel overwhelmed.

"Are we doing the right thing?" I asked Mom, waving my hand over the to-do list, which seemed to grow each day.

Mom simply smiled. "The things that you're working on are important: your vows to Brian, taking care of your family and dearest friends, and celebrating the start of a new life together."

"But still," I protested, "I'm starting to feel a little silly."

"Remember the story of Jesus at the wedding ceremony in Cana?" Mom said, her wise smile bringing to mind the ancient story. "I love that story."

At the wedding ceremony, Jesus' mother, who, like mine, understood the importance of showing guests a good time at a celebration, went to Jesus distraught that the wine was running out, asking Him to do something. And though, as Jesus said, "it's not yet my time," do something He did.

Jesus found the wedding celebration a worthy place for His very first miracle. If He chose to use His awesome power to bless a wedding, why shouldn't I try to do the very best by my dearest friends and closest family?

*Lord, thank You for giving me the opportunity to honor the love of family and friends, and to do so while having a wonderful time with my own mom.*
—ASHLEY KAPPEL

## May

### Wed 11

*She is clothed with strength and dignity; she can laugh at the days to come.* —Proverbs 31:25 (NIV)

Here's the story of the day: A friend of mine who is ninety-six years old, born before the "first of the wars of the world," as she says, still lives in her little beach cottage although she's been blind since the first of our wars in "Persia," as she says. "I hear pretty well, I can move around with minimal creakiness, and people are so kind to me; why would I move?"

One morning her cat captured a sparrow outside and brought it into the house in triumph. My friend heard this dramatic adventure loud and clear while washing the dishes. She barked at the cat, picked up the fluttering bird with a sponge, opened the kitchen window, tossed out the sponge and started back to washing the dishes, only to realize she was using the sparrow, who objected strenuously. "It was all I could do not to fall down laughing," she says, "but at my age falling down is a bad idea. I got the window open again and ejected the bird, but then I laughed so hard, I think I sprained my face."

Now, this is a terrific story from every angle imaginable, it seems to me: the deft, athletic cat; the sparrow who didn't die; the sinewy old lady giggling; the smile on your face; the prayer that your smile is for my friend; and maybe best of all, the helpless laughter of the child you will just have to tell this story to sometime today.

*Dear Lord, for laughter and sparrows and clean dishes and kids giggling and, well, I guess, even for murderous cats, thank You most sincerely.*
—Brian Doyle

## May

### Thu 12

*Thou hast cast all my sins behind thy back.*
—Isaiah 38:17

How did she accomplish so much against all odds? This was always my question about Clara Barton. In fragile health herself, she was so moved by the plight of wounded soldiers during the Civil War that she threw herself into obtaining and distributing medical supplies, eventually gaining permission to travel behind the lines into the battle zones themselves.

After the war, the "Angel of the Battlefield" led the enormous tasks of searching for the missing and identifying the dead. When her doctor insisted she travel to Switzerland for a rest, she joined the newly formed Red Cross Society there and came home to found the American Red Cross. Wherever in the world there was need—the Franco-Prussian war, the yellow fever epidemic in Florida, the Johnstown flood in Pennsylvania, the famine in Russia, the massacre in Armenia, the deadly hurricane in South Carolina—Clara Barton ministered to it.

And all this in the face of entrenched views about "a woman's place." For every achievement, she had to battle dismissive generals, patronizing statesmen, skeptical doctors. How did she do it? One day I discovered at least part of the answer. Among all the loads she carried, there was one weight she was free of—resentment. Her supporters liked to remind her of obstacles deliberately placed in her path. Wasn't she angry at such and such a person, such and such a put-down? To those questions she had an answer that went beyond forgiveness.

"No," she'd reply, "I distinctly remember forgetting that."

In Clara Barton's inner world, the difficulty, once passed, simply ceased to exist. It occupied no emotional space as she turned all her energy to the challenges ahead.

*Father, help me release my small grievances into*
*the vastness of Your great purposes.*
—Elizabeth Sherrill

*May*

## ❋ TO SAY GOOD-BYE

*Fri 13*   *Thy kingdom come....* —MATTHEW 6:10

**STEPS TOWARD THE KINGDOM**

Today, loneliness follows me as I walk through the park. The clouds cover the sun, promising a dreary day of rain.

*What's it all about?* I wonder. *All these years, we've given our life to the church. Soon it will be over. Did the things we've done matter?*

Back on our street, I pause at our mailbox and pull out a letter. "Thank you for the privilege of serving the orphans in Zimbabwe," the letter says. "In praying for you, the Lord led me to Matthew 25." Then, in the careful handwriting of my friend Norma, I read: "I was hungry and you gave me something to eat, I was thirsty and you gave me something to drink, I was a stranger and you invited me in, I needed clothes and you clothed me, I was sick and you looked after me, I was in prison and you came to visit me" (Matthew 25:35–36, NIV).

From the very beginning, my husband David's and my vision had been to bring the kingdom of God to Hillsboro Presbyterian Church. And now, like a clip from an old movie, I see a panorama play out before me: children in Zimbabwe and all around the world being fed through our efforts; homeless people sitting down to Friday night feasts in our fellowship hall, with clean beds and fresh clothes waiting; the faces of battered women and down-and-out families finding shelter in our church; temporary rent money, even new homes built by our congregation. I saw refugees from Vietnam, Poland, Eritrea, Sudan, South America welcomed, housed, fed and educated. I saw old people, sick people, prisoners, an unending line of those in need being comforted, helped, healed by our efforts.

Our vision had become reality, in living color. The things we'd done mattered.

*Father, wherever we go, Thy kingdom come.*
—PAM KIDD

## May

### Sat 14

*He maketh me to lie down in green pastures: he leadeth me beside the still waters. He restoreth my soul....*
—PSALM 23:2–3

After I graduated from college, I traveled for nearly a year as a member of a five-person vocal group. Specializing in 1970s music, we gave ninety concerts on college campuses in ten months. It was an intense time, exhilarating, exciting, fun and quite fatiguing. There were days when I woke up so exhausted that I had to look at the bedside phone book to remember where I was. Traveling all day, performing all night and interacting constantly with students was a recipe for exhaustion.

In the midst of my travels, I asked a veteran musician for advice. "How do you cope with this nonstop lifestyle? How do you expend all your energy and talent every night and refill yourself the next day?"

He smiled at me and said, "I sleep a lot! Whenever the world closes in and I can't handle it anymore, I take a nice, long nap!"

At age twenty-two, the idea of taking a nap was not appealing. But when I did try his remedy, I discovered that the world looked a lot better to me. My emotional vitality returned, and I felt better physically.

Rest deserves to take its place as one of the spiritual disciplines. Along with prayer, Bible study, ministering to others and worship, we also need to restore our spirits with rest and sleep. God created the world in six days and rested on the seventh. And so should we.

*Father, restore my soul through deep and abiding rest.*
—SCOTT WALKER

## May

### Sun 15

*I am the good shepherd, and know my sheep, and am known of mine. As the Father knoweth me, even so know I the Father: and I lay down my life for the sheep.*
—John 10:14–15

Several years ago, in St. John's Cathedral in Hong Kong, I heard the Reverend Canon John Peterson give a sermon on Jesus, the Good Shepherd. Having lived in Jerusalem, a land of shepherds, he shared many of the insights he learned there.

One was that the shepherd carries a bag of small stones with him. He walks behind the sheep, and when one strays from the herd, he throws a stone to hit it in the heel to keep it in line and to keep it moving. Canon Peterson asked if we would be willing to let Jesus so aim a stone at our heel.

He told the story of two men who were invited to recite the 23rd Psalm. The first was a well-known orator with a beautiful, well-modulated voice. He gave a dramatic rendering; the audience cheered and called for an encore so they might hear it from him again.

The second man took the podium and with great humility recited, "The Lord is my shepherd, I shall not want. . . ." In a spirit of reverent prayer, he went all the way through to the final verses: "Surely goodness and mercy shall follow me all the days of my life: and I will dwell in the house of the Lord forever." There was complete silence as the audience sat quietly, many with their heads bowed.

"Ah," the orator said wistfully, "I know the Psalm. He knows the Shepherd."

*Jesus, Shepherd of my soul, hit my heels with stones when I stray, keep me moving on the path You have set before me.*
—Fay Angus

*May*

## Mon 16

*I will praise thee, O Lord my God, with all my heart: and I will glorify thy name for evermore.* —PSALM 86:12

As a magazine editor, I spend most of my time working with other writers' words. I rearrange, replace, polish. But a couple of times a year, I go back to my roots as a reporter and do a little storytelling myself.

One of my recent stories was about midcentury modern furniture. Cultivated by big names such as Frank Lloyd Wright and Ludwig Mies van der Rohe, the look of the furniture is all about clean lines and almost spartan proportions.

As part of my research, I read a book called *How to See* by George Nelson, a giant of midcentury modern who for many years was the design director at the Wisconsin-based furniture company Herman Miller. The book is all about the messages that can be read in our surroundings. One line in particular struck me: Design's "basic rules . . . are not complicated. A designed object has to do what it was made for."

It occurred to me that we are "designed objects." According to the Westminster Catechism, "Man's chief and highest end is to glorify God, and fully to enjoy Him forever." God made us to glorify Him, and He delighted in that creation. The question then is: Do we do what we were made for?

*Lord, day by day, help me to do what You have designed me to do.*
—JEFF CHU

---

### READER'S ROOM

How does God speak to me? Often it's the things of nature and His creation that God uses to draw me to Him: white, fluffy clouds mushrooming in a sky of azure; new buds quietly making their appearance on a rose bush; a full moon in the still of the night; a mama cow quietly nursing her young one in the hazy early morning light. —*Hannah Beiler, Gap, Pennsylvania*

## May

### Tue 17

*"Which of you, if his son asks for bread, will give him a stone?"*
—Matthew 7:9 (NIV)

I tasted hope today. It had a rich, luscious flavor, soothing as the rolling hills around me. It came in the shape of gnarled apple trees and grass.

Andrew and I were visiting a possible new school for our son John. This one was utterly unlike his current school. There was no asphalt basketball court, no chain-link fence, no yellow-painted cinderblock to lend false cheeriness to an otherwise dismal environment. It wasn't the nightmare alternative we had visited the week before, filled with posters warning against guns and domestic violence. ("Things have gotten better," the social worker there told us. "We don't accept so many gang members anymore.") Nor was it the sunny but overly sanitized school an hour's drive away, where every door was locked, even the bathroom.

Here there was a pond and a swimming pool. The class size was eight students per teacher. The grounds were gorgeous. The admissions officer asked insightful questions. She had read John's paperwork, understood his needs and thought this school could help him. My heart cried out, *Yes! Yes! Accept him!*

They did.

After the nightmare years of choosing among bad options, we finally had a good alternative. The city will pay for the school. A school bus will take John door to door. At last our son will be in an environment that is truly therapeutic. It may not solve all his problems, but there is tremendous joy in being able to give your child bread instead of a stone.

*Father, thank You for being patient with me even when I'm not so patient with You.*
—Julia Attaway

## May

### Wed 18

*"The Lord will guide you always; he will satisfy your needs in a sun-scorched land and will strengthen your frame. You will be like a well-watered garden, like a spring whose waters never fail."* —ISAIAH 58:11 (NIV)

Dave was doing his regular volunteer stint at the Salvation Army, where he taught guitar, when he noticed the ugly old yard out back.

A landscaper before he began a twenty-five-year career as a teacher, Dave had a thought: *That could be made into a beautiful garden where our clients could find some peace.*

The idea caught fire. Residents and clients helped clear the land, nurseries donated plants, community organizations provided funds.

During the opening ceremony of "The Healing Garden," I reveled in the beauty of the beds of purple, blue and yellow flowers set against a green hillside with a miniature waterfall trickling nearby. Flowers bloomed from a pair of brown rubber boots and an old blue suitcase. Off to one side were garden plots in which clients grew beets, strawberries, tomatoes and Brussels sprouts to be used in the Salvation Army's kitchen.

A band of six men strummed guitars and banjos and sang "What a Friend We Have in Jesus" and "Amazing Grace." Then Dave picked up his guitar and sang a few of his own songs. The intensity with which they sang really touched me.

"The men sing from personal experience," Dave explained. "As former addicts, they know what living on the streets is like."

"Were you singing from experience too?" I asked.

"I was never an addict," he said slowly, "but I've gone through a lot of other things in my life. I understand their pain."

*Thank You, Father, for using our suffering to grow our love and empathy for others.*
—HELEN GRACE LESCHEID

## May

### Thu 19

*A brother is born to help in time of need.*
—PROVERBS 17:17 (TLB)

One sunny day, my friend Jan suggested we go rowing on the lake in Central Park. We pulled on life vests, attendants shoved us off, and Jan rowed us under the lovely Bow Bridge as tourists leaned over the railing and snapped photos. We glided out onto the large and lovely lake, drifting along until—*bump!*—the rowboat stopped. We were stuck, apparently on a mud-bar.

Nearby rowers offered an oar to try to pull us off; no good. There we sat, not quite in the middle of the lake, but far enough from shore that we couldn't just wriggle ourselves onto land. The water below was cloudy, though I'd sighted some snapping turtles. Goodness knows what else lurked in the depths.

*Now what?* We weren't in danger, but I'd never been crazy about being in small bobbing boats, and, at best, this was embarrassing. I sent up a silent prayer: *Oops, God, could we have a little help here?*

Another boat appeared, this one rowed by a blond young man accompanied by a smiling girl. It pulled alongside, and the young man began to unlace his shoes and roll up his pant legs. "What are you *doing?*" I asked in shock as he stepped over the side of his boat and plopped into water that was just over his knees. He gave our rowboat a big shove and we were free.

I sputtered in astonishment and gratitude. A complete stranger—it turned out he was a tourist from Poland—had gotten muddy for two hapless people he'd never seen before in his life!

*Thank You, Lord, for the kindness of strangers, who appear in our lives to give us a helping hand—or watery shove—when we need it most.*
—MARY ANN O'ROARK

## Fri 20

*He hath put a new song in my mouth, even praise unto our God....* —PSALM 40:3

My neighbor Lonnie is quite a character. Ask her what kind of day she's having and get ready for an earful. Shopkeepers roll their eyes and neighbors sometimes avoid her. She has a good heart, really. It's just that she can be so negative sometimes. I don't think she even realizes she's doing it.

So everyone was surprised a while back when Lonnie appeared walking a fluffy little dog by the name of... Fluffy. The dog had been given as a companion to a sick relative of Lonnie's, but the relative had grown too ill to care for it. "So it looks like I'm stuck with him!" she said.

Fluffy was a good dog but not used to a leash, so there was a lot of pulling and tugging between Lonnie and Fluffy. Lonnie was frustrated, and the dog was confused. "Bad dog, Fluffy!" I would hear Lonnie shouting at him, with Millie, my golden retriever, looking on in disapproval. No, Lonnie and Fluffy were not a happy pair. Finally someone recommended a dog trainer to Lonnie.

The trainer joined Lonnie and Fluffy on their morning walks. "Lonnie," she preached, "positive reinforcement is what's most effective. Praise good behavior, ignore bad, and never lose your patience or act negative. Never say *bad* and always praise."

Praise? I don't think I'd ever heard such a thing come out of Lonnie's mouth. Yet soon enough, there she was on the street with Fluffy, saying "Good dog, good dog!" in the "happy voice" the trainer taught her whenever Fluffy complied with proper leash etiquette. Soon enough, Fluffy was walking like a champion.

Lonnie and Fluffy are now inseparable. There's something else too: Lonnie's not quite so grumpy anymore. She lights up when people stop to admire Fluffy, and she's not so quick to go negative during a conversation. Giving praise has changed her.

*Father, a positive attitude is one of the greatest spiritual gifts. Help me to remember: Praise! Praise! Praise!*
—EDWARD GRINNAN

## May

### Sat 21

*"Do not be afraid, little flock, for it is your Father's good pleasure to give you the kingdom."* —LUKE 12:32 (NRSV)

My husband Charlie and I live on the Thames River in southeastern Connecticut, not far from the US Naval Submarine Base in Groton. Right across the river from our apartment is Electric Boat, the company that manufactures the submarines. We can see the newly minted subs in the massive bay, and we often see them coming from and going to the base. Since the subs don't submerge until they get out to Long Island Sound, we can see them quite clearly. As these large gray monsters move silently through the water, they're beautiful, amazing, and, at the same time, daunting and a little menacing. I always pray for the crew and for the families they leave behind.

When the subs leave base, headed out on a months-long patrol, the sleek vessels move along without any sign of their human occupants. But when they return to Groton, crew members—tiny figures in the distance—frequently climb outside and stand on top of the sub, waving and rejoicing even before they reach their berth.

I always marvel at the sight because it's just a taste of what it must be like to go home to God and find Him waiting for us with open arms.

*Father, let me seek You as eagerly as I seek those here on earth who love me.*
—MARCI ALBORGHETTI

*May*

## Sun 22
*Worship the Lord in the beauty of holiness.*
—I CHRONICLES 16:29

It used to embarrass me to no end when Dad marched all four of us kids and Mom down the center aisle at church to sit in the front pew—granted, we were never on time. And as I was growing up, nobody ever sat up there. Nobody. The church could be packed to the gills and the last seat anybody took was in the front pew. Out of excessive humility or a fear of being blasted out of their seats, everybody else filled up the back first.

In our teen years we couldn't crane our heads around, without being completely obvious, to see some girlfriend three rows back. If we were tuckered out from a Saturday night party, we couldn't sneak in on the side. There we were, right up in front. "Why do we sit here?" I asked Dad.

"It's easier to feel like I'm part of the service," he said to my bewilderment.

I could never figure it out and I didn't really have to. During most of my adulthood I've sung in choirs or shepherded the Sunday school kids, and that meant never sitting in front. But one day when there was no choir and no Sunday school, my wife and I wandered into church early and sat in front for a change. I wasn't sure I liked it. I couldn't swivel around to see who was bellowing on that opening hymn or who was away on vacation. But it was easier to concentrate on the sermon, and during the prayers, I could feel the congregation right behind me. It was as though they were holding me up, keeping me going.

I don't know where you usually sit in church, but I'd recommend the front row from time to time. You'll feel the support of the congregation behind you and know just why you're there.

*Keep me, Lord, in this front-row seat with*
*the perfect view of Your creation.*
—RICK HAMLIN

## May

### Mon 23

*"He reveals deep and mysterious things; he knows what is in the darkness...."* —Daniel 2:22 (RSV)

I have a small collection of nesting dolls, little wooden dolls that open up to reveal a smaller doll, one inside the other. One set is painted like angels and another like players from my favorite baseball team, the Arizona Diamondbacks. My favorite is a traditional set my brother brought back from Russia when I was just a little girl. It's actually seventeen dolls, the smallest one only an eighth of an inch tall. I love opening each one and lining them up, discovering what's inside again and again, studying their slightest differences.

Perhaps I like them because they are made exactly as God created us—complex, layered, sometimes not so easy to figure out from the outside. I think of a new co-worker who at first appeared very serious—cordial but distant. Some thought she was even a little unfriendly. We sat together at lunch one day, and as we talked, she told me how she and her husband were raising their grandson—a layer revealed. As we got to know each other better, she told me about her spiritual searching. We talked about God and another layer was revealed. Months have passed now, and we have discovered several layers within each other that show we have enough in common to become good friends. And the discovery continues.

*Lord, make me the kind of friend who takes time to discover the many layers people have to offer.*
—Gina Bridgeman

*May*

# ADVICE FROM AUNT ANNIE

**Tue 24** *Laying up in store for themselves a good foundation against the time to come....* —I Timothy 6:19

**MAKING THE BEST OF IT**

My Aunt Annie suffered a serious illness when she was seventeen. "When my dearest friend went off to university without me, I was devastated," she wrote. But with help from God and her parents, Aunt Annie made the best of a disappointing situation. The lessons she learned are timeless.

1. *Acceptance is not the same as apathy.* "When I finally accepted the fact that I would be at home for several months," Aunt Annie wrote, "I gave myself over to the task of building my weakened body." She ate nutritious foods, walked as she was able and took her medicine.
2. *Waiting can be productive.* Aunt Annie studied Spanish, read the newspaper to learn modern history and developed good study habits. She also got to know herself. "I am not alone as long as I can read, study and delve into new fields of knowledge and into my own mind."
3. *Cultivating relationships reaps rewards.* "For the first time I got to know and appreciate my parents," Aunt Annie said. "There was time to chat and even to listen."
4. *God will provide guidance.* "Through prayer and meditation, I was convinced that God meant me to be a teacher," Aunt Annie related, "and, indeed, teaching is my life's work."

Fifty years later, Aunt Annie wrote, "I still thank God for the delay that turned out to be one of the most fruitful periods of my life."

*Lord of all times and circumstances, thank You for life lessons from the past.*
—Penney Schwab

## May

### Wed 25

*"First go and be reconciled...."* —MATTHEW 5:24 (NIV)

The doctor had given me good news, but to be safe he suggested a lab test. He sent me back to the waiting room to pick up a container, where I spoke to a receptionist I'd come to know almost as a friend. "I'll alert the lab," she said. We chatted briefly, and I took a seat and waited...and waited...and waited. The lab technician came out several times but called other patients. Meanwhile, the receptionist had gone on a break.

Finally I got up and went over to the relief receptionist. "How long does it take to pick up a specimen container? I've been waiting more than thirty-five minutes!"

She admitted it shouldn't take that long, adding, "I don't know what happened."

"Where can I file a complaint?" I demanded.

Just then the regular receptionist returned. Immediately, she apologized for misunderstanding my request, thinking I'd needed to speak with the technician. "I could have gotten the container myself," she said. "I'm so sorry."

Still fuming, I took the container and left. Afterward, though, I realized I was the one in the wrong. Ashamed, I prayed, *Lord, help me to make this right.*

Not an hour later the receptionist phoned to confirm an upcoming appointment for my wife. "I didn't know if I dared call," she said. I immediately asked her to forgive me for my actions and took the blame for not communicating clearly.

"Then we're still friends?" she asked, her voice brightening.

"You bet," I said.

*Father, whenever I'm in the wrong, help me to do the right thing.*
—HAROLD HOSTETLER

## May

### Thu 26

*Show me your faith without doing anything, and I will show you my faith by what I do.*
—James 2:18 (NCV)

Several months earlier, my friend Patti told me, "Pastor Pablo, you won't believe what happened to me!" At the last minute, Patti had accepted a pair of free tickets to a John Tesh concert. At the concert, Tesh had spoken to his audience about the rewards of volunteering and then handed out ten envelopes, each containing one hundred dollars, to members of the crowd, challenging them to grow the money for a good cause.

Patti was seated somewhere in the middle of her row. *He'll never get to me*, she thought. But amazingly, she found herself holding an envelope, and within minutes she knew what she would do with the one hundred dollars. Patti knew an elderly woman whose home, destroyed by severe storms and flooding, was being rebuilt by Habitat for Humanity, and she had wondered how she could help.

Patti decided to use the one hundred dollars to hold a benefit to help build the new house. The next day she stopped by a local restaurant to ask how to go about it. The owner offered to sponsor the event, providing space and food for two hundred people.

A chain of goodwill began to grow. The musicians at our church heard about the benefit and volunteered to play. Local businesses donated gifts for a silent auction, and people from the church and the community spread the word. Patti raised more than eight thousand dollars.

A pair of tickets and a generous performer—who would have guessed what two simple acts of kindness could do?

*Lord, help me to be open to the challenge
of helping my neighbors.*
—Pablo Diaz

## May

### Fri 27

*He who finds a wife finds what is good and receives favor from the Lord.* —PROVERBS 18:22 (NIV)

The hustle and bustle of wedding planning was almost over; I'd be saying my vows to Brian in less than two days! Now was the time to sit back and enjoy the fruits of my yearlong labor.

The party officially got under way the Friday before the wedding, when my mom, bridesmaids, mother-in-law-to-be, aunts and female cousins gathered for a lunch in my honor. I'd expected to feel a lot of things over the course of the wedding weekend: joy at marrying my heart's true love, peace at the conclusion of a hectic event, awe at such an important milestone and a bittersweet sadness at leaving my family to start a new one of my own. What I hadn't expected was to be utterly humbled.

But there I sat, in my chair at the table of honor, completely humbled as the women in my life rose and one by one read a Bible verse, encouraging and challenging me in the new life on which I was about to embark. Surrounded by strong, amazing, wonderful women who had traveled hundreds of miles to support me in my marriage, I began to feel tears in the corners of my eyes. I'd always thought my wedding day would be magical because of the man I was marrying and the vows we would take, but I had never realized how moving it would be to be encircled by the love of my friends and relatives.

As they read the verses, challenging me to love and support my husband with my whole heart, I knew that I was hardly leaving a family. Mine was just getting a little bit bigger.

> *Lord, give me today so that I can work to be like the leaders in my life. While You're at it, go ahead and give me tomorrow too. I think I may need it.*
> —ASHLEY KAPPEL

## May

### Sat 28

*"Love each other as I have loved you."* —John 15:12 (NIV)

His name is Isaac. His parents call him Ikey, but I call him Yikey. My name fits him best.

He's eighteen months old and the first grandson in our family with lots of little girls who love to have tea parties and play dress-up and pretend they're princesses. When Yikey was born, I wondered if I would be able to relate as easily to a little boy.

And he is all boy! From the moment he could crawl, he was able to move himself to the most unlikely spots—like the top of the stove. He didn't learn to walk; he only learned to run, and now he moves quickly, taking tiny, lightning-fast baby steps. His parents lock any door leading outside, because he can escape from almost anywhere, Houdini-style. And now he's able to move himself more quickly to those unlikely spots.

The other night, his family came over for dinner and we were all gathered in the kitchen. I glanced outside to the patio, where I'd set the table for dinner, and saw Yikey sitting comfortably cross-legged in the middle of the table, lifting a jar containing a lighted candle. Thankfully, it was I rather than Yikey who seemed in need of treatment a few minutes later. I could hardly stop hyperventilating after rescuing him in the nick of time.

Yikey is a fearless, tough little guy, but he's started sharing one incredibly tender gesture with me. "Oma, nose!" he calls to me as he scrunches up his nose. With our faces close together, we touch and then brush noses.

"I love you, Yikey," I tell him. More than I ever could have imagined.

*Lord, Your gift of children teaches us many surprising lessons about love.*
—Carol Kuykendall

## May

### Sun 29
*Better is open rebuke than hidden love.*
—Proverbs 27:5 (NIV)

I left our home in Richland, Mississippi, on a beautiful Sunday morning to drive to Starkville to preach at a church. As I drove, I noticed a green 1972 Volkswagen Beetle parked in a driveway near the road with a For Sale sign on it. My first instinct was to call my wife to say, "Let's check this out!" I felt like a child looking through a toy store window.

However, I could already hear Rosie's answer ringing in my head: "No more VW bugs!" The first three cars we owned after getting married were Volkswagens. We even bought an old VW van and used it for years, and we loved them all. But that morning I realized that as much as I wanted to look it over and see what the owner wanted for it, my wife would simply say, "God has greater things He wants us to use our resources for than satisfying your desire to have a car we don't need."

I didn't have to ask; I knew Rosie and her love for the Lord and for me. She would make sure I kept my priorities straight.

*Lord, help me to keep my eyes on You*
*rather than on earthly toys.*
—Dolphus Weary

*May*

*Mon 30*

*And this day shall be unto you for a memorial; and ye shall keep it a feast to the Lord throughout your generations; ye shall keep it a feast by an ordinance for ever.*
—EXODUS 12:14

This year marks the 150th anniversary of the beginning of the American Civil War. By the end of May 1861, six weeks after the first shot was fired at Fort Sumter, South Carolina, Virginia had joined the seceding states and a series of scuffles had taken place in Baltimore, but no pitched battles had yet been fought. People on both sides of the conflict thought it would soon be over; carriages full of people, carrying picnic lunches, hastened out to watch the first battle at Bull Run in July. But by the time it finally ended in 1865, more than a half-million Americans had died on the battlefields, in field hospitals or in prisons. One of them was my great-granduncle Rufus Hughes, who died of wounds he received at the Battle of Vicksburg.

Memorial Day began from the resolve that the sacrifice of those half-million lives should never be forgotten. In recent years it seems to have lost some of its meaning; it's been reduced to a day for cookouts and picnics, for ball games and visits to the zoo, the unofficial first day of summer. Today, though, before we Attaways do anything else, we're going to take the time to remember such places as Trenton and the Cowpens, New Orleans and Baltimore, Chapultepec and Buena Vista, Shiloh and Antietam, Manila Bay and San Juan Hill, Chateau-Thierry and Belleau Wood, Anzio and Guadalcanal, Inchon and Pusan, Danang and Khe Sanh, Kandahar and Baghdad. And we'll pray:

*Lord, we remember all those who have given their lives for our country, from its earliest days until now. May their memory be a blessing.*
—ANDREW ATTAWAY

## May

### Tue 31

*I have seen something else under the sun: The race is not to the swift or the battle to the strong....*
—Ecclesiastes 9:11 (NIV)

My friend Portia and I met in the admissions office at the University of Maryland in College Park. Two years later, I earned my degree. This past spring, more than thirty years after our first meeting, Portia graduated with her bachelor's degree from the Apex School of Theology in North Carolina. She was afraid to tell people about it and to send out the invitations. "I keep thinking I should wait a little longer, just in case something goes wrong," she said.

Portia may be shy about telling others, but I'm shouting it out loud. Graduation is a major accomplishment for a young person, but it's remarkable and courageous for a fiftyish woman who has had many stops and starts. Each time she began again, the end of the journey seemed farther away.

"Finally," she says, "I realized that graduating is not about how smart you are."

I smile at her. "No, it's about enduring to the end—especially the last semester."

We both groan. My last semester was thirty years ago, but I can still remember the sleep deprivation and running to and fro to make certain everything was done.

"I'm proud of you. You've done good work!" I tell her.

She blushes, struggling to fend off the compliment. Portia has had to juggle being a pastor's wife, working and other priorities that come with life.

Her husband, her father and mother, her nieces and nephews were there. My daughter Lanea and I cheered, despite admonitions not to, when she received her diploma. After thirty years, you need to let your hair down!

*Thank You, Lord, for giving us the strength and courage to complete races and tasks that seem impossible.*
—Sharon Foster

*May*

## SEEDS OF LOVE

1 _____

2 _____

3 _____

4 _____

5 _____

6 _____

7 _____

8 _____

9 _____

10 _____

11 _____

12 _____

13 _____

14 _____

15 _____

## May

16 _____

17 _____

18 _____

19 _____

20 _____

21 _____

22 _____

23 _____

24 _____

25 _____

26 _____

27 _____

28 _____

29 _____

30 _____

31 _____

# June

*We love him, because he first loved us.*

—I John 4:19

*June*

## 💮 A PATH TO SIMPLICITY

*Wed 1*  *Trust in the Lord with all your heart And do not lean on your own understanding.* —PROVERBS 3:5 (NAS)

**TRUSTING IN THE LORD**

I recognized early on that simplifying my life was more than I could handle on my own. So I asked my friend Jenny if she would be my prayer partner. Jenny lives nearby in a big white house with rockers and pots of red geraniums stationed all across her front porch. Her home is a place of peace and prayer, and if you visit early in the morning, you're sure to smell homemade bread baking.

So Jenny agreed to pray with me each step of the way. I knew that many of the things I no longer needed would be of interest to collectors. But there was too much going on at work to think of organizing a sale myself, and I needed the objectivity of a professional. We prayed that God would send someone to host a sale for me, and He did.

The morning of the sale, I scanned the paper for the advertisement. But I panicked when I spotted it. "We've got shabby, Americana and Early Disaster," it read.

*Shabby? Early Disaster?* No one would show up for that!

I went to work, and soon Jenny telephoned me. "You're not going to believe it, Roberta. They're parked up the hill, down the hill and in all your neighbors' driveways!"

That evening the man who handled the sale called. "I've never seen anything like it," he told me. "People bought stuff like there was no tomorrow. Some of them came back three and four times."

I couldn't help laughing. *Shabby? Early Disaster?* Our prayers had been answered after all. Those unappealing words were precisely what was needed to attract a record crowd.

*Help me to trust You in all things, Lord, and to leave the results to You.*
—ROBERTA MESSNER

*June*

## Thu 2
*But Peter was following at a distance.* —Luke 22:54 (NRSV)

I was feeling pretty good about myself the other day. I had just led a Bible study, and several people came up to me afterward to say that they appreciated my words. As I left church, I caught a glimpse of my reflection in a floor-length window and thought, *I'm good!*

About twenty minutes later, while driving home, I yelled at the car in front of me because it was moving slowly. About an hour after that, I found myself scolding my son for no reason at all. Before I finished, a realization hit me like one of those lightbulbs above a cartoon character's head. "I know, I know," I whispered to God. "Thanks for the reminder."

I found myself thinking back to the Apostle Peter. He was one of Jesus' closest friends and yet he deserted Jesus during His time of greatest need. Remember the sermons that Peter preached after the Resurrection and ascension? In Acts 3:13–14, he said, "The God of Abraham, the God of Isaac, and the God of Jacob . . . has glorified his servant Jesus, whom you handed over and rejected." That's the pot calling the kettle black! Only a few weeks earlier, it was Peter who denied Jesus, not once, but three times.

What Peter's life shows me over and over again is that conversion takes a lifetime. I see in him what it means to make mistakes and what it means to be forgiven. I heal. I get better. I experience the Resurrection.

*Teach me anew, Lord, to live a resurrected life.*
—Jon Sweeney

## June

### Fri 3
*Lord, I believe; help thou mine unbelief.* —Mark 9:24

Yesterday, Solomon came home with a flyer from his teacher. "Congratulations!" it said. "You have a wonderful chance to win the class hermit crabs. All you must do to qualify for the drawing is to pledge that you will take good care of them for their natural lives."

"Do you want your class hermit crabs, Solomon?"

"No," Solomon said, shaking his head. "They're creepy."

I sighed with relief because I feel the same about hermit crabs. To me, all those claws emerging from a seashell are the ocean's version of a spider, and I've had more than my share of inheriting pets that scared me. There was my college roommate's mouse, a lizard that ate live crickets, and a black fish I won at a carnival that ate all the other fish in the tank.

Last night, right before bed, my mind wandered to work and our upcoming vacation. *How will I get things done? What if our [twenty-year-old] cat dies while we're away?* Once I opened the door to "what ifs," a parade of new worries showed up. *What if our car breaks down on the way? What if my laptop gets broken on the trip? What if it rains the whole time we're there?*

I got up and went downstairs to make myself a cup of tea. While I waited for the kettle to boil, I walked into the dining room and picked up Solomon's class flyer. *Congratulations,* I thought, *you have the wonderful chance to care for something you're afraid of!*

As the kettle whistled, I laughed at myself. Wasn't my what-if worry game doing exactly that?

> *Dear Lord, help me to remember that when I feed my fears,*
> *I lose sight of my connection to You.*
> —Sabra Ciancanelli

## June

### Sat 4

*Give me understanding according to thy word.*
—PSALM 119:169

My wife Sandee has only two extravagances: Pittsburgh Steelers football and manicures. The guy who does her nails—Tom—is from Vietnam, and he and Sandee have become friends, despite some language issues. On a recent visit, Tom asked what Sandee did for a living. It took a while to explain the concept of "working at a seminary" and "Old Testament instructor," but he got it. "I'm not religious," he said.

Sandee looked around at the artwork adorning the shop, reflecting a deep spirituality. "Oh, I'm not so sure about that," she said.

"No, not me. But you," Tom said, looking up from his work, "you are. I can see it in your face—peaceful. You look like"—he struggled for the right word—"like *Ave Maria*."

Sandee told me this story without comment, but I noticed she was smiling. Turns out that Tom doesn't struggle with the language at all. Some words—*peace*, *friendship*, *insight*—passeth all understanding, and he somehow found exactly the right ones. Sometimes our tongues get in the way of what's really important—and I don't mean Steelers football. Well, not this week, at least.

*Lord, my words so often fail, but Your Word never does, in or out of season.*
—MARK COLLINS

## June

### ❧ TO SAY GOOD-BYE

*Sun 5*  *Sing unto the Lord a new song....* —Psalm 98:1

**UNSUNG HEROES**

"Hey, Mom, did you see who just came in?" Brock whispered to me as the opening hymn began. I glanced back to see one of Nashville's music heroes sitting in the back pew. In a town where music is big business, it's not unusual to run into Dolly Parton at the post office or Amy Grant at the grocery store, and try as we might to treat them as regular people, there's a star-shine about them.

After years of watching the coming and going of great numbers of people in our church—a few famous, most not—I've become quite good at recognizing the people God most certainly sees as heroes.

"Hey, did you see who just came in? It's Penn, the guy who picks up stray animals at the shelter and takes them to visit the residents at a nearby nursing home."

"Wow! Guess who's sitting in the back row? It's Tom. He lost both his parents, and six months later, his wife came down with cancer... I don't know how anybody could soldier through that dark night, but here he is."

"You're not going to believe who's walking down the aisle! It's Everett. A stroke might have taken his voice, but nothing could defeat that smile!"

"Hey, Kristin's in her usual place, divorced with two young children, still teaching Sunday school and making sure our refugee family has a ride to the grocery store."

Unsung heroes, too many to mention, bring a special shine to our Sunday mornings. If I could carry a tune, I'd sing them a song that would knock their socks off.

*Father, we sing the praises of those very special people who never quit saying* yes *to life. Let me be a hero like them.*
—Pam Kidd

## Mon 6

*Even the night shall be light about me.*
—Psalm 139:11 (NKJV)

When I was learning to fly, I lived in dread of my night training. After all, I had a tendency to get lost, even on sunny days. *What if I can't find my way and then run out of gas and crash?*

Then the night came when I had to face my demons. I sat at the end of the runway, praying and idling the engine. Finally, I shoved the throttle forward. The plane shuddered, wove down the runway and climbed into the cool night air. At three thousand feet, I trimmed it out and looked around.

To my astonishment, it was easier to find my way around at night than in the daytime. The towns were all brightly lit up. "Look," I said to my instructor, "I can see everything. There's Salisbury, there's Macon and that must be Centralia." In the daytime I couldn't see these towns, because they were buried in a patch of green vegetation, but at night the invisible was plain.

I still prefer flying in the daytime, but I'm learning that there are some things you can't see clearly in sunlight. At night, you see different things.

Right now our country is going through hard economic times, and I suddenly can see a lot of things more valuable than money: family, sharing, ingenuity, thrift. I can see how rich we are in this country, even when times are tough.

*Forgive me, Lord, for fearing the dark. I should have known You would be there too.*
—Daniel Schantz

## June

### Tue 7

*"My eyes have grown dim with grief; my whole frame is but a shadow."*—JOB 17:7 (NIV)

The whirlwind year of emotions began on the Saturday when I was married to Brian and peaked ten days later, when my dad unexpectedly passed away.

Mom and I were in a haze those first twenty-four hours. Roses from the wedding were still drying in the house. How could this have happened?

Through our fog, we began to compile a list of what needed to be done. One of the things on the list was a guestbook for the service. We decided that we'd rather have a book of family pictures, so off we went to the local craft store to buy a large book with blank pages, a scrapbook.

We must've been a sight, me in the clothes I'd had on the day before (all my belongings had already been moved to my new home, five hours away), and Mom holding the hymnal we'd picked up at the church and forgotten to leave in the car.

A salesclerk walked up to us and asked how she could help. "Where do you keep your scrapbooks for funerals?" Mom asked. The clerk, flabbergasted, had no idea how to respond.

As Mom and I wandered away toward the scrapbooking section, we looked at each other and surprised ourselves with our smiles and then with laughter. The poor saleswoman may have been flustered by our request, but for us it was an unexpected gift from God, a break in the clouds. If we could laugh in spite of what we were going through, we could do anything.

Mom and I marched up to the books and selected a tasteful black one, perfect for filling with photos, family memories and the names of loved ones. I know Dad was watching and probably shaking his head. And I hope he was smiling.

*Lord, when You get a minute, say hi to Dad for me.*
—ASHLEY KAPPEL

## Wed 8

*"But he who endures to the end will be saved."*
—MATTHEW 10:22 (RSV)

In 1937, I was accepted at a college eight hundred miles from home. I was anxious to prove my worth and I dreamed of graduating with honors. On the English placement exam, I poured out my thoughts about my dream, my gratitude and my willingness to work. But when the results were posted, I learned that I had been placed in remedial English. I was crushed and wanted to leave college. But I lacked the courage and the carfare home.

I remained in remedial English until our midterms, when I was recommended for regular freshman English. However, my work schedule conflicted with the class, and I had to remain in remedial English until June. Again I fought against self-pity and feelings of inadequacy. But something else happened: I became excited about writing and fell in love with words. Expressing myself on paper became a joy.

My year in remedial English was painful and frustrating. But from it came the foundation of a lifetime of writing, an opportunity to reach out and touch the lives of others, and the knowledge that words are tools that can sweep away frustrations.

*Guiding Savior, the path You revealed in Your parables is a journey through difficulty. Now, as in the past, I rely on You for the strength to persevere.*
—OSCAR GREENE

## June

### Thu 9

*Call understanding your intimate friend.*
—Proverbs 7:4 (NAS)

On June 9, 1989, I gave birth to Robbie, our third child and first son. More than anything, I'd wanted a little boy. Robbie was born two weeks past due, with a severe birth defect called anencephaly. He lived for twenty minutes.

As the doctors discovered the truth during labor, I wanted to say, "Stop everything! There's been a mistake. We'll come back later." Afterward, I glanced out the picture window at the rain. *Will I always hate rain? Will I ever laugh again?*

After Robbie's birth and twenty-minute life, my husband went home to be with our girls, who were six and eight. My mother-in-law Carolyn offered to stay with me that long night. I didn't think I needed anybody. *I don't have anything to say. I can't talk—only cry.*

Carolyn understood. She plumped my pillow and covered me with a blanket. Without a word, she poured my water and held the straw to my mouth. She didn't ask any questions; she didn't offer Scripture; she didn't even pray. She was just there. I didn't know how much I needed a quiet someone. Maybe that's why I didn't completely reject what she told me a few months later: "God's going to give you another baby."

"I'm not going through that again."

"You're going to have another baby. A boy."

I told her it wasn't going to happen. But deep down, I sensed an unexpected, undeniable flicker of hope.

On August 6, 1991, our fourth child, Richard Thomas, was born—whole and healthy.

*God, thank You for giving me Your quiet compassion and Your healing promise through Carolyn.*
—Julie Garmon

*June*

## Fri 10

*The flowers appear on the earth....*
—Song of Solomon 2:12

When my husband Keith and I lived in Los Angeles, I was vehemently opposed to having any dandelions in our grass. I waged a personal war against them, pulling them up whenever I saw them. It was as if the weeds were an affront to my ability to keep our lawn pristine, like others in the neighborhood.

In Bellingham, Washington, it's a different story. There's so much wild foliage around the driveway, so much untamed growth watered by our frequent rains, that the dandelions are only one part of the picture. We have purple lupine, buttercups, several kinds of ferns, hollyhocks, blackberries, scarlet gilia, Queen Anne's lace, Indian paintbrush and at least two different kinds of dandelions—short ones like the ones we'd seen in our lawn in LA and tall ones with long stalks that let their blossoms sway in the breeze.

At first, Keith teased me for no longer attacking the dandelions with the passion I'd shown before. "You were obsessed by them," he pointed out with a grin. "Don't tell me you've mellowed."

"This is more like wilderness," I said. "And wildflowers look good in the wilderness."

I have to admit, I'm really happy I got to see that dandelions are a lovely addition to our surroundings and not just a bothersome intrusion. It makes me wonder if I might have seen it sooner if only I'd been looking with better eyes.

*Thank You, Lord, for showing me that You really do know how to decorate Your creation.*
—Rhoda Blecker

## June

### Sat 11

*See what large letters I use as I write to you with my own hand!* —GALATIANS 6:11 (NIV)

I suppose most everyone has hundreds of recipes collected over the years and filed somewhere handy in the kitchen. The ones I've typed or pasted on index cards are quick to find and use.

Some of my treasured ones, however, are a motley-looking bunch; ingredients and/or instructions not exact: "Butter the size of an egg." "Salt to taste." "Cook till done." They're not on neat cards either, but handwritten in the middle of what had been letters from long-gone relatives relating things that were important at that particular time: "Mrs. Yoder has a sick cow." "Pa says if the corn don't get rain, we'll lose it." "Edna and the kids are moving to . . . she wants to know if you . . . " (Both sentences left incomplete by the clipped recipe on its reverse side.)

"All those snips sticking out of folders are as unmanageable as jumbled coat hangers!" my older son once remarked.

He was right, of course. Index cards would be neater. But the *snips,* as he called them, are written by hand—each in its owner's distinctive, cursive style—by those no longer living. As with St. Paul in the verse above, Grandma Kate, whose eyes were failing, also wrote in large letters. Aunt Gertie's script reflected its author: tiny, dainty. Cousin Lillian's words sprawled unsightly across the page. But no matter their styles, all shared with their recipients the lessons life had taught them, day by day.

*I shudder to think where I might be today, Father, if those who went before me did not bother to write and pass on the wisdom they learned, especially during their times of walking with You!*
—ISABEL WOLSELEY

## June

### Sun 12

*"That they would seek God.... though He is not far from each one of us."* —ACTS 17:27 (NAS)

I was slicing fresh fruit into a bowl, when I noticed how the morning sun shining through the kitchen window lit up the fruit. Wedges of pineapple and strawberries, grapes and cantaloupe shimmered like gems. They reminded me of Galatians 5:22 (NAS): "But the fruit of the Spirit is love, joy, peace, patience." Playfully, I matched up the first four spiritual fruits with the four fruits in my salad. Suddenly the verse wasn't just another word list; it had color and texture and flavor. I could taste the succulent fruit as I practiced love and joy, peace and patience.

When Jesus taught His listeners, He often wrapped spiritual truth in organic skin. He compared the kingdom of heaven to a mustard seed, "smaller than all the other seeds, but when it is full grown, it... becomes a tree, so that the birds of the air come and nest in its branches" (Matthew 13:32, NAS). Whenever I read about this unlikely seed becoming a huge tree, I think of my cousin's magnificent live oak, offering generous haven to birds and squirrels.

The Bible is not long ago and far away; it's as near as the fruit in a bowl or a tree in the yard, a loaf of bread (John 6:35), a spring lamb (John 21:15), or a flowing stream (Psalm 65:9).

Jesus came from heaven and dug about the familiar things of earth to make known the reality of a loving God Who wants a step-for-step walk with me.

*Jesus, Emmanuel ("God with us"), You have taught me to look for the uncommon among the common, beginning with a "baby wrapped in cloths and lying in a manger" (Luke 2:12, NAS).*
—CAROL KNAPP

## June

### JOURNEY IN THE DARK

*Mon 13*  *To give light to them that sit in darkness and in the shadow of death, to guide our feet into the way of peace.*
—LUKE 1:79

**THE SHARDS OF MEMORY**

That's good news," said my colleague. "So you're going back to work!"

"I hate to ask you this," I replied, "but what floor is our office on?"

"No worries," she said calmly. "It's on the fourth floor."

Memory is like Krazy Glue. Just a touch of it holds together the past, the present and the future. Forgetting the location of your office is a chilling experience. And that was just the beginning of the legacy of electroconvulsive therapy. It vanquishes depression almost miraculously, but as depression heads for the exit, often memory follows right behind. Now I could look at the future without flinching, but pieces of my life were gone—not just temporarily but forever.

"I'm so sorry I missed it," I said to my husband, when he mentioned a memorial service for a friend.

"You were there with me," he replied, looking startled.

The blessing—and there is one—is that some of the memory of how depression had driven me into a dark corner and crumbled the foundations of my life was gone, along with the memory of hospital visits and how to start the car. I pieced some of it together from my notebook and relearned the details of a job I had done for years.

Never have the words *guiding light* meant so much. God tests no limits, asks no hard questions. He asks for no records, needs no introduction or information. I couldn't pray my way out of depression, however hard I tried. I couldn't get back the lost pieces of my life, but the prayers of others kept me safe and the unconditional love of God brought me through.

*Dear Lord, give me the patience to learn my life anew and the spirit to rejoice in Your light.* —BRIGITTE WEEKS

## June

### Tue 14

For God is the King of all the earth: sing ye praises with understanding. —PSALM 47:7

Julia and our eleven-year-old daughter Mary were at a book group last night. After supper I sat on the sofa with a laptop while Elizabeth, John, Maggie and Stephen absorbed themselves in stuffed animals, Legos and elaborate make-believe games.

After checking my e-mail, I clicked over to a blog I follow and opened a video embedded in one of the posts. As trumpets rang from the laptop's small speakers and a choir began singing "God Save the Queen," the children gathered around, and I found myself typing "last night of the proms" into the YouTube search engine.

The Proms, London's summer concert series, traditionally ends with a program of British classics, the choruses sung by flag-waving crowds in the Royal Albert Hall and in parks throughout the United Kingdom. Eight-year-old Maggie and six-year-old Stephen were enthralled as we watched "Rule, Britannia" (sung by a mezzo in an eighteenth-century naval costume), Sir Edward Elgar's "Land of Hope and Glory," Sir Hubert Parry's setting of William Blake's "Jerusalem" and, of course, "God Save the Queen."

By the time Julia and Mary got home, the stuffed animals were arranged on a cardboard box. "That's the orchestra," Maggie told us.

"The dragon plays the trumpet, but he melts it when he breathes fire!" Stephen added. "Here's the conductor," he said as he picked up his stuffed dog, "Sir Stuffy Paul Stephenson!" He propped Sir Stuffy up against *The Complete Sherlock Holmes* and taped a chopstick to his paw. Then Maggie gave out the song sheets she had made, and we all joined in a chorus of "Rule, Britannia."

Oh, and just to make sure I wasn't raising a nest of Tories, we rounded out the evening with "The Star-Spangled Banner" and "Columbia the Gem of the Ocean."

*Lord, whenever I get too enamored with pomp and circumstance, remind me that You are indeed "King of all the earth."*
—ANDREW ATTAWAY

## June

### Wed 15

*Heal me, O Lord, and I shall be healed; save me, and I shall be saved....* —JEREMIAH 17:14

A friend told me that the purring of cats has a healing power. I wasn't so sure. Perhaps it's because our cat, a large Maine coon mix that was rescued from the subway platform, is a less-than-perfect pet. Fred won't sit in my lap for more than thirty seconds and never voluntarily. He likes to wake us up at 6:00 AM for his breakfast, even when there's food still in the bowl. He claws at the sofa. He unloads cat hair in remarkable quantities (you could knit a sweater from the stuff we collect). Fortunately, he's good at purring.

Take out his brush, he purrs. Sit next to him on the bed, he purrs. Scratch him on the flat part of his nose, he purrs so loud I think the neighbors can hear. That his purring can be healing was revealed to me the other night.

It was 3:00 AM, and I wasn't sleeping well. Too many things were going through my mind. I was doing my best to pray through the worries—give them back to God—without much success.

Then Fred leaped up on the bed and meowed. "No, Fred," I whispered, "it's not time for breakfast." He lay down next to my head, his tail twitching, and purred, an incredibly loud, comforting, satisfying sound. It turned out to be just what I needed. I scratched him on the forehead and I'm not sure where the worries went, but the next time I woke up it was 6:10 AM. Fred was letting me know he was hungry.

"Thanks for the extra ten minutes, pal," I told him. And for the purring.

*God, You have so many ways of giving me Your healing touch.*
—RICK HAMLIN

## Thu 16

*The fruit of the Spirit is love, joy, peace, patience, kindness, goodness, faithfulness.* —GALATIANS 5:22 (NIV)

I've heard it said that after many years of married life, couples start to look like each other. I don't know if that's true in Wayne's and my case. However, I can state that an amazing transformation has taken place in the two of us.

When we first married, we were as different as any two people could be. Wayne was a night owl, and I was a morning person. Not only did I wake at the crack of dawn (much to Wayne's annoyance), but I woke up happy. I liked being around people, while he preferred solitude. And yet, after all the years we've been together, our likes and dislikes have blended together. These days it isn't uncommon for us to order the same meal at a restaurant or choose to watch the same movie. Even our political views are the same. And though I'm still a morning person, Wayne seems to take it in stride.

In many ways, I've experienced the same kind of transformation in my walk with Jesus. As I've read my Bible and spent time in prayer, a subtle change has taken place within me: I want to be more like Him; I long for His power in my life.

*Lord, may I grow more like You each and every day.*
—DEBBIE MACOMBER

*June*

## Fri 17

*God Almighty... will bless you with blessings of heaven above, blessings of the deep that couches beneath....*
—Genesis 49:25 (RSV)

My friend Gary headed straight for the steel guitar hanging on the wall in the music store. I knew he would; it was a ritual each time we went. With a look of absolute love on his face, he would hold the guitar and play the blues in the small display room. Each week his paychecks had to go to matters more important than buying a guitar, especially such an expensive one!

Little did he know that the same kind of guitar was waiting for him in his bedroom. His mother had bought it as a surprise. For days, Gary came home late and woke early, too busy and too tired even to notice it.

One day Gary slowed down. He noticed the new, mysterious case sitting in his bedroom and opened it to find the beautiful steel guitar. He was thrilled—and humbled—by the thoughtfulness and generosity of his mother.

"That guitar was sitting there for days!" she said with a laugh. "It just goes to show you that sometimes God has blessings He's just waiting for us to discover, if only we take the time to see them."

*Open my eyes, Lord, to Your abundance. Amen.*
—Karen Valentin

### READER'S ROOM

Father, Your words speak to my heart, quiet it and give me peace. Your Presence in my life is a light at the end of a dark tunnel of difficult situations, guiding me. Your Holy Spirit lifts my spirit to new heights of understanding, acceptance and praise. —*Carolyn Malion, Fairmont, North Carolina*

## Sat 18

*Children's children are a crown to the aged....*
—Proverbs 17:6 (NIV)

"Hold on tight!" my brother Dexter told me as he accelerated his old golf cart through the muddy terrain on the back side of his four-acre plot of land. The family had gathered at his home in the country for a reunion, and he was showing me around the place. I held my eighteen-month-old grandson on my lap, and Dexter's twelve-year-old granddaughter Tianna sat cross-legged in the back of the cart as we bounced around. Recent rains had made the trek a bit treacherous.

Along the way, we passed our grandfather's light blue, gently dented and long deceased luxury car, our family's old travel trailer, and the camping truck in which Dexter and his wife sometimes lived in his post-Vietnam days.

"I hope our grandkids will have some of the same stuff we had," he said. By "stuff," I knew he meant the kind of vision, determination and commitment to family we had.

"Hey," Tianna called as we made a sharp turn, "looks like a cell phone in the mud over there!"

"Couldn't be way out here," Dexter answered. I shifted my grandson on my lap, so I could feel the hard, square shape of my own phone in my pocket.

A while later we doubled back, and again Tianna spoke up. "Stop! I know I see a cell phone over there!" She jumped out and ran through some deep muddy tracks and retrieved . . . a cell phone! *My* cell phone! I felt again in my pocket and pulled out the hard, square shape—my camera.

All the way back to the house, I kept thinking how my cell phone would have been lost forever had it not been for Tianna's bright eyes and dogged determination to help us see what she saw. And especially for choosing to come on this bumpy, muddy ride with us.

*Lord, the youngest people in our families have stuff we don't always have. May I always notice and appreciate their goodness.*
—Carol Kuykendall

## June

### Sun 19

*As you learn more and more how God works, you will learn how to do your work....* —COLOSSIANS 1:10 (MSG)

Think back to when you were a child. Imagine you're walking home from school. You see a pair of roller skates in the front yard of someone you don't know. You take the roller skates, bring them home and hide them under your bed. Your father discovers what you've done. What would his reaction be?

My father would have talked to me sternly about stealing, made me take back the skates and confess what I'd done to the neighbors, and grounded me for a few days.

What would *your* father have done? I've asked this question to dozens of people. And almost without exception, they knew with some assurance what their parent would do in the circumstance. "How do you know?" I asked them.

"Because we lived with him for years and saw and heard what he said and did about all kinds of situations and relationships."

I believe that's how we can learn to know God's will in specific situations. We surrender our lives to God, and as members of His family, we listen to Him in prayer every day, read His story in the Bible and see His values being lived out by Jesus. And we share our questions and our confessions with our brothers and sisters. Over time we absorb God's will, seeing and hearing His way of being honest and loving. And we come to know God's will in all kinds of situations, often without realizing it.

*Lord, thank You for Your Word and for the people all around us from whom we can learn Your will.*
—KEITH MILLER

*June*

## Mon 20

*Every good and perfect gift is from above, coming down from the Father....* —James 1:17 (NIV)

The box the mail carrier delivered was big and square and brown. I checked the return address and saw it was from my young friend Megan, newly graduated from law school and living in Washington, DC.

I opened it carefully and found a layer of green tissue paper. Before I'd even pulled it back, I could smell it. Nested in the box was a wreath made of fresh lavender. Megan's note said simply that she was thinking of me and wanted to send me a "little happy."

I lifted the wreath from the box, its fragrance filling the air around me. When I looked closer, I was distressed to see that the fragile circle had not had an easy trip. Dozens of loose flowers littered the bottom of the box. *How sad*, I thought.

Something else was in the box though—a tiny purple organza bag with a ribbon closure, and a small card with these words: "Because of the delicate quality of lavender, it is not unusual for some of the buds to fall off during shipping. We've included a small pouch so that you can create your very own lavender sachet with the loose buds." I gathered up those loose bits and soon had a lovely sachet bag to tuck into my dresser.

I love my new wreath and enjoy it every day. But I think I'm most appreciative of that tiny bag. The bit of fragrance and beauty is made of scraps, of things someone could have easily thrown out but have now found a new life in my sock drawer.

Yes, Megan's gift did make me more than a "little happy." I'm hoping it made me a bit wiser too.

*Even in little things, Father, may I see opportunity for beauty and service.*
—Mary Lou Carney

*June*

## Tue 21

*For you did not receive a spirit that makes you a slave again to fear....* —ROMANS 8:15 (NIV)

The hotel terrace overlooked a sloping field surrounded by a wire fence. From where I sat with my coffee, I could see, inside the enclosure, a grazing doe and, prancing by her side, a spotted fawn.

Finding his mother indifferent to his capering, the fawn began experimenting with various paces: galloping, bucking, leaping. Now a mincing little dance, lifting each hoof daintily one by one, and then a stiff-legged march, first right legs, then left. Round and round the circumference of the fence he trotted, savoring the newfound delights of four legs, while my coffee grew cold, forgotten.

Suddenly the fawn whirled to face the wire screen. On the other side was a dog about his own size—from his eager pawing at the fence, still a puppy. Both of them shivering with excitement, the two young animals stood nose to nose, tails wagging furiously.

Then the doe thundered down the slope and thrust herself between the fence and the fawn. Prodding him with her head, she drove him swiftly back up the hill. I could almost hear the lecture: *Never, never, ever go near a dog!*

The puppy whimpered; his tail drooped. The fawn stood subdued. But I felt as though for a wondrous moment I'd been given a glimpse of Eden, before the first fear entered the world. Some fears are realistic, of course, on this post-Eden planet. Dogs, the doe knew, kill deer. But what if I could be, most of the time, as trusting and adventurous and full of joy as that fawn?

*Teach me, Father, to distinguish needful fears from the false ones that block full enjoyment of Your world.*
—ELIZABETH SHERRILL

## June

### Wed 22

*Remembering without ceasing your work of faith, and labour of love.... —I Thessalonians 1:3*

Stitch by stitch by stitch, I'm embroidering a wedding sampler for Michelle and Jesse, who will marry next week. I created the simple design myself, using a Celtic alphabet and a heart with filigree and Michelle's colors of red and white—very simple, yet very labor-intensive.

In fact, my gift may not arrive on time as it's taking much longer than I expected. The cross-stitch cloth takes sixteen stitches per inch—that's 256 stitches per square inch—times two for the crossing thread, for a total of 512 stitches per square inch. I wear a magnifier around my neck to be able to see what I'm doing and avoid time-consuming mistakes.

But my project is worth the time I've invested. I've known Michelle since she called me "Mom" at age fourteen, and as I stitch, I remember her growing up with my daughter Trina, her best friend, giggling in pj's during sleepovers, weeping when "he" didn't call, trying on prom gowns in Boston, floating lazily on rubber rafts on the lake, bemoaning homework, harmonizing with Trina in the backseat of the van and in church. Then one day Michelle introduced me to "the one"—and extended her hand to show her diamond ring.

I suppose I could buy an expensive wedding gift, something they can remember me by and really use, like a set of dishes. Or I could buy something from their bridal registry; they'd be sure to like it. Instead, I stitch memories into this little sampler to give a gift of love.

*Loving Father, bless the newlyweds and let their love last longer than my stitchery.*
—Gail Thorell Schilling

*June*

**Thu 23**  *We give thanks to you, O God....* —PSALM 75:1 (NIV)

"You're allergic to wheat? That must be so annoying!" That's what people tell me when they find out about my allergy. It is annoying sometimes, but not really all that bad, relatively speaking. Because everything is relative; I learned that when I was diagnosed.

It was two years ago. I was having stomach pain; a CT scan showed an inflamed intestinal wall. My doctor prepared me for the worst. "Might be cancer," he said.

I've already had cancer once. To have it again would be, well, much more than just annoying. But then the blood tests came back.

"You don't have cancer," the doctor said. "It's celiac disease."

"What does that mean?" I asked.

"You're allergic to wheat."

"Well, I guess that's not so bad."

It wasn't so bad because it could have been worse. And that's what I remind myself whenever I have to turn down a cookie or a slice of pizza.

Celiac disease has taught me to put my problems in context, both the big ones and the small ones. So sure, it's annoying to be allergic to wheat, but it's also really good to be alive, to be healthy, to have friends and faith and a loving family. It all depends on how you look at it.

*God, please give me the perspective to see the blessings You've provided me.*
—JOSHUA SUNDQUIST

## Fri 24

*Am I now trying to win the approval of men, or of God?...* —GALATIANS 1:10 (NIV)

During free time on a silent retreat, I decided to take a walk on a nature trail. As soon as I hit the woods, two pesky horseflies started dive-bombing around my head. I waved a hand over my head as I walked, but soon my arm was worn out. Finally I picked up a three-foot-long branch and moved it back and forth like a cow swishing its tail.

When the trail emerged onto the grassy field behind the retreat house, I encountered a fellow retreat participant jogging toward me. *She must think I'm crazy, walking around waving this branch over my head,* I thought. My embarrassment was compounded by the retreat rule of complete silence, which prevented me from explaining my odd behavior to her as she wordlessly jogged by.

Suddenly I was struck by the absurdity of being so concerned about what the jogger thought about me. How much of my mental energy did I use worrying about how I looked to other people? How much time did I waste every day, needlessly explaining myself so that others would approve of me?

I hurried up to my room, took out my notebook, and came up with a plan to stop investing so much time and energy in what others thought about me. Instead I'd learn how to invest that energy in doing things that please God.

*Dear Lord, help me to do what pleases You and not worry about what others think.*
—KAREN BARBER

## June

### Sat 25

*He who answers before listening—that is his folly and his shame.* —Proverbs 18:13 (NIV)

Julee and I had had a fight. We hadn't exactly hung up on each other, but almost. We were each pretty itchy to end the conversation first.

We don't like being mad at each other, and we certainly don't fight like we used to when our marriage was new. Back then, we were still testing each other's limits and learning how to compromise. Some days I wasn't sure our marriage would survive. But a wise mentor to whom I eventually brought my problem helped me.

"She's too emotional," I told him, as we walked along Central Park West. "She takes everything personally."

After a few minutes of this, he said, "And what about you? A fight takes two and all you've talked about is Julee."

*Well,* I thought, *isn't she the problem?*

"I just defend myself," I said.

I wanted to take those words back as soon as I said them. My friend smiled and then nodded. "That's why most couples fight," he said. "Because they're too busy defending themselves and not listening. If you want to stop fighting, start listening. Here's a trick: Try repeating back to her what you thought she said. See if you both hear the same thing. You won't stop fighting until you start understanding each other."

Listen rather than react. Understand instead of defend. Lo and behold, we stopped fighting and started talking things out more. We had our blowups for sure; now we knew how to call a truce. Through the years we fought less and less. But we had to *practice* not fighting.

*Maybe I'm out of practice,* I thought, picking up the phone to call Julee. It would be good to hear her voice.

*God, You brought Julee and me together for a reason, and it wasn't to fight. Help us keep our ears open so that our hearts may stay open.*
—Edward Grinnan

*June*

## ⌛ ADVICE FROM AUNT ANNIE

*Sun 26*    *"And I, the Messiah, have authority even to decide what men can do on Sabbath days!"*—MARK 2:28 (TLB)

**SUNDAYS SHOULD BE SPECIAL**

When I was a child, Sunday was a "set apart" day. We had Sunday-only clothes: two dresses each for my sister and me, a pair of slacks for our brother. After church, we had a special dinner, usually fried chicken. It was served about 2:00 PM, just when we kids thought we'd die of hunger. Unless we had guests, afternoons were spent resting or reading. Evenings meant leftovers from dinner and church again.

For my family—and, I suspect, for many other families—Sunday no longer follows a strict pattern. We aren't bound by rules regarding activities or travel. After Sunday school and worship, my husband Don and I eat out or have a light meal. We often visit or entertain friends. We may watch a movie or catch up on yard work. But every so often I wondered about the way I observed Sunday. *Is it okay to eat out? Read a best-selling novel? Should my observances be holier?*

Then I read Aunt Annie's article "Sundays Should Be Special." She told of taking home my three-year-old sister Amanda after an overnight visit. The first question Amanda asked Mother was "Did you have Sunday while I was gone?"

"No," Mother answered, "it wasn't Sunday here or anywhere else in the country."

"Oh goody!" Amanda cried. "I didn't want to miss it!" It was obvious that Sunday was already a special day to Amanda, something to look forward to.

Perhaps, Aunt Annie suggested, Sunday should be so special to all of us that we eagerly look forward to it and remember it as a day of worship, thanksgiving and service—always joyful, never dull.

*Please, Lord, don't let me miss Sunday!* —PENNEY SCHWAB

*June*

## Mon 27

*I will lift up mine eyes unto the hills, from whence cometh my help.* —PSALM 121:1

I try to take my two young dogs for a run several times a week, but the word *run* doesn't mean what it did twenty-five years ago. I tell my dogs, between gasps, that they would have enjoyed running with me when I was young. My first two pups accompanied me up and down steep arroyos to a distant ridge before a dizzying descent brought us back to our home, three miles and thirty minutes later.

I still run for thirty minutes—to the top of a very tame Cuchilla Hill, a half mile from our home. My posture has changed as much as my pace. I lean forward and stare at my feet as I plod along, carefully avoiding the rocks and cactus I once ignored.

Last week, though, I saw a hawk perched on the peak of Cuchilla. Its wings twitched nervously, and I knew I would miss its takeoff if I took my eyes off of it. I straightened my back and stared up as I ran. The hawk did not fly away until I was within a few feet of the summit.

It wasn't until it soared out of sight that I realized how much I had missed the past few years by not "lifting my eyes unto the hills." I knew I had been staring at my feet a lot lately, even when I wasn't running with my dogs. Trusting God to guide my footsteps may seem riskier, but He allows me to see so much more when I do!

*Dear God, thank You for helping me to ignore the rocks and cactus while I run with You!*
—TIM WILLIAMS

## June

### Tue 28

*Be careful that you do not forget the Lord your God....* —DEUTERONOMY 8:11 (NIV)

Six years ago, some friends had to move cross-country and needed to off-load their menagerie. They had several reptiles, so I took my children over, thinking maybe we'd adopt something exotic like a frilled lizard. The night before we arrived, my friend's boys knocked over the lizard food: a mail-ordered box of five hundred live crickets. The apartment was hopping when we walked in the door. We came home with a king snake.

King has had plenty of time to grow on me, but instead, he's just grown. He's now about five feet long. Three years ago I persuaded my son John to change King's water as a first step toward getting someone else to take over the snake care. But John accidentally put down the bowl on King's tail, and King bit. I retain my position as chief terrarium cleaner and snake charmer to this day.

King is not an intrusive houseguest. He doesn't scratch the furniture, slobber or make me sneeze. I don't have to feed him often. He doesn't jump up, clamoring for affection. I can forget about him for a few days, and he's still alive. In my busy life, one thing I like about King is that he doesn't demand attention.

That gives me pause though. That other king, the one who adopted me as His own, doesn't force His presence on me either. He takes what is given. If I neglect Him, He doesn't do the squeaky-wheel thing to remind me I'm not paying attention. The measure of our relationship is the measure of my commitment and involvement. It's a scary thing: God doesn't want to be a houseguest, a pet, a visitor; He wants to live with me and be part of my every movement and breath. I want that too. But I forget.

*Oh, Lord, teach me to remember You in all things, every day of my life.*
—JULIA ATTAWAY

*June*

## Wed 29

*"Stand up in the presence of the elderly, and show respect for the aged...."*—LEVITICUS 19:32 (NLT)

A year before Dad turned ninety, my sister, sister-in-law and I began making plans for a big birthday party with all our relatives and my stepmother Bev's friends. I couldn't wait, knowing I'd get to be the master of ceremonies. I was planning to have Dad's friends and relatives roast and toast him in style.

Of course, we were going to make it a surprise party like the big surprise we pulled on Dad when he turned seventy. But something—I think it was Bev recalling how the blood drained from Dad's face when he walked into the banquet hall twenty years earlier—made me rethink the surprise element. I enlisted my sister to talk to Dad. Catherine told him about our plans, including a picnic at a park just for the immediate family the day after the big party. Then she told him we all agreed that the decision would be up to him.

The next morning Dad complained to Catherine. "I woke up at 3:00 AM and couldn't get back to sleep, thinking about that doggone party. Did you really mean it when you said the decision was up to me?"

"Absolutely, Dad. We'll do whatever you want."

"Well, then, no party. I hate being the center of attention. The picnic is okay, but no big party or sit-down dinner."

In the end, Dad agreed to let one of his nephews host a big family reunion at his farm a few weeks before Dad's birthday, where we celebrated with a cake, lots of laughs, good food and more relatives than you can imagine.

*Lord, don't let me always assume that people want things just the way I want them. Teach me to defer to their judgment and their wishes.*
—PATRICIA LORENZ

*June*

*Thu 30*

*For God so loved the world, that he gave his only begotten Son, that whosoever believeth in him should not perish, but have everlasting life.* —JOHN 3:16

Two summers before Dad died, I went over to borrow something and found him sitting on his heels, mopping the sweat off his brow. He was in the middle of laying out a cobblestone patio. He gave me a grin and, sunlight in his eyes, said, "This is the last time I will ever work with cement. It's just getting too hard." We both laughed at his joke.

A few years ago I bought a brand-new house, and the task of landscaping fell to me. I've often sensed Dad's presence as I sought to emulate his creative handiwork. This summer, the project's been a series of cobblestone pathways and patios, like Dad's. How many times have I, like him, set the frame and poured the cement? Sat back on my heels to mop the sweat off my brow? Squinted, sun in my eyes, at the bubble in his level? Patted the concrete into place with his trowel? How many times has a hummingbird, one of Dad's favorites, zipped and zapped over my shoulder?

When I was a child, I struggled with the concept of eternity. Dad did his best to explain, but it wasn't until this summer, sensing Dad's presence in my labor and using his tools, a bird he loved at my shoulder, that I finally began to understand: God has planted eternity within us. "Forever" is in our DNA. For Dad is more than just memory; he's alive, both in me *and* with God.

*Dear God, help me to lovingly nurture the eternity You've planted within my own children so that they, like me, will know I live within them and with You.*
—BRENDA WILBEE

## June

**SEEDS OF LOVE**

1. _____

2. _____

3. _____

4. _____

5. _____

6. _____

7. _____

8. _____

9. _____

10. _____

*June*

11 _____

12 _____

13 _____

14 _____

15 _____

16 _____

17 _____

18 _____

19 _____

20 _____

21 _____

## June

22 _____

23 _____

24 _____

25 _____

26 _____

27 _____

28 _____

29 _____

30 _____

# July

*My little children, let us not love in word, neither in tongue; but in deed and in truth.*

—I John 3:18

*July*

## ❧ A PATH TO SIMPLICITY

*Fri 1*  "*You shall not turn aside to the right or to the left.*"
—DEUTERONOMY 5:32 (NAS)

**TAKING THE PEACEFUL PATH**

I travel a lot, so I recently purchased a global positioning system (GPS) for my car. I couldn't wait to use it, and in anticipation of a three-hour trip from Huntington, West Virginia, to Burlington, Kentucky, I attached the device to my windshield. But when I exited Interstate 75 in search of the address I'd typed, I found myself on an unmarked country road, where the only things I recognized were a few dogwood trees. "Roberta," I muttered under my breath, "you can't even find your way with a personal tour guide."

Then I heard the voice of my ever-patient GPS guide exclaim, "Recalculating... recalculating." Her words were in such sharp contrast to the way I'd been talking to myself that I had to chuckle. The second time I tried her directions, I got to the address just fine. In my first attempt, I'd made a single wrong turn.

In my quest for simplicity, I've made the occasional wrong turn as well. I put a tea set on sale only to discover later that it was just what I needed for a serving tray in my guest bedroom. "It would've gone perfectly with your new wallpaper, Roberta," I grumbled. "Why didn't you think of that?"

And then there were the times I tried to tackle the whole cabin at once instead of going room by room. The day I recognized the error of my ways, I gave myself another good talking-to.

I'm learning that simplicity isn't something I can achieve all at once; I'm liable to make a few wrong turns along the way or even regress. But the next time I flit from one project to the next and end up with a bigger mess than I started with, I'll be saying, "Recalculating... recalculating. Fix yourself a cup of hot tea, Roberta, and look at all you have accomplished."

*Thank You, Lord, for keeping me on the right road.*
—ROBERTA MESSNER

## July

**Sat 2** *Then they were glad because they had quiet, and he brought them to their desired haven.* —PSALM 107:30 (RSV)

I am totally alone this weekend. My husband and son went to a barbershop chorus convention, and my daughter is away with her best friend's family. That leaves me and our dog—and I must admit I'm enjoying it. I love my family, yet there's something refreshing about making my own schedule (or no schedule, if I choose), having cereal for dinner and watching *Field of Dreams* two nights in a row (and crying shamelessly both times).

When I told a friend about how I planned to spend the weekend, she said, "Won't you get lonely?" I wondered why I hadn't thought about that and then I ran across this quote from an unknown author: "The difference between loneliness and solitude is how you feel about who you are alone with and who made the choice."

I feel good about who I'm with because it really isn't just me. These times of solitude provide my very best times with God. In fact, on my rare weekends alone, it feels as if God has made this choice for me, a gift of quiet time so that I will give some back to Him. When I do, I realize that solitude is one of God's best presents, especially in a world that is too busy, too noisy and too crowded. Free of demands and distractions, I sit with my Bible on the back porch swing and rest with God. In the quiet peace that follows, God teaches me that loneliness is simply a space into which He has not yet been invited.

*Lord Jesus, come sit beside me when I am alone;*
*I want to spend time with You.*
—GINA BRIDGEMAN

## July

### Sun 3

> When you come, bring the cloak that I left with Carpus at Troas, also the books, and above all the parchments.
> —II Timothy 4:13 (NRSV)

Two recent encounters with friends—comments about "recommended reading"—have prompted me to reorganize my library.

Last winter I sent my friend Beth a poignant essay, a reminder to invite God into our lives, even in our times of chaos and loss. Beth responded by e-mail: "I keep coming back to this, reading it again and again, passing it on to friends and family. I'm glad to have it in my 'file of fortitude' where I go for comfort and strength." Inspired by Beth's phrase, I set up a new file titled "Fortitude" for memorable lines of poetry or paragraphs of prose.

Then last week another friend inadvertently broadened the scope of my project. Over dinner, she reminded me that more than five years ago I'd recommended a book to her. She'd recently read the novel, and its theme of reconciliation and forgiveness had touched her deeply. When I came home, I pulled my copy from its shelf, eager to reread the last chapter: two pages full of grace.

Tidying up this morning, I returned the book to the bookcase. While there, I rearranged its neighboring titles. I nestled it alongside other books I anticipate reading a second, or maybe third, time. In his *Thoughts in Solitude*, Thomas Merton noted that some books "speak to us like God... they bring us light and peace and fill us with silence." I think that's a long way of saying they give us fortitude, strength for the journey. And next time I need some, I'll know right where to look.

> *Lord, draw my attention today to some written word—*
> *new or old—that will renew my spirit.*
> —Evelyn Bence

## July

### Mon 4

*It is for freedom that Christ has set us free. Stand firm, then, and do not let yourselves be burdened again by a yoke of slavery.* —GALATIANS 5:1 (NIV)

"The Americans are coming!"

The news was exhilarating *and* frightening. As a refugee child of almost ten fleeing from bombs and enemy gunfire, I was painfully aware that not all people were friendly. *What will these soldiers be like? Will they send us to prison? Will they make us go back to Russia?*

But soon we children knew that we had nothing to fear. These soldiers treated refugees with dignity and respect. They easily parted with a meal so we had something to eat. What's more, they gave us chocolate bars, a treat beyond our imagination.

When the order did come for our family to return to Russia, an American officer listened carefully to my mother's explanation of why we couldn't return. "The Communists will send me to Siberia," she said, "and my children to an orphanage. That's what they've done to many of our relatives and friends."

Because of the officer's intervention, we were allowed to remain in Austria. Three years later, a young man from Pennsylvania, working with the American Mennonite Central Committee, reconnected us with some of our relatives. Then the committee made it possible for us to immigrate to America.

The first time my mother was able to vote, she could hardly believe it. She'd lived under Communism, Fascism and now democracy. To be able to come and go as we pleased, to worship in whatever church we chose, to pursue higher education—all this was ours!

And all because 235 years ago, some men got together to write these famous words: "We hold these truths to be self-evident, that all men are created equal, that they are endowed by their Creator with certain unalienable Rights, that among these are Life, Liberty and the pursuit of Happiness."

*Dear Father, thank You for the freedoms we enjoy.*
*May we never take them for granted.*
—HELEN GRACE LESCHEID

## July

### Tue 5

*When darkness overtakes him, light will come bursting in....*
—Psalm 112:4 (TLB)

Not too long ago, I found myself thinking that my life had taken control of me, rather than the other way round.

My job at a creative agency looked glamorous on paper, but in reality it was a cauldron of corporate stress and unending client demands. My home life with my husband Matt and our sons Sam and Ned was a long commute away, and I traveled to distant client offices more than I wanted. All too often I felt I was spending too much time on things I didn't love and missing out on the things that brought me joy.

On this particular afternoon, I once again hurriedly shut down my office computer, packed up my work and climbed into my car for the long ride home. The traffic on the highway was creeping at less than a snail's pace. The air around me was heavy with the haze of city heat and pollution. As I looked over the long line of cars that snaked its way through a marshy area, I saw in the distance a body of water. From where I sat, it appeared to be just littered with trash. I couldn't make out exactly what it was from such a distance, but it seemed like large wads of white paper strewn haphazardly across the water.

*Lord, who could have done this?* I felt heartbroken—the late hour, the stressful day, the creeping commute, the lack of time with my family and now this example of the way we'd marred our world. *Lord, where is the joy?*

As I inched along, the roadway crested above the marsh and gave me a closer look. On the shimmering water below was not trash but hundreds of snow-white swans.

All of a sudden, my heart was light again.

> *Lord, please help me to see the signs of light and love that are always present in my life.*
> —Anne Adriance

## July

### Wed 6
*For with God nothing shall be impossible.* —LUKE 1:37

Going through yet another long-unopened box in the attic as my husband John and I prepared to leave our home of fifty years, I came upon an old photo album, leather binding cracked and discolored. In capital letters on the first page, in my own handwriting, were the words "CAR TRIP TO YELLOWSTONE."

The next page held some faded photographs of various stops in Pennsylvania and Ohio. But there John came down with excruciating shingles, and we didn't make it to Yellowstone. Now, doubtless, we never would.

But that's not what I said to myself. Years ago while visiting my sister in Djakarta, I learned a wonderful word: *belum* (pronounced b'LUM)—"not yet." There in Indonesia, the word *no* is avoided whenever possible—too abrupt, too final and unyielding. *Belum* leaves room for dreams. Asked in a job interview, "Do you have a college degree?" a fifty-year-old man who left school at nine will answer, "Belum." And during a doctor's exam, if an eighty-year-old woman is asked, "Do you have any children?" she'll smile and reply, "Belum."

I like to answer my own questions the same way. Have I learned to sew? Speak German? Play brilliant bridge? Belum to them all.

And so as I added the poor ruined album to the movers' throwaway pile, I used the word that says life is open-ended and nothing is impossible. Have John and I visited Yellowstone?

Belum.

*Let me look beyond limitations of time and space,*
*Father, to the vastness of life in You.*
—ELIZABETH SHERRILL

## July

### Thu 7

*He hath made every thing beautiful in his time....*
—Ecclesiastes 3:11

I jumped for joy when I heard the news: Mr. Stinky was coming to town. Mr. Stinky is not a person but a plant, known to science as *Titan arum* and to plant lovers around the world as Mr. Stinky.

*Titan arum* has several unusual features: It is rare, found only in the Sumatran rainforest and a handful of municipal or university greenhouses; it blooms only once every few years; it is enormous, producing a flower up to ten feet wide and a leaf up to twenty feet long; and, in most people's opinion, it is as ugly as it is large, with a murky-colored blossom and a smell like rotting garbage, the source of its colorful name.

When the great day arrived, I drove to our local college greenhouse and joined the crowd. As the line snaked forward, I could detect a skunklike odor. So far Mr. Stinky was living up to its reputation. Then I entered the exhibit room and saw the visiting celebrity in all its glory. Yes, it was ugly: outsized, malformed, droopy and drab. But it was also breathtaking, even awe-inspiring in its strangeness and enormity. Like a blue whale, it was too large, too ungainly, and yet it had its own peculiar beauty. A favorite quote from Ralph Waldo Emerson popped into my mind: "Nature is too thin a screen; the glory of the omnipresent God bursts through everything."

*Even,* I thought with amazement, *through such a thing as* Titan arum.

*Lord, teach me to see the beauty in every corner of Your kingdom.*
—Philip Zaleski

## July

### Fri 8 *"Surely the Lord is in this place...."*—Genesis 28:16 (niv)

"We can't do this!" I told my friend Elisa as we struggled to lift the heavy canoe off the hooks above our heads on a wall of the garage. The two of us had come to this mountain cabin because both of us felt spiritually depleted, hungry and thirsty for reminders of God's presence. On this first afternoon, we spotted the canoe and decided that paddling around the lake would be a great adventure, even though neither of us knew much about canoeing.

"Look—a pulley!" With a loud thud, we lowered the unwieldy canoe to the ground. We could barely budge it from there. Then we discovered a small dolly. We lugged the canoe onto the dolly and started wheeling it down the path.

"We'll never get it down that steep rocky part." It took all our strength to keep the canoe balanced on the dolly, but somehow we did. We pushed the boat into the water, buckled on our life jackets and clumsily climbed in, just as the canoe glided away. One of us was facing one way and one the other.

Soon we found ourselves headed toward a long sandbar. We figured out how to steer and somehow missed the sandbar. The wind came up, and we quickly drifted farther out into the lake; it was time to head back. We started paddling and realized that we were making little progress. So we figured out a rhythm, paddling on one side of the canoe and then the other. Somehow, we started moving toward the shore.

We didn't think we could get the heavy canoe all the way back up the steep rocky path, up the driveway and back into the garage, but somehow we did. We weren't sure we could lift it back onto the hooks and pull it back up with the pulley. But, thankfully, we did. Somehow.

*Lord, somehow You always remind us that You are near.*
—Carol Kuykendall

## *July*

### Sat 9

*Plant gardens, and eat the fruit of them.* —Jeremiah 29:5

I've noticed something about my generation of suburban kids: We want to grow things. Sometimes we'll sit in our yardless New York City apartments and dream about being gentleman farmers, raising chickens or cultivating herbs.

I have a little house in the country where, every month or so, I can escape from the city for a few days, buy a couple of bags of potting soil and get closer to realizing that fantasy. There's a garden patch out back where a random selection of plants—raspberries, a little rhubarb, some chives—were planted years ago. Last spring, I was up at the house for a week and decided to experiment with a few more things. I added some thyme, some rosemary and some vegetables (cucumber, peppers, chard).

Well, I'm no gentleman farmer. Those of you who are more familiar with growing things may laugh, but on a subsequent visit, I learned that my little plants were still mostly, well, little. The thyme and the rosemary turned out to be hardy, but the cucumbers were tiny and malformed; the pepper plants had become breakfast, lunch and dinner for bugs; and I had enough chard to make the garnish for one plate. Even the raspberries were only producing tiny amounts of fruit.

I realized that my plants needed regular tending—and occasional extra-special care. That little epiphany led to another realization: My garden patch is rather like my spiritual life. I get complacent, busy, lazy. I'm lax about prayer. I'm inconsistent about reading my Bible. And then I wonder why I feel far away from God.

It's been a hectic time at work and in the city, so I'm heading back to my country place soon. During my few days there, I've resolved that I'll prune those raspberry plants and spend some time tending to my faith, giving it some of the attention it needs to get back to good growth.

*Only You, Lord, can grow my faith ... and my garden.*
—Jeff Chu

*July*

## ❈ TO SAY GOOD-BYE

*Sun 10*  *A word fitly spoken is like apples of gold....*
—Proverbs 25:11

**TRUTH TELLERS**

There's a funny thing about being a minister's wife: People say the oddest things to you.

"Pam, I've always wondered why you didn't sing in the choir. But after sitting behind you this morning, I understand."

"You know, Pam, I've always felt sorry for you. People think I look older than my husband too."

"I'm not sure a minister's wife should look *that* stylish."

In a way, I actually enjoy these off-the-wall comments. Well, not the one about looking older. But the others crack me up. I *am* tone deaf and musically inept; I'm so bad, it is funny. As for the "stylish" admonition, I just hope it's true!

Here's a greater truth: I've loved these years in the church. The times I've been part of a worthwhile project or influenced an outcome toward good or even helped craft a sentence to enhance a life-changing sermon. And I've loved the people—even those who have wrapped an arm around my shoulder and told me the naked truth. Those "apples of gold" will remain my treasures. They shine with love. They leave me laughing.

*Father, I have heard Your love spoken in strange words. Bless the speakers.*
—Pam Kidd

## July

### Mon 11
*"Teach them the good way in which they should walk...."*
—I Kings 8:36 (NAS)

This past summer I sat in the audience as my son debuted as a chorus member in his first professional opera with the Cincinnati Opera Company. As I watched Chase, I strained to try to pick out his tenor voice from the others. He is a man now, but summer still reminds me of when he was a boy.

Summer is the sound of motorboats on the lake and lawn mowers in the yard; it's the smell of new grass and sweet flowers. Summer is my memory of my young son pushing a mower across the yard.

I didn't know how to raise a son, how to help him be a man. It was not my plan to raise him alone. I did not anticipate his father dying in a motorcycle accident.

"God, You've got to help me. I can't do this alone." When I finished my prayer, it came to me that we should read the accounts of King David's life. Even as I thought it, I shook my head. The last thing a boy would want to do was sit on the couch and read the Bible with his mom.

But, surprisingly, Chase agreed. Over a period of weeks we read together, taking turns and then discussing what we learned. "There are all kinds of men in the world. Saul was one kind of man, and David was another. You get to choose what kind of man you'll be." That was the beginning, and then there were karate lessons, kickboxing lessons, ballet, football, skateboarding and snowboarding, and lots of conversations and carpools.

Chase survived. He thrived. Now, he is a man. He is driving me places and teaching me new things—about opera, about how men think, explaining Bible passages to me and about how he will raise his son.

*Lord, encourage all those who are raising children.*
—Sharon Foster

### July

### Tue 12

*She makes tapestry for herself....*
—Proverbs 31:22 (NKJV)

When my wife retired a couple of years ago, she had more time to do something she loves: counted cross-stitch. Sharon enjoys watching a picture take shape and then giving it to some young couple as a wedding gift. The walls of our home feature her excellent work.

We are watching an old movie. Sharon sits in her overstuffed chair, surrounded by skeins of embroidery thread and patterns. She strains to see her work through a lighted magnifier.

"Hon," I say, "cross-stitch looks like something they would make you do in a prison cell as punishment."

She smiles. "No, no, it's soothing, relaxing. I love it."

It's almost bedtime now. I'm lying on the living room floor, reading my big, thick car-repair manuals.

"How can you stand to do that?" Sharon asks.

"Stand to do what?"

"Read those repair manuals for hours on end. What do you see in them?"

It's my turn to smile. "It's soothing, relaxing. I love it and I'm learning how to make our cars last longer."

I guess when we're young, we do a lot of things because they're supposed to be fun. They're what "everybody else" is doing. But I think the key to happiness is to find out what really brings us pleasure, even if it would be torture for someone else, and then to do it without apology.

*You made us all different, God. Help me to find joy*
*in doing what I do best, to Your glory.*
—Daniel Schantz

## *July*

### *Wed 13*

*I was thirsty, and ye gave me drink....*
—MATTHEW 25:35

Two summers ago, a missionary came to vacation Bible school to speak about the need for freshwater in Uganda. My daughter Maggie came home awash with enthusiasm and full of grand plans. It wasn't enough to bring in a few dollars to contribute at VBS; she needed to do more.

After much pestering, Maggie talked me into doing some Web surfing to find out who was building wells in Africa. Lo and behold, we could make a personal fund-raising page for a nonprofit called Water Aid. We uploaded a picture, and Maggie pecked out the story about why she wanted to raise money. Then we sent the link to various friends and relatives.

Next on Maggie's list was to get the people at church involved. She wrote a speech, and the pastor gave her permission to read it during the service. Afterward, Maggie stood at the door with a basket to collect money. She raised more than one hundred dollars.

Then my daughter wanted to start a Uganda club and spent an afternoon on the computer, making membership cards. That wasn't quite as successful; her friends weren't eager to join. But a family we know set up a lemonade stand near the playground one hot day and contributed thirty-five dollars in proceeds. Big sister Elizabeth added twenty-five dollars of tutoring money. Relatives chipped in, godparents contributed, some of my husband Andrew's colleagues helped out. In a few months, Maggie raised more than one thousand dollars. Not bad for a seven-year-old!

I'd forgotten about all this until the other day, when Maggie suddenly said, "We really need to do more about building wells." So we reopened her Water Aid Web page.

I don't always remember to give the thirsty something to drink, especially when they're far away. Fortunately, God has given me Maggie to remind me of their need.

*Lord, thank You for those who help me hear You say, "I thirst."*
—JULIA ATTAWAY

*July*

## Thu 14

*Open thou mine eyes, that I may behold wondrous things out of thy law.* —Psalm 119:18

One time, a long time ago, I was on my belly in the bushes and saw a shrew huddled in the leaf-litter. For the longest, shortest instant we stared at each other, completely and utterly astonished. In the normal course of things, one or both of us would have retreated precipitously, but instead we stared at each other, amazed, for what seemed like a very long time.

I remember thinking that the shrew was awfully near my eyes and that shrews are said to be terrors among the tiny. I remember that the shrew was the size of a thumb or a thimble and had a lustrous, dense, shining coat as black as black can be. I remember wondering what it was wondering. I also remember that it was missing one of its front legs, which made me think later about the drama of that loss, epic to the shrew but unknown to the rest of the world, and that made me think for a long time what an incredible welter of things is going on around us that we'll never even know we don't know.

And I remember, too, that there was such an immediacy to the moment. For once I didn't think, I just attended. For a rare instant, I paid attention with every shard and iota of my being. Maybe we couldn't survive if we paid such ferocious attention all the time, but when we do pay attention with all our might, with every scrap of yearning and curiosity, we glimpse things that none of us, in the end, can find the words for.

*Dear Lord, Unimaginable One, Giver of Everything That Is, thank You. There are no small things, are there, Father? Only eyes too closed to see.*
—Brian Doyle

*July*

## Fri 15

*This I recall to my mind, therefore have I hope. It is of the Lord's mercies that we are not consumed, because his compassions fail not. They are new every morning: great is thy faithfulness.*—LAMENTATIONS 3:21–23

I can't believe you're really going to sleep out here," my husband said as he helped me set up the tent and blow up the air mattress. I was camping out in our backyard, something I'd always wanted to try. "I'll keep your side of the bed warm for when you've had enough... say, in about two hours," Whitney said with a laugh.

I admit that I was a little scared as night descended on our property surrounded by woods. Except for my small lantern and a half moon, it was pitch black. I jumped at my own shadow on the tent wall. An owl hooted. Crickets chirped. Something moved in the bushes. I pulled the quilt up around my ears. *It could be a long night,* I thought. Then I fell asleep.

Sometime later, while it was still dark, I awakened to total silence. *Where am I? Oh yes, the tent.* I lay wrapped in a quiet that felt as if the earth were holding its breath. Suddenly a lone bird trilled, as if setting the pitch. From across the way another bird answered, then another and another, till a chorus rose from every treetop. Darkness was receding. Morning was breaking. A new day was beginning.

It happens every day. But out there in nature, on the wings of a song, I heard and felt and received the new day's arrival as the Creator intended: a gift fresh from His hand, filled to the sky with His mercy and goodness.

*Lord, thank You for the birds who awaken me to Your faithfulness in never failing to bring a new day and the hope that comes with it.*
—SHARI SMYTH

*July*

## Sat 16

*I am come that they might have life, and that they might have it more abundantly.* —JOHN 10:10

For some time I've been wanting a small chair, something I can set on the little stoop by my patio door. The door faces west, and the afternoon sun is positively wonderful. But everything I tried was too big or too uncomfortable or just too ugly.

Then, a few days ago, I wandered back to my husband's barn. Our son Brett, whose construction jobs involve rehabbing or tearing down old structures, often drags home items that he finds in abandoned houses. Mostly these things end up in the dump. But something in a pile of recently acquired rubbish caught my eye: a little wooden chair that looked just perfect for what I needed. I pulled it out of the clutter and gingerly sat down. I laughed out loud. It was as though it had been made for me!

The only thing was, it was badly in need of a paint job. And some of the slats were pretty dinged up. Still, it had great lines, it was sturdy and it was just the size I needed. I hustled to the hardware store, picked out a sweet shade of purple paint and broke out a brush. Within hours, the chair was reborn.

I had lunch in that chair today. I sat there contentedly munching on my wheat crackers and hummus, soaking up the sun, wondering where the chair had been when it was new. But then I realized, *It doesn't matter what it was before. What matters is what it has become, what it will be to me for many summers to come—the perfect place to sit in the sun and count my abundant blessings.*

*How wonderful, God, that You see past my scars and dings to what I can be—to what You can make me!*
—MARY LOU CARNEY

*July*

### Sun 17
*He will love you and bless you....*
—DEUTERONOMY 7:13 (NIV)

I graduated from seminary in California in 1971, with a heart to return to Mississippi to work in a rural Christian ministry. One of the challenges my wife Rosie and I faced was to raise funds for our support.

We were introduced to a small charismatic church in Southern California that welcomed us, prayed for us and supported us monthly. Recently, I had the privilege of standing in the pulpit of that church to say "thank you" once again for the many years of love, prayer and financial support they had given us.

We cherish so many memories from our relationship with this little church: our children singing "I Am a Promise" at an evening service almost thirty years ago, the many times the members of the church have prayed for us as we have struggled through some very difficult and painful times. We have never walked into this church without knowing that God's amazing love is flowing from them to us.

*Lord, thank You for allowing us to experience Your love through our connection with Your family.*
—DOLPHUS WEARY

---

### READER'S ROOM

I've felt serenity through interaction with my backyard pets—squirrels and birds—who now trust me and the treats I've given them, and my house pets—my goldfish (who range in color from gold to silver-speckled to black) who recognize my approach to their tanks at feeding time.

—*Linda Brantley, Racine, Wisconsin*

*July*

## ✤ LETTERS FROM THE HEART

<u>Mon 18</u>  *To him who alone doeth great wonders: for his mercy endureth for ever.* —PSALM 136:4

**A CARD FROM A STRANGER**

Back in the spring of 1987, a note from a *Guideposts* reader took me by surprise. It was scrawled on a three-by-five card with a pen-and-ink nature scene. The writer, a professor-minister in Oklahoma, was responding to an article I'd just written about overcoming the depression that follows losing a mate (my husband Jerry had died four years before). The note was kind, polite and brief; it encouraged me to "keep looking up." It was the closing that caused my heart to speed up and my mouth to become momentarily frozen in an *O*: "Good night, Gene Acuff."

Amazing words floated through my mind: *One day he'll be telling you good night in person—every night, for he will be your husband.*

Silly, foolish me! Ridiculous me. The writer lived a thousand miles away and was himself grieving the recent death of his wife.

I'd had a supply of note cards made with a photograph depicting a foggy day. Underneath the picture was a Scripture: "Nevertheless I must walk today" (Luke 13:33). I didn't hesitate to send one to Mr. Acuff.

May 4, 1987

Dear Gene,

Thank you for your marvelous note of encouragement. The battle is fierce in my household again. Thank you for your prayers for Jon and Jeremy. Just returned from a three-day prayer retreat and have peace *right now*. I'm interested in the similarities you say we've experienced.

Looking up, Marion

*Father, I asked You to keep me sensible and sane—remembering that Gene Acuff was a stranger who lived a thousand miles away. But all along, You knew better.*
—MARION BOND WEST

*July*

## LETTERS FROM THE HEART

**Tue 19** *I have loved thee with an everlasting love....*
—JEREMIAH 31:3

"IN HIS LOVE"

Since Gene Acuff had started writing to me from Oklahoma, I watched joyfully for the mail, sometimes waiting at the mailbox till it arrived. My new pen pal answered my letters quickly; it seems we had so much to say to each other. I'd hurry inside with Gene's thick letter in hand, tearing it open even before reaching the door. The sight of his neat, closely spaced handwriting on lined yellow paper always made me smile. He wrote vividly about everyday life on his farm:

I was mowing today on my 1946 Ford N tractor when I came upon a mother killdeer sitting on her nest in the tall grass. As I got closer, rather than flee, she remained steadfast. Admiring her tremendous courage, I went around her.

"Oh, you dear man," I'd wanted to write back, but I was determined to remain casually friendly. I ended my letter with,

I'm looking up, as you said, trying to do the things you suggested. Probably need to concentrate a little more on housekeeping and cooking. Also, I've been neglecting Bible study. I'm grateful for your encouragement and prayers. I battle discouragement. But "The Lord God is my strength, And He has made my feet like hinds' feet" (Habakkuk 3:19, NAS).

I was concerned about how to close my letter. Then I took a deep breath and decided to close mine the way a marvelous woman I knew closed hers to everyone: "In His love, Marion."

*Lord, then and now, I need You to lead clearly and
not let me do something foolish.*
—MARION BOND WEST

*July*

## ❧ LETTERS FROM THE HEART

**Wed 20** *I trust to come unto you, and speak face to face, that our joy may be full.* —II JOHN 1:12

"IN HIS LOVE—AND MINE"

By mid-June, my pen pal Gene Acuff had invited me to come to Oklahoma and stay at his daughter's home. Fear and excitement battled inside me; fear won. "I don't th-think so," I stammered. By the end of the month, Gene and I were talking on the phone daily as well as writing volumes to each other. In a late-night conversation, he told me that he was coming to Lilburn, Georgia, and that we needed to meet and talk. At sunup I wrote to him, trying to hide my excitement:

You are so efficient. You'd have an itinerary made out if I were coming there. I'm not sure I'll know what to do with you. Where do you want to go? What do you want to do? What if we can't talk face-to-face and you have to phone me from Stone Mountain Inn, where you're staying? What if all we can do is talk on the phone and write long, detailed letters? I'm not certain I know how to be with someone as unguarded as you.

The sun was well up when I gathered my courage and signed the letter, "In His love and mine, Marion."

Gene wrote right back:

All I want to do is be with you, without people around us. No parties, no gala events. Can we go someplace with a tin roof and lakes and a wraparound porch with a swing? And cows? I love to listen to cows chew. Hopefully, it will rain on the tin roof. If you'd come here, I'd have taken you to the movies and bought you Milk Duds and a Coke in a bottle and we'd have gone in my '41 Chevrolet.

*Ah, how does he know I love Milk Duds?*

*Father, Helper, Comforter, Friend, Counselor,*
*show me Your will—unmistakably.*
—MARION BOND WEST

*July*

## 🌸 LETTERS FROM THE HEART

*Thu 21*   *"Be strong. Take courage. Don't be intimidated... because... your God, is striding ahead of you. He's right there with you. He won't let you down; he won't leave you."*
—DEUTERONOMY 31:6 (MSG)

"MY LOVE, ETC."

At the end of June, I wrote this letter to Gene Acuff:
For a while it startled me when you popped into my thoughts, but I've come to anticipate that and be comfortable with you. I see you on the tractor or teaching at Oklahoma State University or preaching at the small church where you've been forever. I'm concerned that I may not be what you think I am. I rescue stray animals; desperate people call me or happen by. There's always a crisis with Jon or Jeremy.

No matter what the future holds, I'll always be grateful to you. God's used you in a mighty way in my life. I'll pray for courage for you.

I found a place for our picnic: a renovated farmhouse with a tin roof, three lakes, a wraparound porch with three swings, Black Angus cows—I've never listened to a cow chew; hope it's as great as you say. Jeremy asked me yesterday (gulp), "Mom, do you remember how to kiss?"

Forcing myself to smile calmly, I answered, "It's just like riding a bicycle, Son. You never forget."

He beamed. "Good. I wouldn't want you not to know how."

I like to think God has some neat experiences for you here in Georgia—"something more"—and that you will return to cowboy country tall in the saddle with new power.

My love, etc.,
Marion

*Dear Lord, I couldn't believe Gene was really coming to see me, but You knew he was Your answer to my prayers.*
—MARION BOND WEST

*July*

## 🌀 LETTERS FROM THE HEART

*Fri 22*  *I caused the widow's heart to sing for joy.* —JOB 29:13

**BUTTERFLIES**

Shortly before Gene Acuff arrived in Georgia in July 1987, I wrote:

Thank you for the tape of you preaching. I like your short sentences. I especially like that you don't have all the answers. I'm weary of pastors on mountaintops, soaring through life victoriously.

Do you remember Helen Keller's life story? When Annie Sullivan, her teacher, wrote *Jesus* on the palm of her hand, little Helen beamed and signed, "Oh, I've known about Him for a long time. I just didn't know His name." I feel somewhat like that about you. I told God once, "You know I have this love for someone whom I believe You'll send. I have no idea who he is or where he's from."

Do you know this little poem by Emily Dickinson? I'm paraphrasing: "I can wade in pools of grief, but I don't know how to handle a little joy." That's me right now.

Oswald Chambers says, "We have to get rid of the idea that we understand ourselves; it is the last conceit to go." I don't understand myself at all right now. I can't sleep, eat or concentrate. I have butterflies. Sometimes I sing, "O-Oklahoma, where the wind comes rushing o'er the plain."

I don't care what you do when we meet. Don't plan anything, okay? This is the second letter I've written you today. You make me happy.

My love,<br>Marion

*Father, once You told me that to the exact extent I suffered, You'd make me joyful again. And that's just what You did.*
—MARION BOND WEST

*July*

## LETTERS FROM THE HEART

*Sat 23*  "*And the days of your mourning will be over.*"
—Isaiah 60:20 (NAS)

**AN END TO MOURNING**

On July 21, 1987, I wrote again to Gene Acuff:
   Dear Gene,
This is the last letter before we see each other! I've always relished doing things spontaneously. But now I'm really trying to be sensible. I've forgotten how. I'm fifty-one and feel fifteen. And you're telling me to forget rationality. What we're doing is wild—maybe crazy. But I don't feel like poor, sad, lonely Marion anymore.

I'm enclosing a picture of me in the dress I'll be wearing when we meet. It's not new. It's a beige/white sundress and it matches my beige car. I know you're wearing khaki pants and a yellow button-down shirt, driving a blue station wagon.

I wandered down the stairs early this morning and sat on the sofa and held my cat and cried—happy tears. God sat with me, and I confessed to Him that I'd doubted He could accomplish this. He understood!

I've been looking intently—with a magnifying glass—at the tiny picture of you I just got. I love the determination and sincerity in your face—and your dimple. I like your hands. I love the way your golden retriever is smiling, as though he's telling me that you're somebody really special.

I love you, Professor Acuff.
There! I've said it. Finally.

                                                      Marion

*What a God of total restoration You are, my Father.*
—Marion Bond West

*July*

## 🌀 LETTERS FROM THE HEART

<u>Sun 24</u>   *God proves to be good to the man who passionately waits, to the woman who diligently seeks....*
—LAMENTATIONS 3:25 (MSG)

"ALL MY LOVE ALWAYS"

Gene Acuff came to Georgia to visit me at the end of July 1987. On August 14, we were married. Ten days before the wedding, I wrote:

Dear, dear Gene,

You were worth waiting for—the four years I was a widow and my entire life. I had concerns about my family and close friends; then I watched you win them over—even the strange ones. I loved being with you, talking to you. I'll always want to talk, okay?

What a transformation you've brought to my life. Can I deal with this much wonder and happiness? I guess I'm still amazed that you love me—really love me. It's not such a big deal that I'm willing to move to Oklahoma when we marry; I would have gladly gone with you to Outer Mongolia. I adore the quick, efficient way we bought our rings the day after you arrived.

Tell your marvelous dog, dear, sweet Elmo, that I can hardly wait to meet him, hug him, talk to him. He and I feel the same way about you.

I'm so sorry I never could call you, and you had all those huge phone bills. But Mother never allowed me to call boys. Ever. And I still can't do it.

I'm going to praise our Father forever for the way He brought us together and gave us this powerful love for each other.

Yours soon.

All my love always,
Marion

*Sweet Jesus, how can I ever doubt You again?*
—MARION BOND WEST

## *July*

### Mon 25

*And this I pray, that your love may abound yet more and more....* —PHILIPPIANS 1:9

When my mom was in the early stages of Alzheimer's and still able to live on her own, my wife and I flew out to Michigan to spend a week with her. We brought along our young cocker spaniel Sally, whom Mom took to instantly. Satisfied that Mom could look after Sally, Julee and I felt comfortable spending some time seeing relatives and doing a few touristy things around Detroit.

We noticed right away that Sally had taken an unusual liking to Mom. Whenever we went back to the house, Sally wouldn't leave her side. "What a great dog," I said to Julee.

However, a couple of days into our visit, Julee and I noticed that the dog food we had brought along was disappearing. I took Sally aside and looked her right in the eyes. "What's going on here?" I asked, not actually expecting to get an answer.

You can probably guess. Mom couldn't remember from hour to hour if she had fed Sally, and Sally was always up for seconds. So Mom would feed her again. We put a note on Sally's food, telling Mom not to worry about Sally's meals; Julee and I would take care of it.

That was the end of Sally's amazing gourmet vacation, and I think she held a little grudge over the fact that her scheme had been found out. But here's the good part. Even after Sally got back on her regular feeding schedule, her devotion to Mom didn't abate. She seemed to know that Mom needed all the extra care and attention she could get.

When we left at the end of the week, Mom cried. "Thank you for coming to visit me, Sally," she whispered, hugging her close. "I hope you come back soon."

*Your love takes many wondrous forms, Lord, even a cocker spaniel with a big appetite and a bigger heart.*
—EDWARD GRINNAN

### July

#### Tue 26

*"We remember the fish which we used to eat free in Egypt, the cucumbers and the melons...."*—NUMBERS 11:5 (NAS)

In a casual phone conversation with my seven-year-old grandson Caleb, who lives in Alaska, I mentioned the vegetables I was collecting from farmers' market vendors. "Can you send me some *cukes?*" he asked excitedly.

Caleb's mother doesn't garden, and Alaska's growing season is brief for those who do. So I stuffed a box with fat green cucumbers and sent it off. "How'd you like your cucumbers?" I asked Caleb several days later.

There was a dramatic pause, followed by a one-word crescendo: "Awesome!" I was feeling pleased with myself for pulling off the cucumber sensation when he added, "Next time can you send some ranch dressing?"

When Caleb's eighth birthday arrived at summer's end, he received another "grandma box." Inside were clothes, a chess set (he's a very good player) and, yes, more cucumbers—with a big bottle of ranch dressing.

*Jesus, may Caleb always love cucumbers and seek joy in life's small, often overlooked pleasures. Amen.*
—CAROL KNAPP

## July

### Wed 27

*Give us this day our daily bread.* —MATTHEW 6:11

The day finally came for me to leave Waco, Texas, and drive to Macon, Georgia, to begin a new chapter of my life at Mercer University. My wife Beth and our four golden retrievers would be staying in Waco for five more long months while Beth sold our house and wrapped up her work with international students at Baylor University.

As we stood by the rented truck filled with my books and all of the things I needed for the fall semester at Mercer, I struggled with my emotions. I gazed at our house, our home for sixteen years, where we had raised our three children. Memories overwhelmed me. Turning the ignition key of the truck and releasing the brake, I rounded a corner and watched Beth waving good-bye in the rearview mirror.

I had been driving in stunned silence for a number of miles when I suddenly heard my baritone voice singing over the drone of the truck engine:

> *Strength for today and bright hope for tomorrow,*
> *Blessings all mine, with ten thousand beside.*
> *Great is thy faithfulness! Great is thy faithfulness!*
> *Morning by morning new mercies I see:*
> *All I have needed thy hand hath provided.*
> *Great is Thy faithfulness, Lord unto me!*
> *(Thomas Chisholm, "Great Is Thy Faithfulness")*

For a moment I sat in perfect amazement. Then a smile broke across my face and I sang louder and louder. God had put a song in my heart; I suddenly knew that I could make this journey one day at a time if I truly believed in God's "bright hope for tomorrow."

*Lord, give me strength for this day and bright hope for tomorrow.*
—SCOTT WALKER

## ADVICE FROM AUNT ANNIE

*Thu 28* — *Fix your thoughts on what is true and good and right....*
—PHILIPPIANS 4:8 (TLB)

**THE GOODNESS FILE**

When I heard that a former colleague had said something untrue about me, I exploded. I corrected the misinformation and ticked off a list of the woman's offenses, growing angrier with each word.

At about number seven, I paused for breath. It was then I remembered that Aunt Annie kept a list too: a Goodness File. Instead of dwelling on hurts, she chose to record the spirit-lifters she received through the years.

Her file began in April 1962, when she was sent to interview University of Oklahoma football coach Bud Wilkinson. She was so nervous, she dropped her purse as she entered his office and watched in horror as the contents rolled under Wilkinson's desk. Without saying a word, he crawled under it, retrieved everything and brushed off her apologies. "How good of you to come!" he said warmly. He then answered her questions fully and thoughtfully.

Aunt Annie recorded dozens of other incidents. She received a gift of pink peonies from a student who never spoke in class. An exhausted construction worker, coming off the night shift, gave her his seat on a crowded bus. "You have a full workday ahead of you, while I'm going home to rest," he said. A postal clerk searched the lobby and even the sidewalk to find her missing earring.

I've started a Goodness File, too, and discovered that when I concentrate on people's good points, their faults become much less irritating.

*Help me to look for goodness, Lord, and to recognize it in everyone I meet.*
—PENNEY SCHWAB

## July

### Fri 29

> Be sure to use the abilities God has given you. . . . throw yourself into your tasks. . . . God will bless you and use you to help others. —I Timothy 4:14–16 (TLB)

My first visit to my family in their new home in Morrison, Colorado, was filled with awe: deer grazing in the meadowland that's part of their acreage; an eagle soaring high above hills dressed with evergreens; and the natural formation and inimitable color of the Red Rock amphitheater.

Most memorable was the drive up to Estes Park to see the herds of elk in the National Forest. We were immersed in the grandeur of the Rockies, and the views in every direction were picture-perfect. The trouble was the battery in my camera had run down, and all I had was a hurriedly purchased disposable.

Elk were everywhere. As we joined the spectators clicking their cameras, I bemoaned my inability to get a close-up. A lithe, tawny-haired woman with a friendly smile motioned me over. "Here, take a look," she said, pointing to her telescopic lens. It was focused on a magnificent buck. "Give me your e-mail and I'll send you some pictures," she offered. "Since I was a child I've had such a passion for photography that I'm probably the only girl who took her camera as her date to the senior prom!"

Her pictures arrived, not as e-mail, but artistically printed on canvas—mountains, meadows and the close-up headshot of the large buck, so detailed that I could see the grain of his antlers.

In my frustration the Lord brought me a new friend who continues to expand my view of the glory of nature through a lens I call "the eye of God."

> *How blessed I am, dear Lord, by those to whom You have given*
> *great talent and who have the generosity of spirit*
> *to share it with others.*
> —Fay Angus

## Sat 30

*July*

*Moses built an altar and named it The Lord is My Banner.*
—Exodus 17:15 (NAS)

I'd gotten into a rut with my exercise/prayer time. On most days, I walked the two-mile path around our house, trudging through the same woods and praying for the same things. Surely if I reminded God often enough, He'd get busy.

One sticky summer morning, eager to check off "exercise/pray" on my to-do list, I entered the woods and began repeating my requests to God. As I went deeper into the trees, I spotted the campsite where my twelve-year-old son Thomas and his buddies would be spending the night. Thomas had cut down some small trees and spread pine straw in the clearing. A pile of sticks lay neatly stacked for a campfire, and a plywood paintball target was tacked to a tree. But there was one more thing. At the head of his campsite, Thomas had nailed a cross of two-by-fours to a pine tree and surrounded the foot of the cross with rocks.

I touched the rough edges of the cross. In my dutiful walks, I'd forgotten the most important part of prayer: to praise God for Who He is. Standing there in Thomas' campsite, I began to pray—really, thankfully pray—to my Maker, my Savior, my All-in-All, my Comforter, my Provider and my Friend.

*Lord, thank You for using Thomas' heartfelt worship*
*to bring me back to You.*
—Julie Garmon

*July*

## Sun 31

*When I am afraid, I will trust in You.* —Psalm 56:3 (NIV)

I was having a "sunset moment" one Sunday night, a discouraged feeling I get sometimes after a long week at work. Standing on my patio, gazing up at the sky as the sun went down, I wondered if my being here made any difference at all. *God has so much to worry about. How can He give any thought to me?*

After a while, I heard an odd knocking on my door. A neighbor I'd only nodded to in passing stood there, holding something in both hands. "I had to knock with my elbow," she explained. "Have some cherry tomatoes? I have enough to share."

"Thank you!" Surprised, I opened my hands to receive the bounty; six golf-ball-sized red pearls. "How big a crop did you have?"

"I got twelve."

"Twelve?" I said, confused. "Twelve pints?" I asked.

"Twelve tomatoes."

"You can't give me half your crop!" I motioned to her. "Come inside, please."

Once seated in my kitchen, she said softly, "After my husband passed away and I had to move to a smaller place, I began to wonder if God still cared about me. So to keep myself busy, I planted some tomato plants on the patio. Well, bugs got about a dozen tomatoes and I killed a few more by overwatering them.... But then I realized that it didn't matter to me if I had only one plant left. I tended that one plant and watered it carefully. And it dawned on me then that no matter how small and alone I felt, God was always there, nurturing me."

My jaw must have dropped, for my neighbor said, "I know that sounds strange... but I just wanted you to have them. A gift from me."

*And from God,* I thought.

> *Thank You, God, for the special times You make*
> *Yourself known in my loneliness.*
> —Linda Neukrug

*July*

**SEEDS OF LOVE**

1 _____

2 _____

3 _____

4 _____

5 _____

6 _____

7 _____

8 _____

9 _____

10 _____

11 _____

12 _____

13 _____

14 _____

15 _____

## July

16 _____

17 _____

18 _____

19 _____

20 _____

21 _____

22 _____

23 _____

24 _____

25 _____

26 _____

27 _____

28 _____

29 _____

30 _____

31 _____

# August

*And we know that
all things work together
for good to them
that love God....*

—Romans 8:28

*August*

## A PATH TO SIMPLICITY

*Mon 1*  *Weeping may last for the night, But a shout of joy comes in the morning.* —PSALM 30:5 (NAS)

**BELIEVING IN JOY**

The only childhood photograph I ever saw of my mother showed her wearing a too-small, ragged cotton dress. She was tugging at the hem of it, looking up at the camera with sad, haunted eyes. As a child, Mother hoed corn from daylight to dark, her only reward a beating from her father.

When I happened upon an envelope marked "Mother" while downsizing the cabin, I expected the worst. But instead of heartbreaking images, the envelope held photos of a young adult Mother riding a horse, stretched out on a quilt, enjoying a picnic with friends.

I'd nearly forgotten about those photographs. After Mother died, an old friend we called Aunt Jo had telephoned. "Stop by the house," she said. "I have something I think you'll like." That evening after work, she handed me the envelope full of pictures of Mother. I tentatively removed the first one and surprised myself by smiling. Mother stood before a white porcelain stove with a younger Aunt Jo beside her. Mother's head was tilted back, a look of sheer joy on her face.

I took Aunt Jo's hand in mine. "Mother never talked much about her younger days," I said. "I always wondered what she was like way back when. Most of all, I wondered if she ever had any fun."

Aunt Jo positively glowed. "Well, she sure did when we got together. Sometimes she'd come to the house and stay for days. Whatever we did, we never stopped laughing."

*Thank You, Lord, for those who bring joy to dark places.*
—ROBERTA MESSNER

*August*

## Tue 2

*Watch the road; Strengthen your back, summon all your strength.*
—Nahum 2:1 (NAS)

My husband and I had driven east for a ten-day visit with our children, and just about the time we planned to leave for home, Leo suddenly developed a serious foot infection. We knew from previous bouts that to treat it required daily intravenous antibiotics. Back home in Winnipeg, that just meant an easy five-minute drive to the nearest hospital; in Toronto, it meant a hasty visit to a local walk-in clinic, where a doctor prescribed pills to stave off the infection while we drove home.

The next morning as I got into the driver's seat, I was keenly aware and not a little anxious that ahead of me lay 1,200 miles of winding, hilly roads through northern Ontario's wilderness. We usually take turns driving, but this time most of the responsibility would fall on me.

Leaving behind the bustling traffic of Toronto and nosing the car northward, deeper and deeper into a beautiful landscape of trees and lakes and rocks and hills, I felt my anxiety slowly disappear. I was especially thankful for a special feature in the driver's seat that could be adjusted to alleviate my aching back.

We arrived home safely on the third day, and while Leo's infection was successfully treated, I, too, was healed—of those niggling fears of inadequacy with which I'd begun the journey.

*Thank You, Lord, that I can draw on my experience and
Your strength to help me over the next hurdle.*
—Alma Barkman

## August

### Wed 3

*Finally, brethren, farewell. Be perfect, be of good comfort, be of one mind, live in peace; and the God of love and peace shall be with you.* —II CORINTHIANS 13:11

Looking at the clock with one eye, I jumped out of bed. We had only fifteen minutes to get our son to his swimming lesson.

"Get up, Solomon!" I yelled. "We're late!"

I dashed to the kitchen, started the coffee and found Solomon's towel. Solomon gulped down a bowl of cereal. He got dressed but couldn't find his sandals.

"Let's go," my husband Tony said to him. "Just wear your sneakers."

I was making toast when I heard the car start. My heart dropped; I hadn't said good-bye. I've always felt the need to give my sons a kiss and a hug when we part, and since my sister's sudden death, the need has grown more intense.

Running out the door and down the driveway in my pajamas, I waved my arms. Tony stopped the car.

"What did we forget?" he asked.

I ran to Solomon's window and leaned in. "Good-bye, honey. I love you. Have a good lesson."

"I love you too, Mom," Solomon said.

"Is that it, guys?" Tony said. "We're late."

Solomon smiled. "It's never too late to say good-bye. Right, Mom?"

*Dear Lord, thank You for reminding me that love is eternal and it's never too late to say good-bye.*
—SABRA CIANCANELLI

## August

### Thu 4

*That ye may be blameless and harmless, the sons of God, without rebuke, in the midst of a crooked and perverse nation, among whom ye shine as lights in the world; Holding forth the word of life....* —PHILIPPIANS 2:15–16

When I was ten, my family moved to a Bible camp full of darkness. The woman in charge took in welfare cases, young boys and old men whose families were unable or unwilling to take care of them. Many were overworked, some abused, all neglected. Little compassion was wasted on them until Mother got there.

Mum quickly put my two sisters and me to work, playing dominoes with blind Uncle Earl, though we soon found other ways to entertain this quiet gentleman who loved the Dodgers: walks beneath the eucalyptus, smashing a crop of black walnuts and then helping him separate the meat from the shells, proofreading letters to a daughter somewhere.

Richie was our age. Mum started paying him a nickel for each word he got right on his spelling. She let us skip our own chores to help with his. She cut his hair and patched his clothes.

Joe, developmentally disabled, was a special project. His own mother had died, and Mum took over. She gave him pennies for the birthday bank at church, took him to the cemetery, saved the bread heels just for him.

Mum took them all under her wing: Howard, Jack, Ben.... More importantly, she stood up to the woman in charge. During our first month there, Mum drew a line between us and the darkness—a circle into which no shadow could fall and where we all dwelt safely in her sunbeam of love. We eventually left the ranch, but Mum's love remains—in the lives she forever touched.

*Dear God, You, too, draw a line and create a circle of safety and love into which no shadow can fall, where our hearts and minds can dwell safely in You.*
—BRENDA WILBEE

DAILY GUIDEPOSTS

## August

### Fri 5

> *Oh, Timothy, my son, be strong with the strength Christ Jesus gives you. For you must teach others those things you and many others have heard me speak about....*
> —II Timothy 2:1–2 (TLB)

Because of my heavy travel schedule, routinely attending a Bible study is difficult for me. What I needed, I decided some years ago, was a spiritual mentor, someone who would guide me and be a sounding board for me, someone with a lot of spiritual maturity. I asked a godly woman in our church if she would be willing to meet and pray with me on a regular basis. That was how my friendship with Barb Dooley started. Even now, all these years later, we get together regularly to pray.

Recently I told Barb about a problem I'd been experiencing and the frustration I felt. "I don't know what I'm doing wrong," I said. "I've filled up pages and pages in my prayer journal, pouring out my problem to God. I've brought the matter up daily, waiting for Him to move in my life. I don't think He hears my prayers any longer."

Barb didn't say anything for a long time. Then she smiled and said, "Maybe you should try a different tactic."

"How do you mean?" I said. I was open to anything.

Barb nodded and said softly, "Maybe this isn't a case of God not hearing your prayers, Debbie. I believe He's always available to His children. Perhaps He's just waiting for you to listen."

*Father, open my heart so that I can hear what You have to say to me.*
—Debbie Macomber

*August*

## Sat 6
*"I will not leave you desolate; I will come to you."*
—John 14:18 (RSV)

I opened my eyes to total blackness. I had to go to the bathroom now! My feet slammed onto the floor. *Why is the bed so low? Oh yeah, we're in Fairhope, Alabama, in a B and B.*

I sat very still and listened—nothing. Feeling my way, I remembered a recent doctor's visit. "You've lost a third of your sight in six weeks," he'd said. Or had he said hearing?

I felt a wave of terror. If I lost both my hearing and my sight, I'd be alone.

A familiar Voice whispered, *Keith, can you hear Me?*

"Yes, sir," I said very relieved. "I'm glad You're still with me."

*Don't worry. I'll always be with you. But what will you do if you can't see or hear?*

"Maybe You could help me work out a code to tell my family I'm all right. Maybe I could figure out how to help people like me surrender to You, so they wouldn't be alone."

*How did you think of that in the midst of your own fear?*

"Well, sir, remember in 1956, after my mother's graveside service when I realized that I was alone? You asked me, *What are you going to do?* "I said, 'Maybe You can show me how to introduce other lonely people to You.'"

*So that's what your work has really been about.*

"Yes, sir, I guess so."

Then I heard a concerned familiar voice outside. "Keith, are you all right?" It was my wife Andrea.

"Yeah, I'm okay."

"Can't you find the light switch?"

I smiled in the darkness. "Yeah, honey. I just did."

*Lord, thank You for sending the Light to guide us all the way home to You.*
—Keith Miller

*August*

## Sun 7

*These commandments that I give you today are to be upon your hearts. Impress them on your children....*
—Deuteronomy 6:6–7 (NIV)

The postcard pictured the back of an eighteen-month-old child, walking into her future, one hand held by her mother, the other by her father. "Please join us for Rylie's dedication celebration," the card requested.

So a couple of weeks later, we all gathered in a tree-shaded backyard on a sunny summer Sunday afternoon. Rylie's parents welcomed us and explained their desire to dedicate this little girl to the Lord, just as Hannah had done with baby Samuel in the Bible, saying, "I prayed for this child, and the Lord has granted me what I asked of him. So now I give him to the Lord. For his whole life he will be given over to the Lord" (I Samuel 1:27–28, NIV). Meanwhile, the guest of honor, wearing a pink flowered dress and an infectious grin, danced around her mommy and daddy, blonde curls bouncing in a light breeze.

One of Rylie's grandmothers played the guitar and sang a lullaby about God's tender care in our lives. A grandfather prayed for Rylie, and the other grandparents spoke about the importance of our part in this dedication. "We know that parents don't raise a child alone. Every day, we have opportunities to learn and apply what the Bible tells us and to share that knowledge with another person, especially the children in our lives."

Next came a direct question: "Will you gently remind Rylie about who God is and what He tells us?" With a "yes," each of us received a colorful ribbon bracelet with the words *Gently remind Rylie*.

Today, my bracelet is wrapped around a part of my computer, to remind me of my commitment to the opportunities for reminding Rylie and other children about who God is.

*Lord, You tell us that children are gifts from You. May we remember to tell them about the Giver.*
—Carol Kuykendall

*August*

## Mon 8

*The heart of the prudent getteth knowledge; and the ear of the wise seeketh knowledge.* —Proverbs 18:15

When I was a boy, my dream was to be an outstanding baseball player. I enjoyed attending twilight league games at our school field. To me, the travel, the competition and the adoring fans seemed like great fun. Besides, this was the Depression and the ballplayers were being paid.

During the summer, our fourteen-room home was a haven for African Americans seeking to vacation. When the guests arrived, I carried their bags to their rooms. Then at dinnertime, I donned a white coat and waited on tables. The guests were always received with warmth and hospitality, yet Mother and Father demanded I keep my distance from them. Being overfriendly was forbidden.

One day the barnstorming Philadelphia Black Giants came to town to play our hometown team. The Giants were superb, and my dream glowed brighter. Near the end of the game, I noticed the town officials huddled in the stands, their faces a mass of worry. The Giants needed accommodations for two nights, but the town's inns and guesthouses wouldn't accept them. Father was contacted, and the baseball players came to stay at our home. I was thrilled!

Early on the second morning, one player wandered into the backyard and shook my hand. I threw caution to the wind and questioned him, confessing my desire to be a baseball player. He listened, his eyes glistening, and said, "Go to school, young man, and get an education. I didn't."

My dream of baseball ended, but those words stayed with me.

*Knowing Father, my dreams were for the moment while
Your direction was for a lifetime.*
—Oscar Greene

## August

### Tue 9

*"You are the light of the world. A city built on a hill cannot be hid."* —MATTHEW 5:14 (NRSV)

The forecast had predicted an afternoon and evening of thunderstorms; the skies were dark and glowering, the wind was gusting. My husband Charlie looked outside and said brightly, "Looks like it's going to clear up."

I shot him a look. "You always do that! No matter how bad the forecast, no matter how miserable it looks, you always think it's going to clear up."

"I really think it will this time," he said, and then looking around, added, "eventually."

I rolled my eyes. How could anybody be so blindly optimistic? Charlie ignores forecasts of snow, claiming the meteorologists just want to scare us. He'll endlessly search the sky on stormy days to find one tiny patch that's gray instead of black and then claim that the weather is improving.

A little later as I was looking out the window at a particularly violent thunderstorm, he walked over and put his arms around me. "Don't worry, hon," he said confidently, "I'm sure it'll be over soon."

I looked up at him, incredulous. Then lightning struck me: Charlie was just trying to comfort me. He couldn't care less about the weather; I'm the one who's always anxious about it. For all these years, he's just been trying to make me feel better. I hugged him back silently and together we watched the storm. "Hey," he said after a particularly bright crack of lightning, "I think I just saw a little bit of sunlight."

*Lord, let me see the light of Your hope everywhere I look.*
—MARCI ALBORGHETTI

*August*

## Wed 10

*And I heard a voice from heaven saying unto me, Write, Blessed are the dead which die in the Lord from henceforth: Yea, saith the Spirit, that they may rest from their labours; and their works do follow them.* —REVELATION 14:13

Outside my father-in-law's room, I heard a hospice nurse say, "We usually die the way we lived."

I've held on to what she said, specifically the word *usually*. *Usually*, as in "not always." That means there's still a chance I won't die the way I lived: in traffic, in lines, looking for my daughter's soccer shoes ("No, Daddy, the *red* ones"). I won't die working on my car, filling out forms, watching stupid reruns. I won't die simply waiting... waiting... waiting....

Once, on a beach in Avalon, New Jersey, my father-in-law told me this joke: "I want to die like my great-great-grandpa: peacefully, in his sleep. Not screaming like the passengers in his wagon when he drove it into the river."

I laughed when he told it to me, and that's how I want to go: eyes closed, head back, the sun on my face, throat full of happiness at the sheer absurd joy of it all and hoping the Lord's sense of humor is way more merciful than just.

*Lord, help me to live even the smallest of moments with my eye on eternity.*
—MARK COLLINS

## READER'S ROOM

The piano my mother bought for me years ago was sitting in an empty house. A friend's daughter was interested in learning to play the piano, so I rented a truck and we went to get the piano. The tuner said it was a jewel and tuned it so that it sounded better than it has in years. My friend's daughter is now taking lessons, and I'm blessed to see the old piano revived for use by a beginning musician.

—*Allene DeWeese, Florence, South Carolina*

*August*

## Thu 11

*"I have... only a handful of meal... and a little oil."*
—I Kings 17:12 (RSV)

Goulash. It became a code word for my husband John and me. We were driving down the rutted roads and through the drab towns of Communist Hungary. In the forlorn restaurants, wherever we pointed on the undecipherable menu, what came to the table was goulash, a beef stew long on potatoes and short on meat. For four days, goulash for lunch, goulash for dinner...

So we were delighted, on the fifth day, to be handed a morocco-bound menu in Hungarian, German, French, English and Russian. There were columns of salads, egg dishes, fish, pork, chicken! The elderly waiter stood patiently—we were the only customers—as we debated our choices.

Shrimp salad, we decided at last, and bacon-wrapped scallops. Smiling approval of our selection, the waiter disappeared into the kitchen. Soon he was back, his face a study in shock. The very items we'd ordered, he apologized in excellent English, were unavailable this particular day!

We consulted the extensive menu again. Lobster bisque and stuffed turkey. This time the waiter returned shaking his head in disbelief. These items too—would you believe it!—were not on hand at the moment. When the old man reported that lamb chops and cheese soufflé were also unaccountably unavailable, he looked near tears.

"I know," said John, ever tactful, "why don't you ask the chef what he especially recommends today!"

This time the waiter returned, beaming. The chef did have a suggestion! With a flourish recalling better days, he served the goulash from a porcelain tureen onto plates rimmed in gold. And we had a word to use when our own resources fall short of our desires.

*Help me to accept the goulash in my life, Father,
as willingly as the banquets.*
—Elizabeth Sherrill

*August*

## Fri 12

> They will be called oaks of righteousness, a planting of the Lord for the display of his splendor.
> —Isaiah 61:3 (NIV)

Upstairs in a spare bedroom sits something I've had since I was an infant: a solid oak child's rocking chair stained dark walnut. Not only did I use it when I was little, but my daughters, granddaughter and grandsons have all enjoyed it too.

That little rocker was built just for me by a neighbor in the town where I was born, Rockwood, Pennsylvania, more than seventy-five years ago. I know nothing about the man except that he was a friend of my parents. My middle name, Preston, came from him.

*So who was he?* I've often wondered. *Was carpentry his trade, as it was my father's, or a hobby?* Whichever, he was good at it. The chair is rock-sturdy. Except for some nicks and worn edges, it's almost as good as the day he built it.

I was born during the Great Depression; that's when Preston constructed the rocker with great precision out of good-quality hardwood. About that time my father lost his job and, to survive, was forced to relocate to another town to find work in a coal mine. What happened to our neighbor? I'll probably never know.

But this I do know: Whoever he was, Preston will always be a part of me, in my name and something else. In that chair I see painstaking craftsmanship and endurance. Those are qualities I want in all the things I do.

So, in a way, maybe I do know Preston.

> *Father, help me always to do my best and to concentrate on the things that will last.*
> —Harold Hostetler

## August

### Sat 13

*"How sweet is your love, my darling, my bride. How much better it is than mere wine. The perfume of your love is more fragrant than all the richest spices."*
—Song of Solomon 4:10 (TLB)

It was a hot day in August when my entire family gathered at my cousin Mike's beautiful farmhouse high on a hill in northern Illinois. All but four members of my thirty-member immediate family were there, plus dozens upon dozens of cousins, first cousins once removed, second cousins and spouses.

While the youngsters slid down a gigantic blue tarp spread out across one enormous hill with a couple of hoses at the top keeping the tarp wet, we adults played games, ate, gabbed our fool heads off and laughed like hyenas who hadn't seen each other for ages.

The most spectacular part of the day happened at the beginning of the reunion. My dad, who was three weeks away from his ninetieth birthday, and his darling blonde wife Bev, nearly eighty-five, decided to get married again. Dad and Bev had been married twenty-seven years earlier in a backyard ceremony performed by Bev's Lutheran pastor. But Dad decided it was time to have the marriage blessed by a priest of his own Catholic faith. And since one of my cousins is a priest, Dad thought the family reunion would be the time to do it.

In full regalia, Monsignor Jerry performed the ceremony under the tent in the ninety-six-degree heat. Dad and Bev, dressed in shorts and summer shirts, looked lovingly into each other's eyes and said, "I do." Dad smiled and said, "She's a keeper, isn't she?" We all cheered, and the party continued for hours.

Seeing Dad and Bev share their love for each other in front of all our relatives taught me that it's never too late for love and that no matter how old we are, we're never too old to express it.

*Lord, remind me to show my love every single day to all those I hold dear.*
—Patricia Lorenz

*August*

## ❈ TO SAY GOOD-BYE

*Sun 14*  For every one that exalteth himself shall be abased; and he that humbleth himself shall be exalted. —LUKE 18:14

**THE FRIENDSHIP CLASS**

One Sunday morning I happened by Friendship Class in time to hear Bubba offer a prayer: "God, thank You for being good. Amen."

Friendship Class is one of Hillsboro Presbyterian Church's great joys. Led by Scott, a Nashville educator, the class offers adults with disabilities a special place where they can come learn about God's love. The members of the class have been some of our most profound teachers.

We've learned patience from them, whether it's struggling to get a spoonful of food from plate to mouth or working to form letters on a just-completed art project. We've learned generosity, seeing them place their crumpled dollars in the collection plate. And we've learned kindness and compassion, seeing them rush to the side of someone who is hurt or upset or confused.

Friendship Class has much to teach and we have much to learn, especially in the way we relate to God. In general, we have a bit of a problem: exalting ourselves. From the big giver who wants everyone to know, to the squeaky clean people who like to point out the "sinners," to the spokespeople who decorate their language with so many church-words that they block our view of God, we are all in need of a quick lesson from the Friendship Class.

Bubba, Charles, Virgie, William, Peggy, Tiffany, Seldon, Jonathan and all the beautiful souls we've known through the years speak in one voice: Simply give. Simply pray. Simply care. Simply love. That's the way God loves us. That's the way He wants to be loved back.

*Father, we come as we are and thank You for being good.*
—PAM KIDD

*August*

## Mon 15

*If one falls down, his friend can help him up....*
—Ecclesiastes 4:10 (NIV)

A while ago, I was feeling overwhelmed by the daily demands of work and life. I'd been getting my eight hours of sleep, but I was waking up tired and without the energy to face the new day. Feeling depleted one Friday, I decided to call my friend Todd, who had just relocated to Dallas. While he was living in New York, we developed a special bond through our church. He was one friend I could count on for honest and helpful insight.

I left Todd a voice mail and followed it up with a text message. If need be, I was seriously thinking of driving to Texas to see him. Then on Monday evening the phone rang, "*Hermano*" (the word for "brother" in Spanish), I heard Todd say. "How are you doing?"

"I'm okay," I responded, though the truth was, I wasn't. I paused and then said, "I'm not, really. I'm very tired. I'm trying to balance too many things."

"I knew by the tone of your voice mail that something was up with you," Todd replied. What he said next surprised me. "I'm going to call you every Monday evening. Every week I am going to ask you two questions: Have you taken time to be one-on-one with God? And what one thing did you do last week to take care of Pablo?"

Todd's Monday calls haven't lessened my workload or made any of my challenges go away. But anticipating his questions has given me the focus I need to find ways to replenish my spirit, week by week.

*God, thank You for the friends You give me.*
—Pablo Diaz

## Tue 16

*August*

*And lead us not into temptation; but deliver us from evil.*
—LUKE 11:4

"Stephen," I called to my five-year-old as he skulked down the hall. "What do you have in your hand?"

"Nothing!" he chirped.

"Baloney!" I said. Suddenly it struck me that Stephen has never eaten bologna. It's one of a small group of foods I never eat, like okra, fatty meat and my dad's coleslaw.

Bologna is, in fact, one of the reasons I lead an upright life. On a fourth-grade trip to the city jail, I asked what the prisoners ate for lunch. "Bologna sandwiches," the policeman replied. I knew then that a life of crime wasn't for me; the punishment was too severe.

Now that I'm an adult, avoiding bologna is easy. Unlike sweets, which can push their way into my vision from across the street, bologna rarely enters my mind. I wander through life more or less unencumbered by the fear of being forced to ingest unwelcome foodstuffs. And yet, until today, I never appreciated that freedom.

I was so stunned by this thought that Stephen escaped with whatever was hidden in his hand. It's wonderful to realize that I'm not beset by every sin, nor susceptible to every temptation. There's a small group of iniquities that I avoid because they just don't occur to me: stealing, murder and coveting my neighbor's ox. I'm also not often tempted to gossip, nor am I particularly given to despair. These bologna-like aversions are a gift, small mercies. I only wish my gift list was longer.

*Heavenly Father, thanks for leaving a few things off my list of temptations. Please come to the aid of those who suffer from the trials I've been spared.*
—JULIA ATTAWAY

*August*

## Wed 17

*Cast your bread upon the waters, for after many days you will find it again.* —Ecclesiastes 11:1 (NIV)

A friend of mine once did a favor for someone who showed no gratitude. My friend said, "I cast my bread upon the waters and all I got was soggy bread."

My wife and I "cast our bread" all over Ohio by trying to visit my family (seven brothers and sisters and their eighteen children) in just two weeks. On the last day, we hoped to see a couple who had visited us in Colorado three years earlier. It certainly seemed like a "soggy bread" situation. They lived about fifty miles in the opposite direction from our next destination in Kansas, so we knew *we* were doing *them* a huge favor by including time for them.

Neil and Lorraine greeted us warmly the afternoon we arrived. They took us on a hike in a beautiful hardwood forest next to their home in southeastern Ohio. They prepared the evening meal while Dianne and I sat on their deck and watched the sun set behind a small hill. The hill provided pleasant shade while we ate. Neil and Lorraine provided engaging conversation until the first stars appeared.

We apologized for having to leave before dawn the next morning. Eight hours later, Dianne and I crept quietly upstairs to slip out without waking our hosts. Neil and Lorraine had already prepared a breakfast (eggs, bacon, toast, fruit, pastries, juice and coffee) and packed a lunch for us. My wife and I pulled into a rest stop in Missouri for lunch. The sandwiches were delicious. The bread was perfect—not too dry and definitely not soggy.

*Dear God, thank You for the times when we receive far more than we can give!*
—Tim Williams

*August*

## Thu 18

*Any other commandment... [is] summed up in this sentence, "You shall love your neighbor as yourself."*
—ROMANS 13:9 (RSV)

I live on the seventeenth floor of an apartment building in New York City. My apartment has a narrow terrace, so I sit outside a lot. In the summer, I attach my rainbow-striped umbrella to the railing to block the sun; in the winter I huddle in my parka and watch my breath steam over a cup of coffee.

From the sea of apartment windows, I'll hear somebody practicing the trumpet. In summer, I see children splashing in a rooftop wading pool. One night in a garden far below, a group of men in black suits and broad-brimmed hats sang "Hava Nagila" and danced together around the courtyard. For a long time, a dozen boys and girls would gather every spring for what I finally decided was their end-of-year school picture. From my perch I've seen what must have been baby showers and wedding toasts, retirement parties and building get-togethers.

Usually I'm fairly quiet on my terrace. But today as I sat outside, eating a sandwich, spicy wasabi mustard tickled my nose and I let out a mighty *Ah-ah-ah-CHOOO!* When my dad sneezed in our West Virginia neighborhood, the neighbors would count the number of sneezes—always seven—and shout from their own homes, "God bless you!" So I sneezed again and again—not seven times, but it was close. And it shouldn't have been a surprise when in busy, rushed and impersonal Manhattan, a call came up from somewhere below, "God bless you!"

From the seventeenth floor in one of the biggest, busiest cities in the world, it's clear that God is blessing me like crazy.

*Holy Spirit, let me always listen and rejoice in*
*Your presence, wherever I may be.*
—MARY ANN O'ROARK

## August

### Fri 19
*We have done that which was our duty to do.* —Luke 17:10

The legendary Western *The Magnificent Seven* depicts a poor Mexican village that is constantly raided by bandits. Desperate, the villagers hire seven gunmen to protect them. Not surprisingly, the children of the village see these colorful gunmen as heroes.

Before the final battle, several boys gather round a gunman named O'Reilly, whose courage they admire. "We are ashamed to live here," one boy says. "Our fathers are cowards."

Suddenly O'Reilly scolds the boy. "You think I am brave because I carry a gun? Your fathers are much braver, because they carry responsibility, for you, your brothers, your sisters, your mothers. This responsibility is like a big rock that weighs a ton. It bends and twists them. There's nobody who says they have to do this. They do it because they love you. I have never had this kind of courage."

The boys are humbled by the gunman's sermon and they begin to see their fathers in a different light.

Movies are about dramatic moments, but I think real courage is in the quiet, daily struggle to do what's right. It's about a mother who lives in a difficult marriage for the sake of her children. It's about a husband who is faithful to his wife, even when surrounded by temptation. It's about a teacher who would like to retire but keeps going back because she loves the children in her charge.

*Help me to be brave, Lord, not just in times of danger, but every day.*
—Daniel Schantz

*August*

## Sat 20
*I long to... take refuge in the shelter of your wings.*
—Psalm 61:4 (NIV)

A storm tore through our small town last night, its 150-mile-per-hour winds leaving a trail of devastation more than a mile wide. The roof was ripped off our middle school; trees were uprooted, smashing cars and breaking windows in their thunderous descent; bricks flew off apartment buildings. Pretty scary stuff.

I rode out the storm at my son's house. My husband Gary and I had just stopped by to hold our new grandson. The moment we walked in, the ominous news began flashing on the TV: tornado warnings!

It was Knox Edward's first storm. He's only four days old and he slept through the entire event. I held him close as I watched trees outside the window bend crazily in the wind. The sky was dark and the clouds swirled in a savage dance.

As I cradled Knox in my arms, his even breathing contrasted with the tension in the room, the scrolling warnings on the TV. *Danger? What danger?* Knox was at rest, secure, wonderfully oblivious. And why not? The house was filled with people who would have done anything to keep him safe.

Sometimes, when the storms in my own life come roaring down on me, I tend to panic. *What will I do? How will I handle it? What if* (fill in the blank with the worst possible thing) *happens? If only I had someone who cared for me, someone who would do anything to see me through the crisis....*

I'm between storms just now, walking in sunshine, enjoying my health and my family. Of course I know that the weather can change in an instant. But the next time dark clouds begin to gather, I'm going to remember Knox—and lean hard into God's everlasting arms.

*I'm leaning, leaning, leaning on Your everlasting arms, Lord!*
—Mary Lou Carney

## August

### Sun 21

> But you, O Bethlehem of Ephrathah, who are one of the little clans of Judah, from you shall come forth for me one who is to rule in Israel.... —MICAH 5:2 (NRSV)

*This has to be one of the smallest churches I've ever worshipped in,* I thought. There was room for maybe sixty or seventy people in the pews, and even then, plenty of good seats were still available among the smattering of people present. As I sat through the service, often looking out the window to a broad, windswept plain, I found myself wondering about the future of this place. How does such a tiny congregation survive, let alone make a difference?

When the final hymn was over and the benediction pronounced, I felt a tap on my shoulder. "You're the visitor from headquarters, aren't you?" a man said, extending a huge paw of a hand. At that time, I was working on the national staff of my denomination and was out this way on a visit. "Just wanted you to know, this church saved my life. Bunch of others too. Don't let our size fool you."

Whenever I find myself thinking that the world is too big, its problems too enormous, I remember that little church. It'll never be big or well known or famous. But just like the rest of us, it's called by the One Who came from little, inconsequential Bethlehem; called to make a difference in this vast world by making a difference in its own place. And just like that little church, we're assured that no matter how big the problem and how small our resources may seem, we can accomplish important things.

How can I be so sure? I've seen it with my own eyes in the little church that saves lives.

> *Never let us despair, oh, Lord, of Your Gospel—humble in beginning, humble in character, yet able to change the world.*
> —JEFF JAPINGA

*August*

## JOURNEY IN THE DARK

**Mon 22** *Jesus wept. Then said the Jews, Behold how he loved him!*
—John 11:35–36

### THE SAVIOR'S TEARS

"How are you?" concerned friends asked when they learned of my depression. Why was that question so hard to answer? A small book by minister Barbara Crafton helped me to understand. She had suffered from clinical depression, and being in the ministry had magnified all the hesitations and pain of being deeply depressed.

The title of her book, *Jesus Wept: When Faith and Depression Meet,* refers to the only time in the Bible when Jesus shed tears. When His friend Lazarus, the brother of Mary died, "Jesus wept."

Like us, Christ felt grief and mental anguish and clearly made no effort to hide His sadness from His disciples and friends. We are often less willing to reveal our pain and vulnerability. I know, because I struggled to hide my pain for long enough to make it more serious, more life threatening. I was ashamed of my weakness, ashamed that I couldn't "snap out of it." *If my relationship with God is strong, why am I feeling so hopeless?* I wondered. *Can't my faith vanquish this evil? If I pray hard enough, why doesn't God lighten the darkness?* Questions like these tormented me. I couldn't face down the feeling of shame, imagined or real. I felt as if people saw me as missing spiritual strength.

But quiet words from someone who understands can break through the bleak isolation. I've read Crafton's book four or five times. She knows the pain of trying to reconcile depression and faith. Her healing became a part of mine. Now back on solid ground, I can repeat to myself her words: "We are children of God, put here to delight in the world as long as we are privileged to be here."

*Lord, I need Your care on the good days and the bad, and I trust that You will never leave me alone in the dark. Amen.* —Brigitte Weeks

*August*

## Tue 23

*I have not run in vain, neither laboured in vain.*
—Philippians 2:16

Dad found the perfect spot for himself this year on our beach vacation, at the end of the boardwalk in front of our two-week rental. He sat in his walker, his floppy hat on, a section of unread newspaper in his hands, and all those who passed by wished him good morning or stopped to chat. Some he knew; most were strangers, walkers and joggers doing the loop along the boardwalk. I went out to sit with him.

"They all like to touch the end," he said, speaking slowly, "either with their foot or their hand." It was as though they were in some race and had to touch the end of the old sun-bleached boardwalk for their mileage to count.

"What do you think about, sitting here?" I asked.

"Not much," he said. "There's too much to watch." There were the boats on the water, just visible over the sand; the waves rolling in; the swimmers treading out; and the runners and walkers marking their progress with the quick slap of a hand on the boardwalk wall.

I left Dad in his spot in the sun. He's lived a long, wonderful life and seemed especially glad to have his children and grandchildren close by for these two weeks. I watched him give the boardwalk a gentle tap as though he'd just completed a run. Then he stood up in his walker and came inside to join the family.

*What a precious gift life is, Lord. Help me savor*
*every minute of it and every mile.*
—Rick Hamlin

*August*

## Wed 24

*Let me dwell in Your tent forever....*
—Psalm 61:4 (nas)

I don't own a summer cabin, but I have the next best thing: a tent in the yard pitched near an apple tree. It's furnished with a comfortable cot, a sleeping bag and pillow, a camp chair, and a battery-powered lantern.

The tent is my haven. I retreat there to think and pray and write and read—to be near God, with the sounds and smells and colors of the country all around. I watch the corn crop mature down the street or smell the baled hay in an adjacent field. At night, crickets and tree toads crank up the volume. There are misty sunrises and pearl moons and flashing fireflies. Overhead, flocks of geese gossip and raucous crows chatter.

Once, while I was listening to the vast stirring of wind in the trees, a fanciful idea took hold of me: *I'm listening to the thoughts of God.* As I lay on my cot, my heart was like a tent where Jesus and I could talk together; where, as He says, "I will come in to him and will dine with him, and he with Me" (Revelation 3:20, nas).

I closed my eyes in prayer. When I opened them, something I had never seen before on our property was crawling slowly across the top of the tent: a lovely green praying mantis.

*Jesus, thank You for coming to meet me wherever I may be.*
—Carol Knapp

*August*

## Thu 25 *I will trust, and not be afraid....* —Isaiah 12:2

Last summer, my family and I paid another visit to Pluscarden Abbey, a Benedictine monastery in northern Scotland. We have good friends there, and we love the peaceful atmosphere and rolling Highland landscape. In addition, I have a personal reason for enjoying Pluscarden: It's the only place where I get to practice beekeeping.

I can't keep bees at home; the town in which we live frowns on neighborhood hives. So whenever we head to Pluscarden, I look forward to a day or two of packing honey, scraping combs and inspecting hives with Father Benedict, the abbey's beekeeper. Although I'm afraid of stings, I feel safe wearing a protective suit and with an expert by my side. But I didn't count on what happened my first day back.

We suited up and went to investigate a huge swarm on a nearby tree. As I watched in amazement, Father Benedict—who wasn't wearing gloves—began to sweep the bees into a large box. Just then another monk ran up and announced, "You're needed with the choir!" Father Benedict turned to me, said "Take over!" and rushed off.

I started to edge the bees into the box. But as I rowed my arm back and forth, a cloud of agitated bees took flight and circled my body. I started to panic. Then I remembered Father Benedict's calm demeanor and gentle motions, remembered that I was in a protective suit, and determined to trust in myself, my equipment and the bees.

I began to work with, rather than against, the bees, *guiding* them instead of *forcing* them. They continued to buzz but dropped willingly into the box. And I was no longer scared, just thankful that I had this opportunity, all by myself, to learn more about how to live with a fascinating portion of God's creation.

*Grant me the courage, Lord, to greet the world rather than run from it.*
—Philip Zaleski

*August*

## Fri 26

*The cheerful heart has a continual feast.*
—Proverbs 15:15 (NIV)

When I was a child, I loved going to the butcher with my mother. I think our Brooklyn butcher must have been the first of the stand-up comics.

"Do you have any brains?" a woman once asked him.

"Hey, lady, if you're going to insult me, you can just leave right now!"

I clung to my mother's skirt, thinking that a fight was going to break out, not really understanding why everyone in the store had burst out laughing.

Every time someone would ask for skirt steak, he'd say, "With or without?"

"With or without what?"

"With or without pleats, of course!"

And then there was always the "chicken feet" routine. When a woman, probably planning to make a hearty soup, asked him, "Do you have chicken feet?" he'd act offended and proclaim, "My feet are perfectly normal."

"You're always so good-natured," I remember my mother telling him.

"Hey, I thank God every day for this dream job," he said. "In what other job could a man who looks like me be surrounded by women all day and go home to a steak dinner every night?"

Women (who always did the shopping then) would come in with worry lines creasing their foreheads and crumpled grocery lists written on the back of coupon-stuffed envelopes, but they seemed much more relaxed when they left.

Maybe his jokes weren't new, though they were new to me, but that butcher was an inspiration. He liked people and he showed it, and he helped people who had to count their pennies get through rough days. One of God's helpers on earth, I'm sure.

*God, remind me that I don't have to be in a helping profession to help someone. In any job—or none—I can be a helper and a healer.*
—Linda Neukrug

*August*

## ADVICE FROM AUNT ANNIE

*Sat 27*    *I am a traveler passing through the earth, as all my fathers were.* —PSALM 39:12 (TLB)

**TRAVEL TIPS**

One of Aunt Annie's articles was titled "Personality Bags for Year-Round Travel." I took her suggestions to heart last summer, when my husband Don and I took a cruise through the Inland Passage in Alaska.

"Knowledge acquired before the journey is a blessing," Aunt Annie wrote. So we read two books on Alaska and studied the weather forecast before leaving home. It was cold and rainy every day we were ashore, but clad in heavy rain jackets, we comfortably toured a salmon hatchery, visited a dog musher's camp, saw the stories told by totem poles and were awed by the jeweled icons at St. Michael's Russian Orthodox Church in Sitka.

Aunt Annie suggested packing curiosity and enthusiasm. Sure enough, a question to a young bus driver elicited hilarious stories of only-in-Alaska events such as the Anchorage outhouse races. And could anyone be blasé about viewing Mendenhall glacier or sighting a spouting whale?

Aunt Annie reminded travelers not to neglect the joy of meeting and loving new people. We got to know about the lives of some dedicated ship staff. Our dinner table companions were Mike and Mary Ann from Georgia and Tom and Beverly from eastern Kansas. It was a special blessing to share table prayer each evening.

I plan to stay at home for a while, but Aunt Annie's travel tips won't go to waste. I'm finding out they're also great preparation for each new day of my pilgrimage through life.

*Whether I'm going halfway around the world or just down the street, help me, Lord, to make the most of the journey.*
—PENNEY SCHWAB

*August*

## Sun 28

*Make haste, O God, to deliver me; make haste to help me, O Lord.* —PSALM 70:1

If you board the *Thomas B. Laighton* in Rhode Island's Portsmouth Harbor for the Sunday-morning walkabout cruise, within forty-five minutes you can disembark on Star Island, one of the nine Isles of Shoals. This one-third-square-mile rocky outcropping in the Atlantic Ocean has a few white clapboard buildings, hundreds of gulls and, from the east side, a vista of blue horizon that stretches to Portugal. For me, it has enough wind and sky to quiet my longing for Wyoming, so I visit frequently. Ten miles out in the Atlantic, Star Island offers limitless freedom and release.

During my most recent visit, I explored the tiny stone chapel atop a bluff. As my eyes adjusted to the dim interior, I saw perhaps thirty wooden chairs on a flagstone floor. Nothing adorned the simple wooden altar; only a clear glass window rose behind it. I had paused to pray in thanksgiving for the serenity of the place when I heard a tapping coming from the altar area and saw a sparrow lunging against the window. The poor thing could see its refuge, a spruce tree, just two inches outside the glass, but try as it might, it couldn't reach it. On this windswept island of limitless sky and freedom, the little bird had managed to trap itself.

Since the bird was too high to reach, I slowly unrolled my bandanna and flicked at it. The distraught creature slid down the pane just enough so I could scoop it up in the bandanna, carry it out the door, and toss it into all that sky. It flew away unharmed but stayed in my mind all day.

*Gracious Lord, I don't know how I manage to jam myself into corners. Thank You for Your mercy in gently rescuing me.*
—GAIL THORELL SCHILLING

## August

### Mon 29

*There is no fear in love; but perfect love casteth out fear....*
—I JOHN 4:18

Julee and I have owned four dogs since we've lived in our Manhattan apartment building, and our neighbor Tony has been terrified of every one of them—until Millie. Not that our other dogs were vicious; no, it was Tony. He had a lifelong fear of dogs. Even when our cocker spaniel Sally was hobbling around with arthritis, Tony refused to get in the elevator with us. The mere sight of Marty, our hundred-pound Labrador retriever, was enough to make Tony go weak in the knees. "I don't hate your dogs," Tony tried to explain from a safe distance. "I'm just afraid of them."

For years I tried to keep our dogs away from Tony, pulling them back when we crossed paths with him in the lobby, crossing to the other side of the street when we saw him outside. Then came Millie, our now-three-year-old golden retriever. If you've ever known a golden, you know that they are the sweetest creatures God has created.

During their first couple of encounters, I tried to pull my big puppy back from Tony as he retreated in terror. Millie wasn't having it. She sat down politely, tail swishing on the floor and waited for Tony to pass. Then when they met, she tried to approach him, head down, moving slowly, but determined to show him she was a friend. One day he put his hand out tentatively and patted Millie on the head. Millie was thrilled. Tony couldn't believe he'd done it. "Wow!" was all he could say.

Nowadays Tony gets down on one knee to give Millie a bear hug while she nuzzles his neck. And you know what? Tony stopped me the other day and asked, "Can you recommend a good place to adopt a dog?"

It's only fair, I guess. A dog already adopted him.

*God, Your love abides in many forms—some four-legged—that bring joy to the heart. Thank You for the time we have with them.*
—EDWARD GRINNAN

## Tue 30

*And Jesus increased in wisdom and stature, and in favour with God and man.* —LUKE 2:52

When our daughter Maria started high school, it was hard for me not to try to relive the ups and downs of my high school years through her. I wanted her not to make the mistakes I made, so I was always giving her advice.

"Go to all the football games—don't miss out on things like I did," I told her, even before school started. "Don't go to the dance with a boy you're not crazy about just to have a date" was another bit of my unsolicited wisdom. I couldn't resist it if I thought I could spare her some of the anxiety I had experienced.

Finally Maria said to me, "You know, Mom, if I don't learn some of these things on my own, I won't have any advice to pass on to *my* kids!" She was so right. I wanted her to learn from my mistakes instead of making her own.

God's parenting example is clear. He gives me love and direction, but then lets me go out into the world to fall or fly. What an encouragement for any parent to know that even Jesus, in His humanity, was given the freedom to learn and grow. The best I can do for Maria is love, listen and guide when asked. If she is to grow into the person God created her to be, I need to get out of her way much of the time. Although I'd like to clear the path for her, only she can find her unique way in life.

*Lord, give me the wisdom and the strength to know when to keep silent.*
—GINA BRIDGEMAN

*August*

## Wed 31

*And we know that in all things God works for the good of those who love him, who have been called according to his purpose.* —ROMANS 8:28 (NIV)

I met Lisa, the newly appointed principal at Creekside Junior High, shortly after our schools reopened following Hurricane Katrina. Creekside is a small school located in the town of Pearl River, Louisiana. Lisa had asked our TV station to cover an event at her school. When we arrived, I asked her how her first year there was going.

She said her biggest concern when she was hired was how she would fit into this small, close-knit community, where everybody knew everybody. "I was an outsider. I'd come from another school district. I wanted to be accepted by this community, whose children would be in my care. But I wasn't sure how to do it."

Days later, Hurricane Katrina hit and sent Lisa scurrying to the shelter down the street from the school. She began making sandwiches, serving meals, and doing whatever was needed to help those who had been forced out of their homes feel comfortable and safe.

"Up until the hurricane hit," she recalled, "I'd been trying to figure out what I could do to be accepted in my new job, in my new town, and with my new students and their parents. The storm took care of that. I just rolled up my sleeves and did whatever I needed to do to help out."

When school reopened a month later, Lisa greeted many of the students and their parents by their first names. "We'd worked side by side, preparing meals together and eating together," she said, smiling. "We're family now."

*Dear Lord, thanks for Lisa's reminder that even out of a disaster, something good can come.*
—MELODY BONNETTE

*August*

**SEEDS OF LOVE**

1 _____

2 _____

3 _____

4 _____

5 _____

6 _____

7 _____

8 _____

9 _____

10 _____

11 _____

12 _____

13 _____

14 _____

15 _____

## August

16 _____

17 _____

18 _____

19 _____

20 _____

21 _____

22 _____

23 _____

24 _____

25 _____

26 _____

27 _____

28 _____

29 _____

30 _____

31 _____

# September

*There is no fear in love;
but perfect love casteth
out fear....*

—I John 4:18

*September*

## A PATH TO SIMPLICITY

*Thu 1*  *God loves a cheerful giver.* —II CORINTHIANS 9:7 (NAS)

**GIVING FREELY**

I'd recently replaced my laptop computer, and my old one was on the kitchen table. *I can sell it at my yard sale*, I decided.

That afternoon, the computer store sent a technician to train me on my new laptop. Jake was a friendly guy, and soon we were laughing over our common struggles with attention deficit disorder. "Forget this instruction book," he said with a grin as he tossed it on the sofa. "Get me a sheet of paper, and I'll work you up the cheat sheet of all cheat sheets."

Just then, Jake spotted my old laptop. "Are you selling it?" he asked. Jake's wife, a stay-at-home mom, was an aspiring writer. If she had a laptop, she could write close by while their three small kids played or napped.

I tore a piece of paper for Jake from the notebook I'd unearthed that morning while working in the attic. It held snapshots of my first apartment. The picture of the copper-toned kitchen stove took me back more than thirty years. A physician who made rounds on the floor where I worked as a new nurse had heard that I needed a stove. He barely knew me, but he offered the nearly new stove as if I were his sister. "Why are you giving it away when you could sell it?" I asked incredulously.

"Why sell it when I can give it away?" he answered.

All at once I knew: I had a computer to give away. And I knew just the technician who could refurbish it.

*With You, Lord, there is always more than enough. Help me to give freely.*
—ROBERTA MESSNER

*September*

## Fri 2

*He will teach us of his ways, and we will walk in his paths....*
—MICAH 4:2

Sunshine, clanking cowbells, meadows carpeted with grass and wildflowers—for the first two hours of our Alpine hike, I couldn't help but be thankful. A friend and I were rambling through the mountains above Lucerne, Switzerland, and because trails in much of Europe are well marked, we didn't bother taking the map out of my backpack. We just focused on the view.

Then the signs disappeared. We looked everywhere for the familiar yellow markers that said *Wanderweg*—the German word that literally means "wandering way"—and saw none. Nor could we decipher where we were on the map, which was crisscrossed with numerous trails.

I looked up at the sun, across the valley, to the left, to the right. "I think it's this way," I said.

"Yeah, let's do it," my friend said.

Two hours and two dead ends later, our legs were throbbing. Our patience was running low and so was our water. We turned around, retraced our steps and went all the way back to the crossroads where we'd last seen a sign. In our carelessness, we'd missed the next sign, which was just ten yards from where we'd taken a wrong turn.

There have been many times in my life when I've tried to trust in my own understanding, rather than in God. He's put signs along the path, and in His Word, He's given me a road map. But I have to rely on these tools for them to help me. And I have to rely on Him, not myself, every step of the way.

> *Lord, keep me on the right path, and when I take a wrong turn,*
> *help me to recognize my mistake and go back to You.*
> —JEFF CHU

*September*

## Sat 3

*When the wind did not allow us to hold our course, we sailed to the lee of Crete... and came to a place called Fair Havens....*
—Acts 27:7–8 (NIV)

Niagara Falls! Slowly I turned and looked into the face of a new friend.

Two weeks earlier I had set out on a journey that I thought would lead to a four-week stay at Vermont Studio Center, where I would find peace to work. The center was beautiful, but there was too much peace. The location was so isolated I was unable to receive or make calls needed to conduct research for my project. But all was not lost, because I did meet Dee Dee.

Red-haired and green-eyed, she is 100 percent Californian. Feisty and funny, Dee Dee made me laugh until I cried. At the end of my first two weeks, when her residency was over, I decided to hitch a ride with her to the nearest train station and make my way home to North Carolina. But a storm of excitement blew us off course. Alternately laughing and sighing with awe, we made our way to the Harriet Beecher Stowe Research Center in Hartford, Connecticut. We were so close to Auburn, New York, where Harriet Tubman once lived, that we decided to make our way there and just happened to run into two of Tubman's great-grandnieces. Then the winds of our new friendship blew us north, to Canada, to see the falls.

We talked about husbands, families and God as we drove to Cincinnati, where I introduced Dee Dee to my son Chase. Finally, we arrived in St. Louis, where I boarded a plane for home. Picking me up at the airport, my daughter Lanea expressed shock at my sudden spontaneity. I was still giggling and refreshed. It was the most unexpected fun I've had in years.

*Lord, blow us off course from our usual day to day and help us to see and enjoy the beauty of the fair havens to which You send us.*
—Sharon Foster

*September*

## Sun 4

*Thy word is... a light to my path.* —Psalm 119:105 (RSV)

On the riverbank in the Hudson River town of Cold Spring, New York, I noticed a small sign:

> WARNER SISTERS
> VIEW TO CONSTITUTION ISLAND
> PRESERVED BY AUTHORS
> SUSAN WARNER AND ANNA WARNER
> WHO WROTE THE HYMN
> "JESUS LOVES ME"

Beyond the forested island I could see the US Military Academy at West Point on its dramatic cliffs across the river. *"Jesus loves me, this I know..." Easy words to write*, I thought, *for a well-to-do woman living in this delightful setting.* Then I learned Anna Warner's story.

She and her sister did grow up in wealth. Their widowed father was a prominent lawyer; home was a luxurious townhouse—servants, grooms, carriage house. But in the stock market panic of 1837, when the girls were in their late teens, all this was lost.

Their father bought a derelict old farmhouse on Constitution Island, fifty miles and a world away from New York City's high society. The young women learned to cook, clean, wash, sew, keep a vegetable garden. Among many failed attempts to recoup his fortune, their father tried growing rice. I could still see the channels he dug in the marsh between the island and the shore.

To sustain themselves, Susan and Anna turned to writing stories, hymns, novels (some of them best sellers). But because there were no copyright laws, they lived out their lives in poverty. How did they know Jesus loved them? "For the Bible tells me so." And for forty years they held Bible classes for the cadets at West Point, sharing their love of the book that made their outwardly meager lives rich and joyful.

*Speak to me today, Father, through Your written Word.*
—Elizabeth Sherrill

*September*

## Mon 5

*Aspire to lead a quiet life, to mind your own business, and to work with your own hands....*
—I Thessalonians 4:11 (NKJV)

I spend most of my week at a computer screen, working with words. But on Saturdays I intentionally switch modes and work with my hands in a more tactile way. I look forward to cooking up a few dishes—old favorites or new recipes—from scratch.

In the morning at the grocery store, I linger in the produce section. *Shall I make some guacamole? No, the avocados today are too hard and too expensive. A bunch of herbs for parsley soup? Yes, that would taste good. Apples for pie? Yes, but that means I need to buy shortening.*

I return home and head for the kitchen. I get out my cutting board and chop; my paring knife and peel. With pastry cutter and rolling pin, I transform raw ingredients into tasty baked goods. The soup simmers. I pull a golden pie out of the oven. *It looks good!* Even before tasting or serving, I smile, expressing a joy that flows from deep within.

Ben Sira, an ancient Jewish writer, describes people whose "prayer shall be in the work of their craft." He's referring to farmers, artists, blacksmiths and potters, but I think also of cooks and tailors, builders and gardeners, musicians and machine makers. Whether it's a vocation or avocation, any work can be performed as a prayer to God's glory, a prayer that draws us close to our Creator's heart.

*Lord, draw me today to some project that
I can complete as a working prayer.*
—Evelyn Bence

*September*

Tue 6
*Praise be to the God and Father of our Lord Jesus Christ, who has blessed us in the heavenly realms with every spiritual blessing in Christ.* —Ephesians 1:3 (NIV)

This summer has been eventful for my family. We've welcomed new babies. We've had cookouts and blown a million bubbles (mostly at two-year-old Isabelle Grace's request). We watched grandson Mace blow out one candle on his birthday cake. We've played in the sand and eaten (way too many) ice cream cones. Good times, good memories.

But some of the events haven't been joyful or welcome. My mother-in-law Opal was diagnosed with cancer in her right sinus cavity. She spent the summer undergoing chemo at Vanderbilt Hospital in Nashville, Tennessee. They were hoping the difficult treatments would shrink the tumor and surgery could follow, but that's not what happened. The cancer continues to grow.

There have been a flock of other family problems, too—some physical, some financial, others emotional. I wake each morning and begin praying for the overwhelming needs of those I love. I've even begun to wonder what new calamity might unfold during the course of an otherwise ordinary day. Which is why the sunflowers came as such a welcome surprise.

They appeared one day, twin stalks rising out of the flower bed near my sunroom door. By the time I noticed them, they were knee-high and looked enough unlike a weed to be spared my dedicated pulling. They grew taller and soon big buds appeared. That's when I knew: I was going to have sunflowers to brighten my waning garden!

As I was admiring these beauties this morning, I noticed they had sprung up next to a clump of red geraniums. And nestled in those geraniums is a small gray rock with a single word carved into its face: *Rejoice*.

Good advice; rock solid advice. Because in the midst of sadness and trial, there is always God's eternal love—and some unexpected blessings.

*Keep me from being so downcast, Lord, that I forget
to look for the flowers lining my pathway.*
—Mary Lou Carney

*September*

**Wed 7**  *Now the body is not made up of one part but of many.*
—I CORINTHIANS 12:14 (NIV)

My hands were shaking and my heart was racing. I was about to give a motivational speech at a college that was affiliated with a denomination not my own. I had done some research on their theology to try to make sure I didn't say anything offensive, but still, what if I messed up and said the wrong thing? These people were different from me—would we be able to relate to each other?

As soon as I got onstage, however, I saw that my fears had been unfounded. These students laughed at the same things I thought were funny, and they nodded at the things I thought were true. At the end of the presentation, a few people raised their hands to ask questions.

"What do you do with your left shoes?" someone asked. (I'm an amputee and I don't wear an artificial leg, so I get this one a lot.)

"I throw them away. Funny you mention it. I actually bought a pair of shoes today and I haven't thrown out the other one yet," I said, pulling the left shoe from my backpack.

Someone in the front row raised his hand. "I could use that," he said. Turns out he was an amputee missing his right leg. We have the same shoe size, so I gave it to him. Everyone clapped.

As I drove back to my hotel after the presentation, an observation—albeit in the form of a bad pun—popped into my mind. That other amputee and me? We were *sole* mates. But more importantly, we were also *soul* mates, all part of the same family of God, regardless of the name on the sign at our home church.

*Lord, I ask for unity among Your children on earth.*
—JOSHUA SUNDQUIST

*September*

**Thu 8**  *Then God said, "Let the waters teem with fish and other life, and let the skies be filled with birds of every kind."*
—GENESIS 1:20 (TLB)

The early morning flyby was low and noisy. Many of us ran out to our driveways to watch, some muttering about the nuisance of the wakeup call, others looking skyward in wonder. Our California neighborhood has become a stopover for what we affectionately call the Sierra Madre Air Force: hundreds of large, green, red-crowned parrots.

They line up on the telephone wires, squawking as they jostle for position. They perch in the oaks and sycamore trees. They help themselves to lunch, taking a bite or two out of a piece of fruit and then letting it drop to the ground. Thanks to them, my share of the harvest from our laden fig tree was exactly two figs! Then as suddenly as they arrive, they are gone, the sky filled with a spectacular, raucous mass of flapping green wings.

Old-timers tell us there was a fire years ago in a local aviary, at which time many parrots were set free. After years of nesting and hatching, what ornithologists estimate to be three thousand parrots now swarm throughout our San Gabriel Valley.

Bothersome as it is, the Sierra Madre Air Force brings the dazzling sights and sounds of the Amazon to our skies—and the never-ending wonder of the miracle of flight.

*Praise the Lord from the heavens, praise Him from the skies.*
*The sun by day, the moon by night, drifting clouds and birds that fly,*
*Your glory fills the earth, O God of all creation!*
—FAY ANGUS

*September*

**Fri 9**  *Then the Lord opened the servant's eyes, and he looked and saw....* —II Kings 6:17 (NIV)

When I painted a large mural on a blank wall in our home, I used a sketch I'd done of a vintage Charleston, South Carolina, house and combined it with a picture of a walled courtyard with a fountain that I copied from a book. Because the tranquil fountain in the center reminded me of an oasis of prayer, I named the mural "Morning Prayers."

Four years after I'd done the mural, I suddenly saw that by using two different models, I'd unknowingly composed a picture that was out of kilter. I hadn't followed the rules of perspective; the lines of the house went down one way and the lines of the courtyard wall went up another. Instead of working harmoniously together, both the house and the courtyard looked awkward and out of place.

Then I remembered that the word *perspective* also means our outlook on the events of life, judging things according to their true importance. My mistake had actually enhanced the message of the mural. During prayer, I bring to God my warring perspectives about who I am, what I need and what's really most important. Through prayer, God slowly helps me straighten out my fears and assumptions until everything lines up more harmoniously in the big picture.

*Father, today, please show me how to bring my earthly perspective in line with Your heavenly one.* —Karen Barber

---

**READER'S ROOM**

Last year it dawned on me that I'm a control freak, one of those people who has all the right answers to everything. I knew I needed help, and it came in the precious pages of *Daily Guideposts*. On certain days the writer's words almost shouted, "Janetta, let go and let Me have control!" Finally, one day I let go, and the Lord began to show me how to trust in Him. There are still days when I fall back into my old habit, but soon I'm handing things back to the Lord. Then I'm free to love the ones He gave me, not try to control them. —*Janetta Messmer, The Woodlands, Texas*

*September*

## Sat 10
*The fear of the Lord is the beginning of wisdom....*
—PSALM 111:10

When my father died, I sat beside him, looking around the room, looking for *him*. I heard Mum say to the hospice nurse, "He was a scholar. What happened to all that knowledge? Where did his ideas go?" The blow of losing Dad's creative intellect was almost crueler than physically losing him. Yet I didn't despair, for I knew that Dad's thoughts were very much intact. I knew from personal experience.

I was seventeen when I died from asthma and came back. For years I was confused about this: Why did I see my body from above? Why couldn't anyone hear me talking? Later I came across the evidence that many people have had similar experiences. So I know that when we leave our bodies, our minds remain intact. All of our knowledge, our thought processes, our capacity to learn, even our confusion, remain.

When Dad died, I suspected that he lingered in the room as had I. Could he see me? Was he trying to speak with me? Teach me one last thing? What was he trying to say? I finally kissed his physical self good-bye—a terrible loss—to consciously embrace that which defined him best and would forever live in the eternal presence of God: his curious and capable mind, always eager to learn more of God's character and, when asked, always willing to share. I was going to miss learning what Dad, a PhD in education, could no longer teach me. But what new things was he learning?

Someday, with years of eternal experience behind him, he will once again be my teacher.

*Dear Lord, the beginning of wisdom rests in You and is therefore ours for all eternity.*
—BRENDA WILBEE

## September

### Sun 11

*I have no pleasure in the death of the wicked; but that the wicked turn from his way and live....*
—EZEKIEL 33:11

I sit by the river for a long time, remembering my three friends turned to floating ash on this day ten years ago, murdered by a coward now hiding in a cave. People in the five boroughs of New York City breathed in the sinewy bodies of my friends, strapping hilarious Irish American boys, now dust. Their wives sleep alone, and their children have set one fewer plate at the table night after night, year after year. The scars on those children's hearts....

The rage starts to bubble up in me, and I sit down and watch the birds. "When furious, get curious," as my grandpa used to say. There are finches in the currant bushes, stuffing themselves silly. One finch gobbles so many currants it can hardly get aloft, and I start to laugh as it lurches off its branch and plummets slowly toward the river below like a huge currant covered with feathers. You never saw a fatter flailing finch in your life.

Against the whole welter of death and sadness and grief, there are always finches in the bushes, mooing with happiness at the exquisite forest of fruit laid before them by the Master Orchardist. What could ever be a more eloquent prayer than that?

And while almost every atom in me wishes to wreak vengeance on the man who murdered my friends, the man who sowed such terror and fear and pain among the children of the world that day, a few brave atoms somewhere very deep inside me believe that even he can awaken to the Light that made those finches and made my friends; even he can emerge from the bloody arrogant shell in which he lives his squirming days.

Life defeats death, hope defeats despair, light defeats darkness. There are always finches in the bushes.

*Dear Lord, thank You for really fat finches. Thank You for reaching into dark hearts and planting light.*
—BRIAN DOYLE

*September*

## ❈ TO SAY GOOD-BYE

*Mon 12*   *"Well done...."* —LUKE 19:17 (RSV)

**AN ACHE WITHIN**

In all these years of being a minister's wife, I have yet to lay my head on my pillow at night, thinking, *Ah, well done, Pam. Today you did everything that needed doing.*

My life has been filled with a sense of never having done enough. There's always been at least one lonely person whom I didn't visit, one soul who would have appreciated a hot dinner, one friend who deserved a birthday party, one church member who would have been lifted by an encouraging note.

On the other hand, I've watched over a fair number of people ... fought to keep them in their homes, made sure they had visits and people to care for them. I've cooked a lot of dinners, had a lot of parties, written a lot of letters. Knowing this, why do I feel the way I do? What is the ache that God puts inside us when we see an unkempt child, a homeless woman wheeling a cart down the street, loneliness in a fellow traveler?

As the time to leave Hillsboro Presbyterian Church draws near, I realize that this ache isn't exclusive to a minister's wife. It is, instead, one of the finest gifts God offers us. All I have to do is reach out and accept it. Wherever I go, it's one gift I'll be taking with me: a goad to keep on going and the knowledge—underneath the awareness of all that's undone—that I find deep happiness in doing what I can.

*Father, even when I feel I haven't done enough, help me*
*to keep working toward Your final "well done."*
—PAM KIDD

*September*

## Tue 13

*The man said, "This is now bone of my bones and flesh of my flesh; she shall be called 'woman,' for she was taken out of man."* —GENESIS 2:23 (NIV)

Our first months of marriage were off to a great start. My husband Brian and I had enjoyed a wonderful honeymoon and delighted in the adventure of moving three times in the course of three months, finally landing in Durham, North Carolina, for his final year of law school.

Once settled, we began falling into our roles, finding our footing as we sorted out how to combine two newly joined lives in one modest apartment. I quickly found myself becoming overwhelmed.

I worked from home, so I could easily check my e-mail after hours. I rushed to get the shopping done and dinner on the table by the time Brian finished his evening classes. Like the duck who looks serene floating by on the surface but all the while paddling like crazy underneath, I tried to get everything done, be everything I thought a "good wife" should be and still manage to get the laundry folded before bed.

Finally, Brian stopped me. "You don't have to do all this," he said. "We're part of a team." He reminded me why God created Eve in the first place: to give Adam a companion to share his life, through the ups, the downs and the stack of dirty dishes in the sink.

We're four months in now and still finding our roles, but I'll always remember the lesson Brian taught me. While we're both here to serve God, we're also here to serve each other. Life, I've found, is an awful lot easier with a good helpmate around.

*Remind me, Lord, each day to focus on making the lives of those around me easier and to surround myself with people who strive to do the same.*
—ASHLEY KAPPEL

*September*

## Wed 14

*Comfort ye, comfort ye my people, saith your God. Speak ye comfortably to Jerusalem, and cry unto her, that her warfare is accomplished, that her iniquity is pardoned....*
—Isaiah 40:1–2

Five mornings a week I drive my grandson to prekindergarten in Pegram, Tennessee, the next town over. To get there, I go through three school zones with fifteen-mile-an-hour speed limits. I know the importance of obeying these limits and I'm super careful.

But one morning after I'd dropped off Frank, I got to the second school zone, and before I knew it, I'd crossed the line without slowing down. The earlier activity of buses and children had ceased. All was quiet till I saw the whirling lights of the police cruiser behind me. Pulling over, I immediately began apologizing to the young officer. He interrupted, giving me a lecture that went on and on. I sat there humiliated, feeling the stares of the drivers of the cars crawling by. The bitter icing on the cake was a hefty ticket.

I drove away in tears, alternately beating up on myself and defending myself against the harsh words of the officer. "Lord, what's done is done, and I need to let go of this so it doesn't ruin my whole day," I said. Just then my eye caught something that put it all in perspective: the cross hanging from my rearview mirror.

Its message of unlimited mercy and pardon lifted the weight hanging over my day. Human anger and earthly fines will pass; God's mercy and forgiveness are forever.

*Lord Jesus, on the Cross You paid the debt of all my sins.*
*I can only thank You by receiving Your forgiveness*
*again and again and again.*
—Shari Smyth

*September*

## Thu 15

*The lips of the righteous know what is acceptable....*
—Proverbs 10:32 (NKJV)

It matters how you say something.

William Shakespeare said, "To be or not to be, that is the question." That has a certain panache to it, even after all these years. But my college students would say it like this: "So, like, do I want to go on with this gig, or am I, like, outta here? You know what I'm sayin'?" Somehow it's not the same.

Dylan Thomas said, "Do not go gentle into that good night." My students would say, "When my number's up, I'm gonna go kicking and screaming, man."

John Donne wrote, "Never send to know for whom the bell tolls; it tolls for thee." My students would render that, "Yo, dude, sorry I'm late for class. When my alarm went off, I thought it was my roomie's bell."

When I was first married, I wasn't very tactful. I thought the purpose of a disagreement was to win. I would say things like, "Hon, that's just where you're wrong. You couldn't be more wrong!" Then I would wonder why the rest of the day didn't go well.

After many years of sleeping out on the back porch, I learned to say something like, "Hon, you may be right. You usually are. You're a smart woman, so I'll give your point some more thought before I make up my mind." The day goes much better, and I can sleep in our bed.

To be kind or not to be kind, that is the question.

*Teach me, Lord, to be gracious in my speech, for the sake of those who have to listen to me.*
—Daniel Schantz

## Fri 16

*September*

*Hear my cry for mercy as I call to you for help....*
—PSALM 28:2 (NIV)

I had an odd dream last night. I was driving down a mountain in a car with no brakes. I woke up, convinced myself that I was in bed and fell back asleep. Then I dreamed that I was zooming down a mountain in a car with no steering wheel. This time I woke up and grumbled to God that it didn't take a rocket scientist to interpret these dreams. My life feels totally out of control.

I began to tell God about it, as if He might not know. My husband Lynn has a brain tumor that's affecting the way he thinks and acts and feels. He hates it and I hate it and, most of the time, I'm sure that I'm not doing a good enough job of caring for him.

I told God that all of this makes me both mad and sad, but what's coming out these days is mostly the mad part. And I take my frustration out on whoever's closest to me. Too often, that's Lynn.

Yesterday when I was helping him get dressed, I couldn't guide his arm into the sleeve of his sweater. I yanked at the sweater and made a sound of exasperation, which only made Lynn feel worse. I told him I was sorry, but I'm mad that cancer is robbing him of the ability to get dressed, to do the things he used to do so easily. I'm mad that cancer is changing me too.

I don't remember that God had any clear message to me during my conversation in the dark. But I do remember this: Once I finished my diatribe, I felt better and fell asleep.

And guess what? I woke up this morning knowing that today is a new day.

*Lord, I am grateful that You listen to the mad parts of me and still love me.*
—CAROL KUYKENDALL

## September

### Sat 17

*Let the rivers clap their hands, Let the mountains sing together for joy.* —Psalm 98:8 (NAS)

Making music is awkward for me. My clarinet squeaked in junior high, and once, after singing a hymn, I was told, "Even your 'Amen' is flat." But listening to music is another thing; I love to listen and create connections through what I hear.

Once while I was driving across South Dakota, the big band sounds rolling from the radio undulated like the waves of prairie grain I was passing by. As I sat in a parked car on a rainy day, a lilting classical piece trickled down the windshield with the raindrops. When I was headed into Wyoming, a country singer's scratchy voice seemed to cut tracks into the hardscrabble rangeland. When my last child left for college, the Gregorian chant I played clung with sweet melancholy to the drifting autumn leaves. A spectacular listening-and-landscape connection happened when zither notes played "Rock of Ages" while the magnificent Canadian Rockies slid past my driver's window. On the same trip, I sang (flat, naturally) "I've Got Peace Like a River" as I crossed western Canada's beautiful Peace River.

All the language of music is heard somewhere in God's creation. Birds and animals, land- and sea- and skyscapes, weather systems, human drama—each has a distinctive sound waiting to find its echo in a musician's creativity. How wonderful it is to have the talent to compose and sing and play and perform. But for someone like me without it, what a joy it is to learn to be a talented listener.

*Master Music Maker, teach me to listen for*
*Your original works in all kinds of music.*
—Carol Knapp

*September*

# TIME ON THE RIVER

**Sun 18** *And Abraham was old, and well stricken in age....*
—Genesis 24:1

**HAMILTON**

As we boarded the ship in Antwerp for the journey up the Rhine, I knew I was running away—running away from the fact that moving to a retirement community meant being cooped up with a bunch of old fogies sitting around counting their pills. Of course, I wasn't "one of them," even though what was left of my hair was white and the steps leading up to our stateroom were extraordinarily steep.

Imagine my dismay, on walking into the dining room that first evening, to discover that most of our fellow passengers on the *Viking Sun* were white-haired too. Sure enough, three people at our table immediately got out their pillboxes.

A very old man with two canes was making his painful way straight toward us. As he lowered himself into the seat next to mine, I read his name tag: Hamilton. A waiter offered to get Hamilton's dinner from the buffet. "Thoughtful of you!" boomed Hamilton with a glorious smile.

I saw that smile often in the next ten days. Hamilton never missed a meal or a shore excursion. He beamed on lace makers and glassblowers and clock carvers. He hobbled down church naves and up castle steps.

Watching Hamilton, I knew that in our new community we'd find other men and women whose physical limitations hadn't squelched their zest for living, inspirations for this next stage of the journey.

*As my body grows older, Father, help me respond with grace and cheer.*
—John Sherrill

*September*

## TIME ON THE RIVER

*Mon 19*   *O taste and see that the Lord is good....* —PSALM 34:8

**ALONE IN ANTWERP**

I'd looked forward to everything about the Rhine cruise except the guided tours scheduled for various stops. Ever since boyhood, I'd secretly resisted being force-fed historical facts, dates or the biographical details of long-dead potentates.

The first tour was the city of Antwerp. As I followed the other passengers down the gangplank, I saw to my horror five huge buses lined up on the dockside quay. Tib and I had been assigned to bus five. Beside it stood a guide holding a long stick topped by a dinner-sized paper plate with the number 5 on it, looking for all the world like a giant lollipop.

Everyone trooped off the bus in the center of town where, with a whispered farewell to Tib, and the pang of guilt I always felt at my lack of historical curiosity, I slipped away from the lollipop parade to enjoy the city on my own. I walked through the diamond center on Appelmansstraat and along the rows of houseboats, chatting with cordial English-speaking Belgians. For lunch, I dined at canal-side stalls, sampling raw herring and the Low Countries specialty *erwtensoep*, a pea soup so thick my spoon stood up by itself.

Comparing notes with Tib back on the ship, I thought how differently we'd delighted in the day. Tib learns about a place primarily through its history and its art; I through encounters with the people who presently live there. "Why ever should you feel guilty?" she asked when I confessed feeling that I was missing something others found important. "Aren't yours and mine just different ways of exploring God's world?"

*Help me, Father, to treasure the many ways You've given us
to experience Your limitless creation!*
—JOHN SHERRILL

*September*

# TIME ON THE RIVER

## Tue 20

*For we are members one of another.* —EPHESIANS 4:25

### THE BRIDGE TOO FAR

Near the beginning of our Rhine cruise, we came to a bridge I'd never wanted to see. There it was, just ahead, at the landing near Arnhem, Holland: the "bridge too far," scene of one of the bloodiest battles of World War II. Now the bridge was rebuilt, with a small battle museum nearby. I didn't want to go near it. My own combat had been in Italy, not here, but any reminder brought back the old bitterness toward Germans.

Still, we'd be here for most of the day, and Tib urged me to join her at the museum. So it was that I reluctantly stepped inside. The memorabilia consisted mostly of individual soldiers' recollections. In translation, I read comments by boy after boy whose like I once would have seen as the enemy.

"Vogl was torn open by machine-gun fire," one German soldier wrote. "It was horrendous to see him meet his end in such an appalling way.... He was like a father to us."

Another, Horst Weber, received wounded British soldiers in his headquarters, where a British doctor labored two days and nights without sleep. "We gave our first-aid kits to this fantastic doctor," Weber wrote. "We helped him where we could."

Helmut Buttlar had just lost his left heel when he came across a wounded Brit. "He asked how old I was. I told him proudly that I was nineteen.... We shook hands and wished each other the best."

The Germans' words reflected the horror and sorrow of that ferocious fight. But of hatred I saw none. And in that little room of shared experience and grief, I felt some of my own war tension ease.

*Prince of Peace, teach me to recognize You in everyone.*
—JOHN SHERRILL

*September*

## 🕯 TIME ON THE RIVER

*Wed 21*  *Let us lift up our heart ... unto God....*
—LAMENTATIONS 3:41

**IN THE LOCKS**

I woke with a start. It was unnaturally dark outside our cabin; no lights blinking along the shore. I stepped to the window, where a wall of some sort was moving downward an inch at a time. And then I realized that we were in one of the famous locks that would ingeniously lift our huge ship nine hundred feet from the level of Antwerp to that of Basel.

I went topside to watch. The ship's motors were silent, only its running lights lit the sides of the gray, dripping wall. Slowly our ship rose until we were at the new, higher, river level. The lock gates opened, our engines began to purr and the lights of the control tower slid by.

I have long wondered about four words used when we celebrate the Eucharist at our church back home. "Lift up your hearts," the priest says, and we respond, "We lift them to the Lord." Doesn't this suggest that we are responsible for lifting our hearts, ourselves, out of our troubled spirits?

But perhaps we are responsible only for starting the process, the way the lock master opens the lock's gates, leaving the water to do the rest.

Perhaps when we respond to the command to lift up our hearts by saying that we lift them to the Lord, we're acknowledging that we open the gates. But that's all we do. It's the Lord who does the heavy part, gracefully lifting our loads until we can see our way home.

*Lord, today may I play my role in dealing with the troubles before me—*
*may I open myself to You so that You can do the lifting.*
—JOHN SHERRILL

*September*

# TIME ON THE RIVER

**Thu 22** *Thy word is . . . a light unto my path.* —Psalm 119:105

### THE LORELEI

I was on deck that foggy morning as the Lorelei loomed out of the mist. I'd read about this rocky promontory jutting out into water so treacherous that legends grew up about lovely sirens living on the rock and luring boatmen to their deaths. *Lorelei* means "luring rocks."

The danger was real enough. This was the narrowest reach of the Rhine: a branch floating in the water raced past us almost too fast for my eyes to follow. Submerged rocks have ripped the bottom off many vessels. A sharp bend in the river keeps upcoming peril out of sight.

Today, however, the dangers of the Lorelei are mostly a memory. As I looked left and right, I saw navigation aids everywhere: guiding lights blinking dimly through the fog, buoys marking the safe channel. On a visit to the wheelhouse, the captain had pointed out the radar that lets him spot oncoming traffic even in the worst of weather.

I couldn't help but relate this to the situation Tib and I face as we move away from friends and church and familiar resources into the unknown waters of a new location. Doubtless, there are shoals ahead, hidden snares, blind corners, change coming faster than we can follow. But we, too, have navigation aids. We have praying friends, we have family, we have the Bible, we have nightly reading from the writings of travelers who've marked the channel before us.

*And these things, not the risks ahead*, I thought as the Lorelei slipped silently and safely by, *are what I must keep in mind.*

*As I approach my own Lorelei, Father, show me*
*the navigation aids You will provide.*
—John Sherrill

*September*

## 🕯 TIME ON THE RIVER

*Fri 23*    *Consider the lilies of the field....* —MATTHEW 6:28

**GOING AND BEING**

The first thing I noticed that early morning, wrapped in a blanket on a deck chair, was the primitive, watery smell that hung in the air as our ship glided up the Rhine. What was it? Fish? Diesel oil? The smells of a river! Next there was the cool, moist feel of fog on my face, fog so thick you couldn't see the freight barges until they were almost abreast, and then the cries of gulls, riding our slipstream.

Suddenly we rode out of the mist. And there, on the bike path bordering the river, were scores of cyclists in business suits hastening to work. Behind them on the highway, which paralleled the Rhine, cars and buses sped past. And up in the sky were tic-tac-toe contrails of airplanes moving people to Munich or Tokyo or San Francisco at speeds unimaginable when rivers offered the best way of getting about.

All of these people were *going* somewhere while I had the luxury of *being* somewhere. Most, perhaps, were barely aware of their surroundings as they switched lanes at seventy miles per hour or watched a movie from their airplane seat. I do these things, too, of course. I spend a huge percentage of my time headed elsewhere, and in today's world, speed is inescapable.

But when Jesus traveled the roads of the Holy Land, headed for all-important destinations, intent on His mission, He also took time to enjoy the birds of the air, the rain that fell on the good and the evil, the tall mustard plant that sprang from a tiny seed, the spectacular lilies.

*Help me, Father, bring home from this vacation the wonder of being, even when I have to be going.*
—JOHN SHERRILL

*September*

## 🍇 TIME ON THE RIVER

**Sat 24**  *For I am the Lord, I change not....* —MALACHI 3:6

**AT HOME ABROAD**

From Basel, it was a two-hour drive in our rented car to Geneva, the city where Tib and I made our first home together more than sixty years ago. There it was, just as we remembered it, the stately town rising on its hill above the lake. What a comfort, with the tremendous changes ahead of us, this place that didn't change. Here was the bridge where the Rhone River flows eternally from the lake. There was the *jet d'eau*, still shooting its plume of water 450 feet into the sky, and the white swans forever cruising the riverbank. In Geneva, things stayed the same.

We found a parking place (that was different—a bike rack was all we needed in 1947) and walked up the familiar streets to our old address: 9, rue Calvin. We rang the bell at the massive doors that blocked even a glimpse of the courtyard and the house beyond. We waited a long time, but nobody came. We walked through once-familiar streets now lined with antique shops and boutique hotels. Six times we asked after the de Marignacs, the patrician family who'd opened their home to students in the lean years after the war. Nobody even knew the name.

"I guess nothing stays the same," I said ruefully, "not even Geneva."

"But aren't you glad," said Tib, "that in the years since we lived here, you and I have come to know the One Who doesn't?"

*In all the changes ahead, Father, keep my eyes fixed*
*on Your unchanging love.*
—JOHN SHERRILL

*September*

### Sun 25

*... Abounding with deeds of kindness and charity....*
—Acts 9:36 (NAS)

Mary was a guest speaker at our missionary society meeting, sharing with us her calling to serve as a nurse in equatorial Africa. As she spoke, God seemed to keep prompting me: *Ask her what she needs.* And so as the others chatted over coffee and pastry at the end of our meeting, I approached her.

"Mary, is there anything specific I can do for you?"

"Do you sew?" she asked.

"Yes, I sew almost everything my family wears."

"Would you consider making me a dress? I have everything else ready except for one piece of material for a plain, sleeveless A-line dress."

The following Sunday she handed me a small bag containing a pattern and a folded piece of yellow flowered cotton. Within a few days, I finished the sewing and phoned Mary. "I have your dresses finished," I told her.

"What do you mean, *dresses*?"

"Well, there was enough cloth to make two dresses, so I did."

There was a long pause. "But, Alma, I measured that material, and I wasn't even sure if there was enough for *one*!"

That was thirty years ago, and neither Mary nor I have ever arrived at a satisfactory explanation. "I only know that those dresses were the most carefree, comfortable ones I wore the whole time I served in Africa," she told me when we met again recently.

*Lord, make me responsive to Your Spirit's nudges.*
—Alma Barkman

*September*

## Mon 26
*We must through much tribulation enter into the kingdom of God.* —ACTS 14:22

I've begun to call it Good Idea Hill.

It's the least favorite part of my usual morning run. I jog through our neighborhood, past the school where the teachers are just arriving, past the church and the playground, into the park where, depending on the season, the heather, the azaleas, the dogwood, the peonies, the roses, the daylilies, the poppies, the chrysanthemums bloom. I come around the path to the wide lawn where there's always a jogger or a walker to say "Good morning" to.

But then comes the big hill, a long slow rise on an asphalt road. Sure, there are old elm trees and a blush of impatiens and a view across the Hudson River if I look, but my eyes get glued to the ground and I start thinking, *I'm not going to make it.*

Oddly enough, though, as I push through my fatigue, a lighter stream of thought comes through, telling me, *You should call so-and-so* or *Write a note to such-and-such* or *You should buy your mom X for her birthday.* It's a time when my imagination starts spinning with good ideas. I suppose I could have stumbled on them lying in bed, getting an extra half hour of sleep, but I wouldn't count on it. The combination of endorphins, sunshine, effort and fatigue somehow delivers—and at just the moment when I'm ready to give up. It's like that moment in prayer when you don't think you have anything left to say and you can't imagine what God has to say to you; somehow, prayer happens.

So whatever you're doing, whatever challenges you're facing, stick with the hills. They give back.

*Lord, I will press on and persevere even at those times that are especially tough, because that's often when I come to know You.*
—RICK HAMLIN

*September*

## Tue 27

*What does the Lord require of you But to do justice, to love kindness, And to walk humbly with your God?*
—MICAH 6:8 (NAS)

Sometimes in a darkened room, under the soft light of a reading lamp, an arc of lightning can flash from the page of a book, engraving a sentence in your memory. Some thirty years ago I experienced such a moment while reading Frederick Buechner's short book *Wishful Thinking: A Seeker's ABC*. Buechner was describing the struggle that many of us undergo when we seek God's direction and guidance. He writes: "The place God calls you to be is the place where your deep gladness and the world's deep hunger meet."

Yesterday, a student dropped by to talk with me about her future. She desperately wants to follow God's leadership and is frightened of making a wrong decision. "I don't know whether to go to medical school or to seminary. What should I do?" she asked.

I answered her question with more questions: "Which do you want to do? Which option will bring you the most gladness and joy? Which is the most natural fit for you?"

After a long pause, she said, "Medical school."

And I said, "Go for it!"

God is a god Who creates us uniquely to find and express our greatest gladness and joy. He only asks us to focus our gladness to fill the world's hunger and need.

*Father, give me the courage to follow my gladness and
joy in the service of others.*
—SCOTT WALKER

*September*

## ADVICE FROM AUNT ANNIE

**Wed 28**   *In all thy ways acknowledge him, and he shall direct thy paths.* —PROVERBS 3:6

**CHOOSING YOUR RUT**

When I retired, I abandoned daily routines and schedules. I was slow completing assignments and kept putting off household chores. Where did the time go? It's embarrassing to admit, but I frittered away much of it reading mystery novels and playing bridge on my computer.

Aunt Annie came to the rescue in a story that featured an intriguing sign she'd spotted on a Georgia road: Choose Your Rut Carefully. You'll Be in It for the Next 30 Miles.

I live in the country, and when it rains, each vehicle that makes its way down our dirt roads leaves ruts. I'm two and a half miles from pavement, not thirty, but to avoid getting stuck, I try to choose a rut that's shallow enough so that my car doesn't scrape the road, yet deep enough to have a solid bottom.

Unless you're a car, however, ruts have a bad name. Aunt Annie acknowledged that ruts can be harmful and cause people to stagnate. Nevertheless, she wrote, "My God-directed, carefully selected rut allows me to be productive, efficient and truly enjoy life. If teaching Spanish my whole career is a rut, so be it! New students each year made my twenty-fifth year of teaching just as rewarding as my first."

I've chosen a rut too. It includes routines such as my morning coffee and daily devotions, scheduled periods to complete work projects, and time for household chores. With tasks accomplished, I have plenty of time for family and friends. I even have time to read a few novels and play an occasional game of bridge!

*Keep my rut shallow enough for new experiences, Lord, but deep enough to lead me safely home to You.*
—PENNEY SCHWAB

## September

### Thu 29
*With all thy getting get understanding.* —Proverbs 4:7

We never knew how old my grandfather (*Zeyde* in Yiddish) actually was. He didn't know when he'd been born or how old he was when he left Russia and came to America. When Zeyde was hospitalized for gallbladder surgery, we guessed he was in his late nineties.

Zeyde had worked in his body shop in South Philadelphia, pounding the dents out of car fenders and bumpers, until the day before they put him in the hospital. I hadn't seen him for the past couple of years; I had moved to Los Angeles and it wasn't as if I knew him well. He spoke Yiddish and I spoke none, so we had never really had a conversation. My father and uncles spoke with him, but I never understood what they were saying and I didn't try. Yiddish was an old language; I couldn't see the point.

However, when my father called and told me that the surgery had taken too much out of Zeyde and that it was unlikely he would ever leave the hospital, I flew back to Philadelphia to see him.

In the hospital, Zeyde's three sons had been taking turns translating for him and the doctors and nurses. The afternoon that it was my dad's turn, I went with him, kissed and greeted my grandfather, and then stood quietly in the corner of the room, listening to talk I didn't understand, until it was time to leave.

I turned to go out the door but heard Zeyde call me back. When I got to the bed, he took my hand and asked in heavily accented English, "Rhoda, you got hippies in California?" Surprised, I started to laugh and said we did. He nodded and let go of my hand.

In that moment, he had said good-bye to me and said it very well.

*Help me, God, to remember that sometimes words don't really have a lot to do with communicating.*
—Rhoda Blecker

*September*

*Fri 30*  *Though thy beginning was small, yet thy latter end should greatly increase.* —Job 8:7

I've quit walking—again!" I grumbled to my son Jeremy. "Start over small," he quickly suggested, "and work your way up." I preferred to bellyache.

Days later, I stopped by Jeremy's tiny apartment to share a cake I'd baked with him. He lived in a huge brick complex with no yard whatsoever. A few years before, Jeremy had lived in a neat, older house and had created a magnificent yard. Back then, he owned a landscaping company. All of his customers raved about his green thumb. But bipolar disorder turned Jeremy into someone else; he lost everything. Then, over the past two years, he'd made a grueling turnaround. He took his medications faithfully, attended AA and Celebrate Recovery meetings, went to church, learned to live frugally and simply in his little apartment, and landed a routine job for which he was immensely grateful.

Just outside his front door sat a large clay pot brimming with pansies. As the morning sun welcomed the new flowers, Jeremy hurried out to my car. "Well, how do you like my garden?" he asked enthusiastically. "I found the pot at the apartment Dumpster and the pansies were on sale."

I got out of my car, and together we admired Jeremy's garden in the golden morning. "One day I'll have a real yard again," he said. "But this is a beginning."

I went out for a walk the next day. It wasn't my usual four miles, but it was a beginning.

*Show me, Father, where in my life You want me to take that one small step.*
—Marion Bond West

## September

**SEEDS OF LOVE**

1 _____

2 _____

3 _____

4 _____

5 _____

6 _____

7 _____

8 _____

9 _____

10 _____

*September*

11 ___

12 ___

13 ___

14 ___

15 ___

16 ___

17 ___

18 ___

19 ___

20 ___

21 ___

*September*

22 _____

23 _____

24 _____

25 _____

26 _____

27 _____

28 _____

29 _____

30 _____

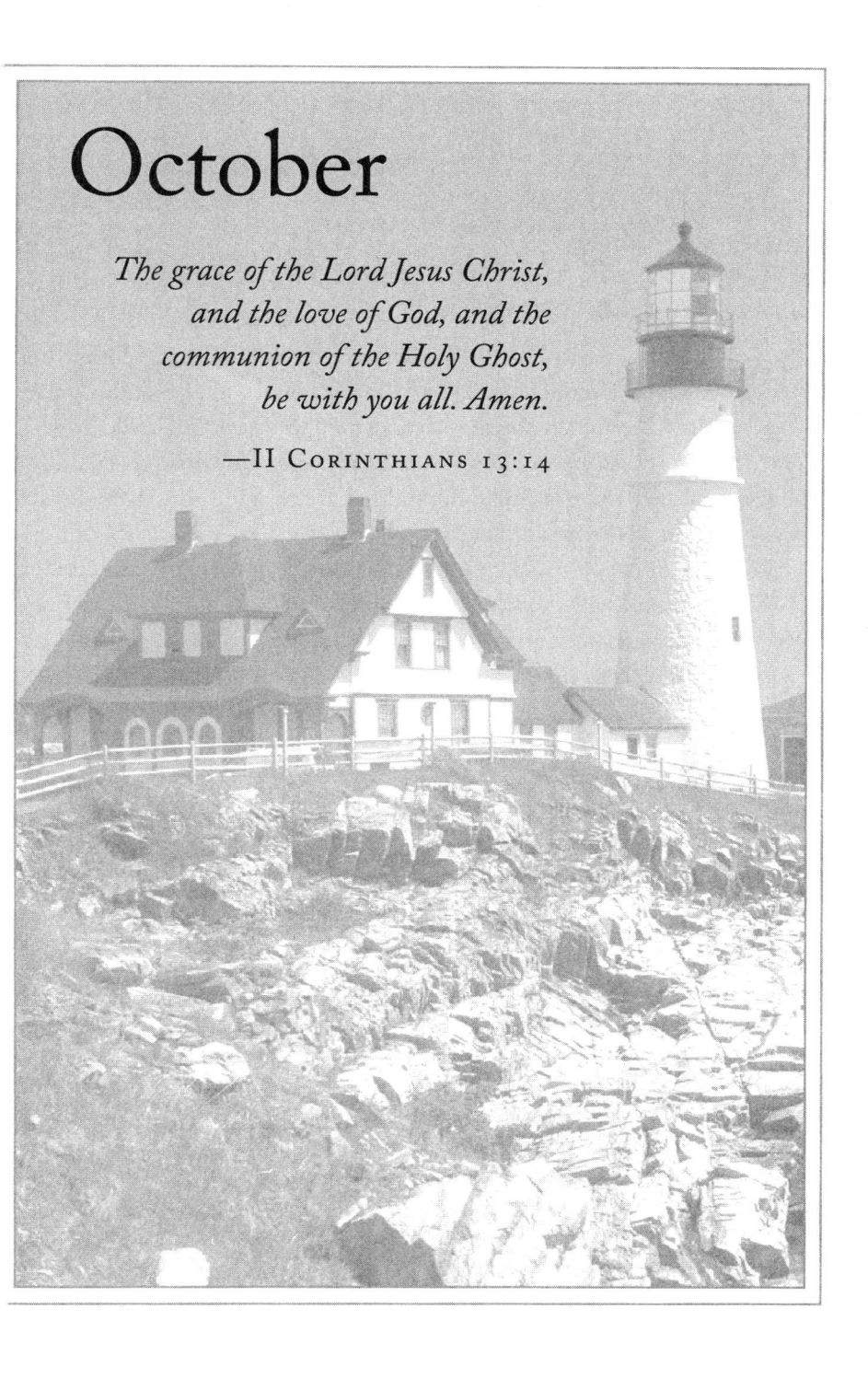

# October

*The grace of the Lord Jesus Christ,
and the love of God, and the
communion of the Holy Ghost,
be with you all. Amen.*

—II CORINTHIANS 13:14

*October*

## ❧ A PATH TO SIMPLICITY

*Sat 1*  *I thank my God in all my remembrance of you.*
—Philippians 1:3 (NAS)

**LISTENING TO MY LIFE**

While giving my home a clean sweep one day, I found myself starting to feel sad. Here I was, living alone in a down-in-the-dumps cabin I called the Leaning Log because everywhere you stood in it, you leaned. *This wasn't where I thought I'd end up, Lord.* Before my divorce, I lived in a newer house, where the plumber didn't have to stand on a ladder to fix the toilet, and the pipes didn't sing.

In a box of papers from college, I discovered an old vinyl jewelry box I hadn't seen in years. Soon I was tackling a tangle of chains, dusty rings and earrings without mates. Once upon a time, the objects had sparkled with promise as they marked milestones: a too-small onyx ring my mother gave me when I graduated from high school; pendants with semiprecious stones an old boyfriend bought me for every imaginable holiday. He had a landscaping business, and one of his customers who owned a jewelry store offered him great deals.

*It's a pity you no longer enjoy these treasures, Roberta.* While most of them weren't terribly costly, treasures they were. I filled a bulging freezer bag with them and went to see a local jewelry designer. "You have a great variety here," he said. "I see these made into a slide bracelet like the Victorians used to wear."

When I picked up the completed bracelet, the jeweler's daughter fastened it around my wrist. "I love the pearl earrings," she said, pointing to a pair of them circled with tiny diamonds that her father had crafted into a single charm. "And this cameo. From your grandmother, did you say? Why, Roberta, you've led a charmed life."

> *As I simplify my house and my feelings, Lord, I can see You there*
> *at every juncture of my very charmed life.*
> —Roberta Messner

*October*

## Sun 2

*When we bless the cup at the Lord's Table, aren't we sharing in the blood of Christ? And when we break the bread, aren't we sharing in the body of Christ?*
—I Corinthians 10:16 (nlt)

Today is World Communion Sunday.

First, our congregation will share in the breaking of bread, symbolizing the Lord's body, which was broken for us, followed by the wine, depicting the blood He shed for us. Before this, each of us will have searched our hearts and asked forgiveness for any wrongs we may have done.

After the service is over, we'll head for the fellowship hall, where my husband and I will join other families pulling out dishes from picnic baskets—or the kitchen's ovens—and putting them on serving tables.

My contribution is always the same: a chicken-rice casserole. We can count on Mrs. Brown's cherry cobbler. And Brother Jim will don his usual chef's hat and apron to bear in a mammoth platter of barbecued ribs. And so goes the food parade until the counters become kaleidoscopes of color!

Children whose eyes are barely level with the tabletops queue up to eagerly await the pastor's blessing and then begin loading their plates.

It's a happy, yet noisy, place, with all of us chatting, eating, visiting... yes, communing together!

*It is truly Your table, Lord, when Your children gather around it, just as You often did with Your friends so long ago.*
—Isabel Wolseley

*October*

## Mon 3

*"All your children shall be taught by the Lord, And great shall be the peace of your children."* —Isaiah 54:13 (NKJV)

My daughter was about to make another trip abroad with just her backpack. I was worried. How was she going to buy food, find safe places to sleep, travel on reliable modes of transportation? All this cost money, much more than she had.

"Mom, you're just going to have to let go of me," she said impatiently.

But how could I let her go so far away? Wasn't that the same as abandoning my duty as a parent?

About this time, a friend gave me a poem by an unknown author to help me understand what letting go really means:

*To let go does not mean to stop caring; it means I can't do it for someone else.*
*To let go is not to be in the middle, arranging all the outcomes, but to allow other persons to affect their own destinies.*
*To let go is not to fix but to be supportive.*
*To let go is not to be protective; it's to permit another to face reality.*
*To let go is to fear less and to love more.*
*When you love someone deeply, letting go is incredibly hard.*
*But I realized I must let go, for I do not own what I love.*

Now, when I look at my daughter happily settled in Australia with the man she loves, doing work she's passionate about, I know that God has done much more than I could have imagined. And it happened because I got out of the way and let Him do it.

*Father, thank You for Your promise that "all your children shall be taught by the Lord, and great shall be the peace of your children" (Isaiah 54:13, NKJV).*
—Helen Grace Lescheid

*October*

## Tue 4

*"Blessed is he who blesses you...."*
—Numbers 24:9 (NKJV)

I called my friend Camilla with a request: "Next time you're in the neighborhood, could you stop by? I'd like a serious prayer session. I need a blessing, and you're such a good prayer."

A few days later Camilla knocked on my door. We soon settled on the couch, across the room from Kitty, who lounged on a ledge. Camilla dabbed oil on my head. We opened our hands, which rested on our knees; we closed our eyes to minimize distractions. Camilla talked to God on my behalf. I silently assented.

After several minutes, I heard a familiar patter. Kitty was on the move. As if she wanted to join our team, she jumped up between us. I opened my eyes to see her licking Camilla's hands. Then she turned and found mine. She briefly settled herself in my lap before quietly stepping down to the cushion. She stopped to give Camilla, still praying, a final friendly lick—an amen. Her mission accomplished, she returned to her perch.

On the church calendar, today is the Feast of Saint Francis of Assisi, known for his love of creation and its creatures. Some churches commemorate the day by welcoming pets and giving each a personal blessing. This morning I placed my hand on Kitty's head and then on her paws. I said a prayer over her that started with gratitude for the blessing I sensed she'd given me.

*Lord, I open my heart to receive the blessings You faithfully give, sometimes even by way of furry friends.*
—Evelyn Bence

*October*

## Wed 5

*What is man that you are mindful of him, the son of man that you care for him?* —PSALM 8:4 (NIV)

Everyone has a friend like Robin—someone who is way beyond wise. We were having lunch and . . . well, we *weren't* having lunch. Kevin, our waiter, was apologetic about the delay and kept us happy with breadsticks and topped-up water glasses. While we waited, Robin inquired about the usual suspects: family, work, writing.

Suddenly I said, "You know, I'm none of those things."

"Sorry?" Robin asked.

"I mean I'm not *only* those things. I'm a dad, I teach, I write, but they aren't who I am. They don't control me. And I'm getting mortally tired—"

Just then Kevin interrupted with another mea culpa and more bread. "I'll do my best to make things better," he said before he left.

"Of being in a box," Robin said, finishing my sentence. "You're chafing at the definitions. You're more than the sum of your parts."

"Yes. I want to get past the dad conversations or the teacher-student conversations . . ."

"And connect on some deeper level," Robin said, reading my mind.

I sat back. "Right." I paused. "Now what?"

She laughed. "Welcome to the human race. People take a lifetime trying to figure those things out."

At that moment, I realized I was a waiter in my own drama—not the chef, not the patron, but the guy running from table to table to attend to the many items that make up a life. I wasn't in control; my job was to serve, as best I could, and see what I could do to make things better, and spend my blessed life—blessed with friends like Robin, blessed with our daily bread and blessed with the prayerful times like this—trying to figure those things out.

*Lord, it's much easier for me to do my job when I'm not also trying to do Yours.*
—MARK COLLINS

## Thu 6

*October*

*And walk in love, as Christ also hath loved us....*
—EPHESIANS 5:2

"Mom, may I do a project from this book?" I glanced up at Maggie and, having ascertained that the project involved neither explosions nor Krazy Glue (it was a computer book), gave my okay. Twenty minutes later, my eight-year-old presented me with four carefully designed coupons. They read:

*This coupon is good for making me make my bed once.*
*This coupon is good for making me clean up fifty things once.*
*This coupon is good for making me do an extra two pages of math twice.*
*This coupon is good for letting you alone for two hours once.*

You can tell a lot about my number-four child—and her relationship with me—from these. Maggie's my artsy girl, the messy one who can't sit still. She has a great heart and a terrible memory for chores. She makes PowerPoint presentations for fun and designs thoughtful cards on the computer. She loses things constantly. She loves to snuggle. She has a temper. Maggie feels life with an intensity I'm not sure I understand. I wish I knew how to reach her better. To that end, I offer the following:

*This coupon is good for having me keep my mouth shut once when you lose something.*
*This coupon is good for one reprieve from picking up that huge mess.*
*This coupon is good for two interruptions.*
*This coupon is good for three extra hugs a day, the tight kind you really like, forever.*

I love you, Maggie. I'm sorry neither of us is perfect, but love doesn't require perfection. It just requires you and me and God.

*Lord, thank You for loving me even in my weaknesses.*
—JULIA ATTAWAY

## October

### Fri 7

*"Do not be afraid; you will not suffer shame. Do not fear disgrace; you will not be humiliated...."* —ISAIAH 54:4 (NIV)

I was very tense when I went into the plumbing supply store. I hate to ask for help, especially when I don't know exactly what I'm asking for. But my sink had a minor leak and, unfortunately, "waiting for it to heal itself" had not been a good plan of action.

I explained what was wrong, and the storekeeper told me what part I seemed to need and kindly wrote down instructions for me. I went home and fooled around with the wrench and the part. But the part was stuck, so I yanked it... and yanked it... until it broke. Now the sink was really leaking, not just dripping. So I had to go back to the store and ask for help again. *Please don't let me feel embarrassed, God.*

I could hear a voice from the back. "Tell her to get a plastic one. They're better."

"But I thought that last time," I protested. "You told me that metal was better."

"Last time? Is that the same lady who was here before?" Everybody in the store turned to stare at me.

The storekeeper came around to the front and peered at me from behind his tortoiseshell half-glasses. "I know exactly what you should do," he said.

"Yes?" I squeaked.

"Call a plumber!"

At that *I* laughed. And he handed me a card with the name of a plumber on it.

By that evening, my sink was fixed, my drip was gone and I'd learned that sometimes asking for help is a very good idea.

> *God, You didn't decree that everything in life has to be a do-it-yourself project. Thank You for letting me know—loud and clear—when it's time to ask for help.*
> —LINDA NEUKRUG

*October*

**Sat 8** *So be sensitive and courteous to the others... Don't eat or say or do things that might interfere with the free exchange of love.*
—ROMANS 14:21 (MSG)

The morning of the annual Texas-Oklahoma football game, I was scheduled to speak to a group of young men in Austin, Texas. However, I had a problem—a little one, I thought. I was a varsity letterman at OU and I wanted to wear my OU ball cap. But something told me that my red cap just might turn that fellowship hall into a bull ring and that my witness would go up in smoke.

I still felt a little uneasy and said to God, "This is a *ball cap* we're talking about, Lord. Do You think my wearing it could possibly cause those young men not to hear what I'm coming to share with them about You?"

God was silent.

With a borrowed UT ball cap in my briefcase and an OU cap on my head, I walked onstage before a hundred young University of Texas fans. "Good morning," I said. "I really love the Lord. I also went to OU. How do you feel about that?"

The reaction was a little wild, an instantaneous and room-filling roar of boos. I was shocked at their intensity.

I reached into my briefcase and switched caps. Then I said, "I also got a degree at UT and I'm a member of the UT Alumni Association. Does that make any difference?"

There was a pause and then cheers and applause that were even louder than the boos.

Ordinarily, no one cares what I wear when I speak. But that morning I just might have lost an opportunity to help some lonely, troubled young men find the new and loving life God offers us all. Thank God for "hat tricks."

*Dear Lord, thank You for reminding me of where my deepest loyalty lies.*
—KEITH MILLER

*October*

## ❀ TO SAY GOOD-BYE

*Sun 9*   *There am I in the midst of them.*
—MATTHEW 18:20

**JUST AS I AM**

It is Sunday morning. Our days at Hillsboro Presbyterian Church are numbered. In just under three months we will go out and find our way to whatever it is we are going to do next. My husband David will no longer be the senior minister; I will no longer be the preacher's wife. I like the idea of being introduced to people by my own name. Beyond this tiny perk, our future is unknown. I sit in a pew (the third from the back) and consider the pleasure of having a husband to sit with in church, at weddings and funerals—one more perk.

As the sermon begins, a moment of quiet clarity comes. The sun falls through a stained-glass window; a shaft of light shoots across the big cross in the sanctuary. Suddenly, in the middle of David's sermon, a stillness falls over the congregation. There are only his words and a hush so distinct it's as though the entire building is holding its breath. In this fleeting moment, I see things as they are.

Through these years, in spite of all our differences, all of us at Hillsboro have come together as one—one people, tired and scarred, often frightened and unsure, beautiful in our humanity, magnificent in our longing for our Creator.

I know each person here. I know their imperfections as well as they know mine. Yet, in this one instant, I see them as God must: just as they are. And just as they are, I love them.

> *Father, let me take this lesson with me: to strive to see others in the way I want You to see me—just as I am.*
> —PAM KIDD

*October*

## Mon 10

*"See, I am doing a new thing! Now it springs up; do you not perceive it?..."*—Isaiah 43:19 (NIV)

My twelve-year-old cousin Grace was visiting from Arizona, and I wanted her visit to go just right. I checked theater times, weather forecasts and bus schedules—frantic to make her visit work out perfectly. Fortified with all this information, I emerged from my bedroom the first morning of Grace's visit and announced I'd created the "perfect plan" for our day ahead. With Grace watching, I wrote out a list titled "The Perfect Plan": "Go out to breakfast on Broadway. Walk to Central Park. Ride double-decker bus to sightsee."

It sounded good. But then Grace and I ended up talking and eating cereal and fruit in my apartment, and it was already ten o'clock. So we revised the list. I wrote, "Perfect Plan #2: Sightsee on bus. Have lunch in Chinatown. Walk in park at 59th Street."

But Grace and I were having so much fun talking in our pj's that suddenly it was close to noon. *Oops.* "Perfect Plan #3," I wrote. "Sandwiches in park. Walk to Rockefeller Center. Check half-price tickets for Broadway show."

But then we started looking at family photographs and had tuna salad out of my refrigerator and played with my cat Sheila and...

You get the picture. By the time we actually put on our clothes, went out and simply wandered around my bustling Upper West Side neighborhood, our itinerary was much more loosely structured. It was just, "Be together and have fun!" The perfect plan!

*Dear God, help me to give up my frenzied overplanning and enjoy each day as it unfolds.*
—Mary Ann O'Roark

*October*

## Tue 11

*They were but flesh; a wind that passeth away, and cometh not again.* —Psalm 78:39

While cleaning my desk this morning, I found a get-well card addressed to my friend Susan. Over the past two years I've tried to support her as she bravely adapted to life with bone cancer. We've shared chats in the break room at work, e-mail jokes, updates on our gardens, assurances in prayer and these greeting cards. I've watched her lose her steady gait, her hair, her energy, her color—but never her wry smile.

Perhaps her upbeat attitude lulled us into denying the seriousness of her condition until she tearfully confided, "I just want to see my son graduate from high school next month." She did. Then, within a few weeks, her health deteriorated and she went home to God.

Now here I am, a month after her funeral, holding a card filled with loving wishes that Susan will never know. Did I become distracted? Need a stamp? Bury her card under other unfinished and perhaps well-intentioned business? I'll never know.

I try to convince myself that Susan knew how much I cared about her, that I did enough, that one card more or less didn't matter. But it hurts to know I missed one last chance to say "I love you" to someone who needed to hear it. With God's help, I'll never miss such a chance again.

*Loving God, help me to follow through in delivering the love in my heart.*
—Gail Thorell Schilling

## Wed 12

*Wait for the Lord; be strong and take heart and wait for the Lord.* —Psalm 27:14 (NIV)

It arrived today: a nice summer shirt, out of nowhere, totally unexpected. Okay, not quite; I ordered it online.

Online shopping is the perfect solution for a congenitally impatient person such as myself: no crowds; no checkout lines; no tables of picked-over items; no taking a number to get a dressing room and then parading yourself in front of a bunch of strangers; no eager young sales associates trying to up-sell you and having to feel guilty about saying, "No, thank you, I just want this." Yes, you have to delay your gratification a little bit, but with express shipping, you get your items pretty fast.

Except for this shirt.

I must have ordered it when I picked out some stuff a few months ago. I vaguely remember something I wanted being on back order, which is usually a deal-killer for me. I'm shocked that I didn't delete it from my shopping cart. Then today the shirt showed up. "I remember you," I said, taking it out of its shipping bag.

I was very glad to see the shirt. It was a kind of delayed instant gratification moment—a long time coming, but a surprise too. Yet I also couldn't help being reminded of all the things I pray for, and my impatience with a timing that isn't my own. I don't want back-ordered answers to prayers; I want express shipping. Yet time and again throughout my life, prayers that I've nearly forgotten have been answered in ways wondrous and unforeseeable. I'm learning to be patient in what I ask and to allow God to work as He sees fit. And what I'm learning most is that the more patient I am, the more I'm able to recognize an answer to prayer. Even in something as inconsequential as a mail-order shirt.

*Lord, help me to learn that all prayers get answered, just not necessarily when I want them to.*
—Edward Grinnan

*October*

## Thu 13

*"You have blessed the work of his hands...."*
—Job 1:10 (NIV)

It's been a full year since I took knitting lessons at our local yarn shop. I'd like to tell you that knitting came easily for me and that I was able to give my family handmade items for their birthdays. But the truth is, I haven't been the quickest learner. And I'm prone to sticking my knitting in the top of my closet for months at a time. But I am working on a project: a scarf, ice blue with charcoal flecks. Inch by painfully slow inch, I'd made my way through two skeins of yarn when disaster struck: a knot—huge, hairy, impossible! I had no idea what to do.

Then I thought of Sue. Sue has been knitting since she was seven years old and creates the most wonderful sweaters and shawls. When I took my snarled yarn to her, she took one look at the mangled mess, smiled and said, "I can fix this." I watched in awe as she did. In and out, over and back, again and again—slowly the tangles disappeared into smooth blue lines.

"I thought you'd cut it," I said as she handed my restored project back to me.

Sue shook her head. "Never cut what you can untie."

It was good advice; advice I could apply to some difficult relationships that had plagued me lately. Maybe with patience—and skill—these things, too, could be restored.

It was something to think about while I knit.

*Keep me, Lord, from being in a hurry to sever what
You would have me work through.*
—Mary Lou Carney

*October*

## Fri 14

*"Their children will see it and be joyful...."*
—ZECHARIAH 10:7 (NIV)

Kassidy, our neighbors' little daughter, knows that her pets are part of the rural food chain. While her cats hunt for mice at night, they are being hunted in turn by larger predators. The cats learn to climb fast and high to survive.

Kassidy awoke one morning to discover that her favorite cat Spook had climbed their power pole and was afraid to climb down. It broke her heart (and mine!) to hear her cat meowing pitifully. "I prayed to God," she said. "He fixes everything. God knows how much I love Spook."

Kassidy put a dish of food at the base of the power pole; Spook ignored it and stayed atop the pole. Owls, hawks and eagles occasionally circled nearby, waiting for the cat to weaken and become easy prey.

When Kassidy's father came home, he passed a loop of rope through a long piece of plastic pipe, lifted the pipe to the top of the pole and lassoed Spook. A very surprised cat was tugged from her perch and lowered to the ground and to a waiting Kassidy.

To Kassidy, her dad now occupies a pedestal far taller than that power pole. She believes her dad is the answer to her prayer, and I agree with her. I can't look at her and come to any other conclusion.

*Thank You, God, for daughters and the fathers who love them.*
—TIM WILLIAMS

### READER'S ROOM

God speaks to me through my cat Charlie. Charlie is about as affectionate as a cat can be. He loves me and he lets me know it every day by rubbing against my legs as I feed him, by running to meet me when I'm outdoors, and by sitting in my lap and purring. I know that Charlie loves me because I first loved him. And I know that's why I love God: He first loved me, met my needs and took me in. —*Linda Parent, Chouteau, Oklahoma*

*October*

## Sat 15

*They will still bear fruit in old age, they will stay fresh and green.* —PSALM 92:14 (NIV)

"Ye-haw!" the young attendant exclaimed as he slowed the chairlift, which scooped up the four of us and began to lift us over a meadow of wildflowers, high in the Colorado Rockies. Here we were, four women in our early sixties, celebrating nearly thirty years of friendship with a festive fall weekend in Beaver Creek.

Once at the summit, we jumped off the lift, checked a trail map and selected a six-mile trek across the mountain to a lake. Soon we were off, following the trail through tall aspen trees and catching up on all that had happened in our lives since our last rendezvous four years earlier. We've added and subtracted family members with weddings, new grandbabies and the deaths of parents. We've faced surgeries, dealt with cancer and the realities of our own aging.

No wonder we were lost in our own chatter as we came out of the trees into an open meadow. Suddenly, Anne shouted, "A bear!"

Sure enough, across the meadow, a bear was on the trail, eating something and totally uninterested in us. Awed and fearful, we snapped several pictures before turning back to choose a different trail through the trees and then down the mountain.

All the way down, we kept pausing and gazing up at the tall aspen trees growing together and towering above us. They were solidly rooted in the ground at our feet but stretched up toward the sunlight where the tippy tops of new green leaves swayed gently in the breeze.

Anne took some pictures of the trees and later gave me a framed copy, which is on my desk, reminding me how good friends grow together: firmly rooted and shielding each other from life's harshest realities, while still stretching toward the sun, where the places of new growth lean into the wind.

*Father, I am grateful for friendships that help
me grow according to Your plan.*
—CAROL KUYKENDALL

*October*

## Sun 16

*I want you to speak confidently, so that those who have believed God will be careful to engage in good deeds....*
—TITUS 3:8 (NAS)

For twenty-three years my wife Ruby and I were chairpersons of seven Trash-and-Treasure tables at our fall church fair. When we volunteered, some of our co-workers objected. They had visited fairs and had seen white-elephant tables. They didn't want such junk-filled tables near the handmade aprons and knits, the food and baked goods, and the country store.

We took their feelings to heart and were careful. Everything—jewelry, glasses, dishes, pots, pans and lamps—was cleaned. Each table was covered with a white cloth. Then we brought in pillows, blankets, tables, chairs, radios and electrical appliances. Somehow we found space for toys, tools, paint and paintings, plus one air conditioner. We spent forty hours arranging and pricing more than five thousand items steeped with memories, donated by people who were moving or downsizing or who had lost a loved one.

Our Trash-and-Treasure tables were a financial success, but more important was the fellowship and goodwill they generated. Over those two days, the parish family—those who worked, those who donated and those who bought—learned how much they were needed.

*Overseeing Savior, thank You for allowing us to serve You by supporting the place where we worship You.*
—OSCAR GREENE

*October*

## Mon 17
*Love never ends....* —I Corinthians 13:8 (esv)

Behind all his rough, tough and rugged ways, my husband John was an incurable romantic.

From the time of our courtship through our forty-five years of marriage, to the very day he died, I was the recipient of love notes—sometimes stuffed in each finger of my gloves—messages scrawled in shaving cream on the bathroom mirror and the delightful surprise of bouquets of "no-occasion flowers." I savor the memory of the first delivery of such a bouquet and replay it over and over to joy my heart, like the lilting refrain from a favorite piece of music.

It was an in-between month, with no holidays, birthdays or other celebrations. Midmorning, I was catching up with the laundry when the doorbell rang. I was greeted by a grinning florist handing me a glorious arrangement of flowers in the soft, romantic colors I love: stargazer lilies, pink roses and fragrant stocks, all framed with fern and baby's breath. My husband's card read, "Just to say, each day I love you more!"

This afternoon when I went out to get the mail, I found a bouquet of handpicked flowers on the front porch with a note: "No occasion, just remembering!" There were tears in my eyes when I phoned to thank the friend who left them.

*You have given me memories of love, blessed Lord, to be the melody of the soul that keeps my heart singing now and throughout eternity.*
—Fay Angus

*October*

**Tue 18**  Then Peter said, *"Silver and gold I do not have, but what I do have I give you...."* —ACTS 3:6 (NKJV)

In my college days there was a student whom no one liked. For one thing, she was bony, with ratty hair and a spotty complexion. Add to that, sloppy dress and an in-your-face personality.

Wherever this student went, she talked about money. "Someday I'm going to be rich," she would boast. "Someday I'm going to live in a big house, drive a Mercedes and wear designer clothes."

It didn't take us long to figure out that what she was really saying was that "Someday I'm going to be loved and respected." She was convinced that if she could just win the lottery, everything else would be fine.

What she really needed (and got) was a wise and caring dorm mother to sit down with her and have a long talk about hygiene and manners. The transformation was slow, but it got a boost when a young man noticed her. The subject of money dropped out of her conversation.

Sometimes it's hard for me to remember that obnoxious behavior in my college students is really a cry for help. It's even harder for me to find the courage to sit down with them and have the long talk. But then I think back on all the family and friends who took the time to challenge me and what a difference it made.

The "long talk" doesn't have to be unpleasant. Sometimes people just need a few gentle suggestions such as, "I think you should clean up your language a bit" or "I know you can do this."

*Help me, Lord, to be a true friend by speaking the truth in love.*
—DANIEL SCHANTZ

*October*

## Wed 19

*When life is heavy and hard to take, go off by yourself. Enter the silence. Bow in prayer. Don't ask questions: Wait for hope to appear. Don't run from trouble. Take it full-face. The "worst" is never the worst.*
—Lamentations 3:28–30 (msg)

My walking partner Martha is sassy, irreverent and just plain fun, so it was something of a shock to see tears in her eyes when we met.

"We lost everything in the stock market," she explained. Martha and her husband are both retired and live on their investment income. Their entire nest egg was gone, and Martha was devastated.

To my surprise, she met me the following morning with a big smile. "It's going to be okay," she said. Her sister had e-mailed her a note that said, "If God brings you to it, He will see you through it." The message lingered in her mind, and later that day as she shopped in a local department store, the most amazing thing happened. Martha had stopped to look at a ring on a counter display. It took her a moment to realize the inside of the ring had an inscription. It read: "If God brings you to it, He will see you through it."

While Martha badly needed the reassurance God offered her that day, it was something I needed to be reminded of too: God is our Father. He willingly, lovingly supplies all my needs. No matter what happens in my life, He will always be at my side.

*You fulfill my every need, Father. May I always turn to You instead of relying on my own resources, no matter what the situation.*
—Debbie Macomber

*October*

## Thu 20

*The Lord, your God, is in your midst....*
—Zephaniah 3:17 (nrsv)

I live in Michigan and work in Chicago. That's about 150 miles each way. On Monday morning, I climb into the car for the two-and-a-half- to three-hour drive; Tuesday evening, into the car and home; Wednesday morning, another long drive; same with Friday evening.

I can't say I always approached that drive with a heart grateful for meaningful work and for a family who graciously made their own adjustments to accommodate my schedule. In fact, there have been many times when I got rather grumbly about it.

Until the morning at church when I was talking with my friend Todd. "Oh, I used to make that drive regularly too," he said brightly. "Good times!"

"Good times?" I responded in that grumbly tone of mine. "How could that drive be good times?"

He smiled. "Maybe I should better describe it as God times," he said. "Three hours just to talk to God—and listen for God talking to me. I could never make that kind of time for myself otherwise."

I can honestly say I'm now less grumbly. And it's not because I don't have to make that long drive all the time; I do. I just try to do it differently: a little less complaining to myself and a little more talking to God.

*In those quiet spaces of my life, oh, God, help me to listen for You instead of filling them with my own noise.*
—Jeff Japinga

*October*

## Fri 21

*And if children, heirs also, heirs of God and fellow heirs with Christ....* —ROMANS 8:17 (NAS)

I was once called a "Lazarus project" by a well-meaning person patiently listening to me run on about what my life was missing. I didn't like the inference. In Luke 16, Lazarus is a poor man covered in sores, begging for crumbs at a rich man's gate.

*I am not a beggar,* I fumed. But what else was I when I hungered for a "happiness handout" from the things I wanted but didn't have? And what did that say about my walk with Jesus?

"I am a fellow heir with Christ in God's kingdom," I reminded myself. "I have every resource of God open to me. What am I doing seeking satisfaction anywhere else?"

Then something inside me began to right itself. Instead of looking in worldly directions for a handout, I felt the power of Jesus like a mighty hand up, lifting me from the longings that were impoverishing me. All the must-haves and should-have-beens in my life seemed to vanish in those breathtaking, timeless words, *fellow heir.* They spoke a deep, rich fulfillment, a completeness that said I didn't need to beg from this world . . . ever.

*Jesus, help me, as a fellow heir, to know the fullness of Your glory.*
—CAROL KNAPP

EDITOR'S NOTE: *Monday, November 21, will be Guidepost's annual Thanksgiving Day of Prayer. Please plan to join all the members of our Guideposts family in prayer on this very special day. Send your prayer requests (and a picture, if you can—but remember that we won't be able to return it) to Day of Prayer, PO Box 5813, Harlan, Iowa 51593-1313, fax them to (845) 855-1178, call them into (845) 704-6080 (Monday through Friday, 7:00 AM to 10:00 PM EDT) or visit us on the Web at OurPrayer.org.*

*October*

## Sat 22

*Blessed are they that do his commandments, that they may have right to the tree of life, and may enter in through the gates into the city.* —REVELATION 22:14

I'd set aside the day to landscape the west side of our house. Armed with heavy-duty leather gloves, clippers, a wheelbarrow and determination, I began to cut down the thick thornbushes.

Clipping was hard work, and no matter how careful I was, thorns managed to pierce through my clothing. Taking a break, I moved on to the trees.

Grapevines and ivy choked the trunks of evergreens, apple trees and a few others I couldn't identify. *How funny,* I thought. *I've walked here so many times, yet I never noticed these trees.* Collecting leaves, I decided to go inside and research the trees on the Internet. Identifying them online was more difficult than I thought it would be. I brought the clippings next door to my mom's house.

"Do you have any idea what these trees are?" I asked.

She went into the other room and came back with a book. "This was your granddad's," she said. "He loved trees."

"Really?" I asked. My grandfather had died long before I was born, and I knew very little about him. As I flipped through the book, pressed leaf clippings emerged from the pages. "Were all these his?"

Mom nodded. "He wanted to collect every leaf in the book."

I held one of the old pressed leaves up and recognized one of our trees. I focused on the drawing and description in the book. "Well, one of our trees is a catalpa."

Later that day, I sat down with the tree book. I picked up the dried clippings and held the stems. I thought of my roots, of my grandfather taking these very leaves decades ago. I looked out the window. The sun was setting, and on the nearly cleared ground I could see the shadows of our trees: apple and evergreen, catalpa, white ash, blue ash and elm.

*Father, thank You for the many ways You lead me to learning about myself.*
—SABRA CIANCANELLI

*October*

## Sun 23

*Each of you should use whatever gift you have received to serve others, as faithful stewards of God's grace in its various forms.*
—I Peter 4:10 (TNIV)

Once the weather cools, autumn in Phoenix brings a different outdoor fair every weekend. One of the most impressive is the Via Colori Street Painting Festival. Streets are closed so that artists can create murals in chalk pastels on the pavement. We watched, mesmerized, as one artist worked hours on a twelve-by-twelve-foot depiction of a Renaissance mother with her child. Her flowing red robe looked real enough to touch, as did her serene face. Of course, the next day traffic resumed and the masterpieces were gone forever.

I was amazed that these artists had given so much of themselves for something that lasted such a short time. They used their talent to create something beautiful for people to enjoy for a day; not one of them thought beyond it.

I can adopt the same attitude toward the gifts God has given me, knowing that I can't always create something permanent; sometimes I'm called just to meet a need today. This morning our church bulletin asked for food bank volunteers, visitors for the homebound and soup kitchen servers. It isn't work that seems to create a lasting result, but that's not the point. A lot of small efforts that seem to wash away almost as soon as they're completed add up to a life that has made a big difference.

*God, give me the generosity of spirit to use everything You've given me in every way possible to serve You.*
—Gina Bridgeman

*October*

**Mon 24** *Blessed are the peacemakers: for they shall be called the children of God.* —MATTHEW 5:9

She was my childhood idol, a secret hero-worship. The name *Roosevelt* sent my father into a table-pounding tirade. For years I kept a hidden scrapbook of clippings about her work for the neglected and needy.

So when I learned at age nineteen that I was actually going to meet Eleanor Roosevelt, I was ecstatic. It was an unforgettable week for me anyhow. I was about to marry a fellow American student at the University of Geneva, Switzerland—now my husband of sixty-three years.

Mrs. Roosevelt was in Geneva to give a speech on behalf of the newly formed United Nations. On the lecture platform with her were to be the prominent men of the city—and me, chosen to represent the thirty-some Americans studying there.

Arriving early at the town hall, I found myself alone with a tall, gracious, gray-haired woman much handsomer than her photographs. I thought Mrs. Roosevelt would talk about her worldwide concerns. Instead, we talked about me. What was I studying? What were my career plans? When I told her I was to be married four days later, she pressed for details. Later I learned that she'd written about me in her newspaper column, "My Day," expressing her pleasure at meeting a young woman about to be married far from home.

I felt a lot nearer home after those moments in her presence, like an only granddaughter whose plans were of great importance. And I thought, listening to Mrs. Roosevelt afterward share her vision of world peace, that caring for the world at large begins with caring for one person at a time.

*Father, what is the work of peace You have for me today?*
—ELIZABETH SHERRILL

*October*

## Tue 25

*O Lord, thou hast searched me, and known me. Thou knowest my downsitting and mine uprising....* —PSALM 139:1–2

My wife Carol got a Kindle e-reader a couple of months ago, and I didn't anticipate what a difference it would make to both of us. First of all, Carol is a huge reader, mostly fiction, and the books used to arrive in monthly stacks and move from dining room table to bedside table to bookshelf or giveaway pile. Monitoring their progress, I could ask, "How's the latest Lee Child?" or "What happens in the Sue Grafton?" and "What was that new novel all about?" Sometimes the books settled in the stack next to my side of the bed.

But with the Kindle, the books don't even come through the front door anymore. They're downloaded from her computer into electronic pages that Carol can read with the flick of a switch. The problem is, I have no idea what she's reading; I can't even borrow a book if she thinks I might like it. A key to her inner life has gone missing. I mean, how clueless should a husband be? The Lord might have searched me out and known me, but couldn't He help me know my wife too?

Then I remembered her blog. "Book group of one," she calls it. She really began it, she says, to keep track of what she reads. Each time she finishes a book she logs on and writes up a quick critique. Anyone can read it; you can check it out at http://carolwallace.wordpress.com. I logged on and there it was, all her wit and wisdom ready for me to quote when I said very casually across the dinner table, "You made a very good point about P. D. James...."

*Lord, help me to know those I love and love them more as I know them.*
—RICK HAMLIN

*October*

## ADVICE FROM AUNT ANNIE

Wed 26

*"'Friend,' he asked, 'how does it happen that you are here without a wedding robe?' And the man had no reply."*
—MATTHEW 22:12 (TLB)

**DRESS FOR RESPECT**

When I learned Aunt Annie once attended a "Come As You Are" party, I laughed out loud. Aunt Annie didn't own any casual clothing—no T-shirts, jeans or sneakers; not a single pair of slacks. She no doubt went to the party in her usual work or home attire: a brown or gray suit, hose, sensible heels and tiny gold earrings.

Wearing formal clothes around the house seems ridiculous today. The dress code for work has relaxed, and most churches are more casual too. In my rural church, jeans and sandals are as common as suits and dresses.

Maybe that's why I was surprised to learn that my grandson Ryan bought new khakis and button-down shirts for his month-long stay in Rwanda as part of a mission team. "We'll wear shorts or jeans when we're painting and for part of our youth work," Ryan explained, "but we don't want to dishonor our hosts by being sloppily dressed when we go into schools and churches. We'll be more effective witnesses for Christ if our dress shows true respect for the people we'll meet."

I know that God isn't concerned with our clothing. In I Samuel 16:7 (RSV), I'm reminded that "man looks on the outward appearance, but the Lord looks on the heart." But there are times when outward appearances reflect carelessness, insensitivity and outright scorn for others—attitudes that most certainly hamper work and witness.

Aunt Annie went as she was. Ryan went as he (normally) wasn't. Both were perfectly dressed to show respect for the occasion, the culture, their hosts and their God.

*Lord Jesus, let my spiritual clothing and outer dress reflect Your love.*
—PENNEY SCHWAB

*October*

## Thu 27

*"Regard your servant's prayer and his plea, O Lord my God, heeding the cry and prayer that your servant prays to you today."* —I Kings 8:28 (NRSV)

Every evening my husband Charlie and I set aside a few minutes for what we call our "daily blessing." We thank God for answered prayers and other blessings, and pray for healing, forgiveness and guidance. It's a part of our routine, and some days, I confess, it can become a bit too routine—my part, that is.

Charlie, on the other hand, always has a fresh thing or two to tell God. He tells God about his day, and if someone has particularly irked him, he'll suggest, "You know what to do about it."

If Charlie's prayers were entered in the Olympics, they'd be categorized as "freestyle." One thing I've learned from him is that sometimes when we talk to God, we're also talking to each other. For example, if he's been working long hours and I've been feeling a bit neglected, he might pray, "Lord, You know that sometimes I get wrapped up in other obligations and don't spend enough time with Marci, so if You would, just let her know that I think about her every day and that I'll be done with this project soon."

Now a marriage counselor might say that we ought to address problems like that head-on. But I like the way Charlie gets God involved; that kind of prayer always makes me smile a little and forget my hurt feelings. And besides, two can pray that game.

*Lord, as You hear me, let me be heard by those I love.*
—Marci Alborghetti

*October*

## JOURNEY IN THE DARK

**Fri 28** *Be joyful in hope, patient in affliction, faithful in prayer.*
—Romans 12:12 (NIV)

**STITCHES OF HOPE**

I love to knit. Many *Daily Guideposts* readers know that and, over the years, have joined me as the needles click to knit wonderful little sweaters for needy children all over the world.

I've knitted blankets, too, for each of my four grandchildren. When I heard about the pending arrival of the fifth, I began her blanket, choosing a very pretty but difficult pattern.

As I knitted, though, my world grew darker. I underwent electroconvulsive therapy. Much of my short-term memory vanished, but not my ability to knit.

The blanket grew longer in squares of alternating pattern. And as I had so often in the past, I began to pray the stitches. Knitting the plain-stitch squares, I prayed for hope, prayed for my vanished self and prayed to stay alive. With the purl-stitch squares, I prayed for the unborn Madeline, that she would make a safe journey into a world where she'd be happy, healthy and grow up unshadowed by depression.

There is a strain of heredity in depression, and I panicked at the thought of bequeathing it. But as I recovered—little by little—I felt a quiet faith, built on hundreds of rows with thousands of stitches, that Madeline, her brothers and her cousins would grow up not only depression-free, but also in a world where new treatments would conquer the demon. The pale green blanket became a blanket of hope. And I was there, smiling, to wrap Madeline into its folds.

*Thank You, Jesus, for sharing our pain and for the
hope and healing You bring to so many.*
—Brigitte Weeks

Editor's Note: *For a copy of the Knit for Kids pattern, please visit www.KnitforKids.org.*

*October*

## Sat 29

*"Therefore do not be anxious for tomorrow, for tomorrow will be anxious for itself...."* —MATTHEW 6:34 (RSV)

Yesterday was a clear, crisp autumn day, and I took a brisk walk around our new neighborhood in Macon, Georgia. The streets are lined with antebellum houses shaded by tall hardwood trees. As I gazed down the sidewalk, I saw a sign in front of a beautiful white wooden house advertising an estate sale. A crowd had gathered and soon curiosity snagged me too.

Inside, people milled around tables stacked with assorted items, leafed through the books lining tall shelves, and examined the mahogany and walnut furniture. I learned that the house was owned by a couple, both university professors, who were moving to the retirement home of their dreams. Now they were downsizing, preparing for one more chapter in their long married life.

As I strolled from room to room, I saw an antique needlepoint motto hanging on a wall. It read, "Today is the tomorrow we worried about yesterday."

I have to admit that I've grown concerned about every approaching chapter of my life. I've died a thousand deaths over problems that seldom materialized. I didn't need anyone to explain the meaning of "Today is the tomorrow we worried about yesterday."

Taking the frame from the wall, I reached for my billfold. I knew that I needed to give this aging bearer of hard-earned wisdom a new home above my desk.

*Father, help me not to be anxious for tomorrow. May I seek first Your kingdom and Your righteousness, and all I need will be provided.*
—SCOTT WALKER

*October*

## Sun 30

*Having gifts that differ according to the grace given to us, let us use them....* —ROMANS 12:6 (RSV)

Long ago we'd been told that if Nellie, our black Labrador retriever who suffered from chronic pancreatitis and was an incorrigible food thief to boot, absconded with one more piece of chocolate, it might well be her last. This evening as we'd washed up the dinner dishes, Nellie began to pace the kitchen in wide circles, panting and eyeing us wildly. We wondered what was wrong until we found an empty, chewed-up box on the back porch. It had once contained a large selection of gourmet brownies. Now, all that was left were tiny shreds of foil and cellophane.

It was the weekend and our veterinarian's office was closed, so I picked up the phone and dialed my sister Katrina, a large-animal vet. Through halting tears, I explained what had happened. "You must get Nellie to the animal emergency hospital *now*," she said.

I kept the cell phone and Katrina's reassuring voice to my ear all through the emergency room evaluation. As the hospital veterinarian told us what could be done, Katrina explained what it all meant. From three hundred miles away, she gave me questions to ask the vet, translated the answers and helped us decide what to do.

Nellie was led away, and for a long hour we could hear her yelping from behind closed doors. Finally the doctor returned to tell us that Nellie would be fine in another twenty-four hours. She also told me that my sister was a remarkable vet.

I called Katrina the next day to thank her for what she had been for me through that trying time. "You're welcome," she said, "but it was easy. That's what I do."

*Dear Lord, You've given all of us our own talents and abilities, and when we share them, we do for each other what we were meant to do.*
—ANNE ADRIANCE

*October*

## Mon 31

*Behold, the heaven and the heaven of heavens is the Lord's thy God, the earth also, with all that therein is.*
—DEUTERONOMY 10:14

We were at loose ends last Saturday, with the weather a bit raw for outdoor activities. Six-year-old Stephen had gone into the kitchen to look for something to eat, and for no particular reason, I started to sing. "Someone's in the kitchen with Stephen..."

Maggie, Mary, John and Elizabeth joined in: "Someone's in the kitchen, I know-o-o-o. Someone's in the kitchen with Steee-phen..."

Stephen popped out of the kitchen and capped the verse: "I think it is a UFO!"

I grew up with a skeptical interest in the outré and the unusual, and I seem somehow to have passed it on to my children, especially thirteen-year-old John. ("Somehow?" I can hear my wife Julia saying.) As a preteen, I hid a radio under the covers so I could listen to an ex-carnival pitchman named Long John Nebel interview people who claimed to have ridden in flying saucers or discovered robot-filled caverns far under the earth.

I'm still fascinated by the strange things some people believe. But at the center of them, I think, is a great sadness: the void left when people no longer have faith in God. In one of his Father Brown stories, G. K. Chesterton wrote, "It's the first effect of not believing in God that you lose your common sense."

If there are other worlds out there inhabited by intelligent beings, I'm confident that they have a part in God's plan. And whether they're there or not, I'll keep singing the praises of the One Who put the great lights in the sky—and occasionally share a laugh with my children about UFOs.

*Lord, how vast is this universe that You have made, and how wonderful beyond all telling that You should have dwelt as one of us on our small green and blue planet!*
—ANDREW ATTAWAY

*October*

**SEEDS OF LOVE**

1 _____

2 _____

3 _____

4 _____

5 _____

6 _____

7 _____

8 _____

9 _____

10 _____

11 _____

12 _____

13 _____

14 _____

15 _____

*October*

16 _____

17 _____

18 _____

19 _____

20 _____

21 _____

22 _____

23 _____

24 _____

25 _____

26 _____

27 _____

28 _____

29 _____

30 _____

31 _____

# November

*But the fruit of the Spirit is love, joy, peace, longsuffering, gentleness, goodness, faith, meekness, temperance....*

—Galatians 5:22–23

*November*

**Tue 1** *The memory of the just is blessed....* —PROVERBS 10:7

A few months ago a friend of ours passed away at sixty after a courageous battle with cancer. Emily had worked as a secretary while raising a large family and keeping active in church and in local charitable organizations. She was always cheerful and kind, with a mellow word for everyone, and I knew that she would be missed.

As my wife Carol and I prepared to go to the wake, however, I confessed to a certain unease: We didn't know Emily's husband or children very well, and I was afraid that if the wake was sparsely attended, we might feel awkward or out of place. After all, Emily wasn't a celebrity, just a good, decent person. What if no one but us showed up? As we left the house, I uttered a quick prayer that everything would go smoothly.

I first realized that something was up when we turned onto the street that held the funeral parlor and ran into a full-blown traffic jam. Navigating our way onto the property to park took several minutes. Then we joined the line to enter the funeral home; there were two hundred or three hundred people ahead of us. The mayor was there, and Emily's state senator, and young and old people from every walk of life. Getting into the building took forty-five minutes—and visiting hours had just begun.

Back home, Carol and I talked it over and realized that we had witnessed something special: the power of goodness. Emily had touched the lives of countless friends and acquaintances, and they had turned out en masse to bid farewell and say thank you.

So long, Emily, and thanks from us all!

*Dear Lord, help me to do good all the days of my life.*
—PHILIP ZALESKI

*November*

## A PATH TO SIMPLICITY

*Wed 2*  *Beyond all these things put on love, which is the perfect bond of unity.* —COLOSSIANS 3:14 (NAS)

**FOCUSING ON THE MOMENT**

In my quest for simplicity, I learned an important lesson: Simplicity doesn't take away from your life; it adds to it. *If only my work life could be simpler,* I mused.

One day, I was discussing my dilemma with the director of the emergency room at the hospital where I'm a nurse. "You have such simplicity in the way you approach everyone," I told him. "How do you do it?"

Dr. Jain told me that he had made a decision that everyone who entered his office would leave feeling cared for.

*Could something so utterly simple make such a huge difference?* I wondered.

When Jill, who's in charge of supplies, came to my office to discuss a purchase, I gave her my complete attention. As I looked directly into her eyes, I asked about her husband, who'd recently received a difficult diagnosis. I recalled how the two of them had looked forward to their retirement years, to selling the deer jerky recipe they'd perfected.

*Dear Lord,* I found myself praying, *give Jill and her husband that precious time together.* As I stayed in the moment, I experienced a new clarity. "My dream for you, Jill, is that the two of you will be able to market that deer jerky together," I said. "I want you to have the time of your lives."

I knew Dr. Jain's advice had been right-on when Jill looked back at me with glistening eyes. "You know what you said about that deer jerky, Roberta? That's *my* dream too."

*Heavenly Father, help me to lovingly offer my work life to You.*
—ROBERTA MESSNER

*November*

**Thu 3**  *Your love has given me great joy and encouragement....*
—Philemon 1:7 (NIV)

At a recent school board meeting, one of our high school principals was promoted to supervisor. He stepped up to the podium to offer his thanks and acknowledged a former mentor who had encouraged him to get into administration. "You always have to have a person in your life who sees something in you that you don't," he said.

When I returned to college to complete a teaching certification, I was thirty years old, with four young children, sitting in classes with eighteen-year-olds who would say, "Yes, ma'am" or "No, ma'am" to me when I'd ask them a question. It was a trying first semester. College algebra was a challenge, since my last math class had been back in high school. I'd never been much of a science student, and my chemistry lab was difficult. When my English professor announced that no one had ever earned an *A* in her class, I was ready to drop the course. I ended up in my adviser's office, ready to quit college. I didn't think I could do it.

Thank goodness my adviser thought otherwise. His continued encouragement kept me in school, and in a few short years I'd graduated with honors, begun teaching and even enrolled in graduate school. My adviser had seen something in me that I had not.

*Thank You, Lord, for the people in my life who encourage me to become more than I think I can be. May we all reach the glorious potential that You see in us.*
—Melody Bonnette

*November*

## Fri 4

*Love one another deeply, from the heart.*
—I Peter 1:22 (NIV)

Emily is white; the Johnsons are black. They got to know each other about twenty years ago when they attended the same church. As Emily's health began to fail, the Johnsons cared for her.

Emily now has Parkinson's disease and lives in an assisted-living facility. The Johnsons take her to church, to the doctor and wherever else she needs to go. My wife Rosie and I visited the Johnsons not long ago and observed how tenderly they care for Emily. We saw them gently put her in a wheelchair and take her shopping, patiently listening to her whispers as she told them what she wanted. We moved from one aisle to the next in the store as she slowly read the labels on the cans. The kindness that the Johnsons display toward this woman is truly phenomenal. No one pays them to do it; no court or agency assigned the job to them. They were moved by God to walk beside a person in need.

As I saw this, I was reminded of I Peter 1:22: "Love one another deeply, from the heart." Here was deep agape, reaching out and caring for a friend, and here I was observing it from a historical barrier of race—no boss, no employee, only God's kind of love.

*Lord, help me to grow in Your love, so I can always be ready to reach out and care for a friend.*
—Dolphus Weary

## November

### Sat 5

*As the Father has loved me, so have I loved you; abide in my love.*
—John 15:9 (RSV)

I'm stressed. My daughter Mary has six hours of ballet a week and an equal amount of *Nutcracker* rehearsal, my daughter Maggie is Jip the Dog in a children's production of *Dr. Doolittle*, and my husband Andrew has been working late. Then there's all the usual stuff: homeschool co-op and parent association meetings to attend, deadlines, children who need attention. Somewhere deep down I can feel a good cry struggling to get out.

Today I dropped Mary off for *Nutcracker* and had three luxurious hours in which to get her birthday shopping done. I knew what I wanted to buy, but I also knew that on New York City's Upper East Side, finding anything I could afford would take a while. I started walking.

I went over to Lexington Avenue and headed south. I found a cute stationery store with a nifty red alarm clock and checked one item off my list. I walked some more, bypassing pricey toy shops and tony boutiques. The combination of brisk weather, solitude and exercise felt good.

I walked some more. And then, nearly a mile from where I'd started, I saw something I'd forgotten was on my route: a church.

My heart leaped. Whatever else I had to find, I needed this more. I climbed the steps and opened the door: silence, warmth, a handful of people on their knees. With a gasp, I threw myself in, gratitude pouring down my cheeks. *Oh, Jesus*, came the cry from deep within, *I am so glad to be here with You!*

I knelt and offered up my burdens, frustrations, puzzlements. Emerging into the twilight and bustle, I resumed my brisk walk, this time not because I was stressed, but because I was filled with joy.

*Jesus, when I am frazzled and frustrated, find me, stop me, heal me.*
—Julia Attaway

## November

### Sun 6

*As she stood behind him at his feet weeping, she began to wet his feet with her tears....* —LUKE 7:38 (NIV)

I had volunteered to pray at the altar with those who came forward with requests at the Sunday evening prayer service. A woman approached and handed me an index card with a prayer request for her parents. She knelt down on the cushion on the front side of the altar rail, and I knelt down on the wooden floor on the other side. She placed her hands on the rail and bowed her head. I placed my hands on top of hers, closed my eyes and began to pray.

Since I knew very few of the details of her situation, I didn't feel I was praying for her as well as I should and my prayers didn't seem very eloquent. That's why I was surprised when I felt a teardrop fall onto the back of my hand. Another came, and then another. An indescribable feeling of sharing a moment of holiness came over me.

After I had finished praying, the woman wiped her eyes and we hugged. I remembered how Jesus had been bathed with a woman's tears and I felt privileged to have been His representative for a brief moment to receive the gift of tears offered to Him from one of His beloved daughters.

*Father, help me to receive someone's tears in Your name today.*
—KAREN BARBER

*November*

**Mon 7** *"You blind men! Which is greater: the gift, or the altar that makes the gift sacred?"* —MATTHEW 23:19 (NIV)

The long skinny package was propped up against my front door when I returned home from the pool. I didn't recognize the name on the return address label, and I was stunned to find a hand-whittled walking stick inside. A typewritten letter from Cecil Lee, age ninety-two, a devoted *Daily Guideposts* reader, told me that he'd whittled and given away some four thousand or five thousand walking sticks and canes in his lifetime. "Now, here's yours," it said.

The walking stick, which is a bit short for my five-foot-seven-inch height, is propped in my office as a daily reminder that I'm heading toward old age and I can do nothing to stop it. But Mr. Lee and his gift are sweet reminders that with a little preparation, getting older doesn't have to be depressing or scary at all. Why, a time may come when I'll be bent over, vertebrae compressed, an inch or two shorter, and that walking stick will be just the ticket.

By then, I imagine, Mr. Lee will be enjoying his eternal reward in heaven. But when he looks down on all the thousands of us who are using his wonderful whittled walking sticks, I hope he smiles and knows what a ministry he created with his talent.

*Lord, bless Mr. Lee and all the oldsters like him who pave the way for us young 'uns to grow old gracefully and with a spirit of giving to others.*
—PATRICIA LORENZ

*November*

**Tue 8** *I am sure that neither... principalities... nor powers... will be able to separate us from the love of God in Christ Jesus our Lord.* —ROMANS 8:38–39 (RSV)

I got up feeling a bit lethargic. The Indian summer skies had gone gray, my house was cold, and I felt a sense of futility over what was happening in our world. I fixed a cup of coffee and headed dully for the computer. I had mail; Rocklin, a college student in Changchun, China, had checked in.

*Hi, Anti Bee. This is Rocklin. Hopefully there is my face in your mind.*

I'd met Rocklin a year and a half before when I visited my youngest son in China. Blake was teaching conversational English on a college campus. Rocklin was seventeen, lonely, suffering from a lifetime of emotional neglect, but he made Blake his friend and spiritual mentor. I inherited some of that role simply because I'm Blake's mother.

Hearing from Rocklin through the wonder of technology, my lethargy vanished, not just because I enjoy hearing from him but because he reminds me that on the far side of the world, in a Communist country, amidst millions of people, God found this young man and gave him to Blake and me to nurture and support and to pray for.

Lethargy, gray skies, a sense of futility—what are these when Rocklin reminds me that through the chaos and fear God calls us by name.

Yes, Rocklin, there is your face in my mind, for you are proof that nothing—neither principalities nor powers—can separate any of us from the love of God.

*Dear God, keep me focused on Your power and love, remembering that amidst the chaos of our times, You hold everyone's faces in Your mind.*
—BRENDA WILBEE

*November*

*Wed 9*  A man's steps are directed by the Lord....
—PROVERBS 20:24 (NIV)

One of the things I love best about being a grandmother is reading books to my grandchildren.

Isabelle Grace is still in the board-book stage. These sturdy books are short and simple, with thick pages perfect for little fingers. Sometimes I read Isabelle longer books with more text and detailed pictures. Usually there are too many words for her liking, and she turns the page before I'm ready. Occasionally, though, a picture intrigues her and she stares at it long after I've finished reading. But one thing is certain: Isabelle is in charge of turning pages. If I forget and flip forward, she emits a squeal, as only a two-year-old can: "Isbee do! Isbee do!"

A few days ago, after Isabelle had gone home, I held the book we'd been reading and thought about how much Isabelle enjoys being the one to set the pace, the one to say when it's time to move forward in the story, the one who determines when a new scene comes into play.

Often I behave like Isabelle, wanting to set the pace for my life. I complain that good times go by too fast. I question why the hard times linger. I want the sunshine-filled pages to stay open forever and those fearsome storm-filled ones to whiz by in a blink. Of course, I'm not the One turning the pages.

I'm old enough to know that grief and illness, disappointment and rejection have their merits. I learn more in shadow than in sun. Still, it's a challenge to surrender control and embrace the pace set by the Author of our lives and cheerfully let Him turn the pages.

*I'll keep my hands off, Lord, and let You take charge*
*of my life—page after page after page.*
—MARY LOU CARNEY

*November*

## Thu 10

*"For they shall all know me, from the least of them to the greatest, says the Lord; for I will forgive their iniquity, and remember their sin no more."*
—Jeremiah 31:34 (NRSV)

I'd been staring at my computer screen for the better part of the morning, with precious few words of the report that was due by the end of the day to show for it.

"I can't seem to focus," I said to my colleague Keith as we headed to the cafeteria for a quick lunch. "Every time I try to draw some conclusions and recommendations, I keep thinking about the report I messed up three weeks ago. And my mind just seems to freeze."

"My basketball coach taught me something that I've never forgotten," Keith responded. Keith had played college ball about twenty years before. "He always said, 'You'll win some games, you'll lose others. But never lose the same game twice.'"

"When you get back to your desk," Keith suggested on the way back from the cafeteria, "print a copy of that old report, say out loud what you learned from it and toss that copy in the trash. And this time, mean it. Then see if you can move on with your current work."

I did finish my report that afternoon. It wasn't half bad.

*Help me to believe, oh, God, that Your grace is greater than my guilt, calling me each and every day to rise above those times when I fail You.*
—Jeff Japinga

*November*

*Fri 11* "For everyone who exalts himself will be humbled, and he who humbles himself will be exalted." —LUKE 14:11 (NIV)

Medal of Honor recipient Bruce Crandall is a neighbor and a friend. He'll be the first one to say he's no hero. The way Bruce tells it, the real heroes didn't come home. He is the last Medal of Honor recipient to receive the medal in person; all the medals since Vietnam have been presented posthumously.

Recently, my husband Wayne and I were on a flight with Bruce that landed in Atlanta. Anyone who travels frequently knows what happens when the airplane door opens: There's a mad rush to get off and hurry to baggage claim or to a connecting flight. In Atlanta, there are a lot of connecting flights.

When it was discovered that a Medal of Honor recipient was aboard, the flight attendant asked the passengers to remain in their seats and allow Bruce to deplane first. I've heard such announcements before, and they're routinely ignored.

Not this time. Everyone aboard the plane remained seated. Then, as Bruce stood and collected his carry-on, a spontaneous burst of applause broke out. As he disembarked, Bruce paused to let three young recruits headed for basic training leave ahead of him.

As I said, Bruce would be the last one to say he's a hero, but I can't help viewing him that way. He's the very best of what it means to be an American.

*Lord, thank You for the people who remind us of the tremendous cost the men and women of our military have paid for our freedom.*
—DEBBIE MACOMBER

_November_

**Sat 12** *And this is the promise that he hath promised us, even eternal life.* —I JOHN 2:25

My dear friend Becky died on Friday morning. She was not yet sixty. She was the greatest science teacher I ever saw. Thousands of kids over thirty years loved and admired her and wanted to be as cheerful and eager and curious and generous as she was. So here's my question for you this morning: Where is my friend Becky? Where is her Beckyness, the salt and pop and swing and song that was her?

We know the principles of physics in this particular universe—all things dissolve, but no energy is lost. So we know that the vessel that was this great biology teacher, this remarkable scholar, the halo of hair and the beaming grin, the ubiquitous ballet slippers and the sweater as big as a coat, that quick, bright, intelligent, amused voice, the twig of a body that once was the high school prom queen, is gone, dissolved, returned to the dust and salt and water from which it came. But the electricity that is that woman—the zest and verve, the laughter and kindness, the wit and generosity—can anyone be absolutely sure it has died? Are your senses so very accurate that you can say she is not traveling farther than we can ever imagine? And I mean this very literally indeed. I believe she *is*, in ways and means and forms and shapes we can only invent childish images for. I believe she lives. I believe that out of the darkness she has danced into an incomprehensible light.

What do you believe?

*Dear Lord, well, finally, half a century after You put me on this planet, I get it that who we really are doesn't die. Thanks.*
—BRIAN DOYLE

*November*

## Sun 13

*Then He arose and rebuked the wind, and said to the sea, "Peace, be still!"....* —Mark 4:39 (NKJV)

When I was a boy, I preferred Sunday evening services because they were more informal. The song leader would often ask for favorites, and my hand would be the first one in the air. "Sing number one-oh-two, 'Master, the Tempest Is Raging'" (Mary A. Baker, 1874).

The dramatic song sent chills through me. It was about the disciples in the boat during a storm on Lake Galilee. When we got to the chorus, I would sing out like a drowning man:

> *Whether the wrath of the storm-tossed sea,*
> *Or demons, or men, or whatever it be,*
> *No water can swallow the ship where lies*
> *The Master of ocean, and earth, and skies;*
> *They all shall sweetly obey Thy will,*
> *Peace, be still! Peace, be still!*

I still think of that song when life gets stormy, when the winds of change rock my boat, when waves of anxiety wash over me, when I feel like I'm drowning in work, when the thunder and lightning of conflict frighten me. At such times I remind myself that nothing can sink my ship because Jesus is in the boat with me. He made the sea and the sky, and He can say, "Peace, be still!" and things will settle down. They always do.

> *Father, the sea is big and my boat is small, but I feel safe*
> *because You are here in the boat with me.*
> —Daniel Schantz

### November

### Mon 14

*"Look to the rock from which you were cut and to the quarry from which you were hewn."* —Isaiah 51:1 (NIV)

I got an e-mail the other day from a man in Italy. Turns out our grandmothers, Angelina and Rosa, were sisters. He tracked me down through a book about Inveruno, the town near Milan where my grandparents were born. Even my dad didn't know about this cousin, because he had moved to another part of Italy long before they could have met. Yet when he sent a photo of himself, I could clearly see the family resemblance.

It still amazes me. In another part of the world, where I've never been, is a man who speaks another language and lives a life very different from mine, and yet we're family. My own genealogy work has shown me that I probably also have family in Germany, Scotland and Canada. Not long ago I discovered a branch in Nebraska that I'd never known about! The rock from which I was cut is a lot larger than I ever imagined.

God has worked this out pretty neatly. It's hard to dislike people or find them strange when they may be family, even if they are different or speak another language.

*Father of all, help us, Your children, to see the family resemblance in each other.*
—Gina Bridgeman

---

## READER'S ROOM

I'm most grateful for family, friends, a growing relationship with God, the knowledge that God covers me with love, my growing ability to see God working every day (He even lets me be a part of it!), and learning to turn my worries over to Him. —*Jo Kruger, Deming, New Mexico*

November

## 🕯 THE ONE WHO IS TO COME

**Tue 15** *Buy the truth and do not sell it; get wisdom, discipline and understanding.* —PROVERBS 23:23 (NIV)

**TURNING ASIDE TO SEE THIS GREAT SIGHT**

The commercial countdown began weeks ago, and today advertisements urge: "Only forty shopping days until Christmas!" In other words, spend! Buy! Get ready!

Forty days has often been a special period for God's people. Jesus Himself fasted and prayed in the desert forty days before beginning His ministry. Although I can't take off to a desert, the coming weeks provide precious opportunity to do some spiritual spending and the Bible gives an interesting shopping list: truth, wisdom, discipline and understanding.

During this hectic season, what I need to seek as doggedly as I search the stores or the Internet for those "perfect gifts" of toys, books and clothing is God's wisdom. It seems no coincidence that discipline is next on the list. Too often I've seen a connection between lack of discipline in my life and a shortage of understanding how to love God and the people around me. This Advent I want to establish a small discipline of taking a few quiet moments each day to think about Jesus, the Wisdom of God. Who is He? Who can He be for me?

Even in this busy time, God wants to come to me in the midst of my everyday life. Moses was busy going about his daily work, tending sheep on Mount Horeb, when he came upon an incredible sight: the Angel of the Lord appearing in a flame of fire from the midst of a bush. Moses' response? "I will now turn aside and see this great sight..." (Exodus 3:3, NKJV).

God, a consuming fire, comes as an infant in a virgin's womb! Forty days isn't enough even to begin to ponder His appearance, but I want to try—to turn aside and gaze on Him a bit more each day.

*Lord, help me to acquire Your wisdom and better understand Who You are.*
—MARY BROWN

## Wed 16

*November*

*Behold, I make all things new....* —REVELATION 21:5

Probably it has to do with my senior citizen status, but I simply cannot keep up with the myriad of new equipment continually coming out to make me more efficient.

A friend showed me something that looked like a lipstick tube smashed flat. "Our company's entire records are on this flash drive." She inserted it into her computer and information appeared "out of thin air," as my mother used to say about things she didn't understand. Mom would've been amazed at knowing cell phones are being used for talking, texting, taking photos, making movies and playing music.

My mind boggles when I try to imagine my words joining billions of other visuals and voices and sounds and radio/TV talk and pictures all swimming around out there in the ether of Earth's atmosphere. What keeps them from mixing? I often long for what we senior citizens refer to as the "simple days." I identify with the slogan, "Stop the world—I want to get off!"

But a little boy helped put my wishes into perspective when I asked him, "What did you learn in Sunday school today?"

He brightened and confidentially told me, "God is good and He loves us kids."

*Dear Father, when I become bewildered with the many new inventions bombarding me, it's so comforting to know You will never be improved upon because You, Your Word and Your workings never go out of date!*
—ISABEL WOLSELEY

*November*

## ❦ TO SAY GOOD-BYE

*Thu 17*   *Your Father knoweth what things ye have need of....*
—MATTHEW 6:8

**A KNOCK AT THE DOOR**

"Hello... anybody home?" I knew his voice long before I made it to the door. The loud pounding was him, knocking on the door with his elbow because his big arms were always full of groceries.

Ministers and their families can know some lean years. But like clockwork, just when our pantry was looking bare, Daddy would appear, his car loaded down with treats that our budget would never allow. In he'd come, filling the house with his enthusiasm, spoiling our children Brock and Keri, taking us all out to fancy restaurants. He was so proud of my husband David and of the things we accomplished in the church. As we near the end of this phase of our lives, I can't help wondering what Daddy would say to us if he were here.

We've been at Hillsboro Presbyterian Church for thirty-seven years. When we came, I was in my early twenties and Brock was nine months old. Keri was yet to be born. We've grown up with this church; we've seen it expand from fewer than fifty members to more than seven hundred. We've been here for every birth, baptism, wedding and funeral.

I know it sounds crazy, but in this ending I sense a beginning. The future seems a bit like a bare pantry at this point, but I wait, fully expecting a knock at our door.

I wait for our Father, with His arms so full of hopeful tomorrows, He has to knock with His elbow.

*Father, I wait. But with You, I know I never have to worry.*
—PAM KIDD

*November*

## Fri 18

*I know, O Lord, that a man's life is not his own; it is not for man to direct his steps.* —Jeremiah 10:23 (NIV)

I was in the office, working through my agenda, when an e-mail arrived: "Greetings! This is Chi from AA flight to LGA. I can't believe it's already been over a week since we met. My time in NY was quite nice and meaningful; especially from the beginning as how God seemed to place us next to each other to connect in many ways."

Our paths had crossed in an airport when her flight was delayed and I was on standby, trying to get home to my family.

During the flight, we enjoyed small talk until she asked me about my work at Guideposts. That opened the door for her to share her faith and the recent loss of her father, who had suddenly passed away, leaving Chi, her mother and her sister. Chi's words were filled with pain, loss and grief. *What if this were my daughter?* I thought to myself. *What would I want someone to say?*

I sensed that this was not a time for me to talk but to listen. Chi spoke proudly. "My father came from Korea and worked hard to give my sister and me a better future in the United States. He valued education, family and faith." The more she shared about her dad, the stronger Chi became.

When the airplane landed at LaGuardia Airport, I promised to pray for Chi and her family and to send her some Guideposts publications. When we said good-bye at the baggage claim, I didn't expect to hear from her again. But when I read her e-mail, I knew that it was no coincidence that God had put us next to each other on that plane.

*Lord, thank You for rearranging our plans so that we can cross paths with those You want us to touch with Your love.*
—Pablo Diaz

*November*

## Sat 19

*They have ears, but they hear not....*
—Psalm 115:6

It began with the mouse in the wall behind our bed. Quiet during the day, the creature liked to scratch on the plaster at 1:00 AM or 2:00 AM, and the sound resonated down the wall, making it impossible to sleep. We asked our cat, Fred the Fearless Hunter, to investigate the fine-line cracks in the plaster in hopes that he'd sniff out a way to trap our tormentor or scare it away. No such luck. I didn't want to put out poison or a glue trap. "Why don't you try one of those machines that make a high-pitched buzzing sound?" a friend said. "No one can hear it but a mouse, and it'll send it away."

I went off to the hardware store and bought the buzzing apparatus for $19.95, plugged it in and turned it on. Fred investigated it, shrugged and ambled off. My wife admired its size and shape. "What about that loud noise?" I said.

"What noise?" Carol asked.

"That buzzing sound," I said. "Doesn't that bother you?"

She had no idea what I was talking about and neither did our son Tim. Turns out I had to wait until the advanced age of fifty-four to discover that I have the hearing of a mouse.

We found a corner of the room to put the machine where it didn't bother me too much, but it bothered the mouse enough that it buzzed off for good. As for my extrasensory hearing? It doesn't seem to do me much good. But it does make me laugh to know that I've got mouse ears.

*Thank You, God, for the many gifts You give me.*
*May I use them to the best of my ability.*
—Rick Hamlin

*November*

# 🕯 THE ONE WHO IS TO COME

*Sun 20*    *"I tell you the truth," Jesus answered, "before Abraham was born, I am!"* —JOHN 8:58 (NIV)

"I AM WHO I AM" (EXODUS 3:14)

One Sunday before Thanksgiving, I phoned my mom to ask how she made her turkey stuffing. After giving me my annual tutorial, Mom exclaimed, "Guess who's coming for Christmas this year?"

Mom hated the thought of anyone spending the day alone and often invited people to share the holiday. Before I could guess, she announced, "Jim and Eileen Connaker!" Hearing the names of my sister Sue's in-laws, I immediately pictured these jolly grandparents—Jim's dry humor and Eileen's lively laugh—and understood Mom's delighted anticipation.

Advent provides a good time to ponder the One Who is coming to all our Christmas celebrations. When Moses asked the Lord His name, God told him, "I AM THAT I AM" (Exodus 3:14). Now that's quite an answer!

Who is coming this Christmas? The One Who exists before all. The One Who beyond all imagination or comprehension makes Himself known. The One Who contains all things yet cannot be contained by anything, Who takes on human flesh.

God told Moses to tell His people, "I have surely looked upon you and all the things that happened to you in Egypt. I will bring you up out of affliction to a land flowing with milk and honey" (Exodus 3:16–17). In sending His Son, God offers to release me from bondage and lead me to a new land. Each day He calls me to begin anew my journey and experience more of His kingdom. Yet like the Israelites, I, too, easily settle for the slavery of this world's ways. What is my Egypt? What are my own afflictions or weaknesses? Where am I stuck? God knows and wants to lead me out.

*Lord, please show me one step I can take this week to come closer to You.*
        —MARY BROWN

*November*

## Mon 21
*And the children of Israel said to Samuel, Cease not to cry unto the Lord our God for us....* —I SAMUEL 7:8

Most mornings find me at the gym in a high-intensity aerobic cycling class—a sweaty, heart-pounding hour of running uphill on a stationary bike. The grunting and groaning of the participants is drowned out by the pounding soundtrack. Today, the one repeated line of a song caught my ear: "Say a prayer for me."

I had to smile through my pain. This was Monday morning, and as we have for decades, Guideposts starts the week at 9:45 with Prayer Fellowship, where we get together as a staff and pray with you. As my friend Van Varner used to say, "If you want to know what's important in people's lives, find out what they pray for."

In my years at Guideposts, I have seen the breadth of spiritual longing in the requests you send in. Last week we prayed for everything from a combat unit in Afghanistan to a sick goldfish in Oklahoma, and we prayed equally for both. We pray for everything from world peace to peace of mind. Most prayer requests are for family, health, finances, forgiveness or simply God's protection in a changing world. In these Monday morning sessions, I have come to understand that prayer not only joins us with God; it also connects us to each other.

*Thank You, Lord, for prayer, by which we stay connected to one another through You.*
—EDWARD GRINNAN

EDITOR'S NOTE: *Join us today for our annual Thanksgiving Day of Prayer. Visit us at www.OurPrayer.org, where you can request prayer, volunteer to pray for others or help support our prayer ministry.*

*November*

## ADVICE FROM AUNT ANNIE

**Tue 22**   *You know how, when you were a small child, you were taught the holy Scriptures; and it is these that make you wise to accept God's salvation....* —II TIMOTHY 3:15 (TLB)

### THE MOST PRECIOUS GIFT

According to Aunt Annie, when I was about four, we were looking at the night sky when I said, "I see a halo around the moon, plus all the little stars of Jesus!" Of course, I don't remember saying that. In fact, I don't remember attending Sunday school or church at that age, or having Bible stories read to me, or even saying bedtime prayers.

But the fact that I don't remember doesn't alter the evidence. Someone—most likely several people—had already introduced me to Jesus and taught me to be grateful for the beauty of His astounding creation.

My children and grandchildren may not remember attending church, hearing Bible stories or saying prayers when they were young. They may not remember Vacation Bible School or singing "I Have the Joy, Joy, Joy, Joy Down in My Heart." But I know without a doubt that nothing anyone does to teach any child about Jesus is ever lost. We have His promise: "And if, as my representatives, you give even a cup of cold water to a little child, you will surely be rewarded" (Matthew 10:42, TLB).

"A cup of cold water"—Christ the Living Water—is the most precious gift a child can ever receive.

*Thank You, Lord, for everyone who teaches little children about You.*
—PENNEY SCHWAB

*November*

## Wed 23
*Go ye therefore, and teach all nations....*
—Matthew 28:19

My grandmother was a woman of great faith. A missionary's daughter and a preacher's wife, she had been a Bible teacher in Hong Kong. After immigrating to the United States, she became a pillar of her church in San Francisco's Chinatown. You could find her there every Sunday, greeting the members of the congregation as they arrived, and every Wednesday, on her knees in prayer, seeking God's guidance for those same people.

During school breaks, I'd accompany my grandmother to the prayer meetings. Afterward, we'd shop for groceries, stopping at the produce stores, with their overflowing crates of verdant bok choy and boxes of red grapes spilling out onto the bustling sidewalks.

As I eyed the fat, round Asian pears—sweet and crisp, they're my favorite fruit to this day—my grandmother would hum hymns and choose oranges. There were always other old Chinese ladies around, and inevitably, she would initiate a conversation. Her typical opening line went something like this: "Do you believe in Jesus?"

At that, I would concentrate even harder on those Asian pears; I loved her, but didn't she realize how embarrassing she was? *How in the world,* I would think, *could she just start talking about Jesus like that?*

Looking back, I realize the proper question is, How could she not? I may quibble with her wording and her strategy, but I can't doubt her heart. My grandmother lived the great commission more than any other person I have ever known. She didn't have to get on a plane to go on a mission trip—she just had to go buy some oranges. And the good news she shared wasn't just meant for those old ladies next to her; it was also for me, as a lesson in what it really means to go and make disciples of all nations, starting at home.

*Lord, wherever I am, give me the boldness to speak about You.*
—Jeff Chu

## November

### Thu 24

*"Your people will be my people...."*
—RUTH 1:16 (NIV)

My first Thanksgiving with my in-laws felt very strange. I wanted to be with my family and I craved the Latin dishes that were missing from the table. I was pregnant and perhaps my hormones were raging, but all I wanted to do was cry. It just didn't feel like Thanksgiving, and the people around me, as kind and welcoming as they were, didn't feel like my family.

The next year I was determined to have a Latin Thanksgiving, surrounded by my own relatives, but as the holiday approached, my husband's sisters decided to fly in from Florida and my mother-in-law excitedly implored us to spend the holiday with them. As much as I wanted to, I couldn't say no. And since they were expecting more people than usual, I offered to host the dinner in our fairly spacious apartment.

On Thanksgiving morning my mother-in-law and sisters-in-law arrived early, and we began to cook. They prepared the turkey and the other traditional dishes, while I made a variety of Latin dishes to go with them. We danced around one another in the kitchen, talking and laughing as we chopped, mixed and fussed over the stove. The bustle and commotion were very familiar to me, and I was beginning to enjoy myself.

The more people arrived, the more fun we had. We played games and enjoyed the delicious food—my Latin dishes were a hit! Everyone held my baby boy, and he giggled in delight all day as they made silly faces and playfully tossed him in the air.

The day was a far cry from the sad, hormonal holiday I'd endured the year before. It was truly a day of thanksgiving—the day my in-laws became my family.

*Thank You, Lord, for Your many blessings, but especially for the love that makes all of us one family in You.*
—KAREN VALENTIN

*November*

*Fri 25*

*"I will lead the blind by ways they have not known, along unfamiliar paths I will guide them...."*
—Isaiah 42:16 (niv)

I recently arranged for my daughter Sarah to take her first unaccompanied commercial plane ride to visit her grandparents in Florida. I ran through all the details: I bought the ticket, arranged for her passport so that she'd have a picture ID, made sure the toothbrush was in her backpack, and set two alarms to ensure that we'd leave for the airport on time.

In fact, we arrived thirty minutes ahead of schedule. I gave Sarah five dollars and told her to go to the newsstand and pick out a magazine. We bought lattes. And then I said to the woman at security: "This is my daughter. She's fourteen and flying by herself today."

As I quickly discovered, the rules for unaccompanied minors have tightened since 9/11. "No, no, sir. You have to get into this other line. There are forms to be filled out and a fee to be paid."

Thirty minutes later, still several people away from the front of the line, I began to panic. By the time we made it to the front, one of the two agents handling customers was closing her window and beginning to pack her things.

"Please... please... I'm sorry... I mean, will you help me before you go?" I stammered, desperate for help. She took one calm look at me and said, "Of course. What do you need?" Ten minutes and fifty dollars later, my problems were mostly solved and Sarah was on her way to the gate.

Despite my best efforts and preparations, things had gotten out of my control—*I* had gotten out of control. But thanks to the graciousness of Rose at Logan Airport, both the situation and I were defused.

*Remind me, Father, to let go of my presumption that I'm in control and to allow You to help me with the people You put in my path.*
—Jon Sweeney

*November*

## Sat 26 *I beseech thee, shew me thy glory.* —Exodus 33:18

Our synagogue in Pennsylvania had a Marc Chagall window, one of those stained-glass masterpieces designed to inspire. In Los Angeles, our synagogue had twelve stained-glass windows, each representing one of the twelve tribes of Israel. They were spectacular.

When Keith and I first came to Bellingham, Washington, on a house-buying visit in November, it was dreary and dark by 4:00 pm. But we could still see, when we went to look at the only synagogue in town, that there were no stained-glass windows at all. I was disappointed. I loved watching sunlight come in through the colored panes and dye the pews and carpets a changing rainbow of hues to complement the prayers.

We moved there the following spring. The first time we attended services was on a sunny Saturday morning, and as we walked up the steps, I braced myself for the plainness of the interior.

We were welcomed by a number of people already in the sanctuary, so I didn't actually get around to looking up at the windows until after the service had begun. I was prepared for a colorless, static view and had been telling myself I would get used to it.

But as soon as I looked out the windows on my side, I caught my breath. Just outside the window was a huge willow tree, its long branches moving gently in the breeze, and a small, bright golden bird clinging to one of the twigs. It was a lovelier and more alive picture than any stained-glass window had ever been, by an artist even more inspiring than Chagall.

*Thank You, Lord, for showing me that windows are
to look through as well as to look at.*
—Rhoda Blecker

*November*

## ☼ THE ONE WHO IS TO COME

*Sun 27*    *"Come, all you who are thirsty.... Come, buy wine and milk without money and without cost. Why spend money on what is not bread, and your labor on what does not satisfy?..."*
—Isaiah 55:1–2 (NIV)

**FIRST SUNDAY IN ADVENT:**
**"I AM THE BREAD OF LIFE" (JOHN 6:35)**

Even though I used my best tricks to persuade her to stay at our dining room table and eat with us, three-year-old Ava knelt on her chair, pointed to her plate and solemnly declared, "I don't like any of this!" Because her mom had put Ava's favorite foods on her plate (fried chicken, cheese bread and strawberries), I suspected her resistance stemmed from the many chips and glasses of lemonade she had consumed earlier, as well as a burning desire to resume playing with her toys.

I hate to admit it, but when it comes to spiritual nutrition, I'm often like Ava. I fill my soul with junk food that suppresses my true hunger. Like Isaiah's listeners, I too spend money, time and effort on much that doesn't nourish me. Jesus invites me to partake of Him: in His Word, in Communion and in what He described was His own food, "to do the will of him who sent me..." (John 4:34).

At bedtime I have the habit of reading something relaxing to help me unwind and fall asleep. Last summer, I decided to read my Bible for at least a few minutes before picking up the novel on my nightstand. What a difference! Those few minutes grew into a peaceful, nourishing time. Lately I've neglected that fragile new habit; it's time to pick up my Bible again.

*Lord Jesus, my Bread of Life, I want You to nourish my soul. Help me receive You today in every way You offer Yourself.*
—Mary Brown

*November*

## Mon 28
*Do not withhold good from those to whom it is due....*
—Proverbs 3:27 (NAS)

Louise was a newcomer at our church when she joined our Monday-evening Bible study. We soon learned that she loved everybody and everything, and had a keen eye for the bright side of life.

During one Bible study, Louise told us something about herself. "I ran away from home and married at an early age. But things didn't work out. My husband's drinking helped to destroy our relationship. But I'm grateful to God that from our union came a beautiful daughter."

When Louise spoke, her father was seriously ill. He died a short time later, and the members of the Bible study attended his wake. During our visit, Louise approached me, accompanied by a tall, attractive young lady. "Oscar," Louise said, "I'd like you to meet my daughter Melinda. She recently graduated from Boston University, and we are so proud."

As I extended my hand, Melinda smiled and said, "I know who you are, Mr. Greene. You came to our school when I was in the second grade."

I blinked as my mind raced back to a spring morning when I sat on a classroom floor surrounded by twenty eager youngsters. I read my stories, and we talked about writing. A boy named Joseph wanted to see a writing contract, and I sent him a photocopy of one the next morning.

I had attended the wake to express my sympathy and to bring comfort. Unexpectedly, Melinda gave me two gifts: remembrance and appreciation. Like her mother, Melinda was beautiful both inside and out.

*Gracious Lord, we learn understanding from each other. All that is required is that we listen, observe and believe.*
—Oscar Greene

*November*

*Tue 29* "These stones are to be a memorial to the people of Israel forever."—Joshua 4:7 (NIV)

A couple of miles from our home, on a well-traveled state highway, sits a vacant service station. Outside its empty storefront, a red-and-white sign still lists the price of regular gasoline as $2.59 a gallon. When the price of gas shot up to about $4.40 a gallon here in 2008, that sign seemed a mocking reminder to my wife Carol and me each time we drove past. Then later in the year the price of gas sank to less than half its highest price. That gave us a different perspective on the unchanging gasoline sign, a reminder of shifting fortunes and an unsettled economy.

There are all kinds of signs that cause us to remember things that are important. In the Book of Joshua, when God parted the waters of the Jordan River and allowed the Israelites to cross on dry ground to enter the Promised Land, Joshua established a memorial. He appointed a man from each of the twelve tribes to gather large stones from the riverbed and set them up as a marker at Gilgal. The stones would be a memorial to the people of Israel reminding them that "the hand of God is powerful."

I like "memorial stones," things that remind me of what's important in life. Passing a church reminds me that I have a lot of brothers and sisters I haven't met yet. Looking at a cross causes me to reflect on what Jesus did for me. And reading God's Word regularly is the best way I know of keeping alive the quiet assurance that God loves me.

*Lord, thank You for the "memorial stones" that assure
me of Your presence and Your power.*
—Harold Hostetler

*November*

## Wed 30

*For by one offering He has perfected for all time....*
—Hebrews 10:14 (NAS)

When I was growing up, we never made homemade Christmas cookies. We had a tree and hung stockings on the mantel, but my mother hated a messy kitchen, so we made slice-and-bakes instead. In grocery-store checkout lines, I'd stare at the holiday baking magazines, their covers filled with cookies shaped like whimsical snowmen, glittery stars and iced candy canes. But messy kitchens were a no-no and, anyway, I knew my cookies wouldn't be picture perfect.

My own children were grown the year my daughter Katie announced, "This December, we're making Christmas cookies."

"Do you know how?"

"We'll figure it out."

"But it's so messy."

"Chill, Mom. Bring a gingerbread-man recipe and the ingredients. I'll handle the sugar cookies."

I found the recipe that night. A flawless gingerbread man with raisin eyes and a knowing smile peered up at me. *You'll never make a cookie as perfect as me.*

"I know," I whispered.

On baking day, I tried to be careful, but a dusting of flour covered Katie's floor. "Sorry," I said.

"Have fun," she said. "We'll clean up later."

I watched as my children decorated their first homemade Christmas cookies. Thomas cut out bells and angels, and Jamie covered them with sprinkles. Katie pulled out some leftover frosting—orange and purple.

"That's not going to look right," I warned.

Katie shrugged and drew silly faces on her gingerbread men. "Who cares how they look? They'll taste good."

And you know what? My daughter was right.

*Lord, no matter how messy my life gets, I can rest in
Your perfect gift of Jesus.* —Julie Garmon

## November

**SEEDS OF LOVE**

1 _____

2 _____

3 _____

4 _____

5 _____

6 _____

7 _____

8 _____

9 _____

10 _____

*November*

11 ___

12 ___

13 ___

14 ___

15 ___

16 ___

17 ___

18 ___

19 ___

20 ___

21 ___

*November*

22 _____

23 _____

24 _____

25 _____

26 _____

27 _____

28 _____

29 _____

30 _____

# December

*Yea, I have loved thee with
an everlasting love: therefore
with lovingkindness have
I drawn thee.*

—JEREMIAH 31:3

## December

### A PATH TO SIMPLICITY

*Thu 1*  *Now faith is the assurance of things hoped for, the conviction of things not seen.* —HEBREWS 11:1 (NAS)

**BECOMING PART OF A FAMILY**

While simplifying my cabin, I found a directory from my childhood church. I scanned the list of names until I found the one that forever changed my life: Inez McGraw. The years fell away as I remembered the day back in 1962 when she planted the seed of a dream in my young heart.

I was nine years old, and to earn spending money, I sold used newspapers to the glass factories in my hometown of Huntington, West Virginia. I had rolled my red wagon to Mrs. McGraw's big brick house to collect her offerings for the week. On top of the stack of papers tied up neatly with string was the tiniest magazine I'd ever seen. "That's for you to keep, Roberta," she said, pointing to it. "I usually hold on to my *Guideposts*, but the stories were so good this month, I told Mr. McGraw, 'I believe our Roberta needs this.'"

"I want to someday tell stories just like this, God," I prayed. "If You'll help me do that, I won't ask You for another thing. Ever."

In 1990, that dream came true. I won a place at the Guideposts Writers Workshop and learned to write the Guideposts way—simply and from the heart. Since then, I've told hundreds of stories in *Guideposts* and *Daily Guideposts* and become a part of a family that has caring members in every state in America.

*Father of our dreams, thank You for listening to the simple prayer of a little West Virginia girl all those years ago.*
—ROBERTA MESSNER

## Fri 2

*His divine power has given us everything we need for life and godliness through our knowledge of him....*
—II PETER 1:3 (NIV)

"I owe you an apology," I wrote to my daughter-in-law in a recent e-mail. "One of the things God and I have been working on in me is to let people feel how they feel without telling them how they should feel. And after I talked to you on the phone this morning, I talked to God and He reminded me that I'd done it again.

"I didn't let you express the frustration that every mom feels in dealing with kids and their stuff. Yours at that moment was the frustration of dealing with a child's shyness, and I tried to be the know-it-all and talk you out of your feelings because (as if you didn't know) shy, sensitive people can grow up to be great compassionate people.

"I hate it when people don't let me feel what I feel for the moment. I would rather they just listen than tell me how I should feel.

"So I'm sorry, because that's one of the things I don't like about me.

"XOXOX"

Later, she wrote back:

"Thank you, even though an apology wasn't necessary. I have to admit that feeling so frustrated in any of my mothering moments is one of the things that I like least about me.

"I appreciate that you're choosing to work on things you don't like about yourself; it's an inspiration for me to do the same."

I was tempted to write her back and thank her for thanking me, but I stopped to thank God first.

*Lord, I'm grateful for the relationships that give me safe places to grow closer to You and closer to who You want me to be.*
—CAROL KUYKENDALL

*December*

## Sat 3

*I even found great pleasure in hard work, an additional reward for all my labors.* —Ecclesiastes 2:10 (NLT)

He starts by reading the third-place winner. Not me. *So I must have won first or second!*

Second place? Also not me. *Great! I came in first!*

But when he reads the winner, the sounds coming out of his mouth don't resemble those of my name. *Is there some mistake?*

It's a long, lonely drive home, thinking about the three months I've put into learning and practicing my new hobby of stand-up comedy. I'd been honing my act in hopes of winning this preliminary contest and advancing to the finals in a few months. But now that's not going to happen.

I took the stage tonight full of confidence. I knew my jokes forward and backward, and I'd practiced them in front of audience after audience. They laughed every time—except tonight.

*I worked so hard. I practiced so much.*

It's raining, and the wipers squeak back and forth. I keep thinking about those hours of preparation, and as I do, I actually start to become less concerned about the loss. What's more important than the result is the work I put in, work that was satisfying and represented my best effort.

When I pull into the parking garage at my apartment building, the weight of the defeat has lifted completely. I did my best work, and the rest was and always will be up to God. Letting a comedy contest ruin my day would be silly—even, you might say, laughable.

> *Lord, I ask for the dedication and energy I need to give my very best effort to the labor You've provided for me.*
> —Joshua Sundquist

*December*

## 🕯 THE ONE WHO IS TO COME

*Sun 4*   *I am the light of the world: he that followeth me shall not walk in darkness, but shall have the light of life.* —JOHN 8:12

**SECOND SUNDAY IN ADVENT:**
**"I AM THE LIGHT OF THE WORLD" (JOHN 8:12)**

A few years ago our family lived in Norway for the month of June. Our most vivid memory is the wondrous evening light. Until I experienced it, I couldn't imagine the effect of living where the sun never sets. It's difficult to describe the energy and sense of well-being that constant sunlight imparts.

No words can adequately depict the light of our Savior. God's light is incomprehensible. After talking with God, Moses' face shone so brightly he had to cover it with a veil so the people would be able to look at him. Christ comes to dispel my darkness, my ultimate blindness: ignorance of God's love and estrangement from my Creator.

On weekday mornings from September to May, I go to the kitchen and plug in a full-spectrum light box on the kitchen counter. Absorbing the brightness, I fill the coffeemaker, make breakfast and pack lunches. This morning dose of light alleviates the seasonal depression I battle each winter. One morning recently, we all overslept, so my son grabbed a protein bar and we raced off to school; no time for the light box.

Once back home, as I went to my prayer corner, I brought the light box with me. Turning it on, I marveled at the beauty of the light illumining the cross on the wall. Then I knew: This time set apart for God to pray and read Scripture is my true light box, the way for His light to fill my soul. His light is greater than the darkness of winter, of lethargy or sadness or all my human foibles.

*Oh, Christ, the true light Who enlightens and sanctifies us,*
*let the light of Your countenance be impressed upon us,*
*that in it we may see Your inestimable light.*
—MARY BROWN

## December

### Mon 5

*Thou shalt not be afraid for the terror by night; nor for the arrow that flieth by day; Nor for the pestilence that walketh in darkness; nor for the destruction that wasteth at noonday.*
—PSALM 91:5–6

I'm a little bit of a germaphobe, I'm sorry to admit, especially during flu season, when every cough and sneeze makes me cringe. So imagine my discomfort the other day when I was stuck on a crowded commuter train and the man in front of me went into a dramatic coughing fit. He would cough violently for a few minutes and then the outburst would subside, only to resume as soon as I thought the coast was clear to start breathing again.

*God,* I prayed miserably, *please make him stop. I can't afford to get sick right now.*

But this man wasn't stopping. I scrunched lower and lower in my seat, trying to stay beneath the thick cloud of airborne pathogens I imagined filling the car. Anger and anxiety roiled within me as I watched the seatback in front of me buck with every cough. Suddenly, the young woman across the aisle reached into her bag, pulled out a bottle of water and handed it to the man. "Here you go," she said. "Might help."

The man took a sip, and another, clearing his throat. "Must have had something stuck," he said to the woman. "Thanks."

"You can keep it," she said with a smile, nodding at the bottle.

And all was quiet, except for the little voice in my conscience. I had a bottle of water in my bag and probably a few mints or cough drops as well—except I hadn't thought of them. I was too busy worrying about the germ cloud.

An uncountable number of germs are in the world, and some of them are going to get me from time to time, no matter what. Maybe I should just relax.

> *Lord, You came into this world and walked among the sick, never fearing. It's flu season again. Grant me protection, but grant me also Your compassion.*
> —EDWARD GRINNAN

*December*

## Tue 6
*Thou art the God that doest wonders....* —PSALM 77:14

I was washing my hands in the women's restroom at a fast-food restaurant when, above the roar of the drier on the opposite wall, I heard squeals of excitement. I turned around to see two little girls, ages perhaps five and three, thrusting their arms in and out of the blast of hot air. Laughing, shrieking, a little frightened, they'd turned what to me was a dull practicality into a great adventure.

As I dried my hands at the machine next to theirs, I, too, let myself enjoy the rush of warm wind on my hands. I remembered how moving air of any kind used to delight my own children. I saw Donnie, age one, chortling with glee each time he felt the breeze from an oscillating fan.

For each commonplace experience, there had to be a first time. Like the winter of 1953, when a friend from Florida came to visit. It was Marcia's first trip north, and as I waited for her train at Pennsylvania Station, I pictured her amazement at New York City's skyscrapers. Instead, what most impressed her was the novelty of seeing her own breath form a white cloud in the frosty air.

"The Empire State Building!" I'd point out. "Rockefeller Plaza!"

She glanced dutifully at these landmarks, but "Look," she kept saying, "I'm smoking!"

*If only*, I thought, as the girls' mother pulled them away from the magical wind machine, *I could learn to recapture that first wonder at the world around us!*

*Let me look with fresh eyes, Father, at all I see today.*
—ELIZABETH SHERRILL

*December*

## Wed 7

*It's harder to make amends with an offended friend than to capture a fortified city....* —PROVERBS 18:19 (NLT)

I recognized the hesitant knock on our front door as belonging to a six-year-old neighbor several houses up the street. Marie often came to play with our puppy because her mother was allergic to animal hair.

My hands were covered with flour, so I called out, "The door's unlocked! Come on in!" I added something else in the way of greeting and continued kneading my huge blob of bread dough.

Marie stayed only a few minutes. Her abrupt exit was puzzling, but I thought, *Kids—can't figure them out,* and continued my baking.

Moments later, the phone rang. The caller was Marie's mother, Virginia, who quickly came right to the point: "What did Marie do that offended you?"

"Nothing," I answered. "In fact, I wondered why she left so soon."

"Marie said you told her to go home."

Virginia and I tried to reconstruct what had happened. Finally I remembered exactly what I'd told her daughter. After inviting her in, I'd added, "Make yourself at home." What Marie heard was, "Go on home."

We ended up laughing at the misunderstanding, but I could have lost my best friend and the trust of a small child had Virginia not determined to resolve a potential rift in our relationship.

*Lord, Your Word tells me how many times You won people to You by simply sitting and talking to them. Help me to be as understanding with Your other children as You are with me.*
—ISABEL WOLSELEY

*December*

*Thu 8*    Let the fields rejoice, and all that is therein.
—I Chronicles 16:32

Winter was just around the corner, and I was feeling slightly blue. Don't get me wrong; I love a lot of things about the cold months: clean air and brilliant skies, ice-skating with the kids and, most of all, the joys of Christmas. But I also love summer for its balmy breezes, lazy days at the shore, and its bumper crop of local fruits and vegetables. *Wouldn't it be grand,* I mused as I entered my favorite café one icy day, *if we could enjoy summer's bounty in the midst of winter?*

The shop was decked out in its Christmas best, with a decorated tree and figurines of angels and Santa. Even the artificial snow looked appealing, although I wouldn't have minded a pinch of beach sand instead. As I sidled up to the counter, a splash of color caught my eye. I glanced at the pastry case and gasped. Within lay a brilliant array of miniature vegetables and fruit: luscious pears, plump strawberries, glossy green peppers, ripe red tomatoes.

"It's marzipan," said the friendly shopkeeper. "Almond paste and sugar, shaped and painted by hand. My family has been doing this for generations."

I could hardly believe my eyes. These tiny creations were perfect replicas of my beloved summer produce. Each was a masterpiece, meticulously shaped and colored, like fruit plucked from a fairy garden. This was better than Christmas in July; it was a bit of July at Christmastime! I bought two dozen pieces, all the while giving thanks to God, Whose abundant love gives rise to every season of the year and to the glorious blessings that each contains.

*Lord, teach me to rejoice in all Your gifts in every season of the year.*
—Philip Zaleski

## December

### Fri 9

*The fear of the Lord is clean, enduring for ever: the judgments of the Lord are true and righteous altogether. More to be desired are they than gold, yea, than much fine gold: sweeter also than honey and the honeycomb.* —PSALM 19:9–10

Years ago, when the kids were young, my wife Sandee and I commissioned a series of Russian Orthodox icons (though neither of us is Russian or Orthodox). The icon painter was an unusual man with an unusually rigid style, but we love what he did—archangels, assorted saints, a Russian monastery.

We love them so much, in fact, that I listed the paintings on my insurance form. I was willing to pay extra just to insure them separately.

The agent was quiet. "Have you ever had the paintings appraised?" he asked.

"No," I said.

"So what do you think they're worth?"

Now it was my turn to be quiet. In my mind's eye, I could see the painting of Mary that hangs at the top of the stairs, or the stoic archangel Gabriel, or the one with the Infant Jesus and His incredibly sad eyes. *What do you think they're worth?* I remembered the care we took in finding just the right places for them in our otherwise messy household, perhaps hoping their beauty would be contagious. *What do you think they're worth?* If the icons were lost in a fire, I could have them repainted, but I could never really replace them.

"Listen," I said finally. "Skip it. We don't need the extra insurance."

*Lord, the most precious things You've given me can't be insured; they rely instead on a different kind of protection—one that appraises value over cost, faith over fate, love over anything else.*
—MARK COLLINS

*December*

## Sat 10
*Glad and merry in heart....* —II Chronicles 7:10

I harbor some Scrooge-like feelings around this time of year. So I secretly hoped no one would mention the Christmas Shop in Dillsboro, North Carolina, where some of us had driven for a day's outing. No such luck; everyone wanted to visit Nancy Tut's store.

I lagged behind and then decided to hurry in and out without buying anything. But once I stepped inside the shop, I sensed an indefinable sweet presence permeating the place. One room contained only Nativity sets; I stayed behind, touching them softly and marveling after the others left.

The spirit of Christmas surprised and captivated my heart to such an extent that I needed help carrying my purchases to the car. "Merry Christmas, y'all!" I called back to the owners. With a new spring in my step and a smile that simply wouldn't stop, I joined our group for lunch.

Back home, as I took my tissue-wrapped purchases out of the festive shopping bags, I noticed a tiny brochure in the bottom of each bag. Printed in red and green, it asked, "What will it take to make yours a merry Christmas? Would good news make you merry? Being cured of a terminal condition? Receiving a gift? Restoring a broken relationship? Being reunited with someone special?" Then the pamphlet listed some Scripture that provided the answers: Luke 2:10–11, John 3:16, Romans 3:23, I John 1:7, Romans 6:23, Ephesians 2:8, Isaiah 59:2, Colossians 1:21, I Thessalonians 4:16–17, Romans 10:9, Romans 10:13.

The house converted into the Christmas Shop some forty-two years ago was about much more than gifts; its purpose was to remind us of the Giver.

*Merry Christmas, Father! I praise You for the greatest Gift ever given.*
—Marion Bond West

*December*

## 🕎 THE ONE WHO IS TO COME

### Sun 11

*He tends his flock like a shepherd: He gathers the lambs in his arms and carries them close to his heart; he gently leads those that have young.* —Isaiah 40:11 (NIV)

**THIRD SUNDAY IN ADVENT:**
**"I AM THE GOOD SHEPHERD" (JOHN 10:11)**

I confess I've never liked thinking of myself as a sheep. Perhaps this comes from seeing the sheep on my husband's family farm: dumb, bleating animals that startle at the slightest sound and aimlessly run after each other.

No, I don't like to think I'm a sheep. In fact, that strong-willed, independent inner me doesn't much like the idea of even needing a shepherd. Yet looking back, I see times my unseen Shepherd led me away from harm and back into green pastures. In college, when I began shedding the faith and morals of my upbringing, I literally bumped into a young man of integrity who became my boyfriend and brought me back to church and a wholesome way of life.

My Shepherd also has carried me through grief. Thirty years ago, when my father died in a snowmobile accident, I felt abandoned—not only by my dad, whom I blamed for taking a foolish risk, but by God, Who allowed it to happen. As our family stood around Dad's casket before it was closed for the last time, we held hands and struggled to pray. My Aunt Helen began speaking: "The Lord is my shepherd...."

From the depth of our sorrow, we joined her: "I shall not want...."

*Yes, my Shepherd, I do want to be Your sheep. Because of You,*
*I fear no evil. Thank You for Your green pastures and still waters,*
*for leading me, restoring my soul, and filling my life with*
*Your goodness and mercy.*
—Mary Brown

*December*

## Mon 12

*Therefore encourage one another and build up each other, as indeed you are doing.*
—I Thessalonians 5:11 (NRSV)

Do you Twitter? Are you LinkedIn? Do you have friends on Facebook?

I don't know about you, but I've been slow to adopt much of the social networking revolution on the Internet. I never could quite understand why a whole bunch of people would want—or especially need—to know what I'm doing or what I'm thinking at some specific moment in the day, in 140 characters or less. (That's Twitter, for those of you who don't "tweet.")

But one of the great benefits of my work is that I get to hang around a younger generation. I was sitting with a group of them one night in the lounge of one of my school's residential buildings, so I started asking them about Twitter and the like—and sharing my skepticism.

"Do you like people?" one of the students asked me.

"Well, of course I do," I said. "But what does liking people have to do with telling them everything all the time?"

She smiled one of those smiles you get when someone knows something you don't. "Sharing hope and joy with people is a great gift. Why wouldn't I want to do that in every way I can?"

I'm still not convinced about tweeting and some of those other electronic communities. But I was convinced that night about something else: As a person of faith, I'm called to share my hope and joy with others all the time, no matter how I do it. That's why, today and every single day, whether on Facebook or face-to-face, I have a goal: offering five friends a kind word, a good thought, a gift of hope.

*Open my eyes today, oh, God, to those who need an encouraging word. And open my mouth (or move my fingers) so that I might offer it.*
—Jeff Japinga

*December*

## Tue 13

*How sweet are thy words unto my taste! yea, sweeter than honey to my mouth!* —PSALM 119:103

Glazed doughnuts are among my favorite things in the world. When I was six years old, I was taken to the hospital to have my tonsils and adenoids removed. After the operation, I awoke in my hospital bed with a very sore throat. I'd been told I could have Popsicles and ice cream, but there was only one thing I wanted. "Glazed doughnuts," I croaked. "I want glazed doughnuts." I couldn't have swallowed them, but the desire was so real that I can still taste the doughy circles with their silky topping. Soon my mother appeared at my bedside. "I have something for you," she said. But it was a little bowl of Jell-O. I fought back tears: This was not what I expected! Still, *hmm*, it tasted pretty good as I took a cool spoonful.

Years have passed, and now my nephew's five-year-old daughter Katie likes doughnuts too. The other day her grandpa—my brother—brought in a big box of them. But when Katie ran to open the lid, it turned out the doughnuts weren't from her favorite bakery. She burst into tears. "This is not what I expected!" she cried. In a few minutes, though, she was testing the "different ones" and seemed to enjoy them.

"I know just how you felt, Katie," I told her later. "So many things in life aren't what we expected. But after the first shock, *hmm*, they're pretty good after all."

*Thank You for glazed doughnuts, Lord. And if they're not available, help me to be grateful for what You do send.*
—MARY ANN O'ROARK

## Wed 14

*"The one who trusts in him will never be put to shame."*
—Romans 9:33 (NIV)

Thousands of Canada geese make their winter homes in Mississippi. The other day I watched a flock of them fly through the air and land on the surface of the water. I'd been having some difficulty adjusting to my new part-time role at work and I envied the geese; they seemed so carefree as they glided along. Then I remembered a song we had sung many times at our church:

> *Trust and obey, for there's no other way,*
> *To be happy in Jesus, than to trust and obey.*
> *Then in fellowship sweet we will sit at His feet,*
> *Or we'll walk by His side in the way.*
> *What He says we will do, where He sends we will go;*
> *Never fear, only trust and obey.*
> *(John H. Sammis, 1887)*

As I looked at the geese and thought about my circumstances, I began to relax, knowing that the more I acknowledge that God is in charge, the more I can trust and obey Him.

Can I be as carefree as the geese? I don't know. Can I be more carefree than I am and trust God more? The answer is a resounding *yes!*

*Lord, help me to strive to trust You more.*
—Dolphus Weary

*December*

## Thu 15

*Thanks be to God for his indescribable gift!*
—II CORINTHIANS 9:15 (NIV)

This week my daughter Elizabeth and I have been eating breakfast by candlelight. I realized we hadn't lit the Advent wreath on Sunday, and it seemed a nice idea to light it Monday in the early morning darkness.

Something about the flickering warmth of candles brings my thoughts around to mystery. Nowadays we illuminate our world brightly and crisply, and it gives us the illusion that we know much more than we do. We operate as if everything is seeable and knowable, or at least *should* be seeable and knowable. But much of life isn't so luminous; people most surely are not!

Gazing at Elizabeth eating her gingerbread in the soft glow of the candles, I remember things that I don't remember under electric lights: the stories of Milky-Milky (a cow) and Walky-Walky (a horse) that I told at bedtime when she was a preschooler; her ocean-themed birthday party when she was four; comforting her the first time she forgot to do her homework; her excitement when her much-beloved mentor Alison arrived at our house to teach her math. By candlelight, it's easy to appreciate that there's a certain miracle in the fact that this marvelous being across the table is my child. How did that happen?

Perhaps part of the reason I've been silently waxing nostalgic during breakfast lately is that Elizabeth is applying to college a year early. Last night we heard from MIT. Among my future memories will be the shout of joy that burst from her as she read that she'd been accepted.

*This is my child. What a gift. What a gift.*

> *Oh, Jesus, the Father's beloved Son, what a gift You are!*
> —JULIA ATTAWAY

## Fri 16

*December*

*Let no one seek his own good, but the good of his neighbor.*
—I Corinthians 10:24 (RSV)

It was such a strange wish among all the SpongeBob and PlayStation requests on the Wishing Tree that the store had on display. I'd stuffed it into my purse without even looking at it; I was running like crazy this year, what with my extra holiday job at a local diner. Still, I wanted to keep to my tradition of buying a present for Brian, whose name and age (seven) were on the tag.

Late again, I screeched to a halt in front of the toy store, raced in and buttonholed an already harried clerk. I hadn't had time to look at the tag, so now I glanced at it and said, "I need an... alarm clock?" Confused, I asked, "Is that the name of a toy?"

The clerk looked puzzled. "Not that I know. And I think I've heard them all."

I made a hurried call to the crisis center, the ones who supplied the names for the tree. A woman sighed and explained, "Brian has to depend on himself to get himself up."

"Wouldn't his parents wake him up?"

"Not all of the parents get up themselves. They're either sick or drunk or addicted."

"I see," I said, asking God to cover in prayer this child I'd chosen, this child who was responsible enough to ask for an alarm clock so that he could get to school on time.

I'd give Brian an alarm clock—and a fun puzzle—as a holiday gift. And I'd give myself the gift of living without a schedule for a few days while I said a prayer for Brian, a boy I'd never meet.

*Dear God, just as You are gracious enough to fulfill my needs, thank You for using me to fulfill a need for someone else this year.*
—Linda Neukrug

*December*

## ⌛ ADVICE FROM AUNT ANNIE

*Sat 17*  *They shall bring gold and incense; and they shall shew forth the praises of the Lord.* —Isaiah 60:6

**THE PERFECT TREE**

My father died of cancer on January 9, 1961, some three months shy of his fiftieth birthday. During his final illness, Daddy continued to practice the generosity that characterized his life. He bought groceries and shoveled snow for a neighbor in great need. When the neighbor heard that Daddy would be spending Christmas in the hospital, she made him a billowy little Christmas tree of red net, decorated with tiny white buttons and topped with a white cardboard star. "I wish I could afford to bring you four dozen red roses," she said wistfully, placing the tree on a dresser so that Daddy could see it.

Aunt Annie thought the tree was a bit tacky, although she was too well mannered to say so. But on the Sunday before Christmas, she was sitting with Daddy when the cleaning woman slipped in. The woman dusted and swept; then stepped to the dresser for a better view of the tree, picking it up and carefully examining it from every angle. "Isn't it beautiful?" she exclaimed. "It's just perfect! I'm going to make one just like it for my grandchildren."

Aunt Annie looked at the tree again, this time seeing it with her heart. It *was* beautiful, she realized. It was beautiful because it represented the bond of love between giver and receiver—a bond that is never broken, not even by death.

*Thank You, Lord Jesus, for Your generous gifts of family,*
*memory and everlasting love.*
—Penney Schwab

*December*

## 🕯 THE ONE WHO IS TO COME

*Sun 18*  We were buried therefore with him by baptism into death, so that as Christ was raised from the dead by the glory of the Father, we too might walk in newness of life.... So you also must consider yourselves dead to sin and alive to God in Christ Jesus. —ROMANS 6:4, 11 (RSV)

FOURTH SUNDAY IN ADVENT: "I AM THE RESURRECTION AND THE LIFE" (JOHN 11:25)

At this point in my journey to Christmas, Jesus reminds me why He was born: so He could die and rise again! Christ came in human flesh not just to be worshipped in a manger but to endure the humiliations of earthly life, to suffer death and to conquer it for us. He lay in the manger as an infant wrapped in swaddling clothes so that one day He would lie in the tomb. The Magi brought the gift of myrrh, foretelling what the women would bring to anoint His body after His Crucifixion and to discover His Resurrection. And His Resurrection gives me hope that I, too, will be unbound from my burial wrappings and raised to life in Him.

Jesus declares to Martha, "I am the resurrection." Then He asks her, "Do you believe this?" Jesus asks me, too, not only if I believe He can raise me to life after my physical body dies, but if I believe I can live a new life, His Life, here and now.

I may know in my mind that Christ has power over sin, but do I truly consider myself dead to sin and alive in Christ? Alive in Christ, I can forgive someone who has wronged me. Alive in Christ, I can draw upon His power to control my anger, to speak calmly and firmly instead of shouting. Alive in Christ, I can admit my mistakes and ask forgiveness. Alive in Christ, I can give Him all my anxieties and trust only in Him.

*Yes, Lord, I believe. Please help me see each day*
*how I can walk in the newness of life.*
—MARY BROWN

*December*

### Mon 19

*The day is yours, and yours also the night.... You made both summer and winter.* —PSALM 74:16–17 (NIV)

We live in a valley. By climbing a hill we call Solstice Point after sunset, I can see the sun re-rise briefly above Black Ridge to the west and then set again a few minutes later. On the depressingly short December and January afternoons, I climb to the top of the hill to savor those few extra minutes of sunlight.

Last year we received a Christmas newsletter from our friends Don and Kathy. They met and married many years ago when they both worked as rangers in the Black Hills National Forest. They looked forward to the short days of winter; being on ski patrol together was more fun than sitting alone in separate fire lookout towers during the long days of summer.

"Last winter's backcountry snow wasn't friendly, so we retreated to groomed Nordic tracks," the newsletter said. "Kathy's feet are still swollen from chemo, so she bought larger boots!" Two pages of cheerful news closed with, "Kathy's been in chemotherapy once a month for two years now. It keeps us nearer to home, but there's still a lot of fun and beauty close by."

I wiped a few tears from my eyes and set aside their letter. Somehow, my complaints about the lack of sunlight seemed irrelevant. If Don and Kathy could rejoice in the midst of their struggle, I could certainly thank God for my December days and long December nights.

*Dear God, please help me be a comfort to my friend Don next winter, his first one without Kathy in fifty-two years.*
—TIM WILLIAMS

*December*

## Tue 20

*A light to lighten the Gentiles, and the glory of thy people Israel.* —LUKE 2:32

This morning I saw the star I've been awaiting, not in the sky, but in my neighbor's window. Surely there's nothing remarkable about a small, star-shaped box about five inches in diameter. Its pale gold offers a speck of visual relief in a monochrome New England landscape of white sky, white ground etched with gray spruces, white house with black shutters. No, not much to look at as a decoration. Yet across the swath of lawn that separates my neighbor and me, I regard this simple star as a symbol of peace and goodwill.

For five years now I've enjoyed kindness from my neighbors: a cup of sugar, fresh bread, a tomato plant, a warm inquiry into my children's activities. I use their clothesline and park in their driveway when mine is slippery. Most of all, I know I can count on them if I'm in trouble. It doesn't seem to matter that my neighbors celebrate Hanukkah and I celebrate Christmas.

Tonight, I'll place my own golden star box in my window—just for my neighbors. In harmony, we celebrate Christmas and Hanukkah—and each other—with our neighborliness and our stars.

*Creator of the moon and stars, thank You for reflected light in kindly neighbors.* —GAIL THORELL SCHILLING

---

### READER'S ROOM

I was introduced to *Daily Guideposts* by Charlene, a dear friend with whom I worked for twenty years. I retired before my friend did, and she continued to give me *Daily Guideposts* every Christmas, as she does to this day. For years I would find surprise notes written throughout the book—special greetings on special days. A very special friend she has been and still is, just as *Daily Guideposts* has been a good friend and still is.

—*Gloe Bertram, Lexington, Kentucky*

*December*

### Wed 21

*The earnest prayer of a righteous man has great power and wonderful results.* —James 5:16 (TLB)

My son had flown in for a pre-Christmas visit and we were at a restaurant, relishing a dessert of trifle after a sumptuous dinner to celebrate the season, when Phyllis, an acquaintance of mine, came up to our table.

"Prime rib, Yorkshire pudding *and* trifle!" Phyllis turned to her husband. "I knew it." Her blue eyes twinkled. "We were at the corner table over there. We saw you come in, guessed at what you'd order and decided to say *hi* on our way out. This must be Ian. Tell me, how are Melissa, Brandon, Luke and Shelby?"

*Amazing,* I thought, *she knows their names and rolls them off with such familiarity!* Phyllis smiled. "Over the past several years I've prayed daily for all of you."

"You have? Without even knowing us?" Ian said. "Wow, Mum, this is some lady." He reached over and gave her a hug. "We have one more child, Tara, born two years ago."

"Beautiful name. Well, as of right now, she's added to my list."

"So dear of you," I stammered. "I had no idea...."

"I know you didn't. And you still wouldn't if we hadn't run into each other. The Lord has put certain families on my heart and daily I lift them up to Him in prayer."

"Oh, Phyllis," I said, "you've given us the ultimate gift. What a joyful Christmas surprise!"

*Beloved Lord, I thank You for the saints among us to whom You have given a ministry of prayer. Strengthen them, anoint them and bless them, even as they bless us by lifting us to Your throne of grace.*
—Fay Angus

*December*

**Thu 22**  *May you rejoice in the wife of your youth.*
—PROVERBS 5:18 (NIV)

God willing, Carol and I will celebrate our fiftieth wedding anniversary this year. As I write, I find myself mulling over a verse I just read as part of my daily Bible reading: "You have stolen my heart... my bride; you have stolen my heart" (Song of Songs 4:9, NIV). Coincidence? More like a divine reminder.

On a snowy afternoon, two days before Christmas 1961, Carol and I stood together before the altar of Pittsburgh's First Presbyterian Church as the pastor, Dr. Robert Lamont, pronounced us husband and wife. I remember looking into Carol's sparkling brown eyes at that moment and being struck by the thought, *We're not here by chance!* Back then I was too spiritually ignorant to understand the significance of that moment. Now I do.

Although I'd never been particularly religious, Carol had a real hunger for God. Eleven years later, in 1972, at her urging, we attended a Methodist Lay Witness Mission where I was transformed by an encounter with the living God.

That new reality of Jesus in our lives has cemented our relationship as nothing else could. He has carried us through illnesses and tough economic times, and on occasion has lifted us to spiritual heights we couldn't have dreamed of before. Together, we've raised two beautiful daughters who have followed us in faith. We've encouraged, taught and prayed with others, and witnessed some real miracles.

So, today, Carol and I, our daughters, son-in-law and three grandchildren will be singing praises to the One Who arranged it all. For He will be there too—and that's no coincidence.

*Father, who knew? You certainly did. And*
*Carol and I will be forever grateful.*
—HAROLD HOSTETLER

*December*

## ❈ TO SAY GOOD-BYE

*Fri 23*  *And on earth peace....* —LUKE 2:14

**A PEACEFUL PARTING**

It's Christmas Eve, our last at Hillsboro Presbyterian Church. There were years when it was almost impossible to get the children to sleep; moments when I held my breath, hoping my parents would arrive in time; days when planning Christmas Eve supper and the next morning's big family breakfast was almost overwhelming. But always on this holiest of nights, I've ended up here.

It's always been the same. I step into the hushed darkness, and peace descends. The sanctuary where my husband David stands is candlelit. Our family gathers in a pew. The sacred silence surrounds us. Finally, we walk as a family to the Communion rail. I can't imagine what's going through David's mind on this night of his last Communion in our beloved church.

At the rail, I am surrounded by the saints. I think of my father and how he loved this place, this night, this church. I think of all the people I have loved, who are with him in that place beyond our seeing.

"Welcome," David says softly, as the candles flicker and glow. One by one, he serves us.

We are all there: our son Brock with his son Harrison, our daughter Keri and her husband Ben with their daughter Abby and baby son Charles, my mother and my stepfather Herb. I am last. I take the cup.

And then it's time to go. I smile at David and whisper, "Hurry home." For the last time, I walk up the aisle toward the light at the doors and out into the beautiful, clear night.

I am not leaving the best behind. I am taking it with me, on to a new year, a new life. I can hardly wait to see what happens next!

*Peace, Father, beautiful peace. Amen.*
—PAM KIDD

*December*

# THE ONE WHO IS TO COME

**Sat 24** *Jesus saith unto him, I am the way, the truth, and the life: no man cometh unto the Father, but by me.*
—John 14:6

## CHRISTMAS EVE: "I AM THE WAY, THE TRUTH AND THE LIFE" (JOHN 14:6)

This is a night of expectation: When we seem to have lost our way, the Way is coming; minds darkened by falsehood prepare to receive the Truth; soon the shadow of death will be dispelled by the light of Life.

One day, after my husband Alex and I had lived in Oxford, England, for several months, I was walking across town to my favorite college garden, through medieval stone archways and winding passageways. I encountered a tour guide telling her group they would soon enter Christ Church College. Flabbergasted, I watched as she led them the wrong way, down an alley with no access to the college.

When I was in college, I found myself like those tourists, naively heading down a wrong path. In desperation, I prayed, "God, if You exist, please show me." That winter, I impulsively registered to go on a church ski trip. Suddenly Michigan was hit with unseasonably warm weather, and I received a call informing me that the ski trip was being replaced by a "Weekend in Christian Living" at a nearby camp. Eager for any chance to get off campus, I went.

Instead of skiing, we walked in the woods and sat by the fire discussing who Christ was and what it meant to be a Christian. After listening to my doubts all weekend, my group leader finally looked at me and said, "Mary, Jesus Christ is the Son of God. This is the truth. He wants you to follow Him and have His life within you. Will you accept it?"

That evening I knelt in the chapel and said, "Yes, Lord."

*Lord, on this holy night I say* yes *to You again. Please be the Way for me, the Truth and the Life.*
—Mary Brown

*December*

## 🦌 THE ONE WHO IS TO COME

*Sun 25* *"I am the true vine, and my Father is the vinedresser.... I am the vine, you are the branches. He who abides in Me, and I in him, bears much fruit; for without Me you can do nothing."*
—John 15:1, 5 (NKJV)

### CHRISTMAS: "I AM THE TRUE VINE" (JOHN 15:1)

Several years ago our family spent Christmas Day in South Africa. On our way home from church in Cape Town, we stopped at a restaurant overlooking a vineyard. On this hot day (December in the Southern Hemisphere is summer), we sat on a shaded balcony, enjoying the lovely view: rows of lush grapevines well-staked, weeded and cultivated. The vinedresser had planted a rosebush at the end of each row to attract pests away from his precious fruit. Not ripe enough yet for harvest, grapes hung from the vines in clusters of pale green pearls, luminous in the sunlight.

It occurs to me now that this unusual setting for our Christmas lunch holds more meaning than the sentimental snowy landscapes back home, which I'd missed as "really Christmas." Before the coming of Christ, the image of the vineyard symbolized Israel as God's cherished inheritance. Now the vine is Christ Himself with each of us as His branches. Today, Jesus reveals how all His "I am" promises can be fulfilled in our lives: Simply remain in Him as a branch on a vine.

How wonderful for each of us to be a living branch of this vine! And what encouragement! The vine does the work, holding onto the branches, pouring nourishment and life through them to bear fruit. All the branches need to do is abide.

*Dear God, what a precious gift You've given me, to be a branch in Your beloved vineyard. Please help me remember, especially during trials and struggles, that You are holding onto me.*
—Mary Brown

*December*

### Mon 26

*What shall I render unto the Lord for all his benefits toward me?* —Psalm 116:12

Christmas Eve came almost three weeks after my heart surgery. I was thrilled to be back at church, delighted to see so many dear friends after the rigors of hospitalization. The minister even announced that I was present. I rose to my feet, my hands in my pockets and a scarf wrapped around my neck to keep me warm, and received a round of applause. I waved to my cohorts in the balcony where for countless Christmas Eves I'd sung with the choir. It sounded like they were managing fine without me.

Sharing a hymnal with my son, I was having a little trouble singing. No doctor had warned me about this. They said it would take a while before I would be walking at a quick pace or running or going to the gym, but they didn't tell me that my breath for singing would go wonky on every other note. I'd sing a phrase and then have to rest to sing the next one. One venerable carol after another, and I was only half present, if that. Usually we like to divide parts as a family and harmonize together. Well, I was pretty useless. *How can I celebrate Christmas if I can't sing?*

Then we came to one of my favorite carols, "In the Bleak Midwinter," and I wanted to throw down the book at the ugly croaking I was making. But there in the last verse was the message I needed to hear: "What can I give him, poor as I am?" The answer from Christina Rossetti, the lyricist: "Give him my heart." Nothing more, nothing less. I didn't have to sing a stirring tenor descant from the loft. All I needed to do was love and be loved.

*What I can give, Lord, I give: my heart, my self.*
—Rick Hamlin

## December

### Tue 27

*There is a time for everything, and a season for every activity under heaven.* —ECCLESIASTES 3:1 (NIV)

I enjoy the holidays and the time with family and friends. I enjoy the laughter, the chatter and the swapping of happy stories. Part of the joy is also the food we share, which doesn't just drop out of nowhere.

For years, on holidays—and usually the night before—I've been one of the millions doing hard time in the kitchen: peeling potatoes, baking pies, basting turkeys and making dressing. I enjoy what comes of all the work. But I have to admit that I've had my weak moments—when my back was tired and my wrists were hurting and I fantasized briefly about going out to dinner.

This year my son Chase volunteered to host our dinner. My friend Portia, her husband Clarence, and my daughter Lanea and I drove up from Durham, North Carolina, to Cincinnati. I still expected to cook, so I carried my skillet with me (have cookware, will travel).

My children took over, and there was hardly anything for me to do. One of Chase's friends cooked a turkey and made stuffing. Chase wrestled a cut of fresh pork, he and Lanea stuffed it with cheese and apples, and then he lassoed it with some string and tossed it in the oven. He made mashed potatoes and sautéed some vegetables. Lanea made mouthwatering macaroni and cheese. I only made sugar-free chocolate cream pie and sweet potato casserole, and everything was complete.

Contrary to popular opinion, it was a joy to have so many cooks in the kitchen. The house was filled with friends and relatives, food and song, warmth and even a movie. It was such a blessing not only to eat but to prepare a holiday meal that way. I hope it's a new tradition, and I wonder why I never thought of it before.

*Lord, thank You for family, friends, food and wonderful holidays.*
—SHARON FOSTER

*December*

## Wed 28

*For now we see through a glass, darkly; but then face to face: now I know in part; but then shall I know even as also I am known.* —I CORINTHIANS 13:12

There are days when I just don't know who my oldest daughter is. When Elizabeth was singing in a children's choir, I'd ride home with her on the subway and get some hint of how her day had been. Lately, though, most of my questions get terse, generic answers: "Fine" or "Okay" or "Not bad."

A couple of weeks ago, we learned that Elizabeth, who is sixteen, had been admitted to college as an early decision/early admission applicant. So next year she'll be going off to another city to start school—and life—on her own.

I had just called home from the office when the news arrived, and I heard Elizabeth's shout of joy in the background. Suddenly I felt like Zero Mostel singing "Sunrise, Sunset." "Come on," I told myself, "you're just being sentimental." But that didn't stop the tears.

So next year I'll have to add a few hundred miles to the teenaged reticence between Elizabeth and me. Not that I'm worried. From what I can see and hear, Elizabeth's inner world is made up of math and physics, William Shakespeare and Sherlock Holmes and the elaborate games based on *Star Wars* and *Star Trek* that she joyfully shares with her younger siblings. She loves music and movies and drawing her own comic books and singing silly songs. And as I sat next to her in church last Sunday and listened to her sing descants on "The First Noel," I knew that her faith had become as much a part of her as her sweet soprano voice. As for the rest, I can leave that—and Elizabeth—in her Father's hands.

*Lord, thank You for this wonder, this mystery You have given into our care. Be with Elizabeth as she goes out on her own, now and always.*
—ANDREW ATTAWAY

## December

### Thu 29

*So do not throw away your confidence, it will be richly rewarded. You need to persevere so that when you have done the will of God, you will receive what he has promised.*
—Hebrews 10:35–36 (NIV)

My sixteen-year-old granddaughter Miriam, who lives in Senegal, West Africa, had been given a jigsaw puzzle for Christmas. It had come in a plastic bag, with no picture to follow. As she dumped its one thousand pieces, all looking surprisingly similar, on the card table, I wondered how she would manage.

Day after day, Miriam spent hours sorting, grouping and turning each piece for a possible fit. She believed that eventually this jumble would make sense and a picture would emerge. Buoyed by her faith, she kept at it long after everyone else had given up. Because Miriam persisted, she was rewarded with a beautiful Victorian painting.

This stubborn trait in my granddaughter comforts me now because she was recently diagnosed with type 1 diabetes. She's a very active teenager, and the news is frightening and unsettling for her. Still, I expect, Miriam has the tenacity to make something beautiful out of it.

"Tenacity is more than endurance," Oswald Chambers wrote. "It is endurance combined with the absolute certainty that what we are looking for is going to transpire. Spiritual tenacity does not mean to hang on and do nothing, but to work deliberately on the certainty that God is not going to be worsted."

God has a wonderful plan for my granddaughter's life, and I know she will find it.

*Divine Shepherd, bless each of my grandchildren today.*
*Comfort them, guide them and when they get discouraged,*
*carry them in Your arms, close to Your heart.*
—Helen Grace Lescheid

## Fri 30

*We have also a more sure word of prophecy; whereunto ye do well that ye take heed, as unto a light that shineth in a dark place, until the day dawn, and the day star arise in your hearts.*
—II PETER 1:19

My sister collected owls: owl pictures, owl ornaments, owl jewelry. After she passed away, I hung one of her Austrian crystal owls in a window where it would catch the rays of the rising sun.

One morning while relegated to an easy chair because of back problems, I watched that tiny owl spin ever so slowly in the current of warm air filtering out of the radiator beneath it. At first, the crystal reflected only the dim light of the early dawn. But as the sun rose higher and higher, the crystal caught its rays, refracting them into dozens of tiny rainbows revolving about the room, their colors becoming more and more intense.

Sometimes in the darker moments of life, I tend to lose sight of what God promises for the future, yet I believe He has plans for this world, even though I can't see them. In the revealing light of Scripture and historical hindsight, however, dozens of His fulfilled prophecies shine out more and more, like tiny rainbows to give me hope.

*Lord, help me hang Your promises in the window of my soul and let the light of Your Spirit shining on them give me courage day after day.*
—ALMA BARKMAN

## December

### Sat 31

*So teach us to number our days, that we may apply our hearts unto wisdom.* —PSALM 90:12

Last night I stopped at a restaurant for dinner. I was alone and brought my datebook to plan for the next day. After ordering, I gazed at the datebook and realized that this year was almost over. I flipped slowly through the pages of past days and weeks and reviewed the last twelve months.

I was amazed to discover all that can happen in a year: I had accepted a new professional position and moved from Texas to Georgia. Beth and I had witnessed the wedding vows of our first child Drew and welcomed our daughter-in-law Katie Alice into our family. Our son Luke had entered the insurance industry, and our daughter Jodi had graduated from Furman University. Somewhere in the middle of all this, I counseled with dozens of students, preached sermons, conducted funerals and wrote a book. These were just the major events; most of my hours were spent in the routines of living: sleeping, eating, exercise, repairing my car, mowing the lawn, preparing our income tax returns, going to movies, and all the other unremarkable events that fill everyone's days and nights.

As my food arrived, I realized that the real question confronting me wasn't, *How did I spend last year?* but *How will I spend the next? How will I use the most precious of God's gifts—life and time?*

I can make long lists of things to accomplish and commit myself to New Year's resolutions. But I really need to do only two things: Love God with all that I am, and love my neighbor as much as I love myself. This is all that really matters.

*Lord, keep me from seeing my days as something I own but rather as a gift that comes from You.*
—SCOTT WALKER

*December*

**SEEDS OF LOVE**

1 _____

2 _____

3 _____

4 _____

5 _____

6 _____

7 _____

8 _____

9 _____

10 _____

11 _____

12 _____

13 _____

14 _____

15 _____

## December

16

17

18

19

20

21

22

23

24

25

26

27

28

29

30

31

## FELLOWSHIP CORNER

ANNE ADRIANCE of Oldwick, New Jersey, says "It's been a year of transitions. June brought the high school graduation of our younger son, Ned, who by midsummer was off to North Carolina for his first year of college. Sam, our older son, rented his first apartment away from home and by September was back in New Mexico as a college junior. I nursed our much-loved cat Chester through his final days. Gratefully, my husband Matt and I enjoy each other's company more than ever, and we're discovering what parenting in this new phase of life means. And, happily, our aging but spunky black Lab Nellie still greets me with a big grin when I walk in the door each night. I feel blessed."

"This is a year when growing in love hasn't been so much an option as an imperative for my husband Charlie and me," says MARCI ALBORGHETTI of New London, Connecticut. "Charlie has a new grandson, Felix, and we were also blessed to be present at the birth of our second godchild, Jett, who joined his family just fourteen months after his brother R.J. was born!" Marci and Charlie still spend time every winter in the San Francisco Bay area, where Marci first worked on her Guideposts book *The Christmas Glass*, as well as the sequel, *Three Kings Day*. They are also volunteering whenever they can on both coasts and are seeing the ravages of the economy on people seeking help and services. "The only answer is for all of us to grow in love and generosity," adds Marci.

FAY ANGUS of Sierra Madre, California, writes, "Stop the clock, time is getting away from me! I need to catch up. This is a significant year for my grandkids. Tara starts kindergarten, Shelby has reached her first decade, Luke enters high school, and Brandon graduates. I'm learning to love by remote control from California to Colorado—special phone calls and personal letters to each. Thanks be to God that love spans all distance and is the melody of the soul that keeps our hearts singing."

*Fellowship Corner*

"It's been quite a hectic year," says *Daily Guideposts* editor ANDREW ATTAWAY. "At work, we're beginning some exciting new ventures, like the *Daily Guideposts* Community of Faith and our special 35th anniversary book *Daily Guideposts Journeys.* At home, Julia and I have seen Elizabeth, our eldest, go off to college at 16; John, 14, blossom at his new school; Mary, 12, stretch mind and body toward the lovely young woman she's becoming; Maggie, 9, tread the boards at our local children's theater; and Stephen, 7, construct amazing inventions from duct tape and aluminum foil. It always seems to me that I couldn't love them more, and yet by God's grace, every year I do."

Life never ceases to be interesting at the Attaway household, and this year was no exception. John started at a new school, Elizabeth is finishing high school a year early, and Mary, Maggie and Stephen are back to homeschooling and are growing up mighty fast. "The way I look at it, there are only two ways to grow: closer to God or farther away from Him," writes JULIA ATTAWAY of New York City. "Every challenge we face, no matter how hard, offers us that choice." In addition to working and homeschooling, Julia's also started a blog that she calls LotsaLaundry. "I think part of the reason I like writing online is because it gives me the illusion that I have time to spare!"

"This year our family literally grew in love with the addition of our first grandchild Kendall," says KAREN BARBER of Alpharetta, Georgia. "She's the daughter of our son Jeff and his wife Leah, and, of course, to us she's the cutest baby ever born! Since we raised three boys and never had a daughter, I'm trying not to go overboard, although I have to admit that I purchased a play kitchen at a garage sale when Kendall was only one week old. It's an added joy that Jeff and Leah live in the Atlanta area, and so does our son Chris, who is out of the Army now and doing MBA work at Emory University. John's not far away, either, off at college about two hours away. I'm blogging now on Ourprayer.org, so come on over for a visit and hear all about our family life as it unfolds."

*Fellowship Corner*

ALMA BARKMAN of Winnipeg, Manitoba, Canada, writes, "The birth of our eleventh grandchild meant the family circle expanding, not only in numbers but in love, to include little Molly. Serving on the executive council of our church seniors group meant reaching out to new folks who have started attending our monthly meetings. Aspiring writers joining the Christian writers group I attend required encouragement and guidance. Although I used to think that love can be stretched to the limit, God has no such restrictions, continually bringing new people across our path for us to get to know, love and include in our prayers. The more we grow in love, the richer my husband Leo and I feel."

"I enjoy hosting an occasional dinner for friends," says EVELYN BENCE of Arlington, Virginia. "It's a way for me to honor my guests, share the fruits of my culinary hobby and hone the lessons in hospitality I learned from my mother. Some years she served more than six hundred guest meals and snacks. Professionally, I continue to work as a freelance editor, poking at people's prose and rearranging their paragraphs." This year for Guideposts Books, Evelyn compiled a new collection of the ever-popular feature *His Mysterious Ways.*

"We rescued a greyhound this year," says RHODA BLECKER of Bellingham, Washington. "We lost Hobo to lymphoma in October and thought that we would be dogless for a while, but it was a revelation to us how a small house with two people and three cats in it could feel so empty. So less than a week later, we brought Anjin home. The adoption agency has placed more than five thousand greys whose racing lives are over and who need forever homes. She has settled in and is a great cuddler. She even helped us celebrate our oldest cat's twentieth birthday in January. Animals truly teach us what love is all about, just in case we couldn't figure it out for ourselves."

Life is indeed good—and very full—for MELODY BONNETTE of Mandeville, Louisiana. "I'm enrolled in the PhD program in education at the University of Southern Mississippi while still directing broadcasting for Channel 13. So I'm really busy!" She still sees her kids and grandkids often. Misty's three boys, Indy, Noah and Micah,

*Fellowship Corner*

are now 8, 6 and 3, and Kristen's daughter Sophia is 7 and son Thomas, 3. Christopher's little girl Mia is a precocious 2. Kevin, Melody's youngest son, is now in the US Air Force and stationed in Germany. "Growing in Love" is a perfect theme for Melody this year. Thanks to husband Johnny Swang, she has two more grandchildren to love, Sky, 3, and Sage, 1.

"Our family stayed busy this year, and love is what kept us going," says GINA BRIDGEMAN of Scottsdale, Arizona. Maria, 16, struggled through another hospitalization, but "the love, support and prayers of family, old friends and new friends at Maria's new school got us through the toughest times, and we all grew closer because of it." Gina continues to work as a communications specialist for a pre-K-through-12 school, and her husband Paul continues as technical director for Arizona Broadway Theatre. Ross, a senior at Belmont University, performed in a production of *Rigoletto* with the Nashville Opera. A highlight of the year: Gina and Paul celebrated their twenty-fifth wedding anniversary in June.

This year MARY BROWN and her husband Alex, of East Lansing, Michigan, celebrated twenty-five years of marriage. Their son Mark, a high school junior, has enjoyed an intensive course in computer-aided design but is drawn in many diverse directions. Mary says, "I'm learning to trust God to bring Mark through these teen years and guide his future decisions." This year their daughter Elizabeth will graduate from Michigan State University with a degree in chemical engineering and a passion to do good for people and the environment. "Our family just lost a dear friend to cancer," Mary notes. "The grief of his widow and three young daughters has been heartbreaking. Yet we cling to the hope that God will comfort them with His tender love and draw each of us closer to Him."

"I've decided to learn something new every year," says MARY LOU CARNEY of Chesterton, Indiana. Last year she took classes in photography and cake decorating. This year's classes are gardening and creating a mosaic birdbath. Mary Lou has also begun "staging" homes for her daughter's real estate company. "It's great fun to transform an empty space into something cozy!" Mary Lou and her husband Gary have

*Fellowship Corner*

five grandchildren, all within a few minutes' drive. "Love? We've got it by the armload in our family. And it's—literally—growing daily. How blessed we are!" Mary Lou partnered with *Daily Guideposts* contributor Debbie Macomber to write a new children's book: *The Truly Terribly Horrible Sweater That Grandma Knit*. You can read about Mary Lou's adventures on her blog at OurPrayer.org.

JEFF CHU of New York City, an editor at the business magazine *Fast Company*, is grateful to still have a job in the incredible shrinking media sector. "In reviewing the past year," Jeff says, "I see growth in two special and not entirely unrelated areas. First, in my love for my two young nephews. And second, in my appreciation for my family's unique history." On a recent trip to Hong Kong, Jeff learned details of his great-grandfather's conversion to Christianity and his grandfather's near-miraculous escape from Communist China. "Reflecting on these long-ago events reminds me of God's power as well as His enduring grace over the generations."

"In this past year of healing from my sister's death, I've learned the true power and strength of my faith," writes SABRA CIANCANELLI of Tivoli, New York. "The upside of grief is its ability to bring everyday blessings into focus: the laughter of my sons, going for a walk with my husband. I'm thrilled to work from home, to sing the 'ABC' song and eat snacks with Henry beneath a blanket tented on two chairs in the middle of our living room. I cherish the look on Solomon's face when he gets off the school bus and smells brownies fresh out of the oven. Last summer we had our first successful vegetable garden, despite a slew of slugs and one very determined rabbit. This year, we're rolling up our sleeves, putting up a better fence and planting even more tomatoes."

"If all you want is simplicity, buy a can opener," advises MARK COLLINS of Pittsburgh, Pennsylvania. "If you want to genuinely live your life, you can forget simplicity and expect chaos. Come to think of it, opening a can is pretty messy too." Mark opened lots of messy cans this year: His wife Sandee took on a new job at her seminary; Faith, 19, survived her first year of college; and Hope, 18, and Grace, 14,

DAILY GUIDEPOSTS   415

## Fellowship Corner

continue to be, *um*, chaotic teenagers. "Maybe a complex life is the Almighty's way of showing us that all we really need is a good can opener."

PABLO DIAZ of Carmel, New York, writes, "Learning to play tennis is lots of fun. It also opened a new world for my wife Elba (who doesn't have much interest in sports) and me. For the first time, we're enjoying a game that we both love. This past year our daughter Christine moved out of our home and is ecstatic about living in New York City. She's happy and so are we—now we have an apartment in the city to stay in when she's out of town! Our son Paul continues to put all of us to shame with his daily workouts. It is great seeing how the things we love fill each of our hearts with joy."

BRIAN DOYLE of Portland, Oregon, writes, "I'm learning the hard way that much of love is letting go—of a daughter off to college (Wasn't I just changing her diapers?), of sons in the thickets of surly teenagery (Can I mail a son to Malaysia?), of the many small sins committed by what is reputed to be a dog but looks like a wolf on steroids. I'm learning fitfully to love by deed, not word; to pay attention; to witness; to savor; to remember—all powerful prayers." Brian edits *Portland Magazine* at the University of Portland. Brian is the author of nine books of essays and poems, and his novel *Mink River* has just been published by Oregon State University Press.

SHARON FOSTER writes, "My daughter Lanea and I sat spellbound in a Cleveland audience, watching my son Chase make his operatic debut as the lead tenor in Strauss' *Ariadne auf Naxos*. At home in Durham, North Carolina, I am equally enchanted as I watch Lanea expanding her plans for homeless advocacy to include an initiative where churches and other organizations each 'adopt' a homeless family for one year. As for myself, after a grueling three years, I have completed *The Resurrection of Nat Turner*, due to be published this year. The historical novel is a departure for me, but I pray my writing—and the speaking and teaching that go along with it—are service and love in action." You can reach Sharon at Sharonewelfoster@aol.com.

## Fellowship Corner

"My husband Rick turned 50 this year," writes JULIE GARMON of Monroe, Georgia. "I'm right behind him. Our youngest is 18; it's his senior year. I want to preserve what counts, what's important. This year we decided to slow down, even if only for a few minutes a day. Rick and I now have parties for two every morning before the sun comes up. We sit on our front porch in rocking chairs, drink coffee and celebrate each morning. I don't think we'd have appreciated the beauty of sharing mornings until now. As our children have grown, so has our love for each other. And we're beginning to discover what matters most. Some truths only come with time."

For OSCAR GREENE of West Medford, Massachusetts, the year was filled with unexpected activities, peace and contentment. Oscar and his wife Ruby have been married for sixty-seven years, and they have lived in the same house for forty-five years. Nearby is their church, a library, business associates and the supermarket. Oscar continues to be asked to teach at writers conferences and to speak at clubs and gatherings. But he declines, preferring to write joyful, encouraging letters and to visit people confined to their homes. Oscar hopes he is still growing in love.

*Guideposts* Editor-in-Chief EDWARD GRINNAN of New York City reports, "I wrote a book on the subject of personal change, both mine and others, and tried to discover how people do what is so hard for people to do—change. In telling my own story, I had to delve into aspects of my past I'd deliberately not thought about in years. Yet in that dark time of my life, when no one would have ever dreamed I'd end up where I did, even then there was an inner light, a light that literally kept me alive and is with me still every day." The book will be out early this year, and Edward would like to thank Millie, his golden retriever, for giving up more than a few hikes in the mountains on weekends when Daddy had to work, and Julee, his wife, who had to put up with a lot more.

RICK HAMLIN of New York City writes, "A couple of mornings a week I jog up and through our local park and start wondering what I'm going to say in my blog on OurPrayer.org or Guideposts.com. Has anything really interesting happened to me? Are there any lessons God seems to be teaching me? Wouldn't you know it, every week

## Fellowship Corner

there seems to be something that I needed to hear. It's like what we say about writing for *Daily Guideposts*. Looking for the devotional moments in your life is good for your spiritual health! Our oldest son William has a job that he really likes and our younger son Timothy has just another year-and-a-half of college. My wife Carol and I sing in our choir, as always, go to museums, get together with our friends, and often think about how much we have to be thankful for."

HAROLD HOSTETLER of Pougheepsie, New York, writes, "The older we get, the more joy Carol and I seem to take in encouraging and seeing the successes of our daughters. Laurel, in Arizona, is the artistic one, building her own copywriting and graphics design business. Kristal, here in upstate New York, is working on a novel, having already won second place for a science-fiction short story in *Writers Digest*'s fiction writing contest. Carol, meanwhile, has finished a biographical photo album for Laurel and is working on one for Kristal, and I continue writing for *Guideposts* and leading Bible studies at church. Our pastor retired recently, and I share in preaching and leading worship while we search for a new minister."

"It's been pretty clear what's made the difference in my life this year," says JEFF JAPINGA. "Seeing God's love and leading so clearly through the people around me. I've experienced that as I've walked my daughter Annie across the lawns of prospective colleges—she'll graduate from high school this year—or as I've traded experiences and ideas with my son Mark, who continues to explore his own vocational callings after college. It's been finding new patterns of life (and growth) with my wife Lynn, first because of my crazy commute between Holland, Michigan, and Chicago, and soon with the new challenge of an empty nest. And it's come through generous McCormick Seminary colleagues who have helped me grow in knowledge these past three years through new and challenging work."

This year, Ashley Johnson took the plunge, married her college sweetheart, and became ASHLEY KAPPEL. Don't be confused by the new name; she's still the same Southern girl at heart. Ashley and her husband Brian live in Durham, North Carolina, where he's finishing his law degree and she works as a freelance writer and a nanny for

*Fellowship Corner*

several area families. As she looks forward to their first anniversary, Ashley is in awe at how the love in her life has grown this year: another niece (that makes seven!) and a husband. God is truly good.

"This past year has marked a time of change accompanied by wonderful growth," writes BROCK KIDD of Nashville, Tennessee. "My father retired from the church that all of my family attended. My son Harrison came into a major growth spurt while hitting the Big 10 birthday mark, and we have grown together in other ways, learning from each other on our night walks, which take the place of TV shows and video games. I also have grown through the love of a new best friend who has pulled me even closer to Christ, an unexpected gift in my life. To quote one of my favorite childhood writers, Louis L'Amour, 'There will come a time when you believe everything is finished. That will be the beginning.'"

PAM KIDD of Nashville, Tennessee, writes, "To celebrate David's retirement, our kids planned a family trip to Mexico. Not only did we find ourselves exploring the exciting possibilities of his next career, but I had a new husband who actually carried in the groceries and emptied the dishwasher, one who has more time to spend with grandchildren Harrison, Abby and baby Charles and with my mother Bebe and my near-father Herb. High on our list is more family time in Zimbabwe, where son-in-law Ben is opening a much-needed dental clinic for AIDS children. In all this, I'm learning that if you love life enough, even in great change, life will find a way to love you back!"

MARILYN MORGAN KING of Green Mountain Falls, Colorado, would like to write one more book while she can still see well enough to do so. She's waiting for the Spirit to touch her and say, "Here's what you should write about." Unfortunately, the Spirit doesn't take orders about such things! In the meantime Marilyn is writing some poetry and has taken a couple of classes—one in fiction writing and the other on "Writing Your Life's Legacy." Marilyn quotes her friend Lucinda who recently said, "As I lay in the hospital all night reading Rilke's *Book of Hours*, I thought to myself, *Despite all the pain and loss, I cherish old age because it is like the final stage of distilling a sweet nectar*." "I agree with Lucinda," Marilyn

## Fellowship Corner

says. "I'm so glad I've had the opportunity to experience some of the precious gifts of growing old!"

"Love has entered my life in countless simple flourishing ways," says CAROL KNAPP of Lakeville, Minnesota. "Daughter Kelly calling to report hearing the first red-winged blackbird's spring song; grandson Clay, 5, and Papa wrestling; granddaughter Tirza, 3, affectionately calling me 'Gram crackers'; mixing up our childhood chocolate no-bakes with my friend Deb at a friends-for-fifty-years reunion; phone conversations with my son Phil over our favorite scenes in recent movies. Learning my thirteenth grandchild (in twelve years!) will be named Natalia for my daughter Brenda's dear teen friend who died. My husband Terry kneeling to gently rub my legs during an inflammation attack. Breathless wonder at a meteor's double flash—God skipping a rock across the night sky. The Bible says that 'love never ends.' I believe this is because God Who is love never tires of giving from Himself . . . in countless simple flourishing ways."

"I used to wonder if a person's love existed in a limited quantity," writes CAROL KUYKENDALL of Boulder, Colorado. "Like, would I have to divide my 'mother love' in half when I had a second child? Now I know that our love grows as we have more people to love, and I am overflowing this year as we are expecting our eighth grandchild, thanks to our three adult children and their families who live nearby. I've also learned that new life is one of God's greatest gifts of love and hope, for which I am specially thankful as my husband Lynn's brain tumor has returned and he is undergoing aggressive chemotherapy treatments. Miraculously, I am still getting good test results for my stage 4 ovarian cancer—and grateful for God's endless source of love."

HELEN GRACE LESCHEID of Abbotsford, British Columbia, writes, "When I think of my five children, I often pray that they will keep growing in God's love, knowing they are loved for who they are and not what they achieve. This past year, Jonathan realized his dream of becoming an orthopedic surgeon and will soon be moving to Vancouver, only one hour's drive from where I live. David, also a medical doctor, has moved to Baden-Baden, Germany. Last fall, I spent five weeks

*Fellowship Corner*

with Elizabeth and Matthew in the outback of western Australia and gained a deeper appreciation of God's creation. Esther and family will be moving from Africa to eastern Canada, where Cathy and their dad live. Besides travel, I've written regularly for an online magazine and updated and revised my book *Lead, Kindly Light*. You can read more about it at www.helenlescheid.com."

"Having lived in five states," writes PATRICIA LORENZ of Largo, Florida, "I've learned that to grow love, I must grow relationships with my family and friends: childhood friends; new friends; younger, older, spiritual, funny friends; the ones who prod me to exercise with them; and the upbeat, off-the-wall, goofy friends. One of my favorite things to do is travel around the country, talking to various groups, because I always meet new friends to cherish. Even the winter-only snowbirds who flock to Florida become friends for three and four months each year. Last year I wrote a book called *Positive Quotes for Every Day*, in which I reflected on 365 famous quotations . . . talk about growing in love from the wisdom of others!"

"Wayne and I are celebrating the birth of Jaxon Paul to our son Dale and daughter-in-law Laurie," DEBBIE MACOMBER of Port Orchard, Washington reports. "Jaxon is God's special gift to our family after Laurie underwent six IVF attempts." An avid knitter, every year Debbie creates something for her grandchildren—all nine of them! In addition, Wayne and Debbie hold Grandpa and Grandma camps each summer. Happy memories, love for Christ, and a close family knit together by love and shared values are the legacy they plan to leave their children and grandchildren. They are part of Guideposts National Advisory Cabinet, and Debbie serves on the boards of Warm Up America! and Point Hope, a medical foundation for children in Buduburam, Ghana, run by her friend Delilah. Debbie's novels continue to top the best-seller lists.

ROBERTA MESSNER unexpectedly fell in love this past year. The object of her affection is an abandoned wirehaired, teddy-bearlike terrier she rescued from a busy road near her home. "I never dreamed I'd love another dog," says Roberta, who lost her beloved Spanky in April 2008. But this little charmer stole her heart. "One unexpected benefit is that my new little Spunkles has made me more active and engaged with life in

## Fellowship Corner

the midst of struggling with intense back pain. I'm learning that's one of the things 'growing in love' does—it makes you fall in love with life all over again."

KEITH MILLER and his wife Andrea live in Austin, Texas, where they work together, communicating through writing books, blogging, hosting small-group meetings in their home (about learning how to accept God's offer to be the motivating center of one's life), and republishing Keith's earlier books. Late in 2009, the second revised edition of *The Taste of New Wine* was released with a new foreword by George Gallup Jr. Keith and Andrea's joint project, a book they call *Square One*, was finished in 2010. For more information about their life and work, visit them at www.keithmiller.com.

LINDA NEUKRUG lives in Walnut Creek, California. She works in a bookstore and also does some substitute teaching, requiring a lot of prayer and some hardy nerves. Linda has two cats, Prince and Junior. While Prince likes to remain at home and gaze at himself in the mirror, Junior is a runner, so over the past year, Linda's exercise has been to chase Junior and entice him home by clicking a can opener. This year, she hopes to make a trip to New York, her home state.

Over the past year, it's turned out to be no cliché: MARY ANN O'ROARK of New York City has felt love growing. "Every morning I pray, 'Open my heart to the gifts of this day,' and no matter how gloomy or cold or empty I've been feeling, all I have to do is pay attention to what's happening in the daily events of my life and lovely things unfold. All of a sudden I notice the ice sparkling on the river and take a walk, or end up chatting with someone on the bus who's admired my Mickey Mouse watch that my parents gave me years ago." This year she added two new furry and rambunctious roommates to her apartment: the Jersey Boys (Ginger and Apolo Kitty Ohno) rescued from a shelter in New Jersey.

DANIEL SCHANTZ of Moberly, Missouri, has lightened his teaching load a little bit and jettisoned some extra duties so he can find more joy in his forty-third year at Central Christian College. Dan's wife Sharon has become librarian of their church library, which has proved to be a big challenge with many side benefits, such as meeting a lot of interesting

*Fellowship Corner*

people and getting to help them personally. Abram, their youngest grandson, was baptized, and granddaughters Rossetti and Hannah got to be extras in the movie *Saving Grace B. Jones,* starring Tatum O' Neal. The movie was filmed in Boonville, right across the river from their home, and the whole family attended the premiere.

GAIL THORELL SCHILLING of Concord, New Hampshire, rejoiced this year as daughter Trina and her beloved Steve married beside Merrymeeting Lake, the family retreat for fifty years. "Tom sang and played guitar, Greg ushered, Tess served as bridesmaid, and granddaughter Hannah scattered petals. I made the cake and floral arrangements; friends prepared the barbecue. My mother, 91, relished memories of three generations of children at her cottage. Mercifully, the sun shone after weeks of June rain. Perfect! A few days earlier I had joined my new church family in a special welcoming ceremony attended by a special guest, whose faithful friendship has now blessed me for nearly a year. I praise God that one can grow in love at any age!"

"Retirement has given me time to nurture relationships with family and friends," writes PENNEY SCHWAB of Copeland, Kansas. "My husband Don and I took our dream trip to Alaska. We enjoyed Christmas in Estes Park with our three children and six grandchildren. My sister Amanda and I hosted a summer get-together for seven of the cousins, which featured trips to a water park and wildlife museum. I've become a regular blood donor. Granddaughter Olivia has ongoing problems related to a bicycle accident that fractured her skull, but we are extremely grateful that she is in school and participating in basketball, volleyball and choir."

ELIZABETH SHERRILL of Hingham, Massachusetts, returned from a trip to the Mideast this year with a list of superlatives. Most beautiful: the Blue Mosque in Istanbul, Turkey. Most meaningful: the spot on Mount Nebo from which Moses saw the Promised Land. Most exciting: a balloon trip at dawn over Egypt's Valley of the Kings. Hardest: a camel ride to a village in the Nubian desert. And the best moment of all? "Returning to see my husband John standing in front of our new apartment building—and knowing that this place has truly become home."

DAILY GUIDEPOSTS

## Fellowship Corner

When JOHN SHERRILL and his wife Elizabeth left their longtime home last year, John shared in the Fellowship Corner his regret at giving up his hobby of cooking. In fact, their new apartment in Hingham, Massachusetts, has a fully equipped kitchen, so his culinary creativity still has an outlet. A much greater regret was leaving decades-long friendships. But here, too, he reports, were pleasant surprises: a welcoming new church, helpful new neighbors. "And tomorrow," he says, "I'll be having coffee with the fellow here who picks up our trash."

SHARI SMYTH of Nashville, Tennessee, writes, "It was a shock for us when Whitney's job, which seemed so secure, evaporated with the economic downturn. It was an even bigger shock that he has not been able to find another job. We've had our struggles. But we also have God, Who has seen us through in amazing ways. Planted in trust, we've found ourselves growing in love, part of which is learning to receive from others, such as our wonderful church family. Of course, our greatest blessing continues to be our four children, our son-in-law and precious grandson Frank, who just turned 5. The other day he handed me a folded note that, in big crooked letters, read, 'I love you.' All the money in the bank couldn't have bought such a treasure!"

"Life is about relationships," says JOSHUA SUNDQUIST, "and on this front I consider myself to be incredibly lucky. My family continues to be a stabilizing force of love and support, and I'm still close with my friends from college. In fact, I've had the same roommate for seven years! We've had a great year hanging out together here in Washington, DC. My motivational speaking career has taken off, and my memoir *Just Don't Fall* came out this year, too, which was a really exciting and special event for both my family and me."

JON SWEENEY of Woodstock, Vermont, had an incredible year: He lost eighty-five pounds and got married! "Falling in love will do that to you," he says with a smile. Jon's books include *Born Again and Again: Surprising Benefits of a Fundamentalist Childhood*, which was given an Award of Merit by *Christianity Today*; *Light in the Dark*

*Fellowship Corner*

*Ages: The Friendship of Francis and Clare of Assisi*, which was a Book-of-the-Month Club selection; and *Cloister Talks: Learning from My Friends the Monks*. He is the associate publisher at Paraclete Press in Massachusetts and writes frequently for magazines.

KAREN VALENTIN of New York City says, "Life with a 2-year-old and a 6-month-old is hectic, to say the least. As I struggle to maneuver my wide double-stroller through doorways, up hills and down subway stairs, I get sympathetic glances from strangers—most times accompanied with the phrase, 'You've got your hands full.' I do. The boys keep me busy starting much too early in the morning, with endless diaper changes, missing pacifiers, tantrums, spitting up and discarded snacks waiting to be swept from the floor. Yes, indeed, my hands are full, and some days I feel overwhelmed. But as I wrap my arms around my children with kisses and hugs, I know that having my hands full is a blessing from God—and a pretty wonderful thing at that!"

SCOTT WALKER writes, "During the first week in January, the contents of our Waco, Texas, home were loaded into a large moving van and taken to our new home, a Victorian house built in the 1840s in Macon, Georgia, where Beth and I are both deeply involved in the lives of students at Mercer University. I am the founding director of the Institute of Life Purpose and am teaching classes; Beth is administering study-abroad programs and working with service-learning projects and curriculum. In a few weeks, our youngest child Jodi will graduate from Furman University. This has been a year of changing seasons and a deepening awareness that God faithfully leads us to continuing challenge and purpose."

"Our trip to Liberia was a life-changing one," writes DOLPHUS WEARY of Richland, Mississippi. "It was our first visit to Africa, and because of fourteen years of tribal war, this country needed to hear a message of reconciliation." He and his wife Rosie fell in love with the people and now have an ongoing relationship with them. "Our daughter Danita continues to practice medicine as a pediatrician in Natchez, while our son Ryan is seeking to become a sound engineer. Little Reggie is

## Fellowship Corner

six and continues to be a vital part of our lives, and we continue to build the REAL Christian Foundation."

"We have all been thinking about 'growing in love' this year," writes BRIGITTE WEEKS of New York City, "and I have been doing just that. Five years ago grandchildren were something I heard others talking about with stars in their eyes. Now I have five of my own—four boys and one (extra joy) girl! I've found that there aren't very many books for learning to be a grandmother, but if I wrote one, 'Don't criticize or judge' would be on the jacket. As a very wise friend told me, 'Get down on the floor with them.' So there I am, sitting on the floor with a six-month-old in my arms and four small boys using me as a climbing gym. And love is growing like Jack's beanstalk."

"It's taken nearly a lifetime to discover the only method of growing in love that works for me," writes MARION BOND WEST of Watkinsville, Georgia. "John 3:30 states, 'He must increase, but I must decrease.' *The Message* paraphrases this as, 'This is the assigned moment for him to move into the center, while I slip off to the sidelines.' I recall a diagram I came across when I was first coming to believe in Jesus. It was a heart with a throne inside. Only one person could occupy the throne, me or Jesus—no compromise. I tend to slip back onto the throne. But when I truly vacate it, His startling love fills my heart."

"Like many who've been caught in the recession," says BRENDA WILBEE of Birch Bay, Washington, "I'm now entering nineteen months of unemployment. I find that old lessons must be reviewed, my faith reexamined. But like Elijah, I've come to the brook called Cherith where I am fed by the ravens God sends. I'm on a narrow creek trail that leads to new trust in God. It proved a good route for Elijah, resulting in the big showdown between the Lord and Baal and a nation turning back to God. I expect no less for me, and I look forward to the new year with fragile but growing hope. Many, I know, suffer similar loss and challenge. I'd love to hear from you. You can e-mail me at Brenda@BrendaWilbee.com or visit my blog at BrendaWilbee.blogspot.com."

## Fellowship Corner

"It's been a busy year," says TIM WILLIAMS of Durango, Colorado. "I've been cutting, splitting and stacking firewood, mulching our two gardens, planting trees, chopping thistle, shoveling snow, fishing, hiking—all things I once saved for weekends! I'm not sure what will happen when Dianne and I are unable to keep up with our isolated rural lifestyle. We're considering moving to a small town in my home state of Ohio, where many of my brothers and sisters and their children live. We hope for specific guidance from God, but we know that 'Love the Lord your God' and 'Love your neighbor' will guide our lives no matter where we are."

"After twenty-eight years living and working in the beautiful Finger Lakes region of upstate New York, my husband Lawrence Torrey and I have returned to the Portland, Oregon, area where our family members still live," writes ISABEL WOLSELEY. "Even though each loved one has become more precious the closer we are, the decision to leave home, church and friends to relocate across country was monumental and emotional for two octogenarians. However, the trip had its light moments. During the three thousand-mile drive while following our moving van, we were amused at fellow travelers' startled expressions when they pulled alongside and saw four pet hens peering out of our station wagon's rear windows! We're now settled in a new home in King City, and our pets have their own mini-Hen Hilton in the backyard."

"Happiness filled our house last year," writes PHILIP ZALESKI of Northampton, Massachusetts, "as John graduated from college and returned home for a much-needed break before continuing on to graduate school in religious studies. His presence has been great fun for all, adding an extra spark to dinner conversations, vacations and sundry family projects. Andy, now in high school, loves having his older brother around to cheer him on as he swoops down the ski slopes and scoots around the base paths. My wife Carol and I continue to teach, write, travel and study. Last summer, we spent a few weeks in England and France, visiting monasteries and seeing old friends. I'm keeping up my Hebrew and Latin lessons, happy to learn at a snail's pace."

DAILY GUIDEPOSTS

# SCRIPTURE REFERENCE INDEX

**ACTS**
1:14, 108
3:6, 327
3:13–14, 175
9:36, 300
14:16–17, 77
14:22, 301
17:27, 185
17:28, 95
27:7–8, 278

**CHRONICLES I**
16:8, 43
16:29, 161
16:32, 385
22:16, 20

**CHRONICLES II**
7:10, 387

**COLOSSIANS**
1:10, 192
1:28, 7
3:10, 14
3:14, 345

**CORINTHIANS I**
9:25, 30
10:16, 311
10:24, 393
12:14, 282
13:8, 326
13:12, 405
13:13, 52

**CORINTHIANS II**
5:7, 58
6:2, 131
9:7, 276
9:15, 392
13:11, 244
13:14, 309

**DANIEL**
1:12, 148
2:22, 162

**DEUTERONOMY**
5:32, 208
6:5, 5
6:6–7, 248
7:13, 224
8:11, 201
10:14, 340
30:19–20, 66
31:6, 228

**ECCLESIASTES**
2:10, 380
3:1, 92, 404
3:1, 4, 72
3:11, 214
4:10, 256
9:11, 170
11:1, 258
12:1, 118

**EPHESIANS**
1:3, 281
4:14–15, 7
4:23, 80
4:25, 295
5:2, 105, 315

**EXODUS**
3:3, 358
3:14, 363
3:16–17, 363
4:2, 101
12:14, 169
17:15, 237
33:18, 369
35:25, 42

**EZEKIEL**
1:16, 147
33:11, 286

**GALATIANS**
1:10, 197
5:1, 211
5:22, 185, 189
5:22–23, 343
6:10, 81
6:11, 184

**GENESIS**
1:20, 283
2:9, 76
2:23, 288
15:1, 18
21:6, 113
24:1, 293
28:16, 215
49:25, 190

**HABAKKUK**
3:19, 74, 226

**HAGGAI**
2:4, 48

**HEBREWS**
6:7–8, 112
10:14, 373
10:16, 134
10:24, 73
10:35–36, 406
11:1, 378
13:1–2, 25

**ISAIAH**
6:8, 90
12:2, 266
30:21, 26
38:17, 151
40:1–2, 289
40:11, 388
40:31, 14
41:10, 47
42:16, 368
43:9, 22
43:19, 319
51:1, 357
51:3, 89
53:2, 16
54:4, 316
54:13, 312
55:1–2, 370
58:11, 157
60:6, 394
60:20, 230
61:3, 45, 253

**JAMES**
1:17, 193
2:18, 165
5:16, 398

**JEREMIAH**
10:23, 361
17:5–7, 54
17:9, 54
17:14, 188
29:5, 216
31:3, 226, 377
31:34, 353

**JOB**
1:10, 322
8:7, 305
12:10, 13
17:7, 180
29:13, 229

**JOEL**
2:13, 27

**JOHN**
1:16, 88
2:4, 149
3:16, 203
4:34, 370
5:8, 75
6:35, 370
6:40, 128
7:38, 49
8:12, 381
8:58, 363
10:3–4, 129
10:10, 223
10:11, 388
10:14–15, 154
11:25, 395
11:35–36, 263
13:34, 53
14:6, 401
14:18, 247
14:18–20, 125
15:1, 5, 402
15:8, 115
15:9, 139, 348
15:12, 71, 167

**JOHN I**
1:9, 86
2:25, 355
3:6, 97
3:18, 207
4:7, 39
4:18, 270, 275
4:19, 173

**JOHN II**
1:12, 227

**JOSHUA**
4:7, 372

**KINGS I**
8:28, 336
8:36, 218
17:12, 252

**KINGS II**
6:17, 284
18:5, 51

**LAMENTATIONS**
1:7, 34
3:21–23, 222
3:25, 231
3:28–30, 328
3:41, 296

**LEVITICUS**
19:32, 202

**LUKE**
1:37, 213
1:53, 24
1:64, 6
1:79, 186
2:12, 185
2:14, 400
2:32, 397
2:52, 271
7:38, 349
7:50, 120
8:2, 119
8:2–3, 121
9:23, 65
11:4, 257
12:32, 160
13:33, 225
14:11, 354
17:10, 260
18:14, 255
19:17, 287
22:54, 175
23:28, 127
23:34, 127
24:52, 130

**MALACHI**
3:6, 299
3:16, 134

**MARK**
2:10, 120
2:28, 199
4:39, 356
9:24, 176
11:9, 122
11:17, 123
12:31, 82

428  DAILY GUIDEPOSTS

## Scripture Reference Index

14:6, 124
14:6, 8–9, 124
14:8, 35
14:36, 62
MATTHEW
2:11, 11
5:7, 56
5:9, 333
5:14, 250
5:24, 164
6:1, 99
6:8, 360
6:10, 152
6:11, 234
6:12, 117
6:19, 8
6:20–21, 84
6:28, 298
6:34, 338
7:3, 63
7:9, 156
10:8, 107
10:22, 181
10:42, 365
13:32, 185
17:22–23, 125
18:20, 318
18:22, 141
19:13, 36
22:12, 335
23:19, 350
25:35, 220
25:35–36, 152
26:39, 126
26:56, 126
28:19, 366
28:20, 100, 109
MICAH
4:2, 277
5:2, 262
6:8, 302

NAHUM
2:1, 243
NUMBERS
11:5, 233
24:9, 313

PETER I
1:4, 91
1:22, 347
2:5, 60
4:10, 332
PETER II
1:3, 379
1:19, 407

PHILEMON
1:7, 346
PHILIPPIANS
1:3, 310
1:9, 232
2:15–16, 245
2:16, 264
3:13–14, 17
4:8, 235
4:11, 14
PROVERBS
3:5, 174
3:6, 303
3:27, 371
4:7, 304
5:18, 399
7:4, 182
9:1–2, 9
10:7, 344
10:12, 83
10:26, 61
10:32, 290
14:23, 41
15:15, 267
16:9, 85
16:18, 40
17:6, 191
17:17, 158
18:13, 198
18:15, 249
18:19, 384
18:22, 166
20:12, 23
20:24, 352
22:6, 14
23:23, 358
24:3, 32
25:11, 217
27:5, 168
31:11, 133
31:22, 219
31:25, 150
PSALMS
8:4, 314
16:6–7, 31
19:1, 55
19:9–10, 386
19:12, 94
23:2–3, 153
23:3, 33
23:6, 132
27:14, 321
28:2, 291
30:5, 242
34:8, 294
35:14, 59

39:12, 268
40:3, 159
40:11, 21
42:1, 46
42:4, 106
42:11, 78
47:7, 187
56:3, 238
61:4, 261, 265
65:5, 93
70:1, 269
73:24, 87
74:16–17, 396
75:1, 196
77:14, 15, 383
78:39, 320
86:12, 155
90:1–2, 100
90:12, 408
90:17, 114
91:5–6, 382
91:15, 111
92:14, 324
98:1, 178
98:8, 292
103:2, 98
103:2–4, 98
104:25, 116
107:15, 50
107:30, 209
111:10, 285
112:4, 212
115:6, 362
116:12, 403
116:16, 79
119:18, 221
119:103, 390
119:105, 279, 297
119:169, 177
121:1, 200
121:5, 146
126:2, 102
127:4, 96
136:4, 225
138:3, 44
139:1–2, 334
139:3, 14
139:11, 179
139:16, 29
139:24, 14
147:3, 67
150:3, 135

REVELATION
3:20, 265
14:13, 251

19:9, 145
21:5, 359
22:14, 331
ROMANS
6:4, 11, 395
8:15, 194
8:17, 330
8:25, 12
8:28, 241, 272
8:38–39, 351
9:33, 391
12:6, 339
12:10, 28
12:12, 337
12:17, 64
13:9, 259
14:8, 143
14:21, 317
RUTH
1:16, 367

SAMUEL I
1:27–28, 248
7:8, 364
7:12, 144
16:7, 110, 335
SONG OF
    SOLOMON
2:12, 183
4:10, 254
SONG OF SONGS
4:9, 399

THESSALONIANS I
1:3, 195
4:11, 280
5:11, 389
5:12–13, 142
5:17, 10
TIMOTHY I
4:14–16, 236
5:4, 140
6:19, 163
TIMOTHY II
2:1–2, 246
3:15, 365
4:13, 210
TITUS
3:8, 325

ZECHARIAH
3:4, 19
10:7, 323
ZEPHANIAH
3:17, 329
3:19, 57

# AUTHORS, TITLES AND SUBJECTS INDEX

Abiding in Christ, 402
Acceptance, 252
Admitting error, 164
Adriance, Anne, 13, 131, 212, 339
Advent: 1st Sunday of, 370; 2nd Sunday of, 381; 3rd Sunday of, 388; 4th Sunday of, 395
*Advice from Aunt Annie* series, 31, 64, 99, 134, 163, 199, 235, 268, 303, 335, 365, 394
Alborghetti, Marci, 11, 83, 160, 250, 336
Alive in Christ, 395
Anger, 123
Angus, Fay, 17, 130, 154, 236, 283, 326, 398
Anticipation of eternal life, 91
Approval, 197
Asking for help, 316
Attaway, Andrew, 7, 78, 169, 187, 340, 405
Attaway, Julia, 24, 89, 109, 156, 201, 220, 257, 315, 348, 392
Availability, 101

Barber, Karen, 6, 79, 144, 197, 284, 349
Barkman, Alma, 35, 98, 243, 300, 407
Beginnings, 305
Beiler, Hannah, 155
Being a comfort, 396
Being busy, 114
Bence, Evelyn, 60, 90, 147, 210, 280, 313
Bertram, Gloe, 397
Best, the: doing, 149; giving, 380; making, 163; taken with us, 400
Bible, the, 9, 14, 185, 279, 370
Blecker, Rhoda, 57, 102, 183, 304, 369
Bonnette, Melody, 22, 91, 148, 272, 346
Boyer, Joan, 58
Brantley, Linda, 224
Bridgeman, Gina, 15, 97, 113, 162, 209, 271, 332, 357
Brown, Mary, 358, 363, 370, 381, 388, 395, 401, 402

Caring: for a friend, 347; for everyone, 56; for one person at a time, 333
Carney, Mary Lou, 12, 53, 95, 143, 193, 223, 261, 281, 322, 352
Change, 16, 19
Children, 36, 96, 167, 187, 191, 233, 392
Choosing life, 13
Christmas, 402
Christmas Eve, 401
Chu, Jeff, 9, 84, 155, 216, 277, 366
Ciancanelli, Sabra, 34, 146, 176, 244, 331
Collins, Mark, 58, 118, 177, 251, 314, 386
Communicating, 304, 384
Companionship, 116
Compassion, 382
Conversion, 175
Courage, 260

Dedication celebration, 248
Designed objects, 155
DeWeese, Allene, 251

Diaz, Pablo, 93, 165, 256, 361
Discernment, 110
Diversity, 294
Doing what one can, 287
Doyle, Brian, 23, 96, 150, 221, 286, 355
Dying, 251

Easter, 129
Easter Monday, 130
Efforts, 112
Elderly, the, 202
Empathy, 73, 157
Encouragement, 225, 226, 346, 389
Endurance, 170, 253
Eternal life, 355
Eternity, 203

Faith, 15, 109, 115, 145, 216, 340
Family, 166
Family resemblance, 357
Father's Day, 192
Fear, 75, 176, 194
Fellow heirs, 330
Fellowship, 282, 325
First words, 6
Focusing on the moment, 345
Following through, 320
Forgiveness, 117, 141, 151
Fortitude, 210
Foster, Sharon, 36, 170, 218, 278, 404
*Free to Love, Free to Follow* series, 119–29
Freedom, 211
Friendship, 42, 62, 162, 324
Friendship Class, 255
Fulfilling needs, 393

Garmon, Julie, 27, 75, 182, 237, 373
Giving: freely, 276; fully, 124
Giving thanks, 133, 142
Gladness: following one's, 302
God times, 329
God's blessings, 190, 281, 313
God's comfort, 27
God's constancy, 359
God's creation, 55, 76, 183, 265, 266, 283, 369
God's faithfulness, 222, 234
God's forgiveness, 289
God's gifts, 23, 264, 362, 385, 387
God's glory, 214
God's goodness, 388
God's grace, 88, 353
God's healing, 67, 182, 188, 243, 263
God's help, 85
God's kingdom, 152
God's light, 247, 286, 381
God's love: as our shepherd, 154; eternal. 351; experienced, 224; in our weakness, 315; relying on, 291; reminders of, 134; sharing, 361; unchanging, 299; unconditional, 186; wondrous forms of, 232, 270

430 DAILY GUIDEPOSTS

## Authors, Titles and Subjects Index

God's mercy, 21, 269
God's miracles, 44, 46
God's omniscience, 29
God's plan, 57, 249
God's presence, 18, 48, 87, 100, 111, 201, 215, 238, 356, 399
God's promises, 84, 407
God's protection, 245, 261
God's provision, 90, 297, 328
God's strength, 45, 74
God's truth, 401
God's voice, 66, 363
God's will, 126, 192, 227
God's wisdom, 358
God's wonders, 405
Good: out of disaster, 272
Good Friday, 127
Goodness, power of, 344
Goodness file, 235
Grace, 63
Graciousness, 290
Gratitude, 390
Greene, Oscar, 41, 107, 181, 249, 325, 371
Grief, 143
Grinnan, Edward, 30, 88, 114, 159, 198, 232, 270, 321, 364, 382
Growing closer to God, 24
Growing old, 350
Growth, 7
Guideposts Good Friday Day of Prayer, 127
Guideposts Thanksgiving Day of Prayer, 364

Hamlin, Rick, 16, 94, 135, 161, 188, 264, 301, 334, 362, 403
Happiness, 140, 219
Hat tricks, 317
Hefner, Ruth, 74
Holy Saturday, 128
Holy Week, 122–29
Honesty, 64
Hope, 12, 26, 132, 156, 250, 337
Hostetler, Harold, 66, 164, 253, 372, 399
Humor, 72

Insight, 58, 177
Irreplaceability, 386

Japinga, Jeff, 65, 115, 262, 329, 353, 389
Jesus Christ: entering Jerusalem, 122; in Gethsemane, 126; in the temple, 123; in the tomb, 128; Mary Magdalene and, 119, 120, 121, 124; Peter and, 125; resurrected, 129; Simon the Pharisee and, 120; the cross and, 127
*Journey in the Dark* series, 62, 108, 186, 263, 337
Joy, 11, 229, 242, 348

Kappel, Ashley, 51, 133, 149, 166, 180, 288
Kidd, Brock, 43–50
Kidd, Pam, 19, 59, 87, 117, 152, 178, 217, 255, 287, 318, 360, 400

Kindness, 158, 165
King, Jr., Martin Luther, 22
King, Marilyn Morgan, 119–29
Knapp, Carol, 14, 76, 145, 185, 233, 265, 292, 330
Knowing others, 334
Kruger, Jo, 357
Kuykendall, Carol, 26, 86, 132, 167, 191, 215, 248, 291, 324, 379

Laughter, 113, 150, 180
Learning about oneself, 331
Learning from mistakes, 118
Lee, Bobby, 21
Lescheid, Helen Grace, 157, 211, 312, 406
*Letters from the Heart* series, 225–31
Letting go, 106, 312, 368
Light, signs of, 212
Listening, 89, 246, 292
Little things, 193
Living fully, 122
Living in the eternal presence, 285
Living monuments, 60
Lorenz, Patricia, 55, 77, 116, 140, 202, 254, 350
Losing one's way, 8
Love: a gift of, 195; all that matters, 408; bond of, 394; eternal, 244; expressing, 53, 254; family, 32; forgiveness and, 120; memories of, 326; speaking the truth in, 327; the greatest virtue, 52
Love and be loved, 403
Loving-kindness, 98

Macomber, Debbie, 28, 80, 189, 246, 328, 354
Making a difference, 262
Making the first move, 41
Making the most of the journey, 268
Malion, Carolyn, 190
Marriage, 94, 198
Maundy Thursday, 126
Memorial Day, 169
Memorial stones, 372
Memories, 34
Messiness, 373
Messmer, Janetta, 284
Messmer, Roberta, 8, 40, 72, 106, 141, 174, 208, 242, 276, 310, 345, 378
Miller, Keith, 56, 192, 247, 317
Mother's Day, 147
Music, 135

National Day of Prayer, 144
Need, 220
Neighbors, 259, 397
Neukrug, Linda, 10, 73, 238, 267, 316, 393

Offering help, 25
*The One Who Is to Come* series, 358, 363, 370, 381, 388, 395, 401, 402
Opening ourselves, 296
Opportunities, 28

# *Authors, Titles and Subjects Index*

O'Roark, Mary Ann, 33, 85, 158, 259, 319, 390
Overplanning, 319

Palm Sunday, 122
Parent, Linda, 323
Parenting, 271
*A Path to Simplicity* series, 8, 40, 72, 106, 141, 174, 208, 242, 276, 310, 345, 378
Paying attention, 221
Payment, 86
Perseverance, 181, 301
Perspective, 196, 284
Positive attitude, 159
Positive changes, 80
Possibility, 213, 223
Prayer: action as, 20; answered, 93, 228, 323, 378; connecting with others in, 364; daily, 65; inspirations to, 10; letting God into our hearts and, 47; ministry of, 398; patience in, 321; power of, 108; praising God in, 237; with others, 336, 349; work as, 280
Present, the, 131, 338
Pressing on, 17
Priorities, 168

Questioning routines, 30

Raising a son, 218
*Reader's Room* series, 21, 58, 74, 118, 155, 190, 224, 251, 284, 323, 357, 397
Reaping what you sow, 83
Recalculating, 208
Receiving, 258
Relationships, 379
Reliability, 61
Relinquishing pride, 40
Replenishing one's spirit, 256
Responding, 95
Rest, 153
Restoration, 230
Role-model moments, 97
Ruts, 303

Saying grace, 77
Schantz, Daniel, 20, 61, 101, 142, 179, 219, 260, 290, 327, 356
Schilling, Gail Thorell, 42, 195, 269, 320, 397
Schwab, Penney, 31, 64, 99, 134, 163, 199, 235, 268, 303, 335, 365, 394
Seeing others just as they are, 318
Seeking God, 160
Self-discipline, 148
Selflessness, 81
Sense of humor, 102
Serving God, 35, 99, 332
Serving others, 267, 300, 314
Sharing, 31, 43, 50, 107, 236, 288, 295, 339, 404

Sherrill, Elizabeth, 29, 82, 111, 151, 194, 213, 252, 279, 333, 383
Sherrill, John, 293-99
Showing respect, 335
Sitting up front, 161
Smyth, Shari, 18, 100, 222, 289
Solitude, 209
Speed bump, 78
Spontaneity, 278
Starting over, 49
Sundays, 199
Sundquist, Joshua, 63, 110, 196, 282, 380
Surrendering control, 352
Sweeney, Jon, 175, 368

Teaching children, 365
Temptations, 257
Tenacity, 406
Thanksgiving, 367
Thinking of others first, 82
*Time on the River* series, 293-99
*To Say Good-bye* series, 19, 59, 87, 117, 152, 178, 217, 255, 287, 318, 360, 400
Transformation, 189, 231
Treasures, 310
Trust in God, 33, 51, 54, 59, 146, 174, 200, 277, 391
Truth tellers, 217

Understanding, 371
Unsung heroes, 178

Valentin, Karen, 81, 190, 367
Valuable things, 179
Veterans Day, 354

Waiting, 360
Walker, Scott, 25, 92, 153, 234, 302, 338, 408
Weary, Dolphus, 21, 74, 168, 224, 347, 391
Weeks, Brigitte, 62, 108, 186, 263, 337
West, Marion Bond, 225-31, 305, 387
*When the Heart Needs Healing* series, 43-50
Wilbee, Brenda, 67, 203, 245, 285, 351
Williams, Tim, 54, 112, 200, 258, 323, 396
Wisdom, 184
Witnessing, 366
Wolseley, Isabel, 52, 184, 311, 359, 384
Wonder, 383
Wonder of being, 298
Woosley, Joann, 118
Working for the Lord, 79
Working through, 322
Working with youth, 92
World Communion Sunday, 311

Zaleski, Philip, 32, 214, 266, 344, 385
Zest for living, 293

> # *Daily Guideposts* 1977–2011
> *35 Years of Faith and Inspiration*
>
> *Daily Guideposts* 2011 is our thirty-fifth edition, and to mark the occasion we've prepared this special gift for our *Daily Guideposts* family. In this chronology, we've woven together the story of *Daily Guideposts* and the sometimes tumultuous times we've lived through. If you've been with us since the beginning, we hope you'll find a smile of recognition and perhaps a tear or two in these pages; if you're new to our family, we hope you'll enjoy what Paul Harvey used to call "the rest of the story." Enjoy the journey!

## *1977*

*Daily Guideposts* was born in 1977. That first edition and the one to follow were written by one man, Fred Bauer, then a book editor at Guideposts.

IN THE NEWS: Deng Xiaoping returns to power in China. The first personal computers go on sale. Elvis Presley dies at age forty-two.

WHAT WE WERE READING: *Oliver's Story* by Erich Segal; *The Thorn Birds* by Colleen McCullough

WHAT WE WERE WATCHING: *Star Wars*; *Annie Hall*; *Saturday Night Fever*; *Close Encounters of the Third Kind*; the TV miniseries *Roots*

COST OF A FIRST-CLASS STAMP: 13 cents

*Daily Guideposts 1977–2011*

## 1978

Like its predecessor, *Daily Guideposts 1978* was the work of Fred Bauer. We were proud to have drawings by Joni Eareckson Tada on our month-opening pages.

IN THE NEWS: Israel's Menachem Begin and Egypt's Anwar Sadat sign the Camp David Accord, for which they receive the Nobel Peace Prize. Pope Paul VI dies at eighty; his successor, Pope John Paul I, dies after thirty-four days in office. Pope John Paul II, the first Polish pope, is elected in his place. Garfield debuts on the comics page.

WHAT WE WERE READING: *The Holcroft Covenant* by Robert Ludlum; *War and Remembrance* by Herman Wouk; *If Life Is a Bowl of Cherries, What Am I Doing in the Pits?* by Erma Bombeck

WHAT WE WERE WATCHING *The Deer Hunter*; *Midnight Express*; *Heaven Can Wait*; *Coming Home*

COST OF A FIRST-CLASS STAMP: 15 cents as of 5/29/78

## 1979

The third annual edition of *Daily Guideposts* was a quantum jump—from one writer to seventy-five, including such standouts as Dr. and Mrs. Norman Vincent Peale, Marjorie Holmes and Catharine Marshall. A number of writers who joined our family in 1979 are still writing for us, including Elizabeth and John Sherrill, Marion Bond West, Marilyn Morgan Helleberg (King), Isabel Champ (Wolseley) and Penney Schwab.

*Daily Guideposts 1977–2011*

Helpful features in *Daily Guideposts 1979* included "Your Spiritual Workshop," a monthly series, and our first Holy Week series by a Guideposts stalwart, longtime New York journalist Glenn D. Kittler.

IN THE NEWS: The Pol Pot regime in Cambodia is ousted by Vietnam-backed forces. Shah Mohammed Reza Pahlavi flees Iran; the Ayatollah Ruhollah Khomeini takes power. President Jimmy Carter and Soviet President Brezhnev sign the Salt II treaty. A nuclear accident at the Three Mile Island reactor in Pennsylvania releases radiation. Louise Brown, the first test-tube baby, is born in London.

WHAT WE WERE READING: *Overload* by Arthur Hailey; *The Matarese Circle* by Robert Ludlum; *Sophie's Choice* by William Styron; *The Dead Zone* by Stephen King; *Aunt Erma's Cope Book* by Erma Bombeck.

WHAT WE WERE WATCHING: *Apocalypse Now*; *All That Jazz*; *Kramer vs. Kramer*; *Breaking Away*

COST OF A FIRST-CLASS STAMP: 15 cents

## *1980*

We welcomed seventy-three writers to *Daily Guideposts 1980*. Among them were three first-timers destined to become reader favorites: Oscar Greene, a beloved presence in all but four editions of *Daily Guideposts* since his debut; Sue Monk Kidd, who has gone on to become one of America's most noted novelists; and Shari Smyth. And there was another notable first that year: our first paperback large-print edition.

DAILY GUIDEPOSTS

*Daily Guideposts 1977–2011*

**IN THE NEWS:** Ronald Reagan is elected president in Republican sweep. Iran hostage crisis continues. John Lennon is shot dead in New York City. Ted Turner launches CNN, the first all-news network.

**WHAT WE WERE READING:** *Smiley's People* by John le Carré; *Princess Daisy* by Judith Krantz; *Key to Rebecca* by Ken Follett; *The Covenant* by James Michener

**WHAT WE WERE WATCHING:** *Raging Bull*; *Ordinary People*; *Coal Miner's Daughter*; *The Elephant Man*; *Tess*

**COST OF A FIRST-CLASS STAMP:** 15 cents

## *1981*

We welcomed an awesome and never-equaled ninety-eight contributors in 1981, including newcomers Karen Barber, Aletha J. Lindstrom and Mary Jane Meyer. We packed in the features, too: "When the Bible Speaks to Me" in the middle of each month, "A Lenten Visit with Norman Vincent Peale," and a Holy Week series by Sue Monk Kidd.

**IN THE NEWS:** Anwar el-Sadat is assassinated by Islamic extremists. Sandra Day-O'Connor becomes the first woman on the US Supreme Court. Major League Baseball goes on strike. Lady Diana Spencer marries Charles, Prince of Wales.

**WHAT WE WERE READING:** *Gorky Park* by Martin Cruz Smith; *Noble House* by James Clavell; *Cujo* by Stephen King, *The Hotel New Hampshire* by John Irving; *An Indecent Obsession* by Colleen McCullough

**WHAT WE WERE WATCHING:** *Raiders of the Lost Ark*; *Chariots of Fire*; *On Golden Pond*; *Reds*; *Atlantic City*

COST OF A FIRST-CLASS STAMP: 18 cents as of 3/22/81; 20 cents as of 11/1/81

## *1982*

Seventy-nine writers graced *Daily Guideposts 1982*; Madge Harrah and Sam Justice made their first appearances. We featured a new series of "When the Bible Speaks to Me" devotionals, as well as our first Advent series and a special three-page Christmas story by Dr. Peale.

IN THE NEWS: The Equal Rights Amendment fails ratification. A permanent artificial heart is implanted in a human for the first time, by Dr. Barney Clark at the University of Utah Medical Center. Princess Grace dies of injuries in car accident.

WHAT WE WERE READING: *North and South* by John Jakes; *The Parsifal Mosaic* by Robert Ludlum; *Space* by James Michener

WHAT WE WERE WATCHING: *E.T.: The Extra-Terrestrial*; *Tootsie*; *Gandhi*; *The Verdict*

COST OF A FIRST-CLASS STAMP: 20 cents

## *1983*

Twenty-two writers joined us for *Daily Guideposts 1983*, and they gave us a real feast, including some very special dishes. Each month featured meditations on the Beatitudes by Marilyn Morgan Helleberg (King); "Journeys in Faith," devotionals on Old Testament figures by Elizabeth Sherrill, whose series would become a *Daily Guideposts* institution; Holy Week with Norman Vincent Peale; and a summer week at the sea with Sue Monk Kidd. Phyllis Hobe and Drue

*Daily Guideposts 1977–2011*

Duke made their first appearances, as did our popular journaling pages.

> IN THE NEWS: Sally K. Ride is the first US woman astronaut in space. Microsoft Word is first released. The final episode of *M\*A\*S\*H\** becomes the most watched episode in TV history. FCC authorizes Motorola to begin testing cellular phone service in Chicago.
>
> WHAT WE WERE READING: *Mistral's Daughter* by Judith Krantz; *The Little Drummer Girl* by John le Carré; *The Name of the Rose* by Umberto Ecco
>
> WHAT WE WERE WATCHING: *The Big Chill*; *Terms of Endearment*; *Fanny & Alexander*; *The Right Stuff*
>
> COST OF A FIRST-CLASS STAMP: 20 cents

## *1984*

An even two dozen writers graced *Daily Guideposts 1984*. For the first time we had a theme, "The Parables," which we learned to appreciate more deeply in Arthur Gordon and Fred Bauer's monthly series "Jesus the Master Storyteller." And each month Guideposts editor-in-chief Van Varner's "Guidepeople" took us behind the scenes at the magazine, while we prepared for Christmas with Marilyn Morgan Helleberg (King) and for Easter with Sue Monk Kidd.

> IN THE NEWS: Soviet Union withdraws from the Summer Olympic Games in Los Angeles. Indian Prime Minister Indira Gandhi is assassinated; President Reagan is reelected in a landslide with 59 percent of vote; Apple introduces the user-friendly Macintosh personal computer.

**WHAT WE WERE READING:** *Who Killed the Robins Family?* by Bill Adler and Thomas Chastain; *Full Circle* by Danielle Steel; *". . . And Ladies of the Club"* by Helen Hooven Santmyer

**WHAT WE WERE WATCHING:** *Amadeus*; *The Killing Fields*; *A Passage to India*; *The Pope of Greenwich Village*

**COST OF A FIRST-CLASS STAMP:** 20 cents

## *1985*

Our twenty-six writers explored "Everyday Discipleship" in *Daily Guideposts 1985*, led by Patricia Houck Sprinkle's series "The Everyday Disciple." Arthur Gordon started each month with some practical pointers to "New Beginnings," and Van Varner—a Kentucky native who became the quintessential New Yorker—invited us to "Meet Me in the City." Marilyn Morgan Helleberg (King) helped us to see "Easter through the Eyes of Jesus and Mary," and Sue Monk Kidd invited us to spend a week with the Lord's Prayer. We traveled down the Mississippi with Fred Bauer, who showed us later in the year "Where to Find Christmas." What's now our Fellowship Corner appeared as The Family Album, with chatty bios and photos of our writers, among whom for the first time appeared *Guideposts* magazine newcomer (and now executive editor) Rick Hamlin.

**IN THE NEWS:** Mikhail Gorbachev becomes the Soviet leader and initiates a broad program of reform and liberalization. Coca-Cola changes its formula and releases New Coke with an overwhelmingly negative response. US budget-balancing bill is enacted.

**WHAT WE WERE READING:** *The Sicilian* by Mario Puzo; *Hold the Dream* by Barbara Taylor Bradford; *Cider House Rules* by John Irving; *Lake Woebegone Days* by Garrison Keillor

*Daily Guideposts 1977–2011*

WHAT WE WERE WATCHING: *Kiss of the Spider Woman*; *Out of Africa*; *Prizzi's Honor*; *The Color Purple*

COST OF A FIRST-CLASS STAMP: 20 cents; 22 cents as of 2/17/85

## *1986*

The theme our twenty-eight writers addressed as we celebrated our tenth anniversary was "Fellowship," and joining our fellowship for the first time was Carol Kuykendall. Sue Monk Kidd shared some ways of "Practicing the Presence of God"; Marilyn Morgan Helleberg (King) took us on a "Wilderness Journey" with children of Israel; we learned about "The Seven Pillars of Marriage" that had blessed Dr. and Mrs. Peale; Arthur Gordon guided us through his beloved Savannah; Jeff Japinga led us through Holy Week, and Patricia Houck Sprinkle through Advent. And to help you find your way through the year's riches, we added indexes.

IN THE NEWS: Major nuclear accident at Soviet Union's Chernobyl power station alarms world. Space shuttle Challenger explodes after launch at Cape Canaveral, Florida. The *Oprah Winfrey Show* hits national television. Fox News, the fourth television network, is born and offers ten hours of prime time programming a week.

WHAT WE WERE READING: *Lie Down with Lions* by Ken Follett; *The Bourne Supremacy* by Robert Ludlum; *A Perfect Spy* by John le Carré; *Last of the Breed* by Louis L'Amour

WHAT WE WERE WATCHING: *Platoon*; *Hannah and Her Sisters*; *The Color of Money*; *The Mission*

COST OF A FIRST-CLASS STAMP: 22 cents

## 1987

Forty writers prepared the bill of fare for *Daily Guideposts 1987*, and a rich one it was. Our theme was "God's Everlasting Love," and Phyllis Hobe's monthly "Lessons in Love" traced it through the year. Eleanor Sass gave us monthly "Bible Echoes," while Sue Monk Kidd traversed Holy Week and Advent. There were special series by Van Varner, John and Elizabeth Sherrill and Elaine St. Johns; Norman Vincent Peale added praises of the four seasons. And new to the family were Patricia Lorenz and Linda Ching Sledge.

IN THE NEWS: Oliver North Jr. tells congressional inquiry that higher officials approved his secret Iran-Contra operations. President Ronald Reagan says Iran arms-Contra policy went astray and accepts responsibility. US Supreme Court rules Rotary Clubs must admit women.

WHAT WE WERE READING: *The Eyes of the Dragon* by Stephen King; *Windmills of the Gods* by Sidney Sheldon; *Fine Things* by Danielle Steel; *The Haunted Mesa* by Louis L'Amour; *Misery* by Stephen King; *Presumed Innocent* by Scott Turow

WHAT WE WERE WATCHING: *Moonstruck*; *Wall Street*; *The Last Emperor*; *Fatal Attraction*

COST OF A FIRST-CLASS STAMP: 22 cents

## 1988

"The Family" was the theme our *Daily Guideposts* family of forty-nine writers addressed in 1988, with special contributions by Carol Kuykendall ("Tandem Power") and Floyd and Harriett Thatcher ("Family Time"). Linda Ching Sledge brought us to "The Wonder of Easter," while Elizabeth Sherrill gave us a unique look at "Advent: Season of Paradoxes." Marilyn Moore Jensen wrote about overcoming loneliness; newcomer Scott Harrison shared the lessons in faith he had learned as a physician in Africa; and Marilyn Morgan Helleberg (King) spent "Three Days in the Psalms." Among the family's new members were soon-to-be-regulars Carol Knapp, who brought the Alaska wilderness to *Daily Guideposts*, college teacher Daniel Schantz, and Indiana's Mary Lou Carney.

IN THE NEWS: George Bush wins the presidential election as Republicans sweep forty states. Benazir Bhutto is chosen to lead Pakistan and is the first Islamic woman prime minister. Pan-Am 747 explodes from a terrorist bomb over Lockerbie, Scotland, killing all 259 aboard. NASA scientist James Hansen warns Congress of the dangers of global warming. Ted Turner starts Turner Network Television (TNT).

WHAT WE WERE READING: *The Bonfire of the Vanities* by Tom Wolfe; *The Icarus Agenda* by Robert Ludlum; *Zoya* by Danielle Steel; *Alaska* by James Michener; *The Cardinal and the Kremlin* by Tom Clancy; *The Queen of the Damned* by Anne Rice

WHAT WE WERE WATCHING: *Rainman*; *Mississippi Burning*; *A Fish Called Wanda*; *Bull Durham*

COST OF A FIRST-CLASS STAMP: 22 cents; 25 cents as of 4/3/88

## 1989

As in 1988, forty-nine writers contributed to *Daily Guideposts 1989*'s exploration of "A Closer Walk with God." Walking with us for the first time were Eric Fellman and Linda Neukrug. We had monthly series by Mary Lou Carney ("Becoming as a Child Again") and Sue Monk Kidd ("Learning to Wait on God"); Phyllis Hobe showed us what Jesus might do in some contemporary situations; Linda Ching Sledge took us to islands she had visited or lived on; Fred Bauer shed light on Jesus' words by thinking about "What Jesus Didn't Say"; Elizabeth Sherrill brought us to "Easter: Road Map for Living"; and Marilyn Moore Jensen took us "On the Walk to Bethlehem." And as a "Back-to-School Bonus," four fifth-graders gave us stories in September.

IN THE NEWS: The fall of the Berlin Wall heralds the end of the Cold War. Army Gen. Colin Powell becomes the first Black Chairman of Joint Chiefs of Staff. Tiananmen Square protests in Beijing result in thousands being killed. Comedian Lucille Ball dies.

WHAT WE WERE READING: *Midnight* by Dean R. Koontz; *Star* by Danielle Steel; *The Satanic Verses* by Salman Rushdie; *While My Pretty One Sleeps* by Mary Higgins Clark; *The Russia House* by John le Carré; *Polar Star* by Martin Cruz Smith

WHAT WE WERE WATCHING: *Glory*; *Born on the Fourth of July*; *My Left Foot*; *Sex, Lies, and Videotape*; *Field of Dreams*

COST OF A FIRST-CLASS STAMP: 25 cents

## *1990*

Our 1990 theme was "Windows," keynoted by Eleanor Sass's "Through an Open Window" and Marilyn Morgan Helleberg (King's) "Windows into Wonder." Carol Kuykendall's "His Final Gestures" took us through Holy Week, Elizabeth Sherrill prepared us for Pentecost in "The Coming of the Spirit," and Terry Helwig

*Daily Guideposts 1977–2011*

encouraged us to "Journey to Inner Bethlehem." It was a year of journeys: We embarked on "A Family Adventure" with Eric Fellman and shared "Our Travels Together" with Ruth Stafford Peale. And we welcomed Arizonan Gina Bridgeman to our family circle.

**IN THE NEWS:** East and West Germany unify into a single Germany. Nelson Mandela is released from prison in South Africa after twenty-seven years. The first McDonald's in Moscow, Russia, opens. *Seinfeld* premieres.

**WHAT WE WERE READING:** *Devices and Desires* by P. D. James; *The Stand* by Stephen King; *The Burden of Proof* by Scott Turow; *The Plains of Passage* by Jean M. Auel

**WHAT WE WERE WATCHING:** *Dances with Wolves*; *GoodFellas*; *Henry and June*; *Reversal of Fortune*

**COST OF A FIRST-CLASS STAMP:** 25 cents

## *1991*

In 1991, our fifteenth anniversary year, we offered "Praise," looking at how the apostles model our own faith journey in Terry Helwig's "The Twelve in Each of Us" and how we might find answers to our life's concerns in "The Questions Jesus Asked" by Sue Monk Kidd. Newcomer Christopher de Vinck bade us to "Come to the Good Shepherd"; Dr. and Mrs. Peale bade us to find strength in "The Timeless Power of Prayer." Elizabeth Sherrill turned our attention to the Epiphany. We spent Easter week with long-timer Eleanor Sass and Advent with first-timer Scott Walker, learned to deal with illness by "Leaning on the Lord" with Carol Kuykendall and to "C.H.A.N.G.E." with Marilyn Morgan Helleberg (King).

*Daily Guideposts 1977–2011*

IN THE NEWS: A cease-fire ends the Persian Gulf War. The South African Parliament repeals apartheid laws. The Warsaw Pact is dissolved. A hard-line Communist coup fails in Moscow. On Christmas, the Soviet Union is dissolved.

WHAT WE WERE READING: *The Secret Pilgrim* by John le Carré; *Cold Fire* by Dean R. Koontz; *The Kitchen God's Wife* by Amy Tan

WHAT WE WERE WATCHING: *The Silence of the Lambs*; *Beauty and the Beast*; *JFK*; *Thelma & Louise*

COST OF A FIRST-CLASS STAMP: 25 cents

## *1992*

"Grace" was our theme in 1992, and our pages were graced by forty-one writers. Our special features included monthly "Grace Notes" from a variety of authors, a monthly series on relationships from Sue Monk Kidd, and a week of "New Lessons in Faith" from Scott Harrison. We spent Holy Week with Scott Walker and prepared for Christmas with Dr. and Mrs. Peale. And as a special treat, we welcomed twelve readers in "Pathways of Praise," the precursor of today's Reader's Room.

IN THE NEWS: George Bush and Boris Yeltsin proclaim a formal end to the Cold War. Bill Clinton is elected president. The Winter and Summer Olympics are held in France and Spain. Johnny Carson hosts *The Tonight Show* for the last time.

WHAT WE WERE READING: *Hideaway* by Dean R. Koontz; *Rising Sun* by Michael Crichton; *The Pelican Brief* by John Grisham; *Jewels* by Danielle Steel

*Daily Guideposts 1977–2011*

WHAT WE WERE WATCHING: *Unforgiven*; *The Crying Game*; *Howards End*; *Glengarry Glen Ross*; *The Player*

COST OF A FIRST-CLASS STAMP: 29 cents

## *1993*

Three dozen contributors explored "The Gift of Hope" in *Daily Guideposts 1993*. Elizabeth Sherrill led off with "The Healing Power of Hope," and we had abundant gifts from other members of our family—Phyllis Hobe, Christopher de Vinck, Carol Knapp and Fay Angus all contributed special series. But two of the offerings that year were most notable: In her Holy Week series, "Transformed in the Broken Places," Marilyn Morgan Helleberg (King) broke new ground in dealing honestly and sensitively with the end of her marriage and how sorrow and suffering can give way to healing and joy. And in October, Sue Monk Kidd said good-bye to *Daily Guideposts* in "Weaving Change into Your Life." But we also said hello to two other Kidds, unrelated to Sue though related to each other: Pam Kidd and her son Brock from Nashville, Tennessee.

IN THE NEWS: China breaks the nuclear test moratorium. An Israeli-Palestinian accord is reached. World Trade Center bombed; five are arrested.

WHAT WE WERE READING: *Dragon Tears* by Dean R. Koontz; *The Bridges of Madison County* by Robert James Waller; *The Client* by John Grisham; *Without Remorse* by Tom Clancy

WHAT WE WERE WATCHING: *Schindler's List*; *The Piano*; *Philadelphia*; *Six Degrees of Separation*; *In the Name of the Father*

COST OF A FIRST-CLASS STAMP: 29 cents

## 1994

In 1994 our family of thirty-eight celebrated "Prayer: The Mightiest Force in the World." Marilyn Morgan Helleberg (King) provided "Gifts of the Season," short poems and prayers to open every month. Pam Kidd followed with "Prayer Can Change Your Life," in which she told us how the classic book of the same name by Dr. William Parker and Elaine St. Johns had changed hers. Eric Fellman accompanied us through Holy Week and Phyllis Hobe did the same through Advent, and Linda Ching Sledge and her son Timothy, Daniel Schantz and Elizabeth Sherrill all contributed weeklong series, as did freed Lebanon hostage David Jacobson, who told how faith had helped him through his ordeal in "Faith: Your Daily Survival Kit." New to our family that year was Dolphus Weary, who continues to inspire us with his work in racial reconciliation and community development in rural Mississippi.

**IN THE NEWS:** Aldrich Ames, high CIA official, is charged with spying for the Soviets. Major League baseball players strike. *ER* and *Friends* debut on NBC. Richard Nixon dies.

**WHAT WE WERE READING:** *Disclosure* by Michael Crichton; *Remember Me* by Mary Higgins Clark; *The Chamber* by John Grisham; *Politically Correct Bedtime Stories* by James Finn Garner

**WHAT WE WERE WATCHING:** *Forrest Gump*; *Pulp Fiction*; *The Shawshank Redemption*; *Quiz Show*; *Nobody's Fool*

**COST OF A FIRST-CLASS STAMP:** 29 cents

## 1995

Our 1995 theme was "Looking Ahead: The Bright and Positive Side of Change." Joining us that year among our forty-four writers

### Daily Guideposts 1977–2011

were Lurlene McDaniel, who contributed a touching series on her fight against breast cancer; Bill Irwin, who hiked the Appalachian Trail with his Seeing Eye dog; and Susan Schefflein. Elizabeth Sherrill helped us in "Facing the Unknown Future"; Sandra Simpson LeSourd told us how her struggles with addiction and failure pointed her "Toward Easter's Joy." We gathered "Around the Campfire" with Mary Lou Carney, went on "Adventures in the Yukon" with Carol Knapp, worked on "Building a Friendship" with Linda Ching Sledge and looked toward Christmas with *Daily Guideposts* editor Mary Ruth Howes. And in devotionals by Arthur Gordon and Ruth Stafford Peale, we celebrated Guideposts' fiftieth anniversary.

> IN THE NEWS: Russian space station Mir greets its first Americans. Israeli Prime Minister Yitzhak Rabin is slain at a peace rally. A Los Angeles jury finds O.J. Simpson not guilty of murder charges. The Rock and Roll Hall of Fame opens in Cleveland.
>
> WHAT WE WERE READING: *Beach Music* by Pat Conroy; *From Potter's Field* by Patricia Cornwell; *The Horse Whisperer* by Nicholas Evans; *The Christmas Box* by Richard Paul Evans
>
> WHAT WE WERE WATCHING: *Babe*; *Braveheart*; *Leaving Las Vegas*; *The Usual Suspects*; *Dead Man Walking*
>
> COST OF A FIRST-CLASS STAMP: 32 cents as of 1/1/95

### *1996*

The theme of our twentieth edition was "Lights in the Darkness," and our fifty-one writers included some exciting new lights: the noted children's writer Katherine Paterson visited us for a year, while then Guideposts senior editor (now editor-in-chief) Edward Grinnan, nurse Roberta Messner, prolific Christian writer Keith

*Daily Guideposts 1977–2011*

Miller (who gave us our Holy Week series) and then Guideposts book division editor-in-chief Brigitte Weeks became permanent parts of the family. Pam Kidd took us through Advent in a "Journey toward the Light," while Elizabeth Sherrill told us monthly about "My Gift Today."

**IN THE NEWS:** Madeleine Albright becomes the first female Secretary of State. Britain is alarmed by an outbreak of "mad cow" disease. More than forty-three million US households (44 percent) own a personal computer, and fourteen million of them are online. Jazz great Ella Fitzgerald dies.

**WHAT WE WERE READING:** *Intensity* by Dean R. Koontz; *Primary Colors* by Anonymous (Joe Klein); *How Stella Got Her Groove Back* by Terry McMillan; *The Runaway Jury* by John Grisham; *Cause of Death* by Patricia Cornwell

**WHAT WE WERE WATCHING:** *The English Patient*; *Fargo*; *Jerry Maguire*; *The People vs. Larry Flynt*; *Shine*; *Sling Blade*

**COST OF A FIRST-CLASS STAMP:** 32 cents

## 1997

*Daily Guideposts* turned twenty-one with a focus on "The Wonder of God's Love." We welcomed a bumper crop of new voices to our chorus of forty-six: Kjerstin Easton (now Williams), then a freshman at Caltech; Mark Collins, a fresh voice from Pittsburgh, Pennsylvania; Roberta Rogers; Julia Attaway and her husband Andrew, the new editor of *Daily Guideposts*. Our special series were from Elizabeth Sherrill ("Love Is...," based on Paul's great hymn to love in I Corinthians 13); Marilyn Morgan Helleberg (King), imagining herself following Jesus through the events of Holy Week; Eric Fellman on "The Candles of Christmas," Mary Lou Carney and Carol Kuykendall.

**IN THE NEWS:** United States, United Kingdom and France agree to freeze the Nazis' gold loot. US shuttle joins the Russian space station. Timothy J. McVeigh is sentenced to death for the Oklahoma City bombing. *Titanic*, the most expensive film of all time, breaks box office records. Princess Diana dies in a car crash in Paris.

**WHAT WE WERE READING:** *Hornet's Nest* by Patricia Cornwell; *The Partner* by John Grisham; *Plum Island* by Nelson DeMille; *Unnatural Exposure* by Patricia Cornwell; *Cold Mountain* by Charles Frazier

**WHAT WE WERE WATCHING:** *As Good As It Gets*; *The Full Monty*; *Good Will Hunting*; *The Ice Storm*; *L.A. Confidential*; *Titanic*

**COST OF A FIRST-CLASS STAMP:** 32 cents

## *1998*

Our fifty-three contributors in 1998 focused on "God's Healing Touch." Our first-of-the-month series featured stories of "The Touch of the Healer"; we made a "Journey to Healing" with Scott Harrison and spent Holy Week with Rick Hamlin. Mary Lou Carney found healing for grief in "My Mother's House," and John Sherrill helped us toward "Healing the Fear of Old Age." And at Advent and Christmas, Marion Bond West took us back to six healing Christmases in her life. Visiting us this year were Bill and Kathy Peel of Nashville, Tennessee, while Rhoda Blecker, then a Californian and now of Bellingham, Washington, settled in for a long stay.

IN THE NEWS: Europeans agree on a single currency, the euro. President Clinton is accused in a White House sex scandal involving intern Monica Lewinsky. An estimated seventy-six million viewers watch the last episode of *Seinfeld*. *Titanic*, the highest-grossing film of all time, captures a record-tying eleven Oscars, including Best Picture and Best Director.

WHAT WE WERE READING: *Paradise* by Toni Morrison; *"N" Is for Noose* by Sue Grafton; *I Know This Much Is True* by Wally Lamb; *The Path of Daggers* by Robert Jordan; *A Man in Full* by Tom Wolfe

WHAT WE WERE WATCHING: *Affliction*; *American History X*; *Elizabeth*; *Shakespeare in Love*; *There's Something about Mary*

COST OF A FIRST-CLASS STAMP: 32 cents

## *1999*

As we approached the end of the nineties and peered ahead toward a new millennium, we took our theme from the Twenty-third Psalm: "He Leadeth Me." Fifty-two writers joined us, among them newcomers Libbie Adams, Melody Bonnette, Helen Grace Lescheid, Allison Sample and Gail Thorell Schilling. Also new this year was "The Reader's Room," where we welcome your comments and stories. Leading us ahead again was Elizabeth Sherrill, who shared "Lessons in Listening." Isabel Wolseley contributed a series about the weekly routines of her growing-up years. In Holy Week, Shari Smyth told us about her struggle to save the daughter she loves. Eric Fellman shared a time of personal decision in "A Fork in the Road," while Julia Attaway led us through Advent on "The Paths of Christmas."

*Daily Guideposts 1977–2011*

**In the News:** The world awaits the consequences of the Y2K bug. US Senate opens an impeachment trial of President Clinton but later acquits him and rejects a censure move. Students Eric Harris and Dylan Klebold storm Columbine High School in Littleton, Colorado, killing twelve other students, a teacher, and then themselves. Doctors in Louisville, Kentucky, perform the first human hand transplant in the United States.

**What We Were Reading:** *Star Wars Episode I–The Phantom Menace* by Terry Brooks; *Harry Potter and the Chamber of Secrets* by J. K. Rowling; *Hannibal* by Thomas Harris; *Harry Potter and the Sorcerer's Stone* by J. K. Rowling; *The Alibi* by Sandra Brown; *Harry Potter and the Prisoner of Azkaban* by J. K. Rowling

**What We Were Watching:** *Blair Witch Project*; *American Beauty*; *Three Kings*; *The Sixth Sense*

**Cost of a First-Class Stamp:** 33 cents as of 1/10/99

## *2000*

The year 2000—Y2K as it was called back then—seemed an occasion of anxiety for many. We chose to look hopefully toward the new millennium and the twenty-first century (yes, we know they didn't really begin until 2001!). So we chose our theme from the Book of Revelation: "Behold, I Make All Things New." New to our family (now fifty-three strong) were Marci Alborghetti, who shared her encounter with melanoma in "Unlooked-for Blessings," Dave Franco and novelist Sharon Foster. Elizabeth Sherrill once again made "All Things New" in a monthly series, while Pam Kidd took us to Jerusalem to follow "The Way of the Cross." Mary Lou Carney shared the memories her mother had left as a legacy for her grandchildren. In Advent, Marilyn Morgan Helleberg (King) shared the memorable Christmases of her life, and through the year, we made regular stops at Van Varner's Central Park West apartment for a story of God's presence in the big city.

IN THE NEWS: Nationwide uprising overthrows Yugoslavian president Slobodan Milosevic. Wary investors bring stock plunge signaling the beginning of the end of the Internet stock boom. Closest US presidential election in decades (Bush vs. Gore) leads to automatic recounts. Charles Schulz, creator of the "Peanuts" cartoon strip, dies. The "I love you" virus disrupts computers worldwide.

WHAT WE WERE READING: *Easy Prey* by John Sandford; *Indwelling* by Tim LaHaye and Jerry B. Jenkins; *Winter Solstice* by Rosamunde Pilcher; *The Mark* by Tim LaHaye and Jerry B. Jenkins

WHAT WE WERE WATCHING: *Chocolat*; *Crouching Tiger, Hidden Dragon*; *Erin Brockovich*; *Gladiator*; *Traffic*

COST OF A FIRST-CLASS STAMP: 34 cents

## *2001*

We celebrated our Silver Anniversary in style, with fifty-three writers joining us in "Reaching Out"—our twenty-fifth-anniversary theme. A plethora of special series included Elizabeth Sherrill's "When God Reaches Out...Through Other People"; Isabel Wolseley's Papua-New Guinea travelogue; Eric Fellman's life-changing experiences in Africa, Kenneth Chafin's Holy Week series; Roberta Messner's search for restoration and renewal in "The Leaning Log"; John Sherrill's look at "Rehab for the Heart"; "A Weekend Away" with Van Varner; Mary Brown's experience with a dying neighbor; and Carol Knapp's look at the "Image in the Mirror" for Advent and Christmas. Marilyn Morgan King and her new husband Robert together told us how they found "A Whole and Holy Love," and we welcomed a very different voice in Brian Doyle of Portland, Oregon.

IN THE NEWS: Hijackers ram jetliners into the twin towers of New York's World Trade Center and the Pentagon. FBI Agent Robert Hanssen is charged with spying for Russia for fifteen years. Budget surplus dwindles attributed to a slowing economy and the Bush tax cut, the largest in twenty years. National Academy of Sciences warns that global warming is on the rise. In Louisville, Kentucky, an artificial heart is implanted in a man.

WHAT WE WERE READING: *A Day Late and a Dollar Short* by Terry McMillan; *1st to Die* by James Patterson; *A Common Life* by Jan Karon; *Chosen Prey* by John Sandford; *Black House* by Stephen King and Peter Straub

WHAT WE WERE WATCHING: *Ali*, *A Beautiful Mind*; *The Fellowship of the Ring*; *Monsters, Inc.*; *Shrek*

COST OF A FIRST-CLASS STAMP: 34 cents

## *2002*

In 2002, we asked our fifty-eight writers—including newcomers Tim Williams, Billy Newman, and recently retired editor-in-chief of *Guideposts* Fulton Oursler Jr.—to reflect on "Praying Together." Elizabeth Sherrill made the familiar words of the Lord's Prayer come alive, while Pam Kidd encouraged us to persevere in "The Practice of Prayer." Other special series included Eric Fellman on his and his wife Joy's twenty-fifth wedding anniversary; prayer at the four seasons

*Daily Guideposts 1977–2011*

with Roberta Rogers; a pilgrimage to the island of Iona with Marilyn Morgan King and her husband Robert; "A Worrier's Way to God" by Marci Alborghetti; a riveting Holy Week series by Roberta Messner; "A Grand Canyon Journey" with Rhoda Blecker; and Advent and Christmas with Rick Hamlin.

IN THE NEWS: The United States and Russia reach a landmark arms agreement to cut both countries' nuclear arsenals by up to two-thirds over the next ten years. UN Security Council passes a unanimous resolution calling on Iraq to disarm or face serious consequences. Kenneth L. Lay, chairman of bankrupt energy trader Enron, resigns with the company under federal investigation for hiding debt and misrepresenting earnings. Bush signs a corporate reform bill in response to the spate of corporate scandals.

WHAT WE WERE READING: *Journey through Heartsongs* by Mattie J.T. Stepanek; *The Nannie Diaries* by Emma McLaughlin and Nicola Kraus; *The Shelters of Stone* by Jean M. Auel; *The Remnant* by Tim LaHaye and Jerry B. Jenkins; *The Lovely Bones* by Alice Sebold

WHAT WE WERE WATCHING: *Harry Potter and the Chamber of Secrets*; *Lord of the Rings: The Two Towers*; *My Big Fat Greek Wedding*; *The Hours*; *Chicago*; *Gangs of New York*

COST OF A FIRST-CLASS STAMP: 37 cents

## *2003*

The events of 9/11 occurred after *Daily Guideposts 2002* had gone to press, so 2003 was our first opportunity to respond to the wounds we had suffered and the uncertainties that lay ahead. To keep our eye on the things God continues to do for us, we chose "Everyday Blessings" as our theme. Our fifty-six writers included a crop of

*Daily Guideposts 1977–2011*

seven newbies: Harold Hostetler, a roving editor for *Guideposts* magazine; Julie Garmon, the daughter of Marion Bond West; Ted Nace, then Guideposts' director of ministries; Evelyn Bence of Arlington, Virginia; Ptolemy Tompkins, then a staff editor at *Guideposts* and *Angels on Earth* magazines; and Joshua Sundquist, then a student from Harrisonburg, Virginia.

Our ten series writers included Elizabeth Sherrill, Roberta Messner, Eric Fellman, Libbie Adams, John Sherrill, Rick Hamlin, Carol Knapp and Mary Brown. Daniel Schantz took us from Palm Sunday to Easter, while Shari Smyth kindled "A Light from the Manger."

IN THE NEWS: In his State of the Union address, George Bush announces that he is ready to attack Iraq even without a UN mandate. US Secretary of State Colin Powell presents Iraq war rationale to UN, citing its WMD as an imminent threat to world security. The space shuttle Columbia explodes, killing all seven astronauts onboard. Supreme Court decisively upholds the right of affirmative action in higher education.

WHAT WE WERE READING: *The King of Torts* by John Grisham; *The Da Vinci Code* by Dan Brown; *To the Nines* by Janet Evanovich; *The Five People You Meet in Heaven* by Mitch Albom; *Blow Fly* by Patricia Cornwell

WHAT WE WERE WATCHING: *Pirates of the Caribbean*; *The Lord of the Rings: The Return of the King*; *Finding Nemo*; *Mystic River*; *Cold Mountain*; *Seabiscuit*

COST OF A FIRST-CLASS STAMP: 37 cents

## *2004*

In 2004, our theme was "The Things that Matter." We featured sixty writers, with special contributions from Elizabeth Sherrill on

*Daily Guideposts 1977–2011*

the hymns that have shaped her faith ("Then Sings My Soul"), Carol Kuykendall on "What Matters Most" to a family, and Roberta Messner ("Consider the Lilies") on God's provision for His children. A lot of travel was in store for us: In June Fred Bauer took us to the Costa Rican rainforest, while Van Varner invited us aboard for "A Voyage North," Brigitte Weeks invited us to join Habitat for Humanity in Central America for "A Time to Build," and Marilyn Morgan King took us on pilgrimage to Wales. In Holy Week, we went "Back to Jerusalem" with Carol Knapp, and we spent Christmas with John Sherrill. Joining us for the first time were Lucile Allen of Van, Texas; Patricia Pingry of Nashville, Tennessee; Philip Zaleski of Middlebury, Vermont; and Pamela Kennedy of Honolulu, Hawaii.

IN THE NEWS: The Democratic convention nominates John Kerry for president; the Republicans renominate President Bush, who wins in November. The US final report on Iraq's weapons finds no WMDs. Martha Stewart is sentenced to five months in prison for obstruction of justice and lying to federal investigators. The Summer Olympics are held in Athens, Greece

WHAT WE WERE READING: *The Last Juror* by John Grisham; *Glorious Appearing* by Tim LaHaye and Jerry B. Jenkins; *"R" Is for Ricochet* by Sue Grafton; *Northern Lights* by Nora Roberts

WHAT WE WERE WATCHING: *The Aviator*; *The Incredibles*; *Kinsey*; *Million Dollar Baby*; *Sideways*; *Spider-Man 2*

COST OF A FIRST-CLASS STAMP: 37 cents

## *2005*

Our theme for *Daily Guideposts 2005* was "Rejoicing in Hope." Sixty writers joined us, among whom were newcomers Debbie

*Daily Guideposts 1977–2011*

Macomber, one of America's all-time-best-selling writers; Sabra Ciancanelli, now the editor of OurPrayer.org; Pablo Diaz, Guideposts' director of ministries; Floridian Rebecca Kelly; and Karen Valentin of New York City.

Elizabeth Sherrill gave us "God Sightings" at the start of each month; Roberta Messner shared her experiences of God's little nudges; Marci Alborghetti faced the recurrence of her melanoma; Julia Attaway took us to the place where Easter truly begins, "At the Foot of the Cross"; Carol Kuykendall found God to be "A Very Present Help"; Marilyn Morgan King shared "The Mysterious Gift"; and Karen Barber showed us the "Simple Gifts" of Christmas.

IN THE NEWS: Former Tehran mayor Mahmoud Ahmadinejad, a hard-line conservative, wins Iran's presidential election with 62 percent of the vote. Hurricane Katrina does catastrophic damage to the Gulf Coast; more than a thousand die and millions are left homeless. British Prime Minister Tony Blair wins a third successive term. Pope John Paul II dies.

WHAT WE WERE READING: *The Closers* by Michael Connelly; *The Mermaid Chair* by Sue Monk Kidd; *The Historian* by Elizabeth Kostova; *Anansi Boys* by Neil Gaiman

WHAT WE WERE WATCHING: *The Chronicles of Narnia: The Lion, the Witch, and the Wardrobe*; *Crash*; *Good Night, and Good Luck*; *Walk the Line*

COST OF A FIRST-CLASS STAMP: 37 cents

## *2006*

For our thirtieth anniversary, we chose "Great Is Thy Faithfulness" as our theme. Ashley Johnson joined our family, an even sixty this year. To celebrate the occasion, we gave you a gift of *"Daily Guideposts*

*Daily Guideposts 1977–2011*

Classics," twelve bonus devotionals from such wonderful writers of years gone by as Norman Vincent Peale, Marjorie Holmes, Arthur Gordon, Eleanor Sass, Glenn Kittler and Catherine Marshall. And our regular series included a look at the mustard seeds of faith by Elizabeth Sherrill; "Turning Points" by Roberta Messner; "Grace Notes" by Pam Kidd; Holy Week with John Sherrill; Marion Bond West's powerful story of her prodigal son, "The Hardest Good-bye"; the moving "Comfort in Our Grief" by Marilyn Morgan King; and "The Hidden Glory" of Christmas with Gail Thorell Schilling.

**IN THE NEWS:** Saddam Hussein is convicted of crimes against humanity by an Iraqi court and hanged in Baghdad. Democrats gain control of both houses of Congress in the midterm elections. An eight-year federal study finds that a low-fat diet does not decrease the risk of heart disease, cancer or stroke. Barbaro wins the Kentucky Derby but suffers serious injury in the Preakness.

**WHAT WE WERE READING:** *The Hostage* by W.E.B. Griffin; *Cell* by Stephen King; *Gone* by Jonathan Kellerman; *Rise and Shine* by Anna Quindlen; *For One More Day* by Mitch Albom

**WHAT WE WERE WATCHING:** *Pirates of the Caribbean: Dead Man's Chest*; *Night at the Museum*; *Cars*; *The Da Vinci Code*; *Happy Feet*

**COST OF A FIRST-CLASS STAMP:** 39 cents

## *2007*

"Strength for the Journey" was our theme for *Daily Guideposts 2007*. Rebecca Ondov and Wendy Willard joined fifty-seven returning writers, who brought us such memorable series as Elizabeth Sherrill's

*Daily Guideposts 1977–2011*

"Lessons from the Journey," Roberta Messner's "God-Finds," Isabel Wolseley's Antarctic journey to "The Beauty at the Bottom of the World," Edward Grinnan's "A Worried Man," Marilyn Morgan King's "Pain and Grace" and John Sherrill's "Eyes upon the Rail." We spent Holy Week with Roberta Rogers and Advent with Daniel Schantz.

IN THE NEWS: The United States begins its "surge" of some thirty thousand troops to Iraq to stem increasingly deadly attacks by insurgents and militias. California Democrat Nancy Pelosi becomes the first woman Speaker of the House. UN panel finds that the Earth's climate and ecosystems are already being affected by the accumulation of greenhouse gases and suggests immediate action be taken.

WHAT WE WERE READING: *Nineteen Minutes* by Jodi Picoult; *A Thousand Splendid Suns* by Khaled Hosseini; *Lean Mean Thirteen* by Janet Evanovich; *World without End* by Ken Follett; *Book of the Dead* by Patricia Cornwell.

WHAT WE WERE WATCHING: *Pirates of the Caribbean: At World's End*; *Harry Potter and the Order of the Phoenix*; *Spiderman 3*; *Transformers*; *Ratatouille*

COST OF A FIRST-CLASS STAMP: 39 cents, 41 cents as of 5/14/07

## *2008*

In 2008 we took a look at some of the many ways we're "Surprised by God" each day. Some of our favorite series writers were back again (no surprise there!), including Elizabeth Sherrill ("Unexpected Blessings"), Marilyn Morgan King ("Letters to Tiny Toes"), two Robertas—Messner ("A Second Thank-You") and

Rogers ("A Way through the Waves"), Carol Kuykendall ("Give Us This Day" on Carol's and her husband Lynn's joint battle with cancer), Pam Kidd (an unforgettable trip to Zimbabwe to find "Bread for the Children"), Scott Walker ("To Abide with Him" in Holy Week) and Penney Schwab ("A Sign Unto You" for Advent, introducing us to the Chrismon tree). Four new writers—Amanda Borozinski, Mary Ann O'Roark, Patricia Pusey and Jon Sweeney—joined our family, while the return of Richard Schneider after more than a quarter of a century brought our number to sixty-three.

IN THE NEWS: Three men wearing ski masks steal four pieces of artwork from the Zurich Museum (a Cezanne, a Degas, a van Gogh, and a Monet with a combined worth of $163 million) in one of the largest art robberies in history. In March, the US government begins to intervene in the US financial system to avoid a crisis. Democratic Senator Barack Obama wins the presidency over Republican Senator John McCain and becomes the first African American to be elected president. Democrats gain control of both houses of Congress in the midterm elections.

WHAT WE WERE READING: *Compulsion* by Jonathan Kellerman; *Unaccustomed Earth* by Jhumpa Lahiri; *The Host* by Stephanie Meyer; *Devil Bones* by Kathy Reichs; *The Story of Edgar Sawtelle* by David Wroblewski

WHAT WE WERE WATCHING: *The Dark Knight*; *Indiana Jones and the Kingdom of the Crystal Skull*; *Kung Fu Panda*; *Hancock*; *Mamma Mia!*; *WALL-E*

COST OF A FIRST-CLASS STAMP: 41 cents, 42 cents as of 5/12/08

## Daily Guideposts 1977–2011
### *2009*

"Living the Word" was the theme our fifty-eight writers tackled in 2009. Daniel Schantz led off with some of the ways "God Speaks" in our daily lives. Roberta Messner's midmonth series "With Eternity in View" shared some of the things living with a chronic disease had taught her. Also appearing monthly was Marilyn Morgan King's "A Time to Every Purpose" on Ecclesiastes. Elizabeth Sherrill's "Living the Word in Holy Week—and Beyond" added Ascension Day and Pentecost to our usual Palm Sunday to Easter series, while her husband John shared "Lessons from an Automobile." We traveled to post–Hurricane-Katrina New Orleans with Brigitte Weeks and to the Mediterranean with Fred Bauer; Brock Kidd presided over our Christmas festivities ("Making Christmas").

IN THE NEWS: The outbreak of the H1N1 influenza strain is deemed a global pandemic. Scotland frees the terminally ill Lockerbie bomber on compassionate grounds, letting the Libyan go home to die despite American pleas to show no mercy for the man responsible for the 1988 attack that killed 270 people. Michael Jackson dies. President Barack Obama wins the Nobel Peace Prize.

WHAT WE WERE READING: *Dead and Gone* by Charlaine Harris; *Gone Tomorrow* by Lee Child; *The Defector* by Daniel Silva; *The Girl Who Played with Fire* by Stieg Larsson; *South of Broad* by Pat Conroy; *The Lost Symbol* by Dan Brown

WHAT WE WERE WATCHING: *Avatar*; *Harry Potter and the Half-Blood Prince*; *2012*; *Up*; *The Twilight Saga: New Moon*; *Sherlock Holmes*

COST OF A FIRST-CLASS STAMP: 42 cents, 44 cents as of 5/11/09

*Daily Guideposts 1977–2011*

## *2010*

Our theme for 2010—our thirty-fourth annual edition—was "The Gifts We Are Given." Among the gifts we were given that year was Jeff Chu of Brooklyn, New York, a pastor's grandson and globetrotting editor-reporter who brought a unique perspective to our family of fifty-seven. Pam Kidd shared "Gifts from Above"; the shadow of blindness prompted Marilyn Morgan King to reflect on "The Gift of Sight"; Roberta Messner presented "Twelve Keys to the Giving Life"; Isabel Wolseley drew on her own most difficult times to share "Comfort for a Hurting Heart." Eric Fellman took a fresh look at Holy Week in "Encountering Jesus," while Elizabeth Sherrill discovered "Words from the Sea," and Marci Alborghetti looked toward Christmas for "The Greatest Gift of All." And most noticeably, we introduced a new page-a-day format to make *Daily Guideposts* more companionable than ever.

As we write this, 2010 is only about a quarter over, so we're going to leave the annual news roundup to you.

## *2011*

Our gala thirty-fifth anniversary edition is the book you're holding in your hand. As we begin what we hope is at least another thirty-five years as your companion on the walk that leads us all, we pray, closer to God, we'd like to ask you to think back over the past thirty-five years and write down some of your own memories. You can send them to us at:

*Daily Guideposts*
Box 35
16 East 34th Street, 12th floor
New York, NY 10016

## A NOTE FROM THE EDITORS

Guideposts, a nonprofit organization, touches millions of lives every day through products and services that inspire, encourage and uplift. Our magazines, books, prayer network and outreach programs help people connect their faith-filled values to their daily lives. To learn more, visit www.guideposts.com or www.guidepostsfoundation.org.